Assumptive Selling

The Complete Guide to Selling More Vehicles for More Money to Today's Connected Customers

••••••••••

For Salespeople, Managers & Dealers

STEVE STAUNING

Contents

"... everyone knows, when you make an assumption, you make an ass out of 'u' and 'umption'."

Mitch Henessey, *The Long Kiss Goodnight* (1996)

Assumptive
Selling

1

INTRODUCTION TO ASSUMPTIVE SELLING

Let's level set before you dive into this book: selling cars is not hard… it just takes work. To the uninitiated, success in car sales appears to be like playing a slot machine. That is, sitting on your butt until you get lucky.

The truth is, success in automotive retail is more like using a vending machine. It's predictable. It's about completing the right steps in the right order to generate your reward. Grab your coins; insert them in the slot; press the right buttons; receive your snack. Rinse. Lather. Repeat.

Assumptive Selling is not about luck, tricks or a magic potion; it's about completing the right steps in the right order to generate your reward. Like all things that lead to success, it is not for the lazy.

Assumptive Selling, to be clear, is not new. Assumptive Selling has been around as long as there've been salespeople; and, despite what you've heard about people who assume, assumptive sellers have always been more successful than their peers. In automotive retail, Assumptive Selling is about knowing what does *not* exist. With Assumptive Selling, there are no tire-kickers; no unqualified buyers. Everyone is a buyer, and everyone is buying today.

Once mastered, Assumptive Selling is the most powerful sales strategy available today. Any seller in any industry will become more successful literally overnight just by learning how to become a true assumptive seller. Assumptive Selling is not about closing; it's about leading. It's about leading the customer down your path (whether on the lot or on the phone). It's about taking charge, being direct and providing guidance; all while understanding that every Up wants to buy and they want to buy today.

Assumptive selling is about believing everyone is a buyer… and knowing that the first time you believe someone is not, you'll be right.

Today's connected customers want to buy; they're just afraid of being sold. They arrive on the lot with all the information they need and they don't like being interrogated. Salespeople who win today are the ones who recognize this, speak to their customers like human beings, and then pull them through a buying process in an efficient manner that makes sense to the buyer.

When you do this with enthusiasm, energy and passion, people want to share in your enthusiasm, energy and passion. They will come along for the ride just because it seems like what the cool kids are doing. Assumptive Selling without this enthusiasm, energy and passion is not Assumptive Selling.

The basic principle for Assumptive Selling is simple: You should always assume the sale. Always. Assume. The. Sale.

A prospect who pulls onto your lot or walks into your showroom is a buyer who is here to buy; and… she's here to buy today. The ringing phone represents a buyer who wants to buy today. The sales lead that's just dropped into your CRM was sent by a buyer who wants to buy today. Everyone is a buyer… and, they all want to buy today.

That guy who opens the door and shakes your hand at church; the waitress; the cashier; the car wash attendant; your friends on Facebook; your kids' teachers… They all represent buyers who are going to buy eventually; and (when you introduce and market yourself properly) they're all going to buy from you.

Assumptive sellers always assume the sale. Assuming the sale gives you confidence that your buyer can sense. Assuming the sale gives you energy that your buyer feeds off. Assuming the sale keeps your thoughts positive in the face of objections. Assuming the sale makes you a more likeable person.

Always assuming the sale helps you sell more cars for more money than you ever dreamed possible… except, of course, during your first full month as a salesperson. It seems every Green Pea starts off strong in the car business. I've seen Green Peas sell 25 vehicles in their first month – all while the average salesperson in their dealership sold 10.

How did they do this? Simple: They assumed everyone was a buyer who was here to buy.

The negative forces in their dealership – the guys sitting around in the smoking circle – laughed at the Green Peas because these newbies were "too dumb to know any better."

Green Peas, because they don't "know any better," assume the sale. They follow the steps their manager taught them as closely as possible, and they sell a bunch of cars. They'll do this until they get pulled into the smoking circle and then realize that every Up is an unqualified tire-kicker who couldn't buy a car today if you were selling them for $1.

If only we could all think like Green Peas forever; if only we could remain "too dumb to know any better" for our entire career in the car business.

Some Quick Caveats/Notes

I know what you're thinking: "Wow, this book is long!"

Yes, but unlike most business and self-help books, this one won't continue to repeat the same concepts over and over and over again. (Well, except for the ones I think are really, really, *really* important.) I tried to keep this book as short as possible to allow you to quickly learn the most important concepts and go to work selling more cars (and making more money).

That said, there is much more to selling cars today than just regurgitating old-school word tracks and knowing how to overcome a few objections. This book attempts to cover as many bases as possible for salespeople, managers and even dealers.

Not every dealership is structured the same way – some will give salespeople access to all Ups and prospects, while others will have these divided among various departments (BDC, Internet Sales, Owner Marketing, etc.) – therefore, some lessons will apply to your position and some will not. I tried to label the chapters and sections to make it easy for you to skip over the parts that simply don't apply to your current situation.

Before you dive into the most important lessons in this book, I want to make a few things clear:

1.   This book may contain advice or tips you're already doing – that's because I cover some very basic information as well as introduce you to the concept of Assumptive Selling. I do this because I don't know how long you've been selling cars versus that guy next to you. Therefore, I wrote this book for everyone who sells cars – from the old car dog to the Green Pea – and their managers.

2.   This is a book written for any vehicle sales team. That is, those who sell cars, trucks, SUVs, minivans, RVs, powersports, boats and everything in between. Selling a vehicle is different than selling furniture or homes; though each of these has some similarities and there may be concepts in this book that help you, the Realtor, or you, the appliance salesman.

3. Just as I did in the point above, I may write salesman, saleswoman, salesperson, he, she or it interchangeably throughout this book because modern society demands diversity; and, damnit, I cannot let modern society down. If I fail to use your gender as much as one of the others in this book and that bothers you, then I'll need to refer you to my first book, *Sh*t Sandwich: Quick & Practical Success Lessons for Practically Anyone.* (It's a real book about learning to get over your drama and faux outrage to live successfully in the real world.)

4. Don't memorize and regurgitate – learn to apply the lessons you learn in this book to various situations. For example, while I might give you a word track for a phone conversation, this doesn't mean you cannot or should not use the same general premise in your in-person, email, text, chat and Messenger conversations (and vice versa), as well. Today's customers are virtually the same regardless of communication channel used; just be a grown up and adapt what I give you for one medium to the medium you're using; adapt what I give you for one situation to your current situation. Got it?

5. An Up is an Up is an Up (see the Glossary at the end of the book for the definition of Up and any other industry term I use that confuses you). Unless I specify what kind of Up I'm referring to (like a "Phone Up" or a "Lot Up"), assume that what I'm teaching applies to all Ups.

6. Although (as of this writing) trucks are more popular than sedans with today's consumers, I will often refer to vehicles as cars throughout this book. Cars, you see, is kind of a generic term to those of us who've been in the business for more than a few years. Cars no longer refers to just sedans; for this book (as in the real world), cars can mean basically anything with wheels and a motor.

7. No style, method or system of selling will close 100% of the prospects 100% of the time. That said, choosing one and mastering it always outperforms flying by the seat of your pants. So, the first time Assumptive Selling doesn't work for you, resist the urge to scrap everything you've learned and understand that sales is and always has been a numbers game… you'll win the next one.

Old-School Assumptive Selling

This book is about assuming the sale, and not the old-school Assumptive Selling practices that (believe it or not) still work today. Typical, old-school Assumptive Selling is effective at getting the prospect to begin taking ownership of the vehicle before the purchase. This occurs when you use trial closes that assume the customer has already purchased with questions like, "How will you be titling *your* Mustang, Mr. Smith?"

The goal is basically to convince him that he's already the proud owner of your vehicle. That's the essence of old-school Assumptive Selling.

With new-school Assumptive Selling, the goal is a bit different. With new-school Assumptive Selling you convince yourself that everyone is a buyer and that they are buying today... from you. No more treating your prospects like suspects. Instead, you're going to assume that:

- Everyone has done a needs analysis
- Everyone has completed their product selection
- Everyone knows the car's features
- Everyone is ready to test drive
- Everyone is a qualified buyer
- Everyone starts the paperwork

You're going to assume they are a buyer until they stop you; then, and only then, should you take them down an old-school road-to-the-sale.

What Will I Get from Assumptive Selling?

As you'll learn in this book, buyers are much different today than they were just a few years ago – they've evolved. And, because they've evolved, your approach must evolve, as well – that is, if you want to close car deals at a high rate for better grosses.

If you fully embrace Assumptive Selling, you should expect to sell more buyers with less friction than ever before. You should expect to close these deals faster, with fewer hassles and at higher grosses. Moreover, because Assumptive Selling results in a great customer experience, you will enjoy higher CSI and you'll always earn the right to ask for the referral.

While today's customer will welcome your Assumptive Selling approach, they're not expecting it. No, they're expecting a hassle every time they deal with a car salesman. You're going to give them something different – something they can't get at any other dealership – and, they're going to reward you for it.

But, When You Assume...

You may have heard the old saying:

When you assume, you make an ass out of 'u' and 'me'.

This doesn't apply here – not in sales; and not today. We're going to use a new type of thinking about making assumptions; we're going to use Assumptive Selling thinking:

When you fail to always assume the sale, you should always assume you'll fail.

This saying must be true, right? I mean, it takes some words from the first part of the sentence and rearranges them in the second part. :)

As I wrote, the old-school assumptive techniques still work today, so let's explore those just a little deeper before we move into today's Assumptive Selling.

Old-school assumptive techniques are trial closes. That is, they are questions designed to get the prospect to start taking ownership in what you're selling by getting them into the habit of answering these trial closes affirmatively. So, while I'm not a fan of having you, the salesperson, talking much at all prior to and (especially) during the demo drive, it is important to include a few trial closes to feel out the customer. Often, the right trial close can seal the deal; other times a trial close might uncover a previously unvoiced objection.

The trial closing questions you use should all be assumptive in nature. This will guide the prospect to a final "yes" after they've responded positively to a few of these. If you begin the sales process assuming that the prospect is going to buy, buy today, and buy from you; your assumptive trial closes won't come off as clumsy or even as if you're selling at all. You will be perceived as someone who is helping them buy the car they want.

One of the reasons that new-school Assumptive Selling works so well is that positive beginnings beget positive outcomes – and, the opposite is also true. Think about it: When you see an Up walk on the lot and you assume they're just a tire-kicker or that they otherwise can't buy, your approach and technique are going to help you prove this.

It becomes a self-fulfilling prophecy. Your attitude is negative, and you'll easily prove your point that "he's just a tire-kicker" or "she can't qualify." Conversely, beginning each encounter with the firm belief that you're dealing with a qualified buyer who is ready to buy right now will result in more sales for more money – and this positive attitude will endear the customer to you.

Additionally, assuming the sale will give you more energy and enthusiasm, because you're confident that this Up will result in a nice, fat commission for you! Your fears of rejection will subside, and you'll breathe positive energy into the encounter.

When you assume the sale the second an Up walks on the lot or the minute the phone rings, you'll also be assuming (by default) that they've already found the benefits in your vehicle and your dealership. You won't need to "sell" these to the prospect, because you know they've already sold themselves on the car and your store.

Any old-school assumptive trial closes you use will just be a way of "taking the buyer's temperature" as you proceed down your road-to-the-sale.

Buying a Car is Exciting!

Whether the customer is here to look at a brand-new car or a ten-year-old vehicle you took in trade isn't relevant – buying anything new is exciting, and your used car is going to be new to them. Of course, while buying a car is exciting, no one wants to be sold. That's why Assumptive Selling works so well: you're not selling, you're guiding and assisting.

When the customer feels like they're being sold, they can become defensive. They begin to create objections they never had; they become more aloof; and they disbelieve anything you tell them. All this because they're starting to feel sales pressure.

Assumptive Selling, meanwhile, is nearly devoid of pressure because you're simply agreeing with their desire to own your car today. In their mind you understand them – and, you might be the first car salesman to ever understand them! This allows you to guide them down your road-to-the-sale – and they'll gladly come along.

Buyers Love Assumptive Selling!

In possibly the best sales movie ever, *Glengarry Glen Ross* (1992), Alec Baldwin's character Blake famously teaches, "A guy don't walk on the lot lest he wants to buy." That's the very foundation of Assumptive Selling.

Since we know buying a car is exciting for the customer – and that every Up is here to buy today – Assumptive Selling is not just a way for you to close more deals, it's also a better customer experience, isn't it?

Assumptive Selling can make this a fun event for your buyers; especially when compared to the ordeal of the old-school, four- or five-hour road-to-the-sale.

Assumptive Selling results in more closed deals that close quicker and with less friction than any of the alternatives. That's why buyers love it.

Let's do this.

2

ESSENTIALS FOR AUTOMOTIVE SALES SUCCESS

Either during the initial job interview or your first week in the car business, you were probably told (as I was) that selling cars is the only career that requires no college degree and no experience yet will afford you the opportunity to create your own small business. Your dealer principal will provide the capital, the marketing, the inventory and the facilities; your sales managers will provide the leadership and (some of) the training; and what you make of this opportunity is entirely up to you.

Guess what? You weren't lied to – this is all true! There are plenty of salespeople today who "own" their book of business. Whether they stay at their current dealership or move across town, many of their customers will never buy from anyone else. Creating your own book of business, therefore, should be one of your goals because this is the only way to ensure both job security and long-term financial success from selling cars.

If you're new to car sales, you probably don't know that most salespeople fit neatly into one of three basic categories: they can be superstars; they can be average; or they can be slugs. You can probably guess right away that you don't want to be a slug.

The great news for you is that this book was written to make everyone a superstar. And, yes, everyone can be a superstar. Regardless of what you're selling, sales is the only profession where the players don't fit on a bell curve. (A bell curve, for the uninitiated, is a typical distribution of values where nearly all the results are bunched together in the middle with just a relative few on the extremes.) For example, if we plotted the monthly results for all the salespeople at a well-run dealership, you'd quickly see that nearly everyone is crowding the right side of the graph. That is, they're all superstars.

Depending on the brand and location, superstar salespeople average between 25 and 100 units a month. Yes, you read that right, there are salespeople like Ali Reda of Dearborn, Michigan who can retail more than 100 units in a month. In fact, Reda reportedly sold more than 1,500 new vehicles in 2017.[1] This, while the average salesperson in America still retails only about 8 to 10 cars every 30 days.

Slugs, you might have guessed, average 8 or fewer units a month. (If this describes you, don't panic. The lessons in this book – when followed – will make you a superstar.)

Interestingly, whatever your success selling cars – whether you're a superstar, a slug, or somewhere in between – you are the sole cause of this. Yes, you and only you decide whether you're going to average 30 units or 8 units. This has been the reality for decades in automotive retail, and it doesn't matter if this is your first month in the car business or if you've been selling for twenty years.

Don't believe me? Let me show you how anyone can go from average (we'll say 8 cars/month) to superstar (let's go with 30 units/month) fairly easily. For this lesson, we'll call our average seller "Alan" and our superstar "Theo."

Eight-Car Alan vs. Thirty-Car Theo

The slugs in your dealership will disagree with my conclusions on what separates your superstars from the rest. But, that's okay; there's a reason they're slugs. While the average salesperson or slug might complain that the superstars are just lucky, the fact is that nearly all the differences between your 8-Car Alans and your 30-Car Theos can be boiled down to two very simple realities: attitude and activity.

More than anything else, attitude and activity are all that separate the 8-Car Alans from the 30-Car Theos. Regardless of what else ails the 8-Car Alans that you may want to add to this simple list, chances are it finds its roots in (and can be solved with) attitude or activity. And, it all starts with attitude.

Simply put: salespeople who sell 30 units expect to sell 30; and they're not satisfied with 29. Meanwhile, the typical 8-Car Alan begins every month expecting to sell 18 (at least that what he tells his manager he's going to sell when asked for this month's goal); yet he is absolutely thrilled when he ends with 12.

While 12 units sold does represent a 50% improvement over 8-Car Alan's average month, it also represents a 33% miss from his forecast. So, to be satisfied with a 33% miss means the forecast was meaningless. Alan never expected to sell 18. In fact, he likely began the month expecting to sell 8; so, any number above that is a success in Alan's mind. His attitude is average; his expectations are average; hence, his results are average. Until Alan resets his attitude, he will never enjoy sustained success.

By contrast, 30-Car Theo would be extremely critical of his own performance and would either triple his efforts next month or possibly seek other employment in the unlikely event he missed his forecast by 33%. His attitude drives his expectations which leads to month after month with 30 units on the board. Short of a two-week hospital stay, there is almost nothing that could cause Theo to ever end his month with just 20 units.

Of course, it's not only the mindset and belief in their individual goals that make up the entire attitudinal difference of top and bottom sellers. 30-Car Theos arrive at work excited and ready-to-go regardless of the day of the week. This is precisely why you'll sometimes witness a 30-Car Theo score a Hat Trick on a Tuesday – they bring their winner's attitude to every single workday.

Theo begins each month expecting to sell 30 or more units. This means Theo begins each week expecting to sell 8 and begins each day expecting to sell 2. Top sellers don't start their month with a wish and then wake up on the last day hoping their wish came true.

Learn to Like Selling Cars – Quickly!

If you don't like selling cars you have only two choices: You can quit, or you can start liking it.

Like, you see, is a verb and not a feeling. You control whether you like something; just as you control whether you walk or run – also verbs. You weren't born knowing how to do many things – you had to be taught. You had to learn to walk, to run and to ride a bike. Some things in your life you liked instantly (like ice cream); while others were more of an acquired taste (like vegetables).

Liking something or not liking it is a choice. Start liking what you do or move on.

30-Car Theos like selling cars; they like the car business and they especially like their customers – and this shows in everything they do. Customers feed off this positive attitude and they enjoy buying from 30-Car Theos. People, you see, like those who like them.

8-Car Alans look at the calendar and lament how "Tuesdays suck around here" as they go on to prove exactly that with their lackluster performance. 8-Car Alans don't particularly like selling cars or the car business. Oh, and ask any 8-Car Alan about difficult customers and they'll bend your ear for an hour complaining about last week's Ups.

Beyond liking what they do, superstars like 30-Car Theo keep their focus on winning – especially when they don't win. When a 30-Car Theo doesn't sell a prospect today – regardless of how difficult the Up was – they count it as a win because they know this prospect will need a car someday (everyone does); and when they do, they'll seek out Theo.

Why? Because Theo's attitude and love for the car business are infectious; and the customer feels that. Everyone wants a friend in the car business, and even though they didn't buy today, Theo's unsold prospects often leave believing that Theo may just be their friend in the business.

Activity Drives Sales Success

When you're in a good mood and you enjoy doing what you do, completing the tasks necessary to sell 30 cars a month comes (relatively) easy. While a 30-Car Theo, for example, might prefer doing something other than making phone calls (wouldn't we all?), he makes his calls because he knows phone calls are an activity that lead to selling 30 units this month.

This is a key point to remember: superstars complete activities that they may not love doing, but that lead to sales success. They do them because their goal depends on it. 30-Car Theos will pick up the phone to call a Be-Back or will send a birthday card to a customer who bought eight years ago; not because these activities are fun, but because they lead to sales success.

Standing outside in the smoking circle, by contrast, might be lots of fun but it's not one of the activities that lead to sales success – just the opposite, in fact. Therefore, you won't see 30-Car Theo joining the daily bitching session.

30-Car Theo gets his 29 or 30 or 35 every month because of activity. 30-Car Theo is always busy doing something productive. He is always active. He is always moving forward; never standing still; never crying about yesterday. Every 30-Car Theo I know keeps busy with moneymaking activities throughout the day.

Show Me Your Moneymakers

So much of success in sales is tied to activity, that I find it odd when I hear salespeople complaining about their lack of opportunities – all while their heads are buried in their smartphones. There is no secret formula for selling – it's pretty simple – those that are the most successful are the ones generating the most sales-focused activity.

In other words: you must do something to sell something!

Pick up the phone and call that lead from yesterday. Send a letter or card to a prior customer on their birthday. Give your business card to the cashier at Burger King and let her know you pay $100 for every referral that buys from you. Walk into the service waiting area and greet your prior customers. Grab your smartphone and start a live broadcast on Facebook showing a cool trade you took in yesterday.

In other words: do something! Anything.

If you're one of those who can't seem to get their month going until the 15th or later, I suspect you're spending most of your time waiting on the Up Bus with a crowd of other 8-Car Alans and/or you have your head buried in your phone.

Instead of wasting your time (and your life) with activities that make you no money, I recommend you start focusing on those actions that drive sales; the activities that can make you money.

Activities, by the way, are not all created equally. There are activities, for example, that feel like work but take you no closer to your goal of selling a car. These might include scrolling through your dealership's CRM tool while endlessly reading notes about unsold prospects. 8-Car Alans will do this to look busy – because they are busy. They're busy wasting time on a non-productive activity; one that does not make them any money.

If you're reading this book, then I'll assume you want to focus on productive activities – that is, those activities that can lead to sales success; those activities that can make you money. I call these your moneymakers.

This is a very simple exercise, but when I'm training a group of sellers doing 8-10 cars a month who genuinely want to get to 20 or 30, I ask them to create a list of their moneymakers. That is, I ask them to create a list of those activities that (if completed) would take them closer to selling 20 or 30.

Moneymakers are simply those activities that make you money. The opposite of moneymakers, of course, are timewasters. 8-Car Alans are great at timewasters and not so good at moneymakers; while 30-Car Theos excel at moneymakers and rarely get caught up in timewasters.

Before we dive into a sample list of moneymakers, it's important to try and understand why 8-Car Alans would rather scroll through the CRM (a timewaster) than pick up the phone and call a Be-Back (a moneymaker). The reason is simple: they're afraid of making money; they're afraid of being successful; they're afraid of hearing someone tell them "no."

The word "no" is music to the ears of a true superstar. They understand (and, as I'll repeat a few times in this book) sales is a numbers game; and while they expect to sell every Up and generate an appointment on every call, they recognize they will not win them all.

Therefore, to be successful – to hear "yes" 30 times each month – they're going to hear "no" more than a few times. They relish the no's because each one brings them closer to the next yes. This makes it vital that you include activities where you may hear "no" to your list of moneymakers.

Create Your List of Moneymakers

Simply jot down those activities that (when done correctly) help you sell more cars in either the short or long term. Unless you are brand new to the business, you know what to do and you should be able put together a list of activities that (again, when accomplished) would easily take you to 30 or more cars in any month. Activities like:

- Calling the sold database and Be-Backs
- Networking – the old-fashioned way
- Networking – via Social Selling
- Asking for referrals
- Sending birthday cards & personal notes via snail mail
- Working the service drive
- Reading a sales training book
- Watching video sales training

This was just my quick list – and we're going to cover most everything above in this book – though your list of moneymakers should include at least one more activity. I don't know what that activity is, but you do. You are the only one who can control your success; so, while you may not be able to think of it today, there is at least one more activity that you could be doing (versus just wasting time) that will lead you closer to 30+ cars per month.

The second part of this activity takes a little more time – that is, every day you remain in the car business! You've created a list of the activities that you know will make you successful, now you need to put the list to work for you. You do this by first keeping a copy of your list of moneymakers always handy.

Given that getting in front of a prospect is how you make your living, your goal should be to always be in front of a prospect. This means, when you're not in front of a potential buyer, your energies should be geared toward getting a butt into that seat in front of you.

How do you do that? By working on one of your moneymakers, of course! The second part of this exercise (the one you'll do for the rest of your car-selling life) is whenever you find yourself just standing around with your hands in your pockets, you need to pull out your moneymakers.

This means taking a quick, one-question test about once every hour or so:

1.   Am I in front of a prospect?
       a.   Yes. Great, pull them through my process.
       b.   No. Pull out my list of moneymakers and choose one of the activities to do next.

Now do it.

Incidentally, you can complete any of the activities on your moneymaker list that you choose; so, pick the one that you like doing the most. You can keep working on that activity until you've exhausted the opportunities from it or run out of To Dos. After all, an activity wouldn't be on the list if it didn't make you money.

There really are no mysteries to becoming a 30-Car Theo. In fact, every 8-Car Alan will admit (when pressed) that they know what to do, they're just not doing it. They prefer the "fun" of timewasters; they prefer activities like standing around complaining.

This is where attitude meets activity – and why you need both to be a 30-Car Theo.

Knowing what to do is one thing. However, you simply won't do those things (or won't do them well) if you don't bring the right attitude to work. This means that if you don't like selling cars, you need to start liking it. This means if you don't like Mondays or Tuesdays or whatevers, you need to start liking them.

As I wrote, liking something is a choice; it's not a feeling. The greatest difference between 8-Car Alans and 30-Car Theos is that the 30-Car Theos have chosen to like what they do; to like coming to work on a Tuesday; to like where they work; to like their customers.

The 8-Car Alans, on the other hand, can tell you why all that sucks.

Your Most Important Moneymaker: You

If a concert violinist wants to be successful, they need to take very special care of their violin. It is their moneymaker – their most important asset – and a broken or out-of-tune moneymaker just won't do. Like a concert violinist, you need to take very special care of your most important asset: you.

If you truly want to succeed at selling cars, then you must ensure your most important instrument is always in great shape and ready to go. You are your own fine-tuned Stradivarius; and if you don't take care of you; you will eventually stop working – just like a broken violin.

If you're currently in your twenties or even early thirties, the advice I'm providing over the remainder of this chapter may seem overly cautious – because you're still indestructible; you're still immortal. Your bell-to-bell lifestyle hasn't killed you yet, so you think it will never catch up to you. It will. It always does.

If you want to sell 30+ units every month this year and also in ten, twenty and thirty years, you need to create healthy habits that can carry your body through the next few decades without breaking down. This means adding lots of boring habits and jettisoning those fun, cool habits you might have. For example:

- Get enough sleep... each and every night. Your body repairs itself when you sleep; and trying to do it all is just not possible over the long term when you deprive your body – and especially your brain – of the sleep it needs to function. Lack of sleep increases your risk of heart disease, diabetes, obesity, and depression. It also negatively impacts your brain's ability to remember (like how to overcome an objection) and its ability to comprehend (like recognizing buying signals).

- Stop smoking. Salespeople who smoke not only stink when sitting across from a non-smoking prospect, but also become agitated more easily when a deal takes too long to complete. I've seen smokers blow deals with their customers because their mood changes as their need for a nicotine fix increases.

- Eat sensible meals. Any one of us can go a few weeks eating nothing but fast food and seem to function properly; the problems arise when you never eat anything other than this crap. The long-term negative impacts of a poor diet are more than just the added pounds and the loss of energy we might notice after eating mostly fast food for a month or so. For those sellers who want to always remain at the top of their game, a great diet wins over the long term.

• Avoid energy drinks. Yep, I went there. Today's energy drinks are akin to the "pep pills" some salespeople routinely took to compensate for their lack of sleep in the last century. Yes, the initial boost of energy is great, but you cannot continue to ask your body to do more for you than it was designed to do by fooling it into thinking you've got energy to spare. If you need more than a couple of cups of coffee in the morning to get your body and brain going, you're likely in for an energy crash that could last for a very long time. Energy drinks are the liquid equivalent of fast food. That is, there appear to be few negative implications in the short term, though they can lead to all the same harmful health consequences when these become your staple beverage for months or years.

• Be happy. Yes, being happy is a habit you can develop. So, be happy for your coworkers, your dealer, your managers and your customers. Your happiness will become contagious and others will be happy for you. If you find you cannot be happy for someone, then just fake being happy for them until it becomes a reality. This means projecting happiness on the outside until your insides match your outsides. Try it; it really works.

• Avoid negative chatter and thoughts. Sitting in the smoking circle complaining about the dealership's advertising or that lady in the finance office might feel like you're bonding with the others, but these negative thoughts will creep into your ability to project happiness to your customers and coworkers.

• Dress up and always be well-groomed. Your customers will never complain when you're clean, fresh and dressed nicely. This doesn't necessarily mean suit and tie, but it does mean wearing clean clothes over a showered, clean body that smells good (use cologne or perfume sparingly).

• Oh, and wear a name tag. You want your customers to remember you throughout the buying process and well into the future. Unfortunately, the distractions of today can be so great that ten seconds after you introduce yourself, your customer has already forgotten your name. They want to call you Steve, but they fear your name might be Scott. This makes them uncomfortable and makes you easily forgettable. Help them remember your name by wearing a simple name tag.

Great habits might be boring, but they are essential for successfully selling over the long term. Moreover, great habits drive your energy levels and your energy levels dictate everything from passion to mood. The bottom line is that passionate salespeople who are in a great mood outsell everyone else.

The great news is that your customers will feed off your passion and your energy. Buying a car is an exciting time for them and no one wants to buy from a smelly, disheveled, moody prick.

Debt Removes Choice

If you're new to the business world – and especially if you're new to selling cars – the best advice I can give you is that debt removes choice.

Wait; what does this have to do with Assumptive Selling?

Not much, but it has everything to do with you becoming and remaining a top salesperson in any field. Salespeople who are living paycheck-to-paycheck lose focus on their priorities, panic and blow up nearly every deal in front of them. True top sellers never panic – they never have to.

When you saddle yourself with needless debt today, you remove your ability to make choices later. You add needless debt when you buy a *want* using credit instead of cash. You may *want* a 64-inch TV, but you don't *need* one. If you cannot pay cash for something like that (or the newest iPhone or the newest gaming system or a cool new drone), you're saddling yourself with needless debt.

Salespeople forced to scrounge between checks find themselves in a never-ending trap – and they feel poor because they are poor. The interest on their credit cards eats up the bulk of their discretionary income. Conversely, salespeople who save their money – and who wait until they have extra income before they buy those cool new toys – are always rich.

Plus, they have choices.

If your spouse got a great job offer in another state, could you afford to move? Could you afford to go weeks without a paycheck while you looked for a new job in this new place? What if your dealership was purchased by new owners who cut everyone's commission in half? Could you afford to take several weeks to find the perfect new job or would you be forced to take the first gig offered?

If you're debt free, you have choices. If you're saddled with debt, you do not. Do yourself a favor (especially if it's still early in your career) and avoid the money stresses that doom so many promising salespeople: stay as debt free as possible.

Strict Sales Processes Will Make the Difference

Top sellers don't freelance with every Up. Quite the contrary – top sellers are known for treating every prospect the same and sticking to a strict sales process every time regardless of which rabbit hole a prospect tries to take them down. They do this because they know that process outsells everything else. It always has, and it always will.

With all the shiny new stuff that gets thrown at dealers on an almost daily basis, I'm often asked why I still focus so heavily on sales processes? Why don't I spend more time helping dealers evaluate and incorporate the latest and greatest magic bean, and less time harping on the basics?

It's simple. Those salespeople who succeed month-after-month, and those dealers that grow share regardless of market condition, have superior processes to those that merely tread water (or worse). Moreover, the dealers with the strictest process adherence are better at evaluating and incorporating the shiny new stuff than those flying by the seat of their pants.

Oh, and the dealers that execute best (with respect to sales, grosses and CSI) also spend the most time coaching, enforcing and improving their processes. Finally, my experience has always been that those stores with the best processes also (not coincidentally) have the best cultures and enjoy the lowest turnover. (These dealerships, by the way, are the ones you should seek out if you're a salesperson looking for a better place to call home.)

I can hear some of you now: "But, Steve; our managers don't teach us a thing; and they don't care whether we follow a process or not!"

This is all too common in automotive retail; but, it's certainly not your problem and it's definitely not the reason you're not selling 30 or more cars every month. It doesn't matter what your sales managers demand since your sales success is driven by you. You're the only one who can get you to 30 units this month… and, you're the only one to blame if you fail.

Your store's lack of process should be looked at as an opportunity. I mean, at least you're not being forced to follow some outdated road-to-the-sale that blows out more buyers than it closes. With no formal process in place, you are free to practice Assumptive Selling and free to create and strictly follow your own good sales processes. For your processes to be considered good, they must be built with simple, repeatable steps that you precisely follow with every Up.

Pros Master the Basics

If you've ever watched an NFL practice, you know that starting quarterbacks spend infinitely more time practicing snaps with the center than they do learning cool, new, trick plays. They do this because they know that without mastering the basics (through repetition) they have no chance of winning.

I focus so heavily on processes (and you should too) because even with all the new, shiny stuff dealers can buy, they will simply fail to grow market share, maintain gross, manage turnover or create a great company culture without strict adherence to process.

For most of the dealerships out there, the digital guy/gal or some vendor or OEM has got your general manager or dealer principal so spun up about which website your competitor uses or what cool, new thing they've just discovered, that these leaders become convinced there must be some secret to profitably growing market share that they've yet to discover.

Hint: There is no secret. Profitable growth and superstar sales results in automotive retail are driven by processes.

For dealerships, I've always found a direct correlation between process adherence and sustained profitability. Interestingly, I've never found any such correlation between website provider and profitability; or digital marketing agency and profitability.

For salespeople, the same direct correlation can be made between process adherence and sales results.

Not only do top dealers adhere to strict processes, they also enforce good business rules to back them up. Sensible rules are welcomed by great salespeople. It's only cheaters and slugs who will resist good business rules; since good employees want structure and they want to know what's expected of them. (If you're already a top seller, then I'm sure you agree with me.)

While this is a book about taking a different approach to selling cars, boring old processes and uninteresting rules still matter when it comes to selling more cars than the dealer up the street. Moreover, they matter way more than the next shiny object someone tries to pitch. The best automotive sales teams I know execute a strategy that consists of tactics that employ rules that are enforced. It's truly not anything special, except that it is special. It's special because they enforce their rules and they actually hold people accountable to those rules.

Top salespeople embrace accountability. Therefore, if you find yourself cringing at the thought of good business rules being imposed on you and your fellow salespeople, you need to get over yourself or find a new profession.

Breaking Out of a Sales Slump

Here's a quick warning for those who rely solely on the Up Bus to bring them much of their business: you will often find yourself stuck in a sales slump. Though, rest assured, everyone in sales hits a slump every now and then. The key to breaking out of your slump is to never panic; instead, do what the pros do.

When I'm speaking of pros here, I'm talking about professional athletes. Like salespeople, superstar professional athletes get paid well; but even the superstars will find themselves in the occasional slump.

When a baseball player is in a hitting slump, the worst thing he can do is swing harder. This, all great players have learned, only prolongs the slump. Likewise, when a salesperson goes 0-for-3 on Tuesday, the worst thing she can do is try harder to sell every Up on Wednesday. That is a guaranteed recipe for another day without a sale. Instead, every salesperson in a slump should follow a few steps that help pro ballplayers break out of theirs:

- Understand that slumps happen. If you're closing 50% of the people you get in front of, congratulations, you're a top seller... however, it also means you're failing to close half the time. Just like flipping a coin (where it's possible to land on tails 10 times in a row), it's possible for a top seller to go 0-for-10 with your next 10 Ups – and then sell the next 10 in a row. Don't panic.

- Prolonged slumps are more mental than physical. When your sales slump hits four or five, it's easy to panic and think something is wrong with your approach. Chances are, there is nothing wrong. However, when your mind starts to overthink the losses, you begin to overthink everything, and you turn a natural dry spell into a prolonged slump. Don't overthink anything.

- It's not you. If you're a top seller, then the prospects you failed to sell today will buy from you tomorrow... you're that good. Remember who you are.

- Can you picture success? Top hitters will often employ visualization to help them break out of slumps. This means they'll imagine the next at-bat or the pitcher they'll face tomorrow as if the situation was happening right now. They'll see the ball leaving the pitcher's hand and they'll follow it in their mind until it meets their bat. Similarly, visualizing the next Up can help top sellers break out of their slumps by imagining themselves using the effective word tracks that move the prospect through the buying process. Visualize your next sale.

- It's a process. Hitting a 96-mph fastball over the left-field fence is not a single, big event. Rather, it's the end result of multiple smaller steps that make up the strict process of batting. Likewise, closing a sale is not a single, big event; it's the culmination of the smaller steps that (when followed consistently) bring success way more often than the alternative. Stay consistent.

- Learn from the best. Sometimes hitters "forget" how to hit. Not really, but a long slump can play enough mind games that ballplayers begin to skip important steps and, basically, forget how to hit. Top sellers can also get stuck in slumps that begin to wreak havoc with their processes. If this happens to you, reread the sales books and re-watch the sales training videos that you've found helpful in the past. Study.

- Practice makes perfect. You've already learned that professional athletes don't practice the trick plays as much as they practice the basics; and the same goes for top sellers in a sales slump. Grab a fellow salesperson and ask them to stand-in as your next prospect. Ask them to throw every objection (verbal and nonverbal) they can at you; and practice pulling them through your road-to-the-sale. Role play.

Why This Chapter?

Success with the methods taught in this book – as with any lesson you learn – depends on you. If you believe you can just use the techniques of Assumptive Selling passively – that is, wait for people to come to you – and not actively seek opportunities, you will have only mild success at best. Moreover, your success will be tied to the traffic your dealership generates.

Today's car seller must generate their own opportunities if they expect to sell 20, 30 or even 40 vehicles a month. Waiting on the Up Bus and dazzling your prospects with perfect Assumptive Selling is, unfortunately, not enough to get you to the top of the sales board each month.

In a couple of chapters we'll cover old-fashioned networking and later we'll tackle Social Selling. Why? Because both are effective in creating 30-Car Theos. Moreover, when you master those lessons, you are truly the master of your own success. If you were forced to, you could leave your current dealership and most of your customers would follow – you will have truly created your own business; one that no one can ever take away from you!

Of course, I'd prefer you never leave your current dealership. I'd prefer your dealer principal and managers do everything they can to create a great culture that produces and nurtures 30-car sellers. They can do exactly that by implementing the lessons in the next chapter.

3

SOLVING DEALERSHIP TURNOVER

No book on car sales success would be complete without a chapter and a few lessons on solving the turnover issues that have plagued most dealerships in America for the past fifty years. Sales team turnover in automotive would be classified as an epidemic; except that even the worst epidemic ever would've ended by now.

It's more accurate (and sad) to say that automotive sales team turnover is both everlasting and omnipresent. But, of course, it doesn't have to be. There are plenty of great examples of well-run dealerships that see fewer than 20% of their sales team leave each year – and many of these salespeople leave for promotions that aren't always available at the better-run stores.

Interestingly, sales team turnover is often blamed for most of a poorly-run dealership's woes. Everything from market share losses to low grosses to poor CSI to you name it, are all caused because the sales managers are forced to constantly recruit and hire new salespeople (instead of spending their time developing and leading the current team). Turnover, some argue, is creating the lackluster leadership efforts you see from most sales managers in the industry.

Of course, for those willing to look beyond the excuses, this isn't a chicken-and-egg scenario. That is, we don't need to waste too much time deciding if the sales team turnover led to the poor leadership or if the poor leadership caused the sales team turnover?

It's the latter. Salespeople – like employees in every industry – don't quit jobs; they quit bosses. Unnecessarily poor leadership drives more good people out of dealerships (and drives some completely out of automotive retail) than all other factors combined.

This doesn't get solved because the excuses for not leading seem genuine to those above. However, every poor manager's excuse for not leading can be summed up in one sentence: "I don't have time to do things right; I'm too busy doing my job."

We know, of course, that in the well-run dealerships – those with miniscule turnover rates – managers do things right… and still have time to do their jobs. Their jobs, you see, become exponentially easier when they're not constantly dealing with sales team churn.

If your dealership could solve its turnover issues, then everything else would be a cakewalk.

Don't believe me? Okay, if you're a manager or an owner, make a list of the top five issues (other than turnover) that are negatively impacting your dealership's profitability. If you're like most dealers, your list probably contains items similar to these:

- Mediocre Online Reputation/CSI
- Competitive Dealer Driving Down Profits
- Higher Discounting/Lower Grosses
- Bad Allocation from the OEM
- Flattening Sales/Loss of Market Share
- Poor Overall Phone Skills/Follow-Up Processes
- Improper Up Tracking/CRM Usage
- Aged Inventory/Floorplan Issues

Now, review your list and honestly answer one question: "If my sales managers spent more time developing and leading, and less time recruiting and hiring, would we still suffer from these ailments?

Hint: All of the above concerns – and virtually every other problem at your dealership – can be traced back to your sales team's turnover issues. That's why I say, "solve dealership turnover issues, and everything else is a cakewalk." Here's the quick and dirty on how sales turnover impacts these items:

- Mediocre Online Reputation/CSI – *Better trained teams mean better customer experiences.*
- Competitive Dealer Driving Down Profits – *All dealers face a "market whore," though dealers with a well-trained staff defend their price and overcome consumer objections in a way that holds more gross.*
- Higher Discounting/Lower Grosses – *Ditto.*
- Bad Allocation from the OEM – *Working deals for top salespeople means fewer pencils and less overall management involvement; leaving the New Car Manager time to focus on factory allocations.*

- Flattening Sales/Loss of Market Share – *Top dealers (those with low to no turnover) grow share in any market condition.*
- Poor Overall Phone Skills/Follow-Up Processes – *Umm, duh.*
- Improper Up Tracking/CRM Usage – *Even if you hire salespeople with experience, they are likely learning your CRM for the first time.*
- Aged Inventory/Floorplan Issues – *Well-trained salespeople know how to move any unit you need moved; though when your managers have time to focus on inventory instead of personnel issues, they make better stocking decisions and your inventory turns faster and more profitably.*

Sales Does Not Cure All Ills

If you examined the data from recent years, there were two puzzling industry trends that took place as the new car market was busy growing to 17+ million units. First, there was the continuing erosion of new car margins as a percent of selling price. Basically, we sold more expensive vehicles for more money, but we decided to let the buyers keep any new-found profits.

Selling more for more and making less should be troubling to dealers and salespeople alike. It begs the question: What's going to happen to margins in a down market?

More troubling for dealers, however, should be the employee turnover trends. It seems that during this same growth market, employee retention decreased. According to NADA, the average dealer saw median employee tenure fall from 3.8 years in 2011 to 2.4 years in 2015.[2]

This is concerning on so many levels, but most of all it means that any lasting improvements contemplated by the dealership must be continually put on hold because your managers are too busy recruiting, hiring and training, right?

But, We Use Vendors for All That!

Outsourcing your staffing or training needs does not mean you're outsourcing your leadership. Unless, of course, your expectations of these vendors is that they'll not only find you the right fit, but also hold that person accountable to your rules, expectations and processes while they groom that new hire into a happy selling machine who will never leave your employ.

Don't laugh. Dealers might not say this out loud, but many of them expect their staffing and training partners to waive a magic wand and solve their leadership issues as well. I hate to write this, but most dealers who outsource their recruiting, hiring and training are actually outsourcing their leadership. (Or, at least trying to.)

The reason that grosses decreased while turnover increased is not because dealers used bad staffing or training firms; it's because no one in the dealership stepped up to truly lead those perfect hires who had just been expertly trained. The issue is not who we're hiring or who is doing the training. The issue is who is leading our people once they join our team or after the trainer leaves.

Give me a great leader and 10 random Burger King cooks, and over the long term that team will outperform a bad manager and 10 perfect hires. (I know this, because the bad manager will blow out your 10 perfect hires in the first 90 days.) Ultimately, the great leader with the 10 fry cooks will end up with a turnover rate near 20%, while the bad manager will continue to hover above 100%.

Okay, But What About My List of Issues?

Think about it, solving the turnover issues on your sales team means you're not having to train and retrain the same rules, processes and expectations again and again. Among many other benefits, a well-trained, stable workforce means a superior online reputation, a reduction in discounting, a growth in market share, great follow-up, and dedication to proper tracking and CRM usage.

If we can all agree that employee turnover negatively impacts our list of top dealership issues, then we can better understand that in order to actually solve any pervasive dealership issue, we need to solve turnover first. In other words, the top five issues you listed are merely symptoms of your dealership's real ailment: an unstable workforce. An unstable workforce, not coincidentally, is a symptom of ineffective leadership.

Of course, rather than offer you yet another hollow "dealers need leadership" lecture, I'd prefer to provide you with a real solution to your turnover issues; which, when followed, will also turn your managers into leaders. (All without having to trot out an expensive leadership "guru" who regurgitates a bunch of meaningless slogans instead of just giving you a blueprint.)

The Blueprint: Six Simple Steps to Solving Dealership Turnover Issues

I really wish it was way more complicated than this so that I could make millions teaching dealership managers how to be better leaders (and thus solve their turnover issues); but it's not. There really are just six simple steps you need to take.

First, write some simple, fair business rules. Don't overthink this and create a 10,000-page company manual; think of these as your Ten Commandments. Simple rules that cover things like skating and the consequences of not following a written process.

Next, write some enduring, fair pay plans. The issue with most dealership pay plans isn't that they change; it's that when they change they can feel unfair to your best people. Therefore, the goal is to write something your team feels is fair and that will only change if a major market disruption occurs.

Then, write some repeatable sales processes. Nothing fancy here, just some simple steps your managers can understand, enforce and easily teach. Of course, you'll need different processes based on customer type (internet, new, used, trade – for example).

Now, you'll want to test your sales processes to ensure they will be welcomed by both customers and employees. The ultimate goal is to ensure your processes can be described as "fun" by everyone from the first-time walk-in to your most seasoned salespeople. (Yes, fun. Given that almost everyone hates the current car-selling processes – including your own team – you should test and refine every process until it's simple, repeatable and fun for all.)

Once everything is in place, you will need to enforce your rules, pay plans and processes fairly. Don't worry about scaring off your good people with a measure of accountability. The fact is that good people like order and great people love structure; while slugs hate having anyone telling them what to do. But, be prepared. Enforcing rules and processes might mean firing those who refuse to comply; and this may include your favorite manager.

And finally, you just need to be nice. It's no secret that people quit bosses, not companies. Therefore, if you provide fair pay plans, good business rules, fun processes and structure – and all of this is delivered in a courteous manner with real respect for the individuals on your team – you will discover very quickly that your best people don't want to leave; and the competition's best people will want to come work for you.

That's really all there is to solving turnover – and I know this because I've seen it successfully accomplished more than once. If you're an owner or manager, stick with this chapter as we'll further explore these steps and other tools necessary for running the kind of dealership the superstars want to join. If you're a salesperson, feel free to jump to the next chapter and save the rest of this one for when you join the management ranks.

You Don't Have Sales Managers; You've Got Deskers!

Most dealerships I work with seem to suffer from too few managers. They don't have enough managers to control the sales floor, monitor phone calls and other activities, oversee the basic road-to-the-sale, ensure the CRM is being used properly or even train their own sales teams.

Why am I complaining? This is probably why they hired me in the first place, right?

Probably; but because they don't have enough managers to run all those day-to-day leadership tasks, they also have no one to reinforce my training or the training the last guy provided or the guy before that or the guy before that or... you get the idea.

It's not that these dealerships need to add headcount – they do not – it's that they need to stop paying deskers as if they were actually managers. (Or, preferably, get their deskers to start acting like managers.)

Don't get me wrong, I love watching a great desker in action. I enjoy being in an active sales tower and observing as a top-notch desker berates an unprepared salesperson for daring to bring him "this garbage," then turns and – without missing a beat – loads the lips of another salesperson with some of the best closing lines ever spoken all while completing a fourth pencil that holds some gross, steals the trade and brings the payments to within $50 of where the customer demanded they needed to be.

Desking for maximum gross is an art form; and great deskers are artists – they really are. Of course, just like most great artists I know, most great deskers make terrible people managers.

Deskers' Days Are Numbered

Let's be clear: America's car dealers won't always need traditional sales managers. (By traditional, I mean sales managers who can desk deals, but couldn't lead their team out of a wet paper bag.) There will come a day when the art of desking is completely replaced by the science (technology and data and firm retail pricing). It's happening more and more every single day; even in dealerships not considered one-price stores.

You see, something happened while you, your 20 Group and your OEM were focused on Facebook and Twitter and Pinterest and... you get it. As we'll learn, the customer became empowered with so much information that they're arriving at your dealership fully armed with what they plan to buy and for how much.

In fact, for some deals, desking has become a mere formality. Some antiquated dance meant to drag the deal on longer than necessary in a way that either blows the sale or eventually lands right on the number the customer calculated from the hours of research they completed before arriving at your lot.

Unfortunately, instead of being focused on processes that can wow the connected customer and get the deal done in under an hour, some deskers are busy trying to hoodwink every prospect by delivering a first pencil that's $3,500 higher than the online price while simultaneously trying to steal the trade for well below the lowest number in the range the customer saw online before they arrived on the lot.

Oh, and while these deskers were trying squeeze the buffalo off the nickel with their fourth pencil, the connected customer has been using their smartphone to find a better deal up the street. And with that, they're gone!

This deal was lost for a number of reasons... here are four possibilities:

1. The desker thinks every Up is an uninformed lay down;
2. They're too focused on traditional desking as the sole generator of front-end profit;
3. They provided zero transactional transparency in-store; and
4. They allowed the customer to sit all alone with their phone.

Because today's connected customer already has nearly all the answers before they arrive at a dealership, all the team needed to do was sell them a car. It's too bad everyone was freelancing their own road-to-the-sale while the deskers were busy outsmarting themselves.

Sales managers, in the traditional sense, will be all but obsolete at most dealerships sometime in the future because there will be nothing left to desk. The deal will be handled from beginning to end by a product specialist on their own tablet at the advertised price. (Oh, and this means dealers won't have F&I managers either, but that's a topic for a different book.)

Don't believe me? Multiple dealers have successfully been selling cars that way for a very long time – some for well over a decade. They're making good grosses, great CSI, and all without desk managers or F&I managers.

Today's prospects are connected and informed; and they chose your dealership largely because of what they learned about you before they arrived. They believe your vehicle is priced right (or they have a price from one of your competitors they plan to use against you) and they believe your vehicle fits their needs.

For most consumers today, there is no reason to visit a dealership unless they've already determined that your offerings meet their needs, including price. Now, they just want someone to treat them with respect, give them a good experience, and sell them the car for what you're advertising it for online.

This is where sales managers (and not deskers) are needed. This book includes multiple processes that create a great customer experience. From proper lead handling to The Perfect Appointment, sales managers have the opportunity to learn how easy it can be to wow today's buyer by providing an efficient, enjoyable experience.

Unfortunately, most deskers are too busy desking deals to try their hand at sales management. They won't reinforce something as intuitive and simple as The Perfect Appointment; even if it means making more money and making their lives easier. Your goal should be to turn your deskers into sales managers because, among other things, true sales managers (in no particular order):

- Ensure the team enters 100% of the Ups in the CRM;
- Oversee every step in your road-to-the-sale in near real time;
- Find the time to shake the customer's hand before the demo drive;
- Observe and train the sales team on phone skills;
- Confirm customer appointments; and
- Gladly turn their slugs into superstars.

In other words, they lead the sales team in a way that improves sales, revenues, profits, inventory turn, and CSI; all while dramatically reducing salesperson turnover.

The Role of Culture

High turnover coupled with market share loss are usually symptoms of a bad company culture. However, telling someone "you need to improve your culture" is utterly meaningless to most people. Since my goal is to help you positively impact your store's culture (and solve turnover), it's better to give you examples of what a great dealership culture looks like.

First, let's agree that the results you reap from having a great dealership culture are worthwhile. That is, it makes sense to pursue a better culture because the rewards far outweigh the effort.

Next, let's agree that we can identify a great dealership culture by examining metrics like market share growth, gross profit growth, employee retention, employee morale, customer retention and, of course, customer satisfaction. When all of these measurements are moving in the right direction, I would argue that the respective dealership has a great culture. When they are not, I would argue the opposite.

Over the years, I've worked with hundreds of dealerships, and it's become easy to quickly spot whether or not a particular store has the makings of a great culture.

For example, when the owner or general manager is highly engaged with their team and their customers, you can bet with certainty that the metrics I mentioned above are moving in the desired direction. In these stores, the leader is someone who is on the floor every single day interacting with salespeople, mechanics, lot porters, service advisors and customers. You see them walking through service at 7:30 a.m. and taking time to greet everyone. You see them chatting with the salespeople in the late afternoon and shaking the hands of their customers.

When I see this, I know immediately that this team has higher morale, lower turnover, better grosses and they are growing share.

Rules Matter

Although it may seem counterintuitive at first, stores with great cultures also have a strict adherence to rules and processes. This helps create a great culture, because deep down employees want structure, order and direction. Moreover, teams that understand what is expected of them happily perform better than teams kept in the dark.

Along with these strict rules and processes, you'll usually uncover that great cultures almost never make wholesale changes to their pay plans. Instead, these dealerships find that static, fair pay plans are generally superior to those where the team sees you as someone who is constantly moving the goalposts. This does not mean great stores never change pay plans, it's just that the best dealerships only touch these when dictated by significant market changes.

You also discover with great dealership cultures that everyone feels appreciated. That is, employees from the receptionist to the general manager feel that their contribution matters and that their contribution is appreciated by those in charge.

Finally, whenever I find myself working in a great dealership culture, it's no coincidence that I can clearly see that they love their customers. This might seem cliché, but the dealerships with the best cultures are actually excited to serve customers. You don't see service advisors, for example, not returning calls in these dealerships. On the contrary, you see everyone proactively working to assist their customers.

More than likely, this is the result of the leadership truly appreciating their employees. With customer service, everything rolls downhill; all the way to the customer. How you treat your receptionist dictates exactly how she'll treat the next person who walks up to her desk.

Great cultures, by the way, cannot be faked. Duplicity is the enemy of a great culture. So, whether it's cheating a customer or lying to the OEM rep just to get him off your back, duplicitous dealers – those who say one thing and do another – create a culture of duplicitous managers and employees.

It's just not possible to build a great company culture without a solid foundation that includes full compliance, rules, processes and clear expectations that we're always going to do what's right, not necessarily what's going to make us the most money in the short term. It's this integrity-driven culture that makes top salespeople want to come to work for you, stay with you and sell you even more cars.

The "A" Word

Accountability is one of those words that consultants, trainers, vendors, OEMs, managers and owners bandy about so much in automotive that it's nearly lost all meaning. We use these words to describe what we need, but we never seem to act on these. For example, think about the number of times you've heard any of the following and what, if anything, changed after the owner or general manager uttered it:

- We need to start *training* more.
- We need to stick to our *processes*.
- We need to provide better *leadership*.

- We need to start holding people *accountable*.

The italicized words have become so overused and so under-executed in automotive retail that they're bordering on becoming punchlines. Of course, you already know that if you want to solve what ails your dealership – and especially solve the turnover issues once and for all – you've got to embrace the "A" word and start holding your team accountable to the standards, rules and processes you've put in place.

Accountability makes everything easier. Managers no longer hem and haw about whether some rule or process is important because they can enforce them all when they employ accountability. Superstars embrace accountability; average sellers begin to sell more when held accountable; and the slugs will slither off to another dealership if you start enforcing your standards, rules and processes.

Accountability is the cornerstone of leadership and the driver of great performance. Accountability is not a bad thing; it's a good thing. Accountability is not stifling; accountability is freeing because it's fair and equitable; and that's the biggest reason to start holding everyone accountable: it's fair!

Accountability is simply enforcing your standards, rules and processes by ensuring there are consequences for performing or not performing according to these. These consequences can be rewarding (an earned bonus) or they can be punitive (a written warning). Though without consequences, your standards, rules and processes are meaningless – because they become unenforceable.

Let's Write Some Good Business Rules

Your dealership is a business; and good businesses have good business rules. Even in the touchy-feely-snowflake world we live in today, we need good (and strict) business rules. Without rules, no business could function.

Most every dealership does a good job of enforcing and holding their teams accountable to the obvious rules. That is, they'll generally fire you if you're caught stealing accessories from the parts department or if you hit a customer; though, shockingly, that's about the extent of the rules that seem to matter in many dealerships. I write "seem to matter" because if a rule is not regularly enforced, then salespeople assume that rule doesn't matter to the store's leadership… and they don't follow it.

So, let's write some basic fair business rules for your dealership. We're not going to rewrite the *Affordable Care Act's* 20,000 pages of regulations, just some good business rules that you can think of as your dealership's Ten Commandments (although, we're only going to write six, not ten, rules in this chapter). As a reminder, you'll want to put these rules into place and enforce them (i.e., hold people accountable to them) if your goal is to solve your turnover issues and sell more cars.

Rule #1: Thou shalt not skate. While every dealer I work with claims to have anti-skating rules in place, the truth is most do not. Most, in fact, reward the thief (the skater) by giving them half the deal when they're caught stealing (skating). That's not accountability, it's madness! And, great salespeople won't stay at a dealership that rewards skaters.

A simple protected prospect rule will not only eliminate any skating but will also encourage your sales teams to start communicating with their database of customers – both sold and unsold. Here's my recommended rule on protected prospects:

ABC Motors operates a 100% open sales floor except in the following instances:

- A valid appointment that shows on time;
- A customer or prospect who asks for the salesperson by name within earshot of a greeter, receptionist or manager;
- A same-day Be-Back.

The three exceptions above are considered protected prospects. Any salesperson who Ups and sells a protected prospect without prior approval from a sales manager will receive no credit and no commission for the sale. No one is authorized to sell a protected prospect without expressed management approval and there will be no split deals in these instances.

Skaters, in other words, would not be rewarded with half the deal; but, rather, would lose the entire deal to the original salesperson.

Besides eliminating the need to "split the baby" in potential skating situations, this rule also encourages your salespeople to call their Be-Backs and their sold database; and to start setting real appointments that show (instead of hoping that your former customers will come back to your dealership and ask for them by name).

This rule rewards your aggressive sellers (those who make phone calls and greet all Ups). This means you'll sell more cars to more people for more money... and all because you put in a fair anti-skating rule that you're going to enforce.

Rule #2: Thou shalt make phone calls. Are you tired of complaining that your floor teams won't make phone calls? Is this one of the reasons you're wasting all that money on a BDC? There are many names for what's happening to your store – and none of them are flattering. This is the tail-wagging-the-dog; this is the inmates-running-the-asylum; this is you and your managers sucking at basic leadership.

Let's put an enforceable rule with real consequences in place... and then – novel idea – let's enforce it! Enforcing a rule that requires salespeople make phone calls is good for everyone. It's good for you (the dealership sells more cars) and it's good for your salespeople (they sell more cars). Here's my simple rule:

> Between the hours of 8:00 – 10:30 a.m. and 2:00 – 6:00 p.m., if you're not with a customer, you must be at your desk making phone calls. No exceptions.

This one is easy to enforce by using the greatest leadership tool ever invented: MBWA. That is, management by walking around.

During your required call times, sales managers should walk around the dealership, ensuring everyone is at their desk, on the phone, calling customers. Those who are not should be asked politely to begin making their calls; and those who refuse (or who are always caught goofing off during these times) should be shown the door. You're not a bad person if you won't make your required calls; you just can't work here.

Rule #3: Thou shalt complete assigned activities. Let's start this section with some questions. Do you remember that CRM tool you're paying so much for each month? Did you know one of the greatest features of any decent CRM tool is that it prompts salespeople to complete activities? Are you aware that the average salesperson has hundreds of past due activities?

You bought and paid for a CRM; you created processes that include activities you deemed important; you expect your team to complete those activities as you know it will help them sell more cars. So, the final question is why the heck don't you require that they complete their activities?

You just need a simple rule with clear consequences (accountability) and your sellers will gladly complete their activities. I like this one:

> All assigned activities must be completed before you leave for the day. If you worked yesterday, and you arrive today with past due activities, you ride the pine today. You get no Ups. You do, however, get to sit at your desk and complete your past due activities, today's activities, and any phone calls you believe will help you set appointments that show and buy.

The pushback from managers on this one is their fear that either they won't have Up coverage (if everyone is riding the pine) and/or their "best guys" will quit the minute they make them sit.

Who cares? Seriously, who cares if you don't have Up coverage today? Remember, you deemed these activities important; so, they must be, right? Moreover, who cares if your "best guys" quit over this? First, if you're delivering good leadership with good business rules, your top sellers will be happy – and, they'll complete their activities every day. Second, what makes you think those who fail to complete required activities are your "best guys?"

Like all of these rules, announce this one a month in advance; monitor for compliance; and then enforce it the very first day you say you will. Imagine the message you'll deliver to the slugs when you sit a superstar on a Saturday! ("Holy crap, they're serious about this activity stuff!")

If your final argument is that some of the activities in the CRM aren't important, then remove these. Get rid of all activities that aren't moneymakers. Doing this allows you to stand firm on this rule.

I've had clients implement this rule (with accountability), and within six months they were able to cut their turnover in half and grow their sales by more than 35% per salesperson per month. Also, there's a great thing that happens when you keep your team busy: they don't have time to gossip; they don't have time to talk about how terrible it is to work here.

Rule #4: Thou shalt use the CRM. A few questions for this rule, as well. Does your CRM tool show all the important notes about all customers and prospects? Does it include details of every interaction? Do your sold units in the CRM match the DMS? No? No worries, the rule for this one is simple:

> All customer and prospect interactions – especially sold units – should be recorded in the CRM as close to real time as possible.

The consequences can be equally simple. Instead of paying for sold units from the DMS, pay only for those marked sold in both the DMS and CRM. This means that at the end of the month, if the salesperson shows 18 sold in the DMS but only 12 in the CRM, they get paid for 12. When they scream bloody murder about their incorrect paycheck, let them know why and pay them for the other sold units on the next check.

Where I've had clients implement this, the issues last exactly one check. After that, the team gets the message that you're serious and your CRM begins to magically match the DMS.

Of course, this rule (like all good business rules) will last exactly as long as your managers enforce it.

Rule #5: Thou shalt record all Ups. Ask any dealer in America if they require 100% Up tracking, and they'll tell you they do. Now, ask them what percent of their Ups make it into the CRM tool, and they'll lament that fewer than half do.

So, you don't really require all Ups be recorded in the CRM, do you? Here's a quick rule with the consequences:

> You must track 100% of your Ups in the CRM. Failure to timely and properly log an Up will cost you one rotation in the Up line. Failure to log a second Up in the same day will put you out of the Up rotation for the remainder of the day and your next scheduled workday.

If you think these consequences are harsh, perhaps you should rethink your career in automotive. Today's Ups are ready to buy, and when you fail to log them in the CRM, you lose all opportunities to sell them today and tomorrow.

The best way to manage this rule is for your desk managers to log Ups as they did when they used paper desk logs. If a guy in a blue shirt walks on the lot and you see Bob greeting them, you write (or enter, if your CRM's desk log works like a paper log) "Blue Shirt – Bob." Later, if you see Bob walking around without the guy in the blue shirt, you bench him for one rotation. Do this a couple of times and you'll soon get 100% of your Ups in the CRM.

Rule #6: Thou shalt T.O. every prospect. Like the 100% Up tracking requirement every dealer claims to have in place, everyone claims to require 100% T.O.s. Of course, just like the Up tracking, this one can sometimes occur less than half the time. Let's put in a similar rule with the same consequences:

> You must T.O. 100% of your prospects – in fact, no one leaves the dealership lest they meet a manager. Failure to properly T.O. every Up will cost you one rotation in the Up line. Failure to T.O. a second Up in the same day will put you out of the Up rotation for the remainder of the day and your next scheduled workday.

We know that T.O.s done properly equal more sold units, so there's nothing harsh or unfair about this rule. Plus, these rules are part of a contract between you and your salespeople. Enforcing these is fair. It's fair to you, and it's fair to the entire team. Everyone wants to know what's expected of them and what to expect. The only ones who complain about these rules are salespeople you can (and should) live without.

Just six simple rules that, when enforced, will greatly reduce your negative turnover (and hasten the exit of slugs not capable of helping you gain share). Of course, you don't want to destroy your existing team by dropping these rules out of thin air. Collaborate with your managers as you write these, identify the roadblocks you expect, address the roadblocks, and then announce these at least a month before you officially put them into place.

Then... and this is the hard part... hold your team (including your managers) accountable to these. No exceptions.

Beware the Prima Donnas

The biggest roadblocks to positive change in your sales department are the Prima Donnas. They poo-poo every suggestion; find fault in every improvement. Yet, they complain constantly about the status quo. Prima Donnas are never your top salespeople; instead, they are those who sell at or just above your store's average, while they believe they're the most valuable employees you have. Plan to share all proposed changes with them first.

Bring your Prima Donnas into your office one by one. Explain the proposed rules and let them know you need their support. Be clear that you hope to get their complete buy-in because you'd hate to lose them. Tell them you genuinely believe they can sell 25 or 30 units a month complying with your rules and processes, but you'd understand if they'd prefer to freelance somewhere else.

Prima. Donna. Solved.

To be effective, these rules must apply to everyone. They apply to your top salespeople; they apply to your Green Peas; they apply to your 8-Car Alans; and, they especially apply to you and your managers.

When you introduce these rules, make sure you highlight the fact that they apply to everyone, including you. Also, ensure that everyone understands three axioms of a leader of any well-run business:

- I will never lie to you.
- I respect you and I respect that you have a life outside of this dealership.
- But, while you're here, these are the rules we're all going to live by.

If someone cannot follow these rules, they're not bad; they're just not a fit, and they need to work somewhere else. As long as you let them work within these rules and manage their activities, the results will take care of themselves. And, the results will be spectacular.

Fair Pay Plans

While it's true that most people quit bosses and not companies, salespeople will leave when they feel your new, new, new pay plan is unfair. Barring a major restructuring of your business, there should be no need to change a fair pay plan.

A fair pay plan is one that equitably compensates the salesperson or manager for the contribution they made. It's also enduring. That is, it remains in place for a long time; regardless of whether the market is up or down. Finally, fair pay plans are those that also drive the results higher. (The pay plan's not fair if it's not fair to the dealership, right?)

When writing a new pay plan or reworking an existing plan, be sure to assume the worst. Determine how someone can cheat your plan and then solve for that. As we know, everyone works their pay plan. So, test your proposed plan the way your most resourceful salespeople and managers will. Find the holes and plug them before releasing it. You want everyone to be able to maximize their pay; you just want them to do this fairly.

Pigs and Hogs

My favorite saying in business is "pigs get fed and hogs get slaughtered." The meaning of this saying is that it's okay to be a pig (and make a little money on this deal or that), but if you go too far and try to take all the money all the time, you're not going to last.

When this saying is applied to pay plans, the meaning is simple: write a fair pay plan where everyone can win. I've encountered managers over the years who felt they could outsmart their salespeople by writing one-sided pay plans that only benefitted the store. They were being hogs and they got slaughtered.

Great salespeople – true superstars – can work anywhere they want; and they know this. They'll tolerate a pay plan where you're being a little piggish, but they'll bolt for your competitor as soon as you try to take all the money. This is not about pay, it's about fairness. Great salespeople won't stay where they feel they're being treated unfairly.

While I'm sure some of you would appreciate a sample pay plan here, I'm not going to provide one. There are simply too many variables for any plan one person provides to have much use to 90% of the dealerships in America. Variables like the brand(s) you sell, the size of the dealership or group, the ability to sell both new and used, your market, the amount of your packs, and whether you have a BDC setting appointments for the floor all matter to creating a fair pay plan.

Besides, if your current pay plan isn't fair to everyone, it's not because you don't know what a good pay plan is. Every manager in the business has worked under fair pay plans and probably has a copy of these lying around somewhere. Go find yours, dust them off, and rework them for your current situation. In the meantime, here are a few guidelines for writing fair, enduring pay plans that attract and maintain great talent:

- Have a protected prospects rule (like the one we've already written) in your dealership. A protected prospect rule ensures you're not paying salespeople for being lucky. Instead, you're paying them for driving their own Up Bus by declaring an open floor for basically everything except appointments that show on time. Remember: this rule rewards the most aggressive salespeople (those willing to make calls and catch every Up on the lot).

- Pack with caution. You might think you're outsmarting your salespeople by putting a big flat pack on every unit, but you're likely just being a hog. If your pack is not directly related to what you've spent on a particular vehicle, then it's just arbitrarily driving down commissions. Flat packs were fine when you set the selling price of your vehicles; but, the market is setting most of the prices today and flat packs aren't helping you hold gross; they're just angering your top sellers.

- Identify exceptions to the plan up front. For example, I know some dealers who claim to pay a 25% commission on the front-end gross, but balk when a salesperson gets sticker + addendum on a specialty vehicle. It's crazy, but some dealers don't want to fairly reward their sellers for getting all the money. If this describes you, then write the exceptions (like "a $1,500 commission cap on any deal") into the original plan. I once saw a rural dealer lose his only 25+ car seller because he didn't want to pay $5,000 on a $20,000 gross; so, he made up a pay plan exception on the spot and only paid the salesman $1,500. The salesman walked the day he got his check; and the $3,500 the dealer saved on the deal cost him at least a dozen units a month for the next year. Pigs get fed and hogs get slaughtered.

- Pay for performance. Your pay plans need to be fair to everyone – especially the dealership. This begs the question, "Why do some dealers pay a full commission to a floor salesperson who closes a BDC appointment?" The only reason you have a BDC setting appointments is because you can't get the floor to follow a process and make phone calls. Therefore, why are you compensating them for something they didn't do? Your floor team deserves a full deal on a deal where they did all the work – that's paying for performance. So, if you're splitting the duties (one person is setting appointments and another person is selling them), then you need to split these deals. Your plan should only pay for actual performance; though, this also means you should be paying for all the little things you want your salespeople to do, for example:
    - If you want them to set the first service appointment, compensate them when the customer shows.
    - If you want them to introduce some F&I products or present accessories while prospects are waiting on the

business office, then compensate them when the customer buys these.

  o If you want to drive better CSI, compensate them for perfect surveys.

• Limit the cuteness. In other words, don't overthink your pay plan. Trying to be too cute with your spiffs can backfire way more often than it helps drive results. I once worked with a dealer who wanted more Saturday appointments, so he paid a $50 spiff on all Saturday appointment shows to his floor team. Immediately, his Saturday appointments increased tenfold. Great, right? Nope; his salespeople just started faking appointments in the CRM to get the spiff. They would take a Traditional Up, put them in the CRM as a Phone Up, set an appointment, then mark the appointment "showed." This cost the dealer a few thousand dollars before he figured it out. So, limit the cuteness and just write simple, fair, enduring plans that cannot be gamed.

• Nobody makes too much. If you've written a fair pay plan and you find that your top salesperson made more than any of your sales managers last month, resist the urge to rewrite the plan – nobody makes too much if the plan is fair. Instead, openly congratulate the salesperson at your next meeting and be sure to tell everyone that she made more than any of your sales managers! (If it were my dealership, I'd go one step further and give the salesperson a check for another $1,000 in front of her peers. This sends the message that we want the team to succeed and we're willing to pay for that success.)

The bottom line on pay plans is this: If you'd like your pay plan to drive positive results and sales team stability at your dealership, then resist the urge to change a fair plan. While salespeople often don't quit over pay, they will quit when they feel that their pay plan isn't fair.

Repeatable Sales Processes

Sales processes always outsell the opposite. The opposite, of course, are no processes; and following a sales process always outsells freelancing. Interestingly, an average salesperson following a bad sales process will outsell those following no process.

Process is what sells cars. Period. Of course, you're probably wondering what this has to do with solving salesperson turnover, right? Everything.

Salespeople who follow processes sell more cars for more money and in less time than those who try to wing it with every prospect. They're more successful and they're happier with their job, you, your dealership and their customers. Good people need guidance and rules and structure and boundaries; simple processes provide these. Great sellers, by the way, will embrace a solid sales process; while the slugs will fight everything you want to "make" them do. Therefore, write sales processes for your superstars and stop trying to appease the slugs.

To be effective, your sales processes need to be simple (easy to understand), they need to make sense (be logical), they need to be repeatable (applicable to any prospect), and they should be fun. Why fun? Because buying a car is an exciting time, and if your sales process is a grind, you're not going to sell as many units as the guys with the fun process across town.

Simple, logical, repeatable, fun sales processes *that are enforced* are the absolute difference maker in dealership staffing. When you teach and enforce good sales processes, you immediately reduce your churn of new salespeople.

Most dealers hire a bunch of Green Peas, have them shadow a salesperson for a week or two, make them watch some training videos, and then send them out to catch Ups. They almost never teach them an actual sales process; though, even when they do, they don't reinforce this process by holding the Green Peas accountable to it.

Amazingly, 60 days later they find that 80% of these Green Peas "just weren't cut out for the car business." Rinse. Lather. Repeat. Conversely, dealers who teach and enforce simple sales processes hire fewer Green Peas because they have fewer openings; though the ones they do hire stay longer and are more successful than their peers at the average dealership.

Reduced Learning Curve

By teaching and enforcing repeatable sales processes – those that are standardized across your sales floor – you reduce the amount of time new salespeople require for training (since everyone is doing it the same way). Moreover, when you have great processes in place, you stop hiring experience and start hiring character. You can do this because you know your processes (when enforced) will help turn almost anyone into a top salesperson. You no longer need to hire your competitor's retreads because your system is what sells the cars.

Enforcing repeatable sales processes also reduces your dealership's need for outside staffing firms, trainers and consultants. Have you ever wondered why we still have major turnover issues today despite the hundreds of thousands of dollars the average dealership has spent over the years on staffing firms, trainers and consultants? The best staffing firm in the world isn't going to solve your turnover issues by making "better hires" if your managers aren't teaching and enforcing simple sales processes.

I'll introduce a few sales processes throughout this book, but I encourage you to write your own. You know your dealership better than I do; and you'll need to live with and enforce the processes you put in place. Your buy-in will naturally be higher for your processes than it will be for mine. Here are just a few tips for writing great processes yourself:

- Great processes are easy. They're easy to follow.
- Great processes are simple. You should be able to explain your process to a stranger in about a minute.
- Great processes make sense. They make sense to you, your salespeople and your customers.
- Great processes are repeatable. Your team should treat 100% of your Ups to the same steps 100% of the time.
- Great processes are enforced. Without enforcement, processes don't exist.
- Great processes are effective. They drive positive results.

Interestingly, the last point is the least important one when writing your sales processes. When you have easy, simple, repeatable processes that make sense and are enforced, you can measure their effectiveness and make changes until these processes are perfected. Once perfected, you continue to measure and continue to improve your processes – this is called continuous process improvement.

Be certain to leverage your CRM tool's capabilities any time you want to employ processes. A good CRM can prompt your team to complete the required steps (the activities); while a great CRM can alert your managers when steps are skipped or faked. When your CRM makes it easy for your managers to hold the team accountable, your processes have a better chance of surviving. Of course, unless processes are driven from the very top of your organization, the first speed bump your team hits will often cause even good processes to be dropped or faked; and the whole thing becomes a box-checking exercise.

Now What?

We've got good business rules; we've got a fair pay plan; we've got great processes that everyone loves... now what?

Managers in business exist for a reason. Plainly stated, they ensure the efforts of their team further the company's interests. If everyone always did what was in the company's interest, we wouldn't need managers, would we?

Now that you have the foundation of a great organization, it's important to realize that your rules, pay plans and processes are meaningless if your sales managers refuse to strictly and fairly enforce these with every salesperson, every day. Owners and GMs can create the best systems ever imagined, but if the sales managers don't support and enforce these, they do not exist. Moreover, when your managers fail to enforce rules and processes that you introduced as important, it undermines your authority and confuses your sales teams.

People want to know what is expected of them; and great people embrace fair rules, pay plans and processes that are strictly enforced. Simply put, if the rules, pay plans and processes are fair, then enforcing these brings certainty and stability to your dealership; and this reduces turnover.

Fear of Enforcement

Some managers are genuinely afraid to enforce even the rules and processes with which they agree. Some want to be the nice guy, while others are afraid that enforcing these may create dissention and lead to turnover. I've heard more than once, "But Steve, my top guys are going to quit!"

Please. Stop. It.

We've already agreed that these rules, pay plans and processes are fair. We know they'll make everyone more successful. We know they'll lead to increases in sales, grosses and CSI. Now you believe that if you enforce these, your good people are going to quit?

Let them. Anyone who leaves over the enforcement of fair rules, pay plans and processes cannot be included in your discussion of "good people." Good people like rules; they like certainty; they like to know what you expect of them and where the boundaries are.

A dealer's "top guys" should be defined as those who have their interests aligned with the dealership's. If they truly are your top guys, they'll embrace the rules, pay plans and processes because they trust you and your managers; and they want to do what's best for both you and themselves.

I once worked with a large dealership that was receiving nearly 2,000 internet leads each month. They hired me to help them sell more to these 2,000 prospects; though they asked me to work with everyone except one particular internet salesperson. This salesperson, we'll call him Ray, was their "top guy," and they were worried he'd quit if they tried to include him in any new pay plan, rules or processes. "Besides," the sales manager told me, "Ray's killing it. He sells over 30 every month."

Given this, I worked with the rest of the team over the next three days and left Ray alone. I was amazed at how many people came in and asked for Ray; and I observed him sell three cars during my visit. What I didn't see – not once in three days – was Ray picking up the phone and calling anyone. From my vantage point in this dealership's phone room I could clearly see into Ray's office. (Ray, like all sellers at this dealership who sold 25 or more units a month, had his own office.) Ray called no one over three days; yet he sold three cars to internet prospects. How could that be?

Two minutes of digging in the CRM showed that Ray was receiving about 450 internet leads each month. To every inquiry, Ray would quickly respond with an email showing the lowest price plus TT&L and all dealer fees. At the bottom of every one of his emails was the following sentence in large, bold letters:

Must ask for Ray and present this email to receive this special price!!!

This was before virtually every dealer showed their expected selling price on their websites. This dealer, in fact, showed MSRP/Book and "Click for ePrice" on all new/used units. It took two whole minutes to discover their "top guy" was just vomiting the lowest price on every prospect and selling to those few buyers who didn't take his email to a competitor to try to beat it.

"But Steve," you exclaim, "Ray was still selling 30, wasn't he?"

Ugh. Yes, Ray was selling 30... to 450 prospects! That's a 6.7% closing percentage! Give those same 450 leads to four good internet salespeople and they'll produce 80 sold units. Give them to two good BDC agents and they'll drive 115 appointments that show on time and ready to buy. Thirty units from 450 valid internet opportunities does not make someone a "top guy;" it makes them below average.

The Show Me Leader

Enforcing your rules, pay plans and processes might mean losing those who refuse to comply; this may include your "top guy" or your favorite manager. If you don't think you have the stomach to enforce these, hire a new general manager to do it for you... or, you could just become a Show Me Leader.

We've all heard "inspect what you expect" and that people "respect what you inspect." The problem for most dealerships is that managers and owners either refuse to inspect anything or they don't know how. As I wrote, it took two minutes to discover Ray's interests were not aligned with his dealership's interests. I simply inspected what the dealership claimed they expected. I do, however, understand that not everyone knows where to look in their CRM tool to ensure the team is following the prescribed process, making calls, setting appointments and selling cars properly (what the dealership expected of Ray). This is where "show me" comes in.

A Show Me Leader doesn't need to know how to uncover cherry-picking, box-checking or price-vomiting in the CRM. Moreover, a Show Me Leader isn't afraid to enforce rules and processes because most people approached by the Show Me Leader quickly begin to self-enforce these... or they leave. Here's how it would've worked in Ray's case:

Show Me Leader: "Hey Ray, do you have all your calls made today?"

Ray: "I sure do, boss."

Show Me Leader: "Great... show me."

When you do this the first couple of times, Ray will give you a puzzled look, so you'll need to add:

Show Me Leader: "Yeah, just open the CRM and show me. I'd love to see where we are with your leads and how I can help."

If you take five minutes each day to ask Ray about these calls, eventually he'll start making them or he'll quit. Either outcome is preferable to a 6.7% closing percentage on valid, non-duplicated internet leads.

To be clear, the Show Me Leader never needs to be confrontational because everything is presented in a way intended to help the team succeed. Using "show me" allows you to inspect everything you expect without having to do any of the work. (The person showing you does all the digging for you.) If you choose to become a Show Me Leader, you'll soon discover "show me" are the two most powerful words you can use as a manager.

Manage the Activities, Not the Results

Not surprisingly, the other internet salespeople at Ray's dealership hated Ray. They knew what he was getting away with and they didn't like it. They also didn't like that he was treated like a superstar and allowed to freelance. To them, it wasn't fair.

I've known lots of Rays over the years, and they cause more good people to leave than their managers ever realize. While Ray was indeed selling 30 units each month, he was costing the dealership at least 50 units; not to mention the production from all the great salespeople he likely chased away. The managers were so focused on his results that they didn't care if he completed the required activities.

If you want your salespeople to overachieve, you should manage their activities and not their results. Salespeople already do a good job of watching the board and tracking their own results. Plus, when you manage the activities, the results will come. Finally, when you manage the activities, your team will stay busy doing those things that you know lead to car sales.

Quick caveat on managing activities: I'm not referring to "counting" the activities – that's called box checking, and it results in worse overall performance than doing nothing as a manager. I'm referring to actively managing the salespeople successfully completing their assigned activities, keeping them busy, and inspecting the quality of their work.

Keeping your salespeople busy reduces turnover in a few ways. Primarily, it ensures their success each month and it keeps them productively engaged instead of destructively disengaged. Disengaged salespeople – you know, the guys sitting outside waiting on the Up Bus; smoking cigarettes; complaining – are always thinking about survival. Disengaged employees are only here for the money and they'll leave you as soon as any opportunity presents itself, even if it's not necessarily a better opportunity.

Conversely, highly-engaged employees – those who are involved in something productive all the time; who are busy the whole day; who look up at the clock and say, "It's time to go home? My gosh, it feels like I just got here" – feel a greater sense of "team" and they deliver stellar sales results. When you manage the activities, you keep your team engaged and productive. They're too busy making money to sit around complaining about how they're not making any money.

The Secret to Holding People Accountable

Did you know there was a secret to holding people accountable? There is; and it's this:

You must hold them accountable.

That's it. That's the secret. The secret is to do it; it really isn't that hard, and you're going to make your good people great and your great people thrilled to work here. And, when your great people are thrilled to work here, they'll always ensure every customer has a great experience buying from you.

4

THE CUSTOMER EXPERIENCE MATTERS

While this book was written to help you sell more cars for more money, this chapter is going to look at examples of customer service and the customer experience from some non-automotive companies. Why? Because dealers and salespeople who want to stand out from the competition need to learn how to create great customer experiences from the experts... and, unfortunately, experts at the customer experience are few and far between in our industry.

Are you truly committed to selling more cars for more money? Are you truly committed to asking for referrals and earning great CSI? Are you truly committed to learning and employing Assumptive Selling to help you get there?

Outstanding! However, just so we're on the same page, let me be sure you understand that you cannot achieve any of this if you don't improve the customer's experience when buying from you. While Assumptive Selling creates a better customer experience by itself, if everything else about buying from you is stuck in the five-hour road-to-the-sale, grind culture of the 1980s, then you're going to struggle to achieve all the benefits of Assumptive Selling.

Without a great overall experience, Assumptive Selling will barely help you move the needle. You won't earn great CSI; few people will send you referrals; your grosses will stink; and your closing percentage will be average at best.

The customer experience matters, and true Assumptive Selling puts you on the right track to provide a great experience for your customers every time.

Of course, I still run into sales managers today that openly question why the customer experience matters? Why, they'll ask, do we need to focus so heavily on doing more than just delivering a good product at a fair price? Why isn't "good enough" actually good enough?

Customer studies are clear: People are more likely to leave you for your competition over a service issue than they are a price or product issue. In fact, a study by Bain & Company tells us customers are actually four times more likely to do so. Moreover, a Forrester Research study tells us that it costs businesses five times more to acquire a new customer than it does to keep an existing one.[3]

If it costs you (in labor) and your dealership (in dollars) five times more to acquire a new customer than to retain an existing one, doesn't it make sense to ensure your current and future customers have a great experience with your dealership from beginning to end?

For salespeople, this is why providing a great experience for every prospect is so crucial. We know that top sellers don't get upset when someone tells them "no" today because they know this person will eventually need a car – everyone does. So, why not make it a great experience to deal with you even for those who don't buy today? When you do, you'll soon discover that those who left your dealership today will often return tomorrow – ready to buy and ready to send their friends to you.

This is also why providing a great experience after the sale matters so much.

Let's say you delivered a great buying experience on Saturday and your customer left the dealership fully satisfied with you and their purchase. However, there was a We Owe on their vehicle for window tinting. The plan was for them to come back on Thursday and leave the vehicle with the service department so that the windows could be tinted by your third-party tint company.

That was the plan, anyway.

Your customer arrives at 7:15 a.m. on Thursday (as planned) and approaches the first service writer she sees. She extends her keys to him and says, "I'm Barbara Jones and I'm here to have my windows tinted."

The service writer looks at her as if she has three heads and replies, "Who told you to come in today? Do you have an appointment?" At this point, is Barbara more likely or less likely to send you referral business? Is she more likely or less likely to buy from you the next time?

Barbara pulls out her We Owe and hands it to the service writer who furrows his brow and sighs while reading it. "Well, no one took the time to put you into the system," he laments, "I'll have to see what I can do." How about now? Is Barbara more likely or less likely to send her friends to come buy a car from you?

Even if Barbara gets her windows tinted today – which, if you've been in the business more than a week, you know is unlikely – does she still feel the same way about you that she did on Saturday? Of course not! All the goodwill you built up with your Assumptive Selling approach on Saturday has been wiped away by your service writer's attitude on Thursday.

Real Customer Service Matters

But wait, won't unhappy customers like Barbara just tell me when they feel they've been treated poorly? Won't she give me a chance to correct everything?

If only. According to the White House Office of Consumer Affairs, the average dissatisfied customer is going to tell 9 to 15 others about their experience; but only 1 out of 26 dissatisfied customers will ever complain to you.[4] This means 96% of your unhappy customers won't ever bother to tell you – but, they have no problem telling their friends and family. (Or, going online and telling the world how much they hate you.)

Real customer service is about not having issues in the first place. If you're committed to this concept, there are rewards for you beyond just what you'll get from Assumptive Selling.

People will not only send you their friends, but most everyone will pay more to ensure a good customer experience. In fact, an American Express study tells us that US consumers will pay 17% more for a great experience.[5] My math tells me this means your prior customers will pay you a couple thousand more in gross when they buy their next car – that is, if you provided them with a great customer experience the last time!

Real customer service – the kind where we never have issues in the first place – leads to customer retention, increased revenue and increased profits. Basically, real customer service and creating a great customer experience costs you less and nets you more… so, let's figure out how to wow every customer every time.

The Customer Is Not Always Right

It's important in your quest to provide a great customer experience that we dispel of the age-old and incorrect myth that the customer is always right. They are not. In fact, in my experience, the customer – especially the one complaining the loudest – is usually wrong.

So, let's agree right now that the customer is not always right, okay?

Of course, they don't have to be right, do they? They are your boss' boss. They pay the bills. The customer is not always right, but they are *always* the customer.

Now that we understand this, let's talk about what we mean by good customer service. To fully grasp what good customer service is, it's important to also know what it's not. Good customer service is not staffing a large customer service department or answering customer complaints quickly. In fact, good customer service is not even solving a customer's issue – this implies a reactive approach to the customer experience.

Good customer service means never having to say you're sorry.

This happens when you focus less on solving customer issues and more on preventing issues in the first place. Lifelong, raving fans are not created by solving issues; they are created by proactively managing the customer experience, understanding that they're always the customer and ensuring they never have service issues.

Think about the companies known for superior customer service. Companies like Chick-fil-A or Ritz-Carlton or Disney. These brands aren't known for solving customer issues; they are known for creating great experiences. In other words, they are known for never having issues in the first place.

So, back to Barbara and her window tinting.

Since we know that We Owes can sometimes get lost in the shuffle from the F&I office to the service drive or parts department, let's work to solve Barbara's customer service issues before they occur. This, so that Barbara will be an even bigger fan of yours on Thursday than she was on Saturday.

After the vehicle has been delivered to Barbara, it's important for you to babysit the We Owe from now until Thursday morning. Since each dealership has their own procedures for getting the We Owe from the F&I manager's desk to the department that is going to fulfil it, I'll give you the steps I would take in virtually any situation.

It's Saturday and Barbara has just driven off in her new car; it's time for you to go to the F&I manager and get a copy of the We Owe (this might be a carbon copy of a multipart form or a photocopy you make yourself). Now, go to your CRM or calendar (whatever you use for reminders) and set a reminder for Monday morning to hand deliver the We Owe to a service advisor that will be working on Thursday.

Monday morning comes, and your reminder alerts you to take care of the We Owe. You walk your copy into the service drive (after the morning rush) and approach the advisor you want to handle Barbara on Thursday. Ask him or her if they've been alerted to this, and if so, if there is anything you need to do to make sure the window tint company will be able to handle this as promised. If everything is a go, then set a new reminder for Thursday morning to meet Barbara in the service drive.

If, as usual, the service advisor looks at you like you have three heads on Monday morning, use the time before your first sales appointment arrives to hunt down the We Owe and babysit it until it's reached the advisor; then set your Thursday morning reminder to meet Barbara.

On Thursday morning at 7:00 a.m. keep an eye out for Barbara. When she arrives, open her car door and ask her how much she loves her new car as you walk her to the service advisor (who now expects her).

This time, given that everything went smoothly with her We Owe, do you think Barbara will still send her friends to come see you when they're in the market? Of course she will! You ensured she had a great experience from beginning to end – not just through the delivery of her car, but all the way through her first experience with your service department. Congratulations!

Become the Chick-fil-A of Salespeople

You may think there's a secret to Chick-fil-A's mind-blowingly great customer service, but the truth is that Chick-fil-A doesn't provide "mind-blowingly great" customer service. What's more is that there's no secret to what they do. The customer experience at Chick-fil-A is good. Compared to other fast food companies, it's great. Compared to a First-Class seat on Emirates Air, it's better than getting a tooth pulled.

But, what Chick-fil-A has discovered (and most salespeople have not), is that you don't have to blow customers' minds with delight, you just have to get things right the first time. Moreover, the average fast food customer just wants to get a good deal on decent food served by respectful people of average intelligence.

That's all your next prospect is looking for from you: a good deal on a decent car delivered by a respectful salesperson of average intelligence. (And, since you're reading this book, you more than qualify!)

Today's consumer is not looking to have a love affair with you, with your dealership, or even with the brand you sell. To help make this point is a great Harvard Business Review study that showed only 23% of consumers said they had a relationship with a brand, any brand.[6] This means that you and the rest of the team at your dealership shouldn't waste time or money chasing relationships that simply will never materialize. Instead, you should just do what Chick-fil-A does.

Think about the experience at Chick-fil-A and compare it to how the average customer is treated at the average dealership. At Chick-fil-A you can take your empty soda cup back to the counter for a free refill; thank them for refilling it and you'll hear "my pleasure." It's a sincere response, even though you'll hear the same response in every one of their stores. The service is good; their team is respectful; they do it right the first time (so they avoid issues that require solutions); and the food is good.

Simply put: Chick-fil-A eagerly provides fast food with manners. That's it. Wanting to serve the customer – being downright eager about it – is easily projected. Customers feel this, and they appreciate it. Moreover, the more eager you are to serve, the more likely customers are to forgive mistakes.

You cannot hide genuine eagerness. Likewise, you cannot hide a lack of genuine eagerness. Being eager, I would argue, is a requirement of good customer service and of good salesmanship. Without it, you have no business being on the front lines. This begs the question: "Are you eager to serve every Up?"

Eagerness, more than any other trait, determines whether or not your customer will feel like you care. That sticky sweetness that we sometimes hear from hotel clerks and waiters and waitresses – you know; that phony concern and forced smile that lacks genuine eagerness – is easy to spot. For many of your customers, this phoniness masquerading as customer service is like nails on a chalkboard. Phony sweetness is so bad, in fact, that I would argue you're better off just being your everyday, boring, miserable, honest self if you can't be eager.

Think about Chick-fil-A for a minute. Yes, they provide a good quality chicken sandwich. It's not the absolute best sandwich any of us have ever had; it's just fried chicken and a pickle on a bun. Yet, Chick-fil-A is world-renowned for blowing away their competition with their customer service.

Here's what I said about Chick-fil-A: they eagerly provide fast food sandwiches with manners. However, this is somehow perceived as mind-blowingly good customer service? By comparison to, say, McDonald's (where they also have a chicken sandwich on the menu), it is.

Here's what I can say about McDonald's: they provide fast food sandwiches. Notice the difference? Oh, and don't just say it's about manners. If the employees at Chick-fil-A were not eager to serve, would the service be perceived as being even half as good? Would hearing "my pleasure" or "please" or "thank you" from employees that hated their job and their customers ring true? Of course not.

What about the food quality? Without the eagerness and the manners, would people rave about fried chicken and a pickle on a bun? Doubtful. The moral here is to be eager to serve or find some other line of work. Being eager to serve your next Up and doing so with manners (and using Assumptive Selling) will make you the Chick-fil-A of salespeople!

Remove the Tiny Hurdles & Miniature Hassles

What Barbara would've faced on Thursday (had you not babysat the We Owe) would've been considered a minor inconvenience at most dealerships. I like to call these minor inconveniences "Tiny Hurdles & Miniature Hassles;" and left unresolved, these can have a devastating impact on your perceived service to your customers. It doesn't matter that "the service department screwed up;" you're the one who will lose the future sales opportunities Barbara would've sent your way.

As much as good customer service is about doing the little things right, good customer service is also about removing these minor inconveniences. To the average salesperson, the Tiny Hurdles & Miniature Hassles seem meaningless; though as we demonstrated with Barbara's We Owe, it's critical to understand that the littlest of things add up to huge inconveniences for our customers.

Think about Chick-fil-A again. What if Chick-fil-A required customers to show their receipt every time they wanted a free refill of pop? This would create an artificial hurdle or hassle for the customer that would, at the very least, make them less likely to return to Chick-fil-A. Miniature hassles are still hassles; and requiring a customer to go back to their table and dig around for a receipt just to get a soda refill would seem unconscionable to most people. It would make for a bad customer experience.

As absurd as the receipt-for-refill policy might sound to you, there are probably customer-unfriendly policies just like this one at your dealership. Think about how inefficient these are. If your store has a policy like this, you need to ask yourself "Are we really that cheap? Are we really that self-destructive? Are we going to treat all of our customers poorly just to catch that one guy out of 500 who is going to try to cheat us by trying to get a soda refill he doesn't deserve?"

Even minor hurdles can frustrate a happy customer or enrage an already stressed-out prospect. If you're a manager, your job is to work to remove the Tiny Hurdles & Miniature Hassles that you and your team might be blind to. If you're a salesperson, your job is to recognize these and remove them before your customer trips over one of them.

Let's go back to Barbara for a moment. What if, as happens with so many deals in automotive, after you and Barbara agreed on the numbers and signed the deal, she had to wait for over an hour to get into F&I? Barbara thinks she's bought the car; she assumes she owns it; she has $40,000 she wants to give you, but you're making her wait around to complete the paperwork.

To Barbara, this is madness! To your F&I manager, this is just a minor inconvenience. It's an artificial hassle that you'll need to remove if you want Barbara to be a raving fan who sends her friends to buy from you.

How do you remove it? As you'll learn later in this book, you need to keep her engaged. If you're the salesperson, it's likely you do not have the power to speed up the F&I department, so you need keep Barbara busy while you both wait on F&I. If you're the manager, you need to create a customer-friendly way to make the time waiting on F&I feel necessary and fulfilling to Barbara.

Perception is Reality

Think what you will about your in-store processes, but the customer experience is exactly what your customer says it is. Their perception is their reality, and their perception is all that matters. To put it more succinctly: the perceived experience is what matters. Since we know people will pay an average of 17% more for a great experience, doesn't it make sense to ensure they perceive this buying process as a great experience?

But, what defines a great experience with your dealership? It's exactly what the customer says is a great experience; and (if you're an average salesperson at an average dealership) it's likely you're not currently providing one.

Let's look outside of automotive for an example of this. Let's look at two successful hotel chains; one known for a great customer experience and the other known for providing no-frills, though clean rooms. Let's compare Ritz-Carlton to Fairfield Inn.

Both Ritz-Carlton and Fairfield Inn provide a comfortable bed. (I know, I've stayed at both.) Interestingly, that's really about all they have in common. Fairfield Inn provides free breakfast, free Wi-Fi and free in-room coffee. Ritz-Carlton does not. Yet, Ritz-Carlton commands rates at least two times higher than Fairfield Inn. How can that be? Isn't free breakfast a great experience?

Nope. Not according to the customer – and the customer's perception of a great experience is all that matters.

The customer experience at these two hotel chains is defined not by the amenities, but by the intangibles. Ritz-Carlton doesn't need to give away breakfast and Wi-Fi; they win hands down on the intangibles. I describe what Ritz-Carlton does as simply this: every employee greets and assists every customer with an eager, genuine interest in serving. Nothing magical or mystical; but just as the customer experience at Chick-fil-A is defined by good manners (not a good sandwich); the experience at Ritz-Carlton is defined by attentive service (not breakfast or coffee or Wi-Fi).

Those who work for Ritz-Carlton understand that those closest to the customer create the customer experience; and the same is true for your dealership. Frontline employees (salespeople, service writers, cashiers and receptionists) and frontline managers (sales and service) control the experience for your customers. Knowing this, how can you ensure you're perceived as providing a great experience (via the intangibles) and not just the free stuff Fairfield must provide?

For salespeople, it's simple. You need follow just three simple rules:

Rule 1: Love your job.
Rule 2: Love your customers.
Rule 3: If you can't comply with Rules 1 and 2, then you need to get a new job.

In all seriousness, anyone who doesn't love selling cars and who doesn't love their customers has no business being in a dealership; you should leave and find something you truly love. True customer service is all about being genuine and authentic. It's simply not possible for your customers to enjoy a great experience with you if you don't absolutely love what you do and for whom you do it.

The customer experience, after all, is what the customer says it is. Their perception of the experience is the reality. Moreover, people like people who like them. If you love your customers, they'll feel this, and they'll want to do business with you.

Disney Has the Best Customer Service on the Planet!

Most people think Disney is pretty good at customer service, don't they? They have the pedigree; and they certainly must have a reputation for effectively solving customer issues, right? Well... no. Disney is not that much better than most other companies at *solving* customer issues. It's not just Disney, by the way, but Ritz-Carlton and Chick-fil-A are also not that much better at *solving* customer issues than say Fairfield Inn or McDonald's.

"But," you exclaim, "Disney and Ritz-Carlton and Chick-fil-A are well known for providing the best customer experience in their respective industries!"

Yes, they are indeed. But, none of these three spends much time solving customer issues... because they are known for *never having issues in the first place*. And, as we learned, good customer service means never having to say you're sorry. Disney, you see, almost never has to say they're sorry.

Creating a great customer experience is everyone's job; and if you want to be successful in the car business, you need to be in charge of creating these for your customers. As frontline employees, salespeople control the customer experience, but the drive and desire (and processes and rules and incentives) for providing great customer experiences start at the top.

Disney understands this at the highest level; and, moreover, lives it at the highest level. Earlier, I shared the expression "crap rolls downhill." Indeed, it does; it rolls downhill all the way to the customer. Coincidentally, so do admiration and respect.

As we know in the car business, everything rolls downhill. With Disney (as with your dealership), how management treats frontline employees can dictate how they treat customers. This means that if your managers are jerks, you need to find ways to stop this from impacting how you treat your customers. This, because jerks usually beget jerks.

When managers are fair, thoughtful, and respectful with their frontline teams; they can expect their teams will be fair, thoughtful, and respectful with the customers. Conversely, if managers are jerks; they're going to unleash a team of jerks on those very same customers. Your job is to not let your manager's deficiencies become your deficiencies.

"But," you exclaim, "No salesperson would ever let how their manager treated them impact how they treated a customer!"

Let me give you a real-world example of just how easily the crap from above can roll down to the customer – even in a job with almost no stress when compared to selling cars.

In the mid-1990s, I was working for a beer distribution company and happened to be in the receiving area of a grocery store with one of our delivery drivers. Right in front of us, one of the grocery chain's vice presidents was loudly scolding the store manager. The VP was abusive; and watching this display was brutal and embarrassing for us and the manager.

After the VP left, I watched that same store manager berate the liquor department manager. Not five minutes after getting his tongue-lashing, I watched the liquor department manager unfairly reprimand the first employee he saw.

The recipient of this scolding was a nice, middle-aged cashier who was stocking shelves in the liquor department. She was almost in tears as the liquor manager verbally tore her down. Within a few minutes, she composed herself and went to the liquor department checkout stand to help a customer. Without warning, this nice, middle-aged cashier became rude, unpleasant, and short with the customer. Barely speaking, with a scowl on her face the entire time — and all of this happened in about fifteen minutes.

If a vice president's one-time backroom tongue-lashing can translate into a bad customer experience in just 15 minutes, imagine the long-term effects of this kind of abuse. Crap rolls downhill all the way to the customer; and you simply cannot allow your manager's issues to become your issues if you want to provide the kind of customer experience that's possible with Assumptive Selling.

A Note for Managers and Owners

Carl Buehner once said, "They may forget what you said, but they will never forget how you made them feel." The store manager, the liquor manager, the cashier, and the customer all surely remember how they were made to feel that day. If this had been your dealership and not a grocery store, a pissed-off cashier or receptionist would not just have created a bad customer experience but would likely have lost you thousands in future profits — all from one avoidable negative interaction that started at the top.

While you can never expect your employees to care as much as you care, you can certainly never expect them to care after a beating. Think about this the next time you're being a jerk to your entire sales team at your Saturday morning meeting 15 minutes before you open the doors.

Being a jerk just creates more jerks; and if any of those newly created jerks deals with your customers, you can expect they'll be jerks to them, as well. Incidentally, your best people simply won't stand for you being a jerk. They have too many options. In the end, jerk bosses are left with a bunch of poor-performing jerks as frontline employees... making the bosses turn into even bigger jerks.

This becomes a vicious circle... of jerks – one that I see repeated in underperforming dealerships all across the country.

You Control the Experience

Great customer service from a salesperson comes from being aware: aware of your surroundings; aware of the rules; aware of your strengths; and, especially, aware of your customer.

Great salespeople, like great poker players, have a common trait: they can read people. Moreover, they use their ability to read others to benefit themselves by modifying their approach when the opportunity arises. They are selfish and that's not a bad thing in poker or in sales.

When you're a selfish salesperson, you're not going to escalate issues; you're going to solve them. You'll solve them, because you'll recognize them early as minor inconveniences – well before they become issues. You're going to selfishly solve these issues, because it means a better customer experience, more closed deals and higher commissions. Of course, you must be aware of the customer and the possible Tiny Hurdles & Miniature Hassles they could face. Solving these before they occur keeps them from becoming major events causing a bad customer experience.

This customer awareness includes how you address everything; because, how you say things is often way more important than what you say. Let's look at how a typical (unaware) employee response to a customer inquiry can create a bad experience:

Customer: "I'm looking for Blue Widgets."

Typical Employee: "Sorry, Blue Widgets are reserved for VIP Customers only."

Ouch. This frontline employee just told a potential customer why we cannot help them, instead of offering a way we might be able to help. In this case, the employee has taken a customer that wants to spend money with us – someone who had a specific need that they felt we could solve – and turned them into an enemy of our company and our alleged VIP program.

Let's look at this same exchange when the frontline employee is aware of how they articulate their responses:

Customer: "I'm looking for Blue Widgets."

Aware Employee: "Excellent. All I need is a little bit of information from you and you'll become you a VIP Customer eligible to purchase Blue Widgets."

Both employees essentially said the same thing, right? *You must be a VIP Customer to purchase Blue Widgets.* But, the employee who was aware of the customer detailed how she could help the customer, not how she could not. This is a subtle difference to most employees, but a huge difference to the customer.

As a top salesperson employing the fundamentals of Assumptive Selling, your words must always pull the customer through the purchase, not become an impediment to purchasing. In a dealership scenario, I've seen the exchange play out like this:

Customer: "I'm interested in the zero percent financing Ford is offering."

Typical Salesperson: "That's only for people with great credit. How's your credit score?"

Congratulations; you've just taken someone who gave you a clear buying signal and insulted them with your clumsy qualification question. Good luck closing this deal!

Instead, try to frame the discussion in a way that genuinely pulls the customer through your road-to-the-sale:

Customer: "I'm interested in the zero percent financing Ford is offering."

Aware Salesperson: "Outstanding! That's a great program. Let's get some quick paperwork done to make sure we get you the absolute best rate available."

With Customers: Always Expect the Unexpected

Any real fan of the movie *Road House* (1989) knows that when Patrick Swayze's character Dalton gives his famous "Three Simple Rules" speech, he actually combines two rules into the first rule, giving his bouncer team four rules:

> "All you have to do is follow three simple rules. One: never underestimate your opponent. Expect the unexpected. Two: take it outside. Never start anything inside the bar unless it's absolutely necessary. And three: be nice."

Expect the unexpected in retail is best translated this way: "If you want your customers to feel welcome, you should actually expect them." Contrary to the popular belief of some dealership employees (think desk managers, cashiers, service advisors and receptionists), a customer visit is not an inconvenience, and it should never be a surprise. This means taking the modest steps of noticing them immediately and acknowledging them as soon as you notice them. Let's examine how this should look in your dealership:

> The receptionist is on the phone when a customer walks up to her desk. She should look at them immediately, smile and acknowledge them by covering the receiver and whispering something like "I'll be right with you."

As we'll learn later in this chapter, this simple acknowledgement by the receptionist resets the customer's clock. This gives the receptionist a bit of extra time to finish her call and then assist the customer in front of her.

You see, customers expect to be expected. They assume that your dealership actually wants customers. So, when someone on your team acts surprised to see them; or, more importantly, doesn't notice or acknowledge them; they're immediately creating a negative experience that the salesperson must now work to overcome.

Salespeople should take note: Ups on the lot want you to acknowledge them; they are indeed looking for help. Giving them a few minutes to browse your inventory worked okay in the past, but today they arrive with a vehicle already in mind. Acknowledge them immediately (by upping them, of course).

If you're a manager or owner, you need ensure everyone on the frontlines at your dealership understands that without those pesky customers, we don't need employees. So, they should expect them, notice them, acknowledge them, and assume that they're where they are supposed to be. Moreover, if they're arriving for a pre-scheduled appointment or if you otherwise already know who they are, you should greet them by name and don't make them repeat anything you already know about their visit.

Studies have proven that if you can greet people by name, they immediately assume you are more competent. It doesn't matter if you're a barista, a dentist, or a dealership service advisor; when you use your customer's name (and especially if you already know why they're on your premises), their perception of your business improves and their confidence in your abilities grows.

This is an especially important lesson for salespeople who have a customer in their dealership's service drive. Most good CRM tools today will alert you when a previous buyer is in the dealership. Walking to the service waiting area, locating your customer, and confidently greeting them by their name makes them feel appreciated and increases the chances that you'll be their first choice the next time they're in the market for a vehicle.

Aligning Customer Expectations

Superstar salespeople are great at aligning their customers' expectations with reality. In other words, they manage the customer's expectations so that whatever they deliver meets (or exceeds) the customer's needs.

Think about Barbara's We Owe on the window tinting. What if you were told by your sales manager that she could bring in her new car and wait on the tinting because it would probably only take about an hour to complete? If you told her this and she arrived to find out it was going to be four hours, her expectations would not have been met, and you'd have a customer service issue on your hands. An issue, like most customer service issues, that was fully avoidable just by properly aligning her expectations.

Misaligned expectations are the number one cause of customer service failures. (They also happen to be the number one cause of relationship failures, but that's a lesson for another book.) Therefore, keeping your customer's expectations top of mind and under control is critical. You can do this by simply following one of the oldest lessons in customer care: under promise and over deliver.

Managing expectations is often best described as the need to under promise and over deliver. In essence, this means don't promise more than you are certain you can deliver. To ensure you always create a great customer experience, you must also ensure you always deliver more than the customer expects. If the customer expects a 7 and you deliver an 8, you're a hero. However, if they expect a 9 and you deliver an 8, you're a failure. In both cases you delivered the exact same thing, but their expectations dictated whether or not you provided a good customer experience.

When possible, you want to align their expectations early in your process; as this is the easiest way to avoid future customer service issues. There's a sign I've seen in a few establishments that sets expectations early and in a friendly, funny way. It reads:

We offer three kinds of service: good, cheap, fast... but you can only pick two:

Good and cheap won't be fast.
Fast and good won't be cheap.
Cheap and fast won't be good.

Believe it or not, this sets expectations, while it also puts people in a good mood. Moreover, it allows you to take your time if you're known for providing high quality products or services. For salespeople, properly setting the customer's expectations around time is often the difference between closing a deal or not.

The Customer's Clock

No one ever wanted to waste five hours on a Saturday to buy a car. That said, this is still the reality in some dealerships today. Dealerships, by the way, that close far fewer deals for less money than those who can both shorten their road-to-the-sale and manage the customer's clock.

Basically, as the seller, your clock is different than the customer's. More importantly, only the customer's clock matters. Your clock is not important; and reality is not important. Your clock is on the wall and the customer's clock is in their head. Oh, and the customer's clock has only two settings: *Right Freaking Now* and *This Is Taking Forever*.

While speed isn't as important in the customer experience as quality, customers want to know that you value their time; and you must always meet or exceed their expectations (including their expectations on time). Your job, in managing the customer's clock, is to properly set it or reset it (as your receptionist did earlier in this chapter) so that time does not create a bad customer experience. Let me give you a quick example of a company in another industry successfully resetting the customer's clock:

> My wife and I stopped at a small-town café for a quick bite to eat. It was about 2:30 in the afternoon on a Saturday and we had about 30 minutes to kill. As we walked in, we noticed that the place was fairly busy. The manager seated us and immediately informed us that not only did they have a packed house, but that they were severely understaffed. She explained that the service would be incredibly slow; that the kitchen would be slow; but that she would keep us informed throughout.
>
> Although we only had about 30 minutes to kill, we left the restaurant 120 minutes later. Full and satisfied with both the food quality and their service; I even gave them a five-star review online.

Why did I give them a great review for a meal that took four times longer than I originally expected? Because they managed my expectations from the beginning by properly resetting my customer clock.

Imagine if the manager hadn't said anything when she sat us at our table. Imagine if she'd just gone through the motions and said something like, "Your server will be right with you." We would have been livid, and they would've received a one-star review. Instead, she aligned our expectations with their reality, so we settled in, changed our plans and enjoyed the slow service.

For your buyers, there will be times when the process of buying a car is excruciatingly slow. Your job is to keep your customer's clock running along with reality. If the used car manager is backed up and can't appraise their trade during the test drive, be sure to let them know this with a simple, "I spoke with our appraiser and it's going to take him a little longer than usual to properly appraise your trade-in. However, rest assured that it's a priority for him and our goal is to get you a firm written offer as soon as possible."

Houston, We Have a Problem!

So, you're ready to make sure everyone has a great experience with you, right? Therefore, this means everyone will always have a great experience, right?

Wrong. Sometimes, no matter what you do and no matter what you say, you're going to have a customer blow a gasket for no reason. This is called a heat case in automotive retail; and even the best salespeople must deal with these from time-to-time. In these instances, you need to kill your customer with kindness.

I know you've heard "kill them with kindness" before, and I know a lot of you don't fully understand what that means; so, here's precisely how you kill your heat cases with kindness:

- The angrier they get, the calmer you get;
- The louder they get, the quieter you get;
- The more words they use, the fewer words you use; and
- The meaner they get, the nicer you get.

When you kill the unreasonably angry customer with kindness, you take away their only weapon: their power over you. The unreasonably angry customer has a problem... but, it's their problem, not yours. Their problem is they need to feel superior and they can only do that by making others feel small. Killing them with kindness disarms them. Only you can make yourself feel small. If you allow an angry customer to get to you; if you start to take anything personally; or (worse) try to go toe-to-toe with them; you'll lose, and they'll win.

Usually at the beginning of interactions with unreasonably angry customers, you're on an even footing. They have an issue and you want to help them resolve it. Once they try to take control over you by making you feel small, you're faced with a choice. Only you can decide to give them control over you (and force you to react angrily). Or, you can decide to kill them with kindness – giving you all the control.

I understand you probably want to solve all issues, but I also understand that even when you do everything right and properly try to kill them with kindness, there are still those heat cases who are simply too far gone for you, the salesperson, to help. In these instances, you should escalate their issue (i.e., get it off your plate and onto someone's with a bigger paycheck).

However, if you want to close more deals and create customers for life, ensure you're only escalating the real issues. When you push every issue up the chain to your manager, you reduce your value to the customer. You're no longer their friend in the car business – your manager is. Your goal should not only be to create a great customer experience every time (because, after all, the customer experience matters), but to be certain your customer knows that you have their best interests at heart.

5

OLD-FASHIONED NETWORKING

For today's top sellers – as was the case with yesterday's top sellers and the top sellers for at least the last eight decades – the business generated from repeat customers and referrals are the most profitable sales they make. Furthermore, the sales from these two sources can often equal 80% or more of the closed deals for those who routinely sell 25 or more units a month.

In fact, virtually every automotive salesperson I've ever met who averaged more than 25 vehicles a month depended on their repeats and referrals to hit their numbers and make better than average commissions.

They treated their customers right, which earned them repeat business and allowed them to ask for the referral. The great part, of course, is that their sales from repeats and referrals were the easiest and highest grossing deals they made.

Unfortunately, living off referrals seems to have become a bit of a lost art for many in automotive retail; and it's a shame. Every top salesperson you meet today still lives off these, because (as I wrote) they close at high rates and the grosses are better. And, while most every store has at least a couple of salespeople doing a good job with referrals, the reality is that the clear majority of sellers enjoy little to no repeat/referral business today. Couple this with the Up Bus making fewer stops, and you'll understand why many sales managers are struggling to get their average and below average salespeople to sell more.

Of course, these same sales managers know that to sell more in this environment, their salespeople must begin to generate more of the business themselves. If you're new to selling cars, then you're not going to benefit from repeat customers just yet; but, there's nothing stopping you from generating 30 or more units a month from referrals – if, that is, you're willing to do some old-fashioned networking.

(We'll discuss asking for referrals from your sold customers in a later chapter. Here, we're going to focus on generating new business out of thin air by channeling the great salespeople from the past.)

Networking Takes Work

There's a reason "work" can be found in the middle of the word "networking" – networking takes work. Of course, because it requires work, most salespeople won't do it… and this is great news for you! As top sellers know, when there are moneymakers that others are unwilling to complete, their own opportunities grow exponentially.

As was the case pre-internet, those salespeople earning great grosses and leading their teams today simply outwork their contemporaries. One way top sellers grow their book of business faster than the average salesperson is through old-fashioned networking.

The first step in proper networking – regardless of your profession – is to make sure everyone you meet knows what you do for a living. It goes without saying, but it's pretty damn hard to generate a referral from one of your friends if your friends don't know that you sell cars, right? Top sellers then and now blur the lines between their work and personal lives – everyone knows what they do, and they are always working, as it were. This doesn't mean they're always selling; they're not. It means they're always networking; and the blend of personal and work seems natural and even fun to them.

So, beginning right now and continuing throughout your entire car-selling career, you need to be certain every single person you meet, encounter, or pass on the street knows that you sell cars. Moreover, you should be proud of selling cars and tell everyone you meet three things:

1. I sell cars;
2. I'm honored to be selling cars; and
3. I'm your friend in the car business.

When you do this (along with handing your business card to literally everyone), you'll have people coming to you asking for help. People you don't even remember meeting, but who were so impressed by your passion (and who have your business card in hand) that they're going to give you a chance to earn their business.

Don't let them down. Sell them a car that fits for them, make a good commission and then make sure they know you live off referrals by asking them directly for help:

> Salesperson: "I'm not sure if you know this, but most of my buyers are referred by my customers. If you feel like I worked hard for you, would you do me the honor of passing my card to any of your friends or family who might be in the market?"

Then hand them five business cards. If you work in a state that allows bird dog fees, be sure to let them know how much you pay for these referrals. For many of you, your dealership will be the one actually paying for the referral business; so, ask your managers if they will do this. Given that the average dealer spends more than $600 in marketing costs per vehicle sold, asking them to foot the bill for a $100 referral you generated is just sound business for your dealership.

Quick note about referral fees paid for by your dealership: I meet salespeople all the time who work for a dealer who pays this on behalf of their sellers, yet the salespeople don't leverage this to their advantage. In fact, I've met salespeople who've never enjoyed a paid referral... because they don't use this important tool. If your dealership pays your bird dog fees, you should be leading with this information everywhere with everyone you meet.

Why Am I Teaching Old-Fashioned Networking?

As much as this book is about assuming the sale with today's buyers, it's essentially more about how to sell cars in today's market. This means there will be lessons like this one that seem to run counter to my "new-school methods." Don't sweat this – old-fashioned networking, you'll find, contains lots of Assumptive Selling, for example:

- You assume everyone is going to buy (at some point in their life);
- You get out in front of them early;
- You treat them like they're a qualified buyer; and
- You ask for their business!

This – and asking for a referral that you've yet to earn – is the essence of old-fashioned networking.

"Wait, I need to ask for referrals that I've haven't earned?" You're thinking, "What the heck is that all about?"

Relax, when you begin telling everyone you meet what you do, you need to be very clear as to why you're telling them this. Simply put: you want to help them (and all their friends) buy their next vehicle. You want all the business and, more than anything else, you deserve all the business.

Remember: you sell cars; you love selling cars; and you're their friend in the car business. Now, let's follow these three steps with a very quick sales pitch where you ask for the referrals that you haven't yet earned. You're paying your bill in a restaurant and you're leaving the waitress a very nice tip; you'll want to share with her what you do:

Salesperson: "Now, I know you're probably not in the market today for a new car, but when you are, I want you to know that I'm going to help you avoid all the hassles and haggles; and make sure you get the best overall deal right from the start. So, be sure and call me first, Okay? Also, it would be a big honor for me if you would pass my card to any of your friends or family who might be in the market."

Just like you did when you asked for the referral that you earned (after the sale), hand her five business cards; and be sure to let her know how much you pay for these referrals (if bird dog fees are legal in your state).

Your Business Card

Yes, business cards (at least for car salespeople) still matter – especially when you're planning to conduct some old-fashioned networking. Given this, let's level set on the four most important aspects of your business card:

1. Your message
2. Your name
3. Your number
4. Referrals made easy

Because we're talking about *your* business card, it's important to make sure that *your* message is the one the consumer remembers.

I emphasized *your* in that sentence to make sure you understood that this is your card, not the dealership's; so, you need to be in control of all four important aspects. If your dealership won't allow you to include your message and/or your personal mobile number on the business cards they supply, that's okay. They're allowed to dictate what's on the marketing materials they pay for. Your dealership can (rightfully so) demand you only include their information on these. Of course, the great news is that business cards are cheap and easy to design online.

Your message on your card should be simple and should address at least one of the chief concerns people have with car buying. Newsflash: Most people don't like buying cars; though understanding "why" is critical to selling more vehicles for more money. Primarily, consumers dislike car buying because of any combination of the following:

- Lack of trust
- Fear of getting a bad deal
- The hassles of dealing with a dealership
- The time it takes to complete the process
- Haggling
- Pushy salespeople

Given this, let's address at least one of these with your message on your business cards. Here are a few of my favorites that I've seen over the years:

- Your friend in the car business!
- I'm your no-hassle, no-haggle way to get the best deal!
- Call me first to get your best deal upfront!
- I work harder for my customers!
- Your Vehicle Guy!

Next, let's get your name right. Yes, some salespeople overlook the importance of including their actual name on their business cards.

Wait? What? Everyone puts their name on their cards, right?

Nope, not everyone. My legal name is Stephen Michael Stauning, but only my sister and mother call me "Stephen;" everyone else calls me "Steve." Putting my full name on my cards just means I'm going to either be correcting my prospects (a bad idea) or having people call the dealership asking for "Stephen" (a better idea but could still confuse the receptionist).

The best idea is to call myself "Steve Stauning" on my cards. If I had a cool-sounding, non-offensive nickname (like Spike), then this should also be on the cards. In other words, you want *your* name on *your* cards – and the more memorable the better.

Since you want your networking efforts to pay off today and tomorrow, be sure to include your personal mobile number on your cards. This is usually not an issue – dealers don't want to pay for your mobile phones, so they'll allow you to use yours; and in most cases, allow you to include this number on your business cards. If they do not, of course, you'll need to pay to print your own cards. It does you no good to hand someone a card today and ask for a referral, only to have someone else answer their call in three months (when you're working up the street).

Finally, since the primary reason you're handing out your card is to generate referral business, be sure your business card makes generating referrals intuitive and easy. This means ensuring there's a call-to-action and an area for the referrer to write their name. Here's a sample business card that includes this and the other three important areas:

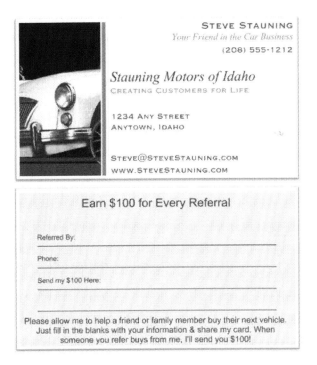

Don't overthink your business card. It exists primarily to remind prospects of who you are and what you do; and to drive referral business for you. The front of your card should relay the former and the back of the card should relay the latter. Be sure to turn your card over when asking for the referral, so the customer will know exactly what they need to do to send you your next client.

Birthday Cards & Personal Notes

Yes, your CRM prompts you to call your customers on their birthday. Guess what? Unless your customer also happens to be a friend whom you've known most of your life, chances are your customer doesn't want to hear from you on their birthday! No offense, but do you want a call from your Realtor on your birthday? How about the guy who sold you your washer and dryer? Again, unless you were lifelong friends, the answer is an absolute "no."

So, instead of letting technology assist you in completing an impersonal, contrived activity that your customer will see right through, why not try some old-fashioned sales techniques that will stand out and will truly drive repeat and referral business? Of course, I'm referring to using snail mail to send handwritten birthday cards and notes.

Create CRM Reminders

Your CRM tool, used properly, will help you sell more cars. Period. End of story.

For some reason, many salespeople regard their CRM as some sort of management "Big Brother" or a bunch of bureaucratic bullshit where they just "need to check a bunch of boxes to get the boss off my ass!" The fact is that your CRM is one of the greatest selling tools ever invented.

However, just as a golfer's putter won't sink shots on its own, your CRM will not sell you any cars by itself. But, just like that putter, when you learn to follow a few basic, repeatable rules and you use it properly, it will most certainly help you sell more cars.

We'll touch on using the CRM in other chapters, but for the purposes of old-fashioned networking, the CRM can make the task of sending the right snail mail at the right time easier and more efficient. You do this by creating reminders for these tasks in the tool.

All CRMs are a little different, so I'll save you the step-by-step instructions for these reminders and just give you the basics that you can employ in the tool your dealership uses:

1.   **Sold Customer Anniversary Cards** – once a year, in the month that your customer bought their vehicle, sending them a nice, handwritten thank you card will keep you top of mind when they're ready to buy again. Including a couple of your business cards and asking them to share these with their friends who happen to be in the market is perfectly okay. Your reminders (if not set automatically by the CRM) should be set to trigger an activity on the 1st or 2nd day of their anniversary month. This means all the anniversaries for a given month will trigger on the same day, allowing you to print this list with names and addresses to create your cards for the month. Drop these in the mail as you complete them throughout the month.

2.   **Birthday Cards** – once a year, very close to or on their birthday, all sold customers should receive a nice, handwritten birthday card. This will, again, keep you top of mind when they're ready to buy. Some managers will tell you to include business cards and ask for referrals in these; I, however, do not recommend you make any such request. Feel free to include a business card, though refrain from asking them for a favor lest the birthday card will seem contrived. If your dealership will allow it, including a coupon for a free oil change can be a welcomed and appropriate birthday gift. Your reminders (if not set automatically by the CRM) should be set to trigger an activity on the 15th day of the month prior to their birthday. This means all the birthdays for a given month will trigger on the same day a couple of weeks before anyone's birthday. Print this list with names, dates of birth and addresses to create your cards. Given that it probably takes two days for the post office to deliver a card in your market, drop these in the mail a couple of business days before each respective birthday.

3.   **Christmas and Other Holiday Cards** – When your card list gets really big, your holiday card efforts will become overwhelming. Top salespeople have a plan for this: they personalize and sign the respective holiday cards at the same time they address the birthday cards to these customers. This means you'll be writing lots of "Merry Christmas" greetings in April and May. Of course, you'll be thankful you did this when December 1 rolls around and your Christmas cards for the year are ready to be dropped in the mail.

If you're paying attention to your lists, you can stop yourself from sending a thank you card and a birthday card during the same month. Just move your anniversary reminders for anyone having a birthday in the same month to a month later. This way every card will have its desired impact.

"But Steve, I have too many customers! I don't have time to purchase, handwrite and send all these cards!"

Wow, what a great problem to have! Time to hire an assistant to help you manage all this business! Great sellers throughout the history of automotive have employed assistants to help them manage their database and other general tasks; so, don't overthink this. At first, enlist the help of a relative or friend who wants to make a few bucks to organize and address these. You'll still want to include your own handwritten notes (unless your handwriting stinks) for as long as you can.

Once you've sold more than about 600 customers, however, you'll likely need the assistant to handwrite the notes, as well. (Six hundred customers means 50 birthday cards and 50 anniversary cards each month – that can be a lot of writing for someone also selling 30+ units.)

Plan Ahead

To keep the costs of this undertaking manageable, you'll want to plan ahead and purchase your cards in bulk. While the thank you cards can be fairly generic, the birthday cards should appear as if you went to the Hallmark store yourself and selected the card. Of course, you don't want to pay $5 or more per card when you might be sending out hundreds each year. Luckily, we have the internet to help us find cost-effective birthday cards in bulk.

In less than ten seconds, I was able to find nearly 400 listings of "bulk birthday cards" on eBay, with the average price per card around $0.30. This keeps your cost per card under $1 – including the stamp!

Keep it Personal

The note you include in these cards should contain something personal, when possible. You accomplish this by jotting down an interest or two in the CRM that you noticed about or overheard from the customer while they were buying. When you're writing your personal note, try to find a natural way to weave in something you know the customer will find interesting.

For example, let's say your customer is wearing a sweatshirt from an obscure local college. You ask her about it and you find out that she attended that school on a lacrosse scholarship. Before sending her the personal note, check online to see if there've been any interesting events around the ladies' lacrosse team for her college. If there have been, feel free to include a tidbit about it:

Hi Barbara,

I wanted to drop you a quick note to wish you and your Camry a Happy Anniversary!

:)

Yep, it's been two years since you purchased your Camry; and I just want to be sure everything is running smoothly. If there is anything I can help you with regarding your Camry, please let me know.

By the way, I saw that the Lady Wildcats are headed to the Division 2 playoffs this year! Go Wildcats!

As a reminder; if any of your friends or family are looking for help with buying a car, I'm hopeful you would send them my way. I promise to treat them fairly and honestly... and without any sales pressure. Plus, for each one who buys from me, I'll send you $100.

Thank you for your continued business and support - I really appreciate it!

Best wishes,

Steve

Yes, that's a lot of writing. But remember, if you're so successful that you cannot find the time to do these for yourself, hire someone to write these cards for you. You might be shocked to learn how many top sellers don't even sign the handwritten notes and cards that are sent on their behalf. That said, you should continue to write these yourself if (1) you have the time; and (2) your penmanship is legible.

Clubs & Associations

No chapter on old-fashioned networking would be complete without a discussion about community involvement. Great networkers get involved! They join their local chamber of commerce, they help at their kids' school, they join local clubs, and they help local charities. More than this, they're truly involved in these organizations. That means they not only join the chamber and local clubs, they also attend the meetings and work the events.

If you're of Hispanic descent, join the Hispanic organizations in your market. If you're from Pakistan, get deeply involved in the local Pakistani community. If you're... you get the picture. Everyone wants a friend in the car business, and they're especially happy if they speak the same language and have the same interests as that friend.

Your community involvement will expose you to business and civic leaders that you otherwise would not have met; and these connections will bring you even more connections. Plus, until you meet them, they won't know that you sell cars and that you're honored to sell cars and that you're their friend in the car business.

Oh, and be sure and ask your general manager or dealer principal to pay your membership dues. Most dealerships are so thrilled to have their salespeople involved in the community that they'll usually pick up this cost without a problem. Additionally, many dealerships will gladly sponsor the events that your organizations hold – especially when one of their salespeople will be in attendance gaining customers.

As I wrote at the beginning of this chapter, today's top sellers often generate 80% or more of their monthly sales from repeats and referrals. Given this, these should be your primary focus; though unlike Ups, these people aren't just going to show up at your dealership. It takes work to cultivate referrals and to keep customers buying from you again and again. This, of course, is good news; because anything that requires work won't be practiced by the bulk of the sellers out there!

6

TODAY'S CUSTOMERS ARE DIFFERENT

Though true in the past, there's an adage in automotive that continues to circulate among old-school sales managers that goes something like this: "Price is only an issue in the absence of value."

The idea behind regurgitating this to your sales team today is to somehow blame them for failing to create enough value in the product or service whenever the customer has a price objection. It's a diversion; it's a way to keep from actually admitting to your team that their job of selling cars at maximum grosses – when faced with pricing transparency and increased competition – is harder today than it was yesterday.

While it's true that before the internet, price was only an issue in the absence of value, today this is simply not the case. The more correct saying your sales managers should be repeating today is that "Price is only an issue in the absence of value, in the face of competition and/or when selling to a well-informed prospect."

Today's customers are different; they really are.

Value, Relevancy & Authenticity

To sell any big-ticket item (cars, homes, furniture, etc.), the buyer must find value, relevancy and authenticity. This was true 50 years ago and it's true today. The difference in car sales, of course, is that 50 years ago the salesperson was allowed to establish all three. Today, you can only confirm the first two. Let me explain.

Value is the easiest of these three pillars of sales success to explain. Simply put, value is the *relative worth* of an item. For example, if two identical vehicles were priced $1,000 apart, you could say that the higher-priced vehicle is a bad value, while the lower-priced one is a good value.

The value of the lower-priced one, you see, is good *relative* to the higher-priced vehicle. Therefore, when your sales managers say that "price is only an issue in the absence of value," they are partially right. If a customer does not find the value in what you are selling, then the price will always be "too high" in their mind. The problem, of course, is that in today's world you no longer establish the value of the average vehicle, the market does.

To be clear, this is not to say that there won't be occasions – especially with used cars – where great salesmanship can drive the perceived value higher of a given vehicle. This, however, is the exception and not the rule. We deal primarily with rules in this book because rules will dictate your overall success more than the few exceptions you'll encounter.

Before the internet, customers arrived on the lot armed with no knowledge. They had no idea what the expected selling price was of your new cars; they had nothing to compare the price of your used vehicles; and they had no clue what their trade-in was worth. Salespeople had the privilege of establishing value. Great salespeople earned great grosses, and marginal salespeople earned great grosses – they just did so on fewer deals.

You see, when you're in control of establishing something's value, there are few limits on the profits you can earn.

Today, virtually every used car is priced-to-market. That is, dealers are now pricing their inventory online at or near their expected selling price. Gone are the days when a buyer could haggle away for hours to knock $2,500 off the price, while the dealer still grossed $2,500 on the front-end. In today's market, if the average dealer has an extra $250 to give on a used car, it's likely because the unit is aged and will be headed to the auction next week.

As most consumers are discovering, the days of haggling over the price of a used car are long gone at most dealerships. The primary reason it still happens today is that consumers were taught for a hundred years that they had to haggle. Assumptive Selling changes that dynamic and holds what remaining gross you have left.

Value, simply put, is now established before the prospect ever connects with you. In fact, if your vehicles are priced too high online (in the minds of today's buyers), most will simply avoid your dealership. They have too many options available to waste time trying to uncover your actual selling price; again, because value is established before the prospect ever picks up the phone to call you or steps on your lot.

Relevancy

The concept of relevancy comes down to fit, if you will. The buyer is trying to answer the question "Is this vehicle a fit for me?" That is, is it relevant to the buyer's needs? Does it satisfy the bulk of what the buyer believes she wants?

An easy example to understand is to look at the number of seats and amount of cargo space a vehicle provides compared to the needs of the buyer. For example, if the buyer was a single mother with three children and this was to be her only vehicle, then a Mazda Miata would not be a good fit for her. She would not find relevancy in the two-seat Miata. The comparably priced Mazda CX5, by contrast, would likely provide most everything she needed. The buyer, you could say, would find relevancy in the CX5.

Looking deeper at this example: if these were her only two choices, would it matter that the Miata had a special rebate that brought the price down $2,000 below the CX5? Of course not. The Miata is not relevant to her needs. Buyers must find both value and relevancy before they'll consider a big purchase like an automobile.

Again, just like with value, today's buyers find relevancy before they connect with you. While in the past, the salesperson was able to build both value and relevancy, today you can only confirm these two.

This is not bad news, per se. Understanding and remembering that today's Phone Up, Lot Up, Internet Up, etc. has already determined that your vehicle is a good value and that it is relevant to their needs will help you close more deals more quickly (and with better CSI and higher grosses).

Authenticity is the Difference Maker

Given that today's buyer has already determined value and relevancy before they connect with you, your only job (if you want to sell a car) is to provide authenticity. Authenticity is the least clear of the three pillars of sales success; in that, it can be the hardest to explain. But, just like what Supreme Court Justice Potter once said about pornography, "I know it when I see it."

Authenticity (and especially the lack thereof) is easy to spot.

Authenticity refers to how both you and your dealership rank (in the buyer's mind) when it comes to important factors like honesty, integrity, friendliness, transparency, credibility, genuineness and reliability, among others.

Are you authentic? Is the brand you sell a good brand? Is your dealership a good place to buy a car? Are you a good person? Can the buyer trust you? Are you being honest with the buyer? The buyer wants to (subconsciously) get a "yes" to each of these questions before moving forward with the purchase. This is all about what the buyer perceives. To be clear, this means the buyer's perception of (for example) your transparency is more important than your actual level of transparency.

I know what you're thinking: "Can we still sell a car even if we're inauthentic?"

Absolutely! It's done every day in the car business. For example, when a vehicle is truly scarce, is priced below the market value or the buyer has few options (for example, a credit-challenged customer standing on a Buy-Here-Pay-Here lot), the salesperson can be an inauthentic rat bastard and still sell the car.

But, why would you ever want to be a rat bastard to your buyer? I mean, just because you can do something doesn't mean you should. In the examples above, if the salesperson was truly authentic in the buyer's mind, he would earn repeat business and referrals; and perhaps the dealership would earn higher back-end grosses on these deals.

In the world of Assumptive Selling, the authentic salesperson is the one who wants the customer to have a great experience before, during and after the sale. She's the one who wants to ensure the customer is treated fairly throughout the process. She helps the customer buy, she doesn't have to sell. She's the customer's "friend in the car business."

By being authentic you'll close more deals today at higher grosses and earn the right to ask for referrals. Though I know some readers are still confused about what it means to be authentic – and while we'll touch on authenticity in your responses when we deal with the different types of Ups in their respective chapters later – I can give you the very essence of authenticity in one sentence:

Address every prospect as if you're speaking with a close friend.

For example, if a friend walked on your lot today, would you give them the third degree that is so common with a traditional road-to-the-sale? Would you interrogate them with needs analysis questions like these?

- Why are you in the market for a new vehicle?
- What's more important to you, style or price?
- What do you dislike about your current vehicle?

- What are the top 3 things you must have in your new vehicle?
- Is this vehicle primarily for business or pleasure?
- How do you intend to use the vehicle?
- Do you do most of your driving around town or on the highway?
- How important is safety?

Customers have always hated this part of the car-buying process. In the past, many just wanted to be left alone to look for the vehicle they believed met their needs (that is, provided relevancy). Once they found the right fit, they wanted to get the best price (find the value). Thankfully, our old-school road-to-the-sale process kept them from doing this. Why thankfully? Because; if prospects were allowed to just aimlessly wander the lot, they'd never buy... at least, not from us. They'd gather information and then go home (or go to the next dealer on the street).

Today's customer hates these needs analysis questions because, in their minds, they're unnecessary and the entire process feels like an interrogation. Before they ever walked on your lot they found value and relevancy; now, they're just looking for someone to sell them the car.

Think about it. There are millions of cars for sale online at tens of thousands of dealerships; yet, today's Up chose your dealership and your vehicle. Why? Simple: they found it to be priced right and a good fit for their needs. They're here to buy the damn car; so, let's be authentic and sell it to them!

This is why Assumptive Selling exists and why it drives so many sales that would otherwise have been lost by the old-school methods. To be authentic today, we need to treat every Up as a friend and as a buyer. A buyer who is going to buy today. A buyer who is going to buy from us.

Today's Car Buyers

Today's buyers – all of whom are connected consumers – know what they want before they arrive on your lot. In fact, according to Autotrader, in 2015, 68% of used car buyers purchased the vehicle they intended; while 77% of new car buyers purchased the vehicle they intended.[7] These stats are eye opening for many dealers as the sheer volume of those who've made up their mind at home is unlike anything most of us faced when we sold our first car.

Of course, when you share these statistics with most traditional sales managers, they'll tell you, "You're crazy. No, we flip everybody."

No, you don't. Not anymore. Not today.

If you believe you "flip everybody," then you're likely flipping people out of the store and down the block straight to your competition. Today's buyers know what they want because they've spent hours researching online in advance of their visit to your lot.

Trying to move today's buyers to something more profitable for you is the reason most dealers are still closing just 20% of their Traditional Ups on the first visit. Today's consumer showed up ready to buy and you chased them away.

Today's buyers do not like the old-school road-to-the-sale; and many will avoid your dealership altogether if this is your reputation online. The need for a shorter buying process is clear, as many dealerships are experiencing higher closing percentages, higher grosses and happier customers by working hard to replace the old-school, four-hour grind with a buying process that understands where today's consumer is on the road-to-the-sale and pulling them the rest of the way through.

Open-minded sales managers are beginning to treat every Up like an informed, connected buyer – someone who already knows what they want – instead of trying to flip them using an old-school road-to-the-sale. They're shortening their processes to make the purchase a great experience for all. The need to improve the buying experience is clear. In fact, according to DrivingSales.com, 99% of consumers say they *expect* a hassle when they start the car-shopping process.[8]

It's time to change. We already knew that virtually everyone is online; now we know that everyone pretty much knows what they want and that they all expect a hassle. Employing Assumptive Selling concepts will help you make this change in a seamless way that reenergizes salespeople and excites today's customers.

Online Car Buying

Be prepared to be shocked, but despite what Wall Street and Silicon Valley think, not everyone wants to buy their next car online. Not even close.

While there are certainly consumers who want to fully buy new and used vehicles online today, those who actually will do so, likely represent no more than ten percent of total buyers. Moreover, just because someone says they want to buy online doesn't mean they will. Companies like Tesla and eBay have made bypassing the traditional dealership and buying 100% online easy for over a decade; and yet, even counting the online startups, (as of this writing) online buying is still a tiny fraction of the vehicle purchases in America today.

This means you'll be around for a long time and that your skills as a salesperson will be needed. The online consumers are an important group of buyers to court and cater to, but not numerous enough for traditional dealers to shutter their lots and move to 100% online car selling.

While most consumers dislike most everything about today's car-buying process, they still like *shopping* for cars. They still want to see the actual vehicle and they still want to test drive it. So, while many consumers may begin the process of buying online (vehicle selection, feature presentation, and even completing the credit application), this just means you and your dealership must be all-in on a great experience; whether the deal is completed online or offline.

Most deals will eventually be a hybrid of online and offline. That is, the consumer will complete some important steps online and these will be shared with the dealership before they arrive. Your goal is to assume the sale and help them complete the buying process. It does you no good to take someone who's already determined their payment back to an old-school needs analysis – they'll walk.

When you assume everyone is a buyer who is buying today, you're better equipped to handle (and sell) the prospect who arrives with their completed credit application in hand expecting to start on the sixth step of your road-to-the-sale. Assumptive Selling, you'll find, helps you sell cars today (when the buyer arrives unannounced) and in the future (when the buyer arrives with their deal already loaded on their iPad).

7

COMMUNICATING WITH TODAY'S UPS

In the last chapter, I revealed that today's Ups have all the information necessary (in the form of value and relevancy) to make an informed decision. Given that all you now need to provide is authenticity – and that the best way to provide this is to speak to them as you would a close friend – communicating with them should be easy... and it is.

First and foremost, honesty matters; it's appreciated, and it will be rewarded by today's buyer. Just as you would not lie to or mislead a close friend, you should never lie to or mislead an Up. Your goal is to pull them through your process and sell them a car; and doing so with authenticity will make all the difference.

To be clear, even if you're 100% authentic, this does not mean your buyer will always be honest with you. In sales, we like to say that "buyers are liars." We say this, because it's often true and it rhymes. (Somehow, when something rhymes it makes it feel truer.) The fact is that buyers are still going to lie to you in the face of your honesty. They'll claim they're "just looking" or that they're "just gathering information" and that they're "not ready to buy."

They're lying. But, with Assumptive Selling you don't need to worry about this. With Assumptive Selling, every Up (whether on the phone or on the lot) is a buyer, despite what they say; and, they're going to buy today from you.

Communication Channels

I want to take a few pages to review the different channels you might use when communicating with today's Ups. This is important because I want you to know that there is not a one-size-fits-all approach to communicating with prospects. When I'm training salespeople on how to use the phones, for example, I'll usually have one or two in the audience who want to challenge me with statements like, "Millennials hate talking on the phone; we use text messaging to connect."

My answer is that this is great – but don't discount the phones. Don't discount email or even direct mail when we're talking about getting our message through to today's car buyers. And, even though texting is vastly more popular today than phone calls, this does not mean we shouldn't be using all communication channels available to us.

Please, don't get hung up on popularity. All communication channels are valid because all communication channels are in play. This means email is in play; phones are in play; direct mail is in play; Messenger is in play. They're all in play. They all have a place and they all can show you a return on your investment. Also, it's important to note that the same basic structure and goals apply whether customer conversations are via phone, text, chat, email or Messenger. All two-way communications are treated the same and will have the same overriding goal: an appointment that shows.

Texting Today's Ups

It's true that most of today's Ups prefer texting over other forms of communication. They like to text with their friends because texting is flexible. Unlike an incoming phone call, with text they can respond when they want. Today's Ups also like texting because it limits unnecessary greetings and the exchange of irrelevant information.

I'm going to let that last point sink in for a second. Today's Ups like texting because it limits unnecessary greetings and the exchange of irrelevant information. To put this more plainly, most of today's Ups don't want to hear sticky-sweet greetings or get bogged down in an irrelevant back-and-forth with you. They want to get to the point and texting forces others to do this. I'll remind you of this when we discuss communicating via the phone with a prospect.

Of course, just because most of today's Ups prefer texting over other forms of communication, this doesn't mean they want *you* to text them. In fact, according to the Telephone Consumer Protection Act (TCPA), for the most part, you must have permission before texting a prospect.

DISCLAIMER: To be clear, I am not a lawyer and nothing in this book should be taken as legal advice. You should check with your dealership's legal counsel before implementing any advice provided by me or anyone not acting as your legal counsel. Moreover, the laws and regulations concerning texting are fluid and information may have changed since this book was published.

(Caution: In my opinion, you're about to enter a particularly boring part of this book. Important stuff… so hang in there; we'll get to more Assumptive Selling later in this chapter.)

As of this writing, the TCPA has been relaxed to allow for more sensible uses of texting between a salesperson and a prospect. I'll attempt to explain how I interpret these; though again, I'm not a lawyer and you should check with your own legal counsel before implementing any of my advice.

As a salesperson, you should want to text your prospects because it provides a more immediate response than an email or voicemail. When you have a new sales lead, for example, your first goal is to make a connection. Often, that connection will come more quickly via a text message than through other means. Data from the dealerships I've worked with shows that the first dealer to connect with a new prospect is more than twice as likely to sell them a car than the dealer who connects second; so, texting should be an important tool in your Assumptive Selling approach.

The best way to keep your texting activity compliant with the TCPA is to keep your texting communications on point. For example, if a service customer provided their mobile number to the advisor when they brought their vehicle in for repairs – and you've had no sales communication with them – you will likely be in violation of the TCPA if you send them the following unsolicited text:

> Great News! We have 0% financing on all new Tundras in stock!

This is a marketing message that is wholly unrelated to why the customer provided their mobile number. Moreover, it's an inauthentic, unwanted communication that will not help you create a great customer experience.

In the past, it was not a violation of the TCPA to send a marketing message via text to a customer where you had an established business relationship. This changed in 2013, requiring you to have prior express written consent to send these types of messages. This is an especially important distinction when your plan is to send a marketing message as a mass text from your CRM. The TCPA is very clear on the use of software to send these messages in an automated fashion, and you must receive prior express written consent from the customer to do so.

The good news is that this consent can come from a checked box on a lead form, called an opt-in. If your dealership does not already use a disclaimer that contains this opt-in on your website lead forms, I recommend that you add one. Here's a very simple example of how this might read:

> "By providing my phone number, I authorize ABC Motors to send text messages to my mobile phone related to this inquiry. I recognize I'm not required to enter into such an agreement as a condition of purchase, and that I could receive multiple text messages and that standard message and data rates may apply."

Again, I'm not a lawyer, though this is a very simple online opt-in that you can include on your website's lead forms so that consumers understand when they submit the form, they're agreeing that you may text them information related to this purchase.

This, however, is not enough (in my opinion) to keep you compliant when it comes to new prospects using a lead form to opt-in. The reason? Consumers completing lead forms can and do enter incorrect phone numbers on occasion. Whether by accident or intentionally, if a prospect enters the mobile number of another individual, the other individual has not yet given express permission for you to text. To ensure compliance, I recommend the first text you send to any new lead be a double opt-in. Here's a quick example of what that text might look like:

> ABC Motors is confirming a request to send messages. Reply A to allow, S to stop, H for help. Message and data rates apply.

This double opt-in is where using your CRM to manage these communications comes in handy. This message can be created as a texting template, sent from you, and your prospect's affirmative response is recorded in the CRM.

There is some discussion that an employee using their own phone to text a prospect does not require the same express consent. I disagree with that assumption, since the technology of the average smartphone can mimic automated software by sending these rapidly, using templates and to sequential numbers. My advice is that it's better to be safe than sorry when dealing with an agency like the FCC. (The FCC enforces the TCPA.)

If you're a manager or owner, you'll want to ensure your salespeople never use their own phones for texting (unless it's through the CRM's mobile application); they should always use the CRM. Using the CRM for texting gives you some control over the templates your team uses and allows for the documentation of the back-and-forth with a prospect.

Not everything about the TCPA is bad for salespeople and dealerships. In fact, when someone provides their mobile number to the salesperson (perhaps as part of the paperwork for their trade appraisal), they are demonstrating their consent for the salesperson to send non-marketing texts relevant to the reason they gave the number. This means, for example, that if the customer leaves without purchasing, the salesperson has an implied consent to send a text message asking them to come back and let the dealership have another look at their trade.

Whether this implied consent would also apply to announcing a one-day sale on F-150s is doubtful, in my opinion. Additionally, if a prospect scheduled a test drive appointment and provided their mobile number, the current interpretation of the TCPA indicates it's fine for you to send them appointment reminders via text messaging.

Finally, most texts that are considered transactional in nature are usually allowed. This would cover messages that relate specifically to a given situation or a response to a customer's specific inquiry. For example, sending a thank you text as a follow-up to a lot visit is likely not a violation even when you do not have a prior express written consent.

Salespeople should be careful how they respond to a customer's initial, unexpected text message. While it may seem like any text received from a customer means that customer is fair game to be bombarded with any messages the salesperson chooses, the truth is that without express consent, the salesperson should refrain from marketing pitches in these return texts.

For example, if a prospect had the salesperson's mobile number and texted them a question about the mileage on a particular used vehicle, the salesperson would be allowed to answer the question, but would need to send an opt-in request if he wanted to also send the prospect photos of the car and the current sale price (as these last two items could be considered marketing).

Confusing, I know. That's why I always recommend texting via your store's CRM tool. Most of these tools have safeguards to keep you compliant with the most current TCPA regulations. Plus, given that the current penalties can be as much as $1,500 per offending text message, dealerships who allow unmonitored texting can open themselves up to tremendous liability. For example, if just 5 salespeople sent just 10 noncompliant texts per day for 5 days, the dealership could face a fine as high as $375,000.00!

That's for just 5 days of noncompliant texting!

Texts are not Mini Emails

For those applying the principles of Assumptive Selling, it's important to stress that texting, chat and Messenger conversations should not be treated as miniature emails. These are back-and-forth discussions that should more closely resemble miniature phone calls. Think of these as walkie-talkie conversations. This means that the direction you take a prospect should be similar to what you'll do when you have someone on the phone.

It's easy to think of these as emails when you're using your CRM or chat program to manage these communications – especially when you're in front of your computer creating or editing your text and chat templates. Just remember that when you use these templates you'll be involved in a dialogue and not a monologue.

Additionally, the texting opt-in is not a license to spam. It is a privilege, and you need to use this privilege sparingly. To today's Ups, texting is the most personal form of communication, and any seller wanting to create a customer for life – one who believes you are their friend in the car business – won't stand for your spam texts; so, keep your messages relevant and on point.

Emailing Today's Ups

We'll explore sample emails to your prospects and customers in other, more appropriate chapters of this book. For now, let's level set about your dealership's emails.

No offense, but most every dealership today is a spammer. That is, you send blast emails to your entire database so often that most of your recipients have already labeled you as spam or junk in their inboxes. When this happens, your important emails wind up in the spam folders of new prospects who truly would like a price quote. For most of the dealerships I work with there is a never-ending battle with trying to keep their email addresses whitelisted.

The only real remedy for this is to stop blasting your database. Think about your own personal email. Do you enjoy getting unsolicited offers from companies that have no relevance to your current needs? Of course you don't; yet some dealerships will send a mass email to all the addresses in their database to announce a huge weekend sale. If I just purchased a new car from you last month, do you think I want to start seeing these in my inbox today?

Your emails must provide a value to the recipient or they'll quickly label you as a spammer. So, while an oil change coupon might be of value to a recent new car buyer, a lease special would not. Likewise, most of your database doesn't want your newsletter. If you're a manager, I recommend you examine the value this email delivers versus the potential loss of future business. If you're a salesperson, I recommend you ask if you can opt any of your customers out of the newsletter. At a minimum, your newsletter should allow for a specific opt-out; that is, there should be a clear message that the customer can opt-out of future newsletters, but still receive important updates about their vehicle.

When you do have a targeted email that you want to send to your database – for example, you want to send a Value Your Trade message to anyone whose vehicle is more than 36 months old – be sure to divide the database in a way that allows you to properly respond to those who are interested in your offer. Let me give you an example why that's important.

Let's say you have 10,000 customer and prospect emails that fit the example above. If you send the Value Your Trade message to all 10,000 today, you could easily have 300 who complete the trade-in form over the next couple of days. Does your dealership have the resources to properly respond to 300 interested customers in two days? Probably not. Therefore, instead of blasting all 10,000 in one day, divide the list by 20 and send the email to 500 customers per day for the first 20 weekdays in the month. On average, you'll have a manageable 15 form completions per day; and you'll be able to treat each one of these to a true VIP experience in your dealership.

Phoning Today's Ups

When we explored texting, we learned that most of today's Ups want to eliminate unnecessary greetings and the exchange of irrelevant information. This also means your phone conversations should get to the point (the essence of Assumptive Selling); and you won't have time to check off every step on one of those antiquated Phone Up cards your dealership bought from a phone trainer in the 1980s.

You should approach every Phone Up as if the person on the other end of the phone has already found value and relevancy, and now they just want an authentic person to sell them a car. Unfortunately, when you talk on the phone using old-school word tracks, you use a lot of unnecessary greetings and you exchange a lot of irrelevant information.

For example, when a prospect calls and asks, "I'm looking at this white Taurus that you've got listed on UsedCars.com; is it still in stock?" and you pepper them with questions asking how they're doing and how their day is going and are they looking at any other vehicles, you're going to cure them of their new car fever. They found the one vehicle that meets their needs at the right price and they're trying to buy it from you – stop eliminating yourself from the equation!

The 4 Rules

There are four rules to keep in mind when speaking to a Phone Up that also apply to any communication with today's connected customers. For those using Assumptive Selling, these rules will govern most everything we say on the phone, in email and on the lot; and they are the quickest way to get today's prospect to purchase a vehicle.

Rule #1: Take Charge

Interestingly, this rule was the most important rule in selling when the first Up walked on the first dealer's lot over 100 years ago; and it's still the most important rule in selling cars today. You need to take charge and stay in charge of every conversation you have with a prospect or you'll see them driving by your dealership in the vehicle they bought from the guy across the street.

What's more, is that today's Ups want you take charge. They're trying to buy a car and despite all the research they've conducted, they don't know how any of this works. Today's Phone Up wants you to take charge, pull them through the phone and sell them a car. They just don't want to be hurt in the process. So, take charge and stay in charge of every conversation.

The best way to take charge on a phone call is to avoid the typical questions that BDC agents and salespeople often confuse with politeness. Questions like "When would you like to come in?" might sound polite, but they're not; they're weak. You think you're being polite and giving the prospect the courtesy of choosing when they want to see your vehicle; but you're just ceding control of the call to the caller.

We'll discuss the proper way to handle a Phone Up in a later chapter; though for now, let's examine what you really just told this prospect when you asked, "When would you like to come in?" You just told them:

- "There's no rush."
- "We're never busy."
- "We don't care when you buy."
- "That car is going to be here forever."

Is that the message you want to convey to your Phone Ups? I would hope not. The only goal you have when you have a prospect on the phone is an appointment that shows. There are no other goals! To get the prospect to show for an appointment, you must create a sense of urgency; though by asking them when they want to come in, you just removed all urgency from the purchase.

Taking charge is the first rule for a reason – and not just when you're on the phone. Any time you're communicating with today's connected customer, whether it's via phone, email, text or in person, you must take charge and keep control, or they will take you down their own path until they've eliminated you and your dealership from their consideration set.

When someone submits a sales lead or calls your dealership about a vehicle, they are trying to buy a car... but, they're also trying to eliminate you. Since yours is not the only vehicle for sale, you should assume they have a couple of other vehicles they would like to consider. If you allow them to eliminate you with a weak question – and the guy across the street sets a firm appointment that shows – you're never going to get a chance to sell them a car.

The leads and calls you receive today are generally from ready buyers, but most of them have at least two other options they're considering. They're reaching out in advance of going to these three dealerships (yours and two others) in hopes of further narrowing their search. You just made it easy for them to put you third on their list; basically guaranteeing that you'll never see them.

You must be their first stop if you want the best chance of selling them a car; and you cannot become this if you don't create the necessary urgency by taking charge of the call. As you'll learn when you read about The Perfect Appointment later in this book, being the first dealer in line gives you an 80% chance of closing this deal. Thus, always take charge of the conversation so that you can create the necessary urgency to set an appointment that shows.

Rule #2: Be Direct

As we know, today's consumers don't want a lot of unnecessary greetings or the exchange of irrelevant information. They also don't want to be talked to like they're some tire-kicker from the 1970s. They need you to be direct; they want you to speak to them the same way you would if a friend was on the other end of the phone.

They've already found value and relevancy in your vehicle, and they want to buy it today. Being direct with them is the cornerstone of authenticity; so, asking them questions they find offensive or irrelevant is the antithesis of being direct. Let me give you an example.

Imagine that a friend calls you about a 2017 Honda Odyssey you have on your lot. Would you ask that friend any of the following?

- "What is it you like most about the Odyssey, is it style or price?"
- "Are there any colors you wouldn't consider?"
- "Is it just minivans you're considering or are you also looking at mid-size SUVs?"
- "Are you primarily going to use the Odyssey for business or pleasure?"

No! You'd tell your friend "Come! Now! Buy!" Your responses would be authentic, because you would be direct with your friend. Why would you treat a ready buyer any other way?

Being direct resonates with today's buyer. They're looking to buy, they found your minivan, and they're just calling to see if the price is real and if it's still available. Rather than use old-school word tracks that seem irrelevant to buying your vehicle, just help them buy it. If something doesn't resonate with today's Up or if they feel they're being sold, they're going to eliminate you and find an alternative.

<u>Rule #3: Provide Guidance</u>

When we introduced the first rule, I wrote that today's buyers don't know how any of this works; and they don't. That's the reason they sent in the lead; that's the reason they called. Your job is to guide them through the purchase. This is a little more than taking charge, in that you need to be certain your words help guide them through your process.

Whatever your buying process, you must stay focused on the next step and not the last step. Often, salespeople are so eager to sell a car (the last step in the process) that they try to do this over the phone. Let me be clear: you cannot sell the car over the phone. Trying to sell the car over the phone is the same as trying to sell the car to the Up who just walked on your lot – you'll fail. You need to guide them through your process from one step to the next.

I wrote it earlier and I'll write it at least a few more times in this book: your only goal when you have someone on the phone is an appointment that shows. That's it. This means, your next step after the phone call is a shown appointment, right? So, let's be sure that's how you guide them using the first three rules of communicating with today's Ups:

> Customer: "I'm looking at this 2017 Honda Odyssey that you've got online. Is it still in stock?"

> Assumptive Seller: "I saw that minivan this morning, but at the price we have it listed at it's not going to make it through to the weekend. Now, I do have two test drives open on that minivan this afternoon. I've got a 12:15 and 12:45. Which one works better for you?"

In this exchange, you took charge, you were direct, and you guided the prospect to the next step; that is, an appointment that shows.

<u>Rule #4: You Lose All Pre-Visit Information Exchanges</u>

You may have heard a sales manager put it this way, "You can't sell an empty seat." The point he or she was trying to make is that the customer needs to see your vehicle (in person) to buy it. When you try to sell it over the phone, you're going to lose.

But, it's not just attempting to sell the car over the phone that's the problem, this saying also applies when you find yourself just exchanging lots of information on the phone, via text, or email with the prospect. In these cases, you're going to give the prospect just enough information to eliminate you.

To be clear, I'm not saying that you should not answer questions. You should always answer all questions truthfully and completely (just as you would when speaking to a friend); but, you need to avoid the "tennis match" many BDC agents and salespeople find themselves in on the phone. This tennis match usually goes like this:

> Customer question sends the ball in your court. You answer, sending the ball back. Next customer question puts it back in your court. You answer… Rinse. Lather. Repeat.

I cringe when listening to these exchanges because I know the salesperson believes they're being helpful; though, ultimately, they just end up eliminating themselves from consideration. They were caught in an endless information exchange; and when these information exchanges take place pre-visit (before the customer arrives on your lot), you will lose virtually every time.

Think of any pre-visit information you provide as being on a continuum. At one end, you give no information; you just "get 'em in." This, of course, is not a very good customer experience and you're not going to set very many appointments that show. At the other end of that continuum, you give every prospect all the information they need about your vehicle, their credit worthiness, their trade and your terms. Congratulations, you've given them enough information to eliminate you. The key on pre-visit information is to live somewhere in the middle; somewhere in that sweet spot where you can generate appointments that show and buy.

It may sound a bit customer unfriendly, but you don't get paid for information. If you're a BDC agent, you're usually paid on shown appointments; and if you're a salesperson, you're paid to sell the car. Getting caught up in an 11-minute information exchange is not good for you or the prospect. Think about it:

- Are you a good person?
- Is your dealership a good place to buy a car?
- Do you sell a good brand?

If you answered yes to all three questions, then why in the world would you just vomit information all over the prospect until they decided to buy somewhere else? Isn't it better for everyone if they buy from you?

Again, I'm not telling you not to answer questions. I don't want you to play dumb or be coy on the phone. Transparency – in both pricing and process – is key to a great customer experience; so, you should answer all questions.

But…

Every answer (whether to a question or an objection) should set up the next step in your process. When you're on the phone, this means an appointment that shows. For example, if your prospect asks about the current interest rate offered by your OEM, how you answer will determine whether you get caught in an information exchange or set an appointment that shows:

> Typical Salesperson: "Currently, Dodge is offering 1.9% for up to 72 months to qualified buyers."

> Assumptive Seller: "Currently, Dodge has rates as low as 1.9% on some vehicles. Of course, the promotional rates can expire at any time, so we should see how this current promotion affects you. Our next step should be to test drive the Challenger and then run the numbers together. As I said, we have two test drives open on that Challenger this morning, we have a 10:15 and a 10:45, which one of these works better for you?"

In the first example, the typical salesperson was inviting more questions by not circling back to his goal of setting an appointment that shows. Whereas, the assumptive seller assumes the customer is not calling to gather a bunch of information; but wants to buy the new Challenger. Taking charge, being direct, providing guidance and avoiding a pre-visit information exchange pulls the buyer through your process – right through the phone and onto your lot.

Why Buy from Me / Why Buy from Us

Why would anyone want to buy from you or your dealership? If you cannot easily answer this question, there's no need to panic; but, there is a need to develop your "why buy" messaging. Being able to answer "why buy" questions – even if just to yourself – helps you understand and highlight the unique advantages you and your dealership deliver for your customers.

Creating your "why buy" list doesn't have to be a major undertaking; simply write down some of the reasons someone should want to buy from you. Perhaps you're friendly and you'll always work to get them the best deal. Maybe you deliver a no-pressure buying experience and your customers give you rave reviews. Whatever it is about you that makes buying a good experience should be on your list.

Now, create the same sort of list for your dealership. Do you offer free loaners in service? Do you have a vehicle exchange policy? Are you open late? Believe it or not, these are all proper "why buy" messages – despite that they may seem unimportant to you.

Your lists don't need to be extensive or elaborate, just accurate. Once you've created your lists and done a good job of reviewing why anyone would want to buy from you, you'll be able to interject some of these into your customer conversations in ways that overcome objections or move someone off the fence and into a new car.

Words Matter

A final note on communicating with today's Ups is that the words you choose matter; so, speak carefully. You're trying to help someone purchase the second most expensive thing they'll probably ever buy; and this should be a fun and exciting time for them. They're stressed, and they already believe car buying is going to be a hassle; so, be careful to avoid the negative words and phrases that will dampen their mood and potentially lose you the sale.

Here are just a few examples of negative speak and replacement phrases that can put a positive spin on what you're really trying to convey to today's buyer:

Instead of saying:	Say:
"We don't…"	"I'd love to help with that …"
"I can't…"	"I will definitely…"
"If you only had…"	"We'll make it work…"
"We don't have time…"	"We're going to…"
"I don't think…"	"I'm certain…"
"But, you…"	"I'm going to ensure…"
"No, we can't…"	"We're going to do everything we can…"

8

THE POWER OF PERFECT DATA

Communicating properly with today's Ups is just not possible if you try to wing it – this is where relying on a well-maintained CRM gives top sellers an advantage.

Your CRM is the most important sales tool you'll ever use; though it has one severe limitation: It's only as good as the information you put into it. Your goal, therefore, should be to have a perfect CRM filled with perfect data. Achieving perfect data can make the difference between profitably growing share in any market condition or wondering where your customers went.

I define perfect data as the recording of every customer and prospect interaction in near real time. This means Ups go into the CRM soon after they arrive on the lot, and the visit is closed soon after they leave. The customer record is complete with every important step they took while on the lot, including copious notes about what they liked and didn't like about you, your dealership and the vehicle.

I get it, entering every customer and prospect interaction in the CRM takes time. Plus, trying to get that data in there in near real time is almost impossible with the hectic schedules we sometimes find ourselves working in. That said, there seems to be no profession with more down time than car sales. When it's busy, it's busy. But, when it's not busy, it's dead.

My point is that those who want perfect data in their CRM will always find the time to include it. Moreover, those who strive for perfect data sell customers and prospects in less time with fewer errors – which, of course, gives them even more time to accurately represent in the CRM what is happening in real life.

Perfect data helps you sell cars today and tomorrow; so, I'm going to make my pitch for it in this chapter and perhaps motivate you and your teams to care about what goes into and comes out of your CRM.

Perfect Data is Important

Not only does perfect data matter, it matters more than the Up getting out of their car right now. In fact, compared to perfect data in your CRM, that Up is worthless.

The sooner the leadership team at your dealership or group realizes this, the faster you'll be able to navigate the changes in automotive retail. Not only will perfect data be a game changer in the future, but dealerships willing to insist on perfect data today in their CRM tool from the variable side of the business will enjoy an almost immediate competitive advantage that makes them less vulnerable to market mood swings.

Perfect data is not Big Data. Perfect data is actually Small Data. It's the data you can use to make meaningful decisions with your business from day-to-day and year-to-year. It's the data that only you own; and it's the most important data for every retail business in America – especially car dealers.

Perfect data is exactly what the name implies: information that is accurate, up-to-date and (above all else) a true representation of what happened and what is currently happening on your lot. While getting perfect data may sound like a hard task, it's actually easier than the alternative.

There is a broad misconception with America's desk managers that perfect data gets in the way of working a deal or somehow makes the job of being a sales manager harder. The opposite is true. Perfect data makes every job in the dealership easier.

With perfect data you can decide which salesperson is best suited to handle the next Up and which one needs help getting folks to take a test drive. Without perfect data you spend every sales meeting screaming at the entire team about manager T.O.s instead of being laser-focused on the two guys struggling the most at getting a manager involved early in their lost deals.

With perfect data, you know which marketing vendors are helping you sell cars and which ones are just stealing from you. Without perfect data, you'll keep wasting tens of thousands of dollars on the latest brand of snake oil. The more perfect your data, the better your decisions and the more focused your energies and training. Period.

To understand where best to concentrate to ensure your efforts for perfect data are not wasted, let's look at how perfect data impacts your business over time. For example, there are numerous instances where perfect data in the CRM can mean higher sales, lower turnover and better grosses; here are just a few:

Perfect Data Today:

- Knowing at a glance how long a prospect has been on the lot and where they are on the road-to-the-sale allows a sales manager to make a proactive T.O. and close more deals.
- Knowing where a prospect is stuck in the sales funnel (whether offline or online) allows managers to proactively pull them towards a sale.
- Managers are able to get closer to 100% of the Ups in the CRM simply by comparing the current Showroom Log to the actual showroom. (This is a great coaching opportunity to ensure salespeople enter their prospects timely and properly.)
- Managers, floor salespeople, BDC agents and internet salespeople know instantly when appointments are running late. This allows them to call to reconfirm the prospect's status and increase show rates.
- Floor salespeople are reminded who they upped this morning, where they are in the sales funnel, and what to say when they make their follow-up calls. (Yes, you make your Be-Back calls the same day for unsold prospects, given that the average buyer visits fewer than two lots before they purchase.)

Perfect Data Tomorrow:

- With 100% of the Ups from yesterday in the CRM, a robust Be-Back process can be initiated, followed and managed.
- For dealers conducting true save-a-deal meetings, perfect data from yesterday allows the managers to focus on the prospects most likely to buy. (For dealers not holding save-a-deal meetings: what in the world are you waiting for?)
- If you're using a separate equity mining tool (not provided by your CRM), you're occasionally calling customers based on a CRM prompt, despite the customer telling your equity mining team yesterday to stop calling them – all because your team failed to make sure the data in the CRM was perfect.

Perfect Data at the End of the Month:

- A typical dealership treats two salespeople who each sold 15 vehicles this month exactly the same – they provide the same amount of coaching to each. With perfect data, it's easy to pinpoint which salesperson is properly following your road-to-the-sale and which one needs additional coaching. For example, would your coaching still be the same if you discovered that one salesperson who sold 15 units handled 50 Ups (30% close) and the other who sold 15 worked with 100 (15% close)?
- Perfect data allows for comparisons of salespeople by their performance at each step in the road-to-the-sale. For example, you might have salespeople who do a great job of getting demo drives but fail to get these same customers to the write-up (relative to the other salespeople). This would indicate they are saying or doing something during the test drive that turns off their prospects. You wouldn't know this unless you had perfect data in the CRM.

Perfect Data Over the Longer Term:

- By properly recording trade-in and desired vehicle information for every Up, the dealership could easily target (based on current inventory and incentives, for example) phone campaigns, email marketing and direct mail to those who did not buy in an effort to bring these people back into the store months after they first visited.
- Imagine if the contact information from every Up from three years ago was collected and stored in your CRM. Then imagine that a real Be-Back follow-up process was completed for those who did not buy. Imagine that during the Be-Back calls, you discovered who bought elsewhere and you asked them what they bought, where they bought it and why they did not buy from you; and you put all of that data in the CRM. Your salespeople or a BDC could include these people in their Buy Back (Owner Marketing) efforts and create sales opportunities three years after you lost the deal.

Perfect Data: Enforcement

Ensuring you have perfect data in the CRM may seem like a daunting task (especially when you consider how few dealerships have anything close to perfect data), but the opposite is actually true. Collecting and maintaining perfect data is easier than always flying by the seat of your pants. In fact, the only thing that makes perfect data "more work" than what you're doing now is that you'll start selling more cars because of it.

If you're serious about striving for perfect data, there are a few simple ways to dramatically improve the accuracy of the information in your CRM, including:

1.   Daily Checks. This is where the leadership asks a few questions about the current state of the CRM Showroom Log to check for accuracy. This is the most proactive way to improve the data and allows you to get closer to perfect data more quickly. Practicing Show Me Leadership will help you drive perfect data in your dealership. For example: You see four different customers on the lot, yet your CRM shows only two. Asking your desk managers how many people are on the lot and following that question with "show me" forces them to reveal that only two are being properly tracked at this time.

2.   Manual Up Tracking. Tasking your greeters and/or receptionists with a simple "Up Tracking" scoresheet is an easy way to see which salespeople are entering their Ups in the CRM and which ones are not.

3.   Daily Managers' Meeting. A good Daily Managers' Meeting is one that reviews the business data from yesterday and includes a true save-a-deal function. In this meeting, the leadership should be able to see at a glance where data "fudging" has occurred and take corrective action.

4.   Monthly Reports. Applying a "sniff test" to the monthly reports is a reactive approach, but like the Daily Managers' Meeting, the leadership should be able to easily spot bad data. For example, if your closing percentage of Traditional Ups is greater than your closing percentage of appointments, this is a red flag that proves you're not getting enough Ups entered in the CRM. Likewise, if you have any salesperson closing above 50% of their Traditional Ups, they are either true superstars or they're entering fewer than half of the prospects they encounter in the CRM.

Of course, perfect data (like everything) is easier said than done, so here are a few final tips to get you started today:

1.   You may know that the second-best time to plant a tree is right now. Stop worrying about the data from yesterday, last week, last month and last year. Start right now and commit to perfect data.

2. Perfect data is boring both in a book like this and in practice. Get over it. In this case, boring is good and can be very profitable (if done right).

3. Perfect data requires constant oversight from the top. Automotive retail tends to reward lazy, seat-of-the-pants decision making in the short term; and perfect data is a much-needed cultural change that will not happen on its own. It will not be easy, but it will be incredibly rewarding for those willing to do it right.

4. The opposite of perfect data is not no data; the opposite of perfect data is something called box checking – also known as bad data. For far too long, dealers and their OEMs have rewarded sales managers when they check boxes. This was done to avoid conflict, real work and to keep some sort of weird balance in the universe. Stop with the box checking, okay?

The big dealer groups are actively working toward having and feeding off perfect data. If they beat you to it, you may never recover. I know that sounds drastic, but the truth is that relationships matter less every day. Those gaining market share today are the ones with great processes; and great processes are fueled with great data.

9

SOCIAL SELLING IN AN ASSUMPTIVE SELLING ENVIRONMENT

At this very instant, there are vehicle salespeople on Facebook enjoying 25 or more sales a month just by talking about their accomplishments and taking pictures of their lunch. Marketing themselves via Facebook has made a huge difference in their results; and all they've had to do is allow a huge intrusion into their lives, give up much of their privacy, and be ready to tell anyone and everyone that they love selling cars.

Welcome to new-school networking.

Social networking, just like old-fashioned networking, can help motivated salespeople deliver stellar results. But, just like old-fashioned networking, this takes work; and you must be proud of what you do and be ready to tell anyone and everyone online that:

1. I sell cars;
2. I'm honored to be selling cars; and
3. I'm your friend in the car business.

When you do this (along with following some basic guidelines that I'll lay out in this chapter), you'll have people showing up at your dealership telling you, "I saw you on Facebook; can you help me buy a car?"

Beyond what social media can do for the hardest working salespeople in your organization, it's an often overlooked, though extremely fruitful way to occupy a bored salesperson's time, as well.

Sales managers wanting to motivate those in the smoking circle could do much worse than encouraging them to begin driving their own Up Bus via Facebook Live (and other social media channels/tools). The industry calls this "social selling" (as will I); though it's really more a form of personal social media marketing and branding.

Of course, if you want to argue semantics, then social selling is probably not for you. However, if you're ready to start generating real business via your Facebook account, then this chapter will help you do just that.

Quick disclaimer: This chapter is not *The Complete Idiot's Guide to Social Media Marketing* or *Facebook for Dummies*. I'm going to assume you have some knowledge of this medium, as this will not be a step-by-step guide on how to upload photos or what time of day is best to post a video. In this chapter, we're going to combine the social media best practices of some great social sellers with Assumptive Selling to show you how you can use (primarily) Facebook to drive Ups to your door.

Social Selling is Free

Done right, social selling shouldn't cost you anything. While top social sellers may occasionally pay to have some of their posts seen in their market, this is not a requirement of social selling. There are plenty of social sellers today who use the tools they already own (their iPhone and a selfie stick), use their existing social media profile, and perhaps add a free tool or two (like Krutchit.com) to help them profitably sell to buyers they've never met; buyers who just show up at the dealership and ask for them by name, just because someone shared their post.

You've already learned about value, relevancy and authenticity; so, I won't bore you with a regurgitation here. Your presence on Facebook and other social channels is your chance to prove authenticity. That is, it's critical that your Facebook "you" match the real you. When you're using social media correctly, you have the chance to prove authenticity well in advance of the prospect discovering value and relevancy. Let me explain how this works and why this is great news for you.

The typical consumer today – one without a friend in the car business – finds a car they like online at a price they think is fair. They've discovered value and relevancy; now they need to try to buy that car. They might pick up the phone, send an email lead, or they might just walk on your lot. Regardless of how they came to you, they've already found what they want. Your job is to confirm value and relevancy while you prove authenticity. In these cases, your grosses are (for the most part) controlled by the market because you couldn't build the value in the traditional sense.

When the consumer has a friend in the car business, they often go to that friend first with just a general idea about what they want. They trust their friend to find value and relevancy because the friend has already provided the authenticity. In these cases, the salesman-friend can make a fair profit on the vehicle because, well, they're friends. When done right, social selling (just like old-fashioned networking) makes you their friend in the car business.

With social selling, you generate the buyers for yourself; keeping you in control of the process from beginning to end. Of course, you must remain authentic throughout the process because you want your newfound friends to recommend you to their friends after the purchase. It does you no good to generate a sales prospect from Facebook and then take their head off.

Don't get me wrong, I want you to earn a fair profit on every deal. Profit is not a dirty word; and without it, there would be no cars, no dealerships and no you. However, you need to look at every sale as an opportunity to sell five more from the repeats and referrals. If you destroy a customer, you destroy all the repeat and referral business that customer would've delivered you.

The worst salespeople I know are the ones who look at each sale as a single transaction. They're the ones who bounce from dealership to dealership because they don't have the skills to develop their own book of business. (Yes, if you have your own book of business, you can move anywhere in your market; but, the truth is that those salespeople who develop a true loyal following often enjoy staying put.)

Why Facebook?

There are literally scores of active social networks that someone could argue are important for you to consider if you're going to try your hand at social selling. However, as of this writing, I recommend you initially focus solely on Facebook. I recommend this for many reasons, but not the least of which is that it's the most popular. Moreover, your posts have the ability to go viral more readily there than on any other large social network.

Twitter, for example, just doesn't provide the same multiple-day lift that a great Facebook post can earn. When you Tweet something that's pure genius – even if you're properly using hashtags – your post can fall on deaf ears. That is, your post is missed by nearly all your followers and it gets buried in their stream. It's gone.

Plus, Facebook rewards great posters. This basically means that if your last few posts were well-received (lots of likes, shares and comments), your next post stands a better chance of being at the top of your friends' and followers' respective news feeds.

Finally, there are just too many social networks and places to share user-generated content to try to be everywhere all the time. To help prove this point, here is an alphabetized list of just some of the active social networking sites (as of this writing):

43Things, 500px, About.me, Academia.edu, Advogato, Ancestry, AngelList, aNobii, AsianAvenue, aSmallWorld, Athlinks, Audimated, Badoo, Bebo, Biip.no, BlackPlanet, Bolt, Busuu, Buzznet, CafeMom, Care2, CaringBridge, Cellufun, Classmates, Cloob, ClusterFlunk, CouchSurfing, CozyCot, Crokes, Cross.tv, Crunchyroll, Cucumbertown, Cyworld, DailyBooth, DailyStrength, delicious, DeviantArt, Diaspora, Disaboom, Dol2day, DontStayIn, douban, Doximity, Draugiem.lv, Dreamwidth, Dronestagram, DXY.cn, Elftown, Elixio, Ello, English,baby!, Eons, Epernicus, eToro, ExperienceProject, Exploroo, Facebook, Faceparty, Fetlife, FilmAffinity, Filmow, FledgeWing, Flickr, Flixster, Focus, Fotki, Fotolog, Foursquare, Friendica, FriendsReunited, Friendster, Fuelmyblog, FunnyOrDie, Gab, GaiaOnline, GamerDNA, Gapyear, Gather, Gays, Geni, GetGlue, GirlsAskGuys, Glocals, Gogoyoko, Goodreads, Goodwizz, Google+, GovLoop, Grono.net, Habbo, hi5, HospitalityClub, Hotlist, HR, HubCulture, Hyves, Ibibo, Identi.ca, Imgur, IndabaMusic, Influenster, Instagram, Internations, IRC-Galleria, italki, Itsmy, iWiW, Jaiku, Jiepang, Kaixin001, Kickstarter, Kiwibox, Lafango, LaiBhaari, Last.fm, LibraryThing, Lifeknot, Line, LinkedIn, LinkExpats, Listography, LiveJournal, Livemocha, Makeoutclub, MEETin, MeetMe, Meettheboss, Meetup, Meetup, Messenger, MillatFacebook, Minds, mixi, MocoSpace, MOG, MouthShut, Mubi, MyHeritage, MyLife, MyMFB, MyOpera, Myspace, Nasza-klasa.pl, Netlog, Nexopia, NextDoor, NGOPost, Ning, Odnoklassniki, OpenDiary, Orkut, OUTeverywhere, Partyflock, Path, PatientsLikeMe, Photobucket, Pinboard, Pingsta, Pinterest, Pixabay, Plaxo, Playfire, Playlist, PlentyofFish, Plurk, Poolwo, ProductHunt, Qapacity, Quechup, Quora, Qzone, Raptr, Ravelry, Reddit, Renren, ReverbNation, Ryze, ScienceStage, Sgrouples, ShareTheMusic, Shelfari, Shutterfly, SinaWeibo, Skoob, Skype, Skyrock, Smartican, Snapfish, SocialVibe, Solaborate, Sonico, SoundCloud, Spaces, Spot.IM, Spring.me, Spybirds, Stage32, Stickam, StudentsCircleNetwork, StudiVZ, StumbleUpon, Tagged, Talkbiznow, Taltopia, Taringa!, TeachStreet, Telegram, TermWiki, TheSphere, Tinder, Tournac, Tout, TravBuddy, TravelBuddy,

Travellerspoint, tribe.net, Trombi, Tsu, Tuenti, Tumblr, Twitter, Twoo, Tylted, Untapped, Uplike, Vampirefreaks, Viadeo, Viber, Vine, Virb, VK, Vox, Wattpad, WAYN, wechat, WeeWorld, WeHeartIt, Wellwer, Wepolls, weRead, Wer-kennt-wen, WhatsApp, Wiser.org, Wooxie, WriteAPrisoner, Xanga, XING, Xt3, Yammer, Yelp, Yookos, YouTube, Zoo.gr, Zooppa, Zynga.

Reviewing this list makes it easy to understand that trying to be everywhere is just not possible. Even though sharing content on the overwhelming majority of these sites is free, the time required to manage these profiles and posts ensures you receive a negative ROI of your efforts. Of course, if you're already a member of and active on any social networks, be sure that your profile clearly states:

1.   I sell cars;
2.   I'm honored to be selling cars; and
3.   I'm your friend in the car business.

ROI of Social Selling

Your investment with social selling is going to be measured in terms of time and effort. Your goal is to minimize both while you maximize the sales that great social selling can drive. The reason you want to minimize your time spent on social selling is because your time is not limitless. There are a finite number of work hours in the month, and if you dedicate nearly all of them to social selling, then you have little time for other moneymakers.

You'll want to measure your return on this time and effort investment in a number of ways. First, you'll want to ensure you gain the necessary engagement to make this effort worthwhile. Engagement, of course, is in the eye of the beholder. That is, it's up to you to determine if your efforts produce the engagement you're looking for.

For example, if you post something to Facebook that produces no likes, no shares and no comments, then you have no engagement; no interaction. Posts like these can hurt you (because Facebook's algorithms begin to see your posts as irrelevant to your friends and followers), and these should either be avoided in the future or should be tailored to your audience in a way that generates engagement the next time. Without engagement, your posts cannot go viral.

Beyond the engagement, of course, your ultimate goal – and your ultimate ROI measurement – should be on the results these posts produce. That is, are you generating referrals, leads, calls, store visits and especially sales from your activity on Facebook?

The most important rule on any sales efforts you make is to measure something... anything. Measuring allows you to improve your efforts. Without some form of measurement, you're just throwing a bunch of crap against the wall and hoping that some of it sticks. Hope, as has been said again and again, is not a strategy – especially not in sales.

The second rule on all your networking efforts (but, certainly with your social selling efforts) is to be patient. You might make a sale based on the first business card you hand out, for example, but you should expect to hand out 100 cards or more before the first referral roles in. Likewise, with Facebook, your first post could generate a sale, though it's more likely that it will take many hours of working on your Facebook posts before you start to see a return. Again, be patient, the sales will come.

Ultimately, any sales effort you make needs to pass the DISC Test. That is, Does It Sell Cars? With social selling, it could take some time before you can honestly answer that question. Though, I can tell you there are vehicle salespeople selling cars today with relatively little effort on Facebook.

Social Selling is not for Everyone

Although there are social sellers selling cars with relatively little effort on Facebook today, this doesn't mean they didn't have to work hard to get to that point. They did. As I wrote earlier, social selling, like old-fashioned networking, takes work. This means that social selling will not be a fit for you if you look at it as some sort of dodge; a way to avoid working.

If you can't break away from the negative cliques and the smoking circles in your dealership, then social selling is probably not for you. It's not a lazy man's way to sell 30 cars a month. (Hint: Unless you can get a sweet gig like the guy Ray I described in chapter three, there is no lazy man's way to ever sell 30 cars in a month.) The top social sellers I know are the busiest people in their respective dealerships. Social selling requires work, but the rewards are great and the best part about social selling is that it's fun. It really is.

There are a few common traits that the great social sellers of today share with the great salespeople of the past. The first one is activity. It doesn't matter if they're social sellers or they're traditional salespeople, top sellers generate a lot of activity. They're always doing something; they're always working. What's more is they're always working towards their goal. In the world of social selling, they're always generating content.

Another common trait among all top sellers is they follow a process. They are deliberate about what they do and how they do it; and they repeat the process over and over; improving it all the time. Because of this, their first week of the month is often as successful as their last week of the month.

Contrast that with the typical 12-car per month seller:

- Week One = 1 unit sold;
- Week Two = 2 units sold;
- Week Three = 3 units sold; and
- Week Four = 6 units sold.

You simply cannot sell 30 cars month in and month out if the first half of every month generates you just 3 units. The math just doesn't work. In fact, for top social sellers, the only reason they would sell demonstrably more units during the last week of the month versus the earlier weeks is because management drove more traffic that week. If not for that, their month would be steady and predictable from beginning to end.

Top social sellers are never desperate. They know that by following and sticking to their processes they will reap the rewards. They know that for every five prospects in the funnel, they're going to sell one. They just keep lots of prospects in the funnel. All top salespeople I've ever met, including top social sellers, approach every opportunity with confidence, because they know that desperation will show; and no prospect wants to buy from a desperate salesperson.

Don't take this the wrong way, but top social sellers, like all top sellers, are constantly dissatisfied. But, this dissatisfaction is a good thing. They never beat themselves up; but, when they come off a 30-unit month, they don't sit back and relish in the satisfaction for a week. No, they immediately start to plan how they can hit 31 this month. They know they can do better; they know they can work harder.

Top social sellers work for themselves, not the dealership. Again, this is a good thing – especially for the dealership! Dealers should want their salespeople to work for themselves; they should want them to be selfish.

When salespeople are selfish, they sell more cars; they make more money and they satisfy more customers.

So… is social selling for you? It is if you're willing to work; if you'll follow a process; if you're not prone to desperation; if you're dissatisfied; and, especially, if you're selfish!

Less is More

While I wrote that social selling takes work, this does not mean you should post 42 times a day. That is, unless you have something important to share with your audience 42 times a day. With proper social selling, less is often more.

There is certainly a value in being prolific on social media. You want to be productive and you want to be active, but you shouldn't be posting for the sake of posting. You need to have something to say with each post. And, because you need your posts to gain interactions to go viral, posting crap no one wants to see is worse than not posting.

When I look at the mistakes new social sellers make – the ones I want to make sure you do not repeat – the biggest mistake I see is they get unfollowed because of their posts. (Hint: Just because someone is friends with you on Facebook doesn't mean they're seeing any of your posts. If a friend unfollows you, you remain friends, but they never see another thing you post.)

There are many reasons you might be unfollowed (or even snoozed), but the most prevalent reason for social sellers is they over-post. They basically vomit pictures of their inventory on Facebook – sometimes posting 15 or 20 cars a day, just because they can. When your friends see inventory post after inventory post, they get bored and they feel like their news feed is being spammed by you. This means limit your inventory postings! Less is more – especially when it comes to inventory posts.

The only inventory you should ever post to your Facebook profile (as opposed to the Marketplace) are true deals and the Batmobile. If the car you're ready to share doesn't fit one of these two categories, then just don't do it.

True deals are just that: true deals. A cash car priced $1,000 below KBB is a true deal. A brand-new $65,000 truck with a $2,500 rebate is not. Everything in between is up to you to determine if it's a true deal or not. When you do post inventory that you believe to be true deals on your social feeds, be sure to always include the price. Not including pricing online breaks trust with today's consumers because it feels like old-school car sales. You won't appear to be anyone's friend in the car business if you're perceived to be an old-school car salesman.

The real Batmobile is unique; there's (technically) only one and Batman drives it. Your lot, however, might be full of Batmobiles; you just need to look. Batmobiles on your lot are unique vehicles that may interest your friends. For example, if you're a Dodge dealer and you have a Challenger SRT Demon in your showroom, congratulations, you have a Batmobile. Share photos and perhaps even conduct a Facebook Live event to show off this thing. This vehicle is unique and will be interesting to lots of your friends and followers.

Likewise, if you have a ten-year-old minivan with 53,000 miles on it sitting in your used car inventory, you have another Batmobile. Why is this old minivan a Batmobile? Because it's unique! Limiting inventory posts to true deals and Batmobiles will keep your engagement up and reduce the number of friends who unfollow you.

As bad as over-posting can be to your follower count, a sure way to get unfollowed en masse is to post anything political – even if it's funny. Social selling is about selling, and politics has no place here. When you dive into the political discussion, you're bound to make someone angry. Therefore, no matter how angry you are at the president, the congress, the governor, the mayor or even the local dog catcher, keep it to yourself! Politics and sales have never mixed, and they certainly don't mix on social media.

Finally, be clean. Keep your posts to G and PG rated material only. No one is ever going complain that you only post wholesome, fun and interesting things. But, many will certainly object to foul language and posts in bad taste. So, for the sake of maximizing your sales from social, stay clean.

Stop Selling; Start Helping

Interesting fact, but social selling is not about selling at all. It's about building relationships; it's about letting people you've never even met know that they have a friend in the car business. Friends in real life are helpful, not salesy; so, emulate this online.

Your job is to help people find the right vehicle at a fair price. They want your help and they'll gladly pay for that privilege. They won't, however, appreciate it if you appear to be selling them. This goes for your posts, as well. Before you post anything on Facebook, ask yourself,

"Would my friends want to see this? Would my friends appreciate this post? Will this post help someone?"

You and your friends should be able to look back on your posts and agree that the content was compelling or funny or helpful. Social selling is about generating engagement that leads to a sale; and the more genuine you appear – that is, the more authentic you come across – the more likely someone is to contact you for help in buying their next car. More than that, they're more likely to recommend you to a friend or family member.

Social selling is about transparency. You're going to provide outsiders with an inside look at the car business. They're going to see that you're a normal person with normal challenges. Your posts should be honest and full of mistakes; and, you should be ready to laugh at yourself as you make these mistakes. That's authenticity; and when a prospect finds authenticity first, you get the chance to build the value.

The typical Up fears sales pressure; they're afraid of salespeople – especially car salespeople. Your honesty should come through in your Facebook posts (especially in your live videos) because this will reduce the fear someone has in dealing with you before they've ever even met you.

To accomplish much of this, be sure to craft your overall message (and your online image) to convey the following:

- I'm your friend in the car business.
- My friends get better deals.
- I'm a humble expert when it comes to car buying.
- I'm not going to attack you when you get to the lot.
- I'm going to work hard for you.
- I'm going to be completely transparent and upfront with you throughout the entire process.

Social Selling Warriors

All sales activities, including social selling, have a cumulative effect over time. Plainly stated, what you do today matters today and tomorrow. Complete enough activities over a long enough period of time and you'll grow your sales at a rate higher than you ever imagined. If you're toiling at 10 cars a month right now, you likely won't sell 20 next month if you just started social selling, but these efforts will eventually get you to 20, then 30, then 40, and so on.

Think of it like this: What you sell today – provided you gave the customer a great experience – will lead to at least two sales down the road. So, keep plugging away at those sales activities; keep plugging away at posting great content on Facebook. Eventually, you will become a true Social Selling Warrior.

Those who succeed at social selling – the true Social Selling Warriors – are often performers at heart. They don't mind speaking up in public (not the same as public speaking), they're passionate about their beliefs, and they're especially passionate about selling cars.

Performers don't mind looking silly if it's for the good of the show – and putting on a show is often what you're doing when you broadcast live video on Facebook. This means that if you're a little camera shy, you'll need to cure yourself of this, work through it, or choose a different sales activity to get you to 30+ cars a month.

A great example of an online performer – at least as of this writing – is Ling Valentine from LINGsCARS.com. Her website is noisy, filled with distractions and (most of all) authentic. Ling's willingness to put herself out in front and in comical situations is a big reason she is so successful.

Of course, this black and white screenshot does not do her website justice, so I encourage you to visit LINGsCARS.com for yourself and check it out. When you do, you'll find that while Ling is wacky and zesty (my words), she's also authentic and transparent. It's the wacky and zesty that gets her noticed, but it's the authenticity and transparency that sell her to the public.

For true Social Selling Warriors, social media marketing was not their goal. Their goal was and is to sell cars; they just found success going directly to their market to create their own Up Bus, rather than waiting for the regular Up Bus.

Social Selling Warriors are skilled old-fashioned networkers. In fact, they spend more time handing out business cards and shaking hands than they do crafting Facebook posts. For them, social selling is merely an extension of their other networking activities.

They are marketers and they are self-promoters. But, their self-promotion is not necessarily an outcropping of an overactive ego. In fact, most Social Selling Warriors I know are humble people. They truly care about others and would likely prefer that someone else was doing the promoting. However, they know that without their self-promotion, they would be selling fewer cars and helping fewer people. Self-promotion is just another job requirement to them. A job that they love.

Storytelling

One of the best ways to ensure you're only posting compelling content to your social media channels is to focus on storytelling. With storytelling, your posts convey some message other than "buy this car" or "buy from me."

Storytelling on social media is not complicated and you don't have to be a good writer. Storytelling on social media is simply talking to a friend. It's explaining what happened, what is happening, and what will happen. It's talking about the who, what, when, where and why in authentic terms.

Let me give you two actual examples of social posts where one tells a story and the other does not. See if you can guess from my description which post is the one telling the story:

Post A: There is a picture of the inside of a car with the following text above it: "BMW has been recognized by J.D. Power for having the most user-friendly technology out of any other luxury brand. See which BMW models came out on top here."

Post B: There is a picture of a snowplow on a snow-covered BMW lot with the following text above it: "Snow Day! We are open."

Both updates were posted by the same dealership and yet only one of them tells a story. If you chose Post B as the storytelling post, you are correct. It was the only post of the two to have any engagement (one comment and eight likes), as Post A reads like a magazine ad. No one is interested in Post A – apparently not even the employees at this BMW dealership, since the post received zero interaction.

Post B tells a story by showing what happened (snow), what is happening (we're plowing), and what will happen (we're gonna be open today). It doesn't matter that it tells this story with one picture and five words, since the post is authentic; it's genuine; it's exactly what you'd post for your friends to see (if you were the one running the snowplow that day). It doesn't matter that there is no beginning, middle and end like a fairy tale; Post B tells a story. Post A just regurgitates some OEM ad. (To be clear, these posts were on a Facebook business *page*, so neither should be expected to gain as much exposure as your posts to your Facebook personal *profile*.)

Post A is spam.

Post A is spam because their followers say it's spam. They didn't like it, share it or comment on it. To the average follower of this BMW dealership, Post A is spam; and no one likes spam. Your spam test should be to answer the following question with a yes before you post: "Will my friends (or the friends of someone in the picture/video) like this post?"

If it was a salesperson who added Post A on their personal Facebook profile, it might get a little interaction, but over the long term these types of posts would stop earning engagement. When you post spam, you're costing yourself views because Facebook's algorithms are going to assume your posts just aren't popular enough to share at the top of everyone's news feed. You cannot afford to have your posts ignored.

Let's look at some quick examples of what is and what is not storytelling so that you'll be able to begin with a guide of what and how to post:

Test: Is it storytelling?

- Three-year-old Honda Civic we got in trade. – NO
- Three-year-old Honda Civic we got in trade from a couple who've purchased 6 Honda Civics from our dealership over the last 15 years. – YES (and, try to get a photo with the couple, their trade-in and their new Civic)

- Ford just announced 0% financing on some models. – NO
- Ford just announced 0% financing on these specific models and I can help determine who qualifies. – YES

- I pay $100 for referrals. – NO
- I pay $100 for referrals and here's a picture of me handing a giant $100 bill to Barbara Jones who sent me a referral. – YES (and, be sure to tag Barbara Jones so her friends will see this in their news feeds, as well)

- We have doughnuts in the coffee area this morning. – NO
- We have doughnuts in the coffee area this morning and I need you to come get one now because I've been known to eat a whole box! – YES

The point of this brief exercise is to let you know that many boring posts can be fashioned into stories by just adding a little more detail (if it exists). Again, we need to answer the question, "Will my friends (or the friends of someone in the picture/video) like this post?"

Understanding this, let's look at some posts from Social Selling Warrior Joey Book of Lewis Automotive in Fayetteville, Arkansas. Joey is well-known to many in the car business because of his enthusiasm for the industry, his work ethic and his mastery of social selling. A mastery, by the way, that he would likely disagree with. Joey, like most great social sellers, is humble and is always learning.

Although he's now a sales manager, about four out of every five vehicles Joey sold in his last year as a salesman were to people he met through Facebook. This wouldn't have happened if his Facebook posts didn't see lots of engagement.

This engagement (likes, shares and comments) multiplied Joey's exposure and generated referrals because of the genuineness of the stories he told. (I included a random sample of some of Joey's social media activity; though please note that these are much more entertaining in color; so follow Joey on Facebook and run through his timeline to check out his posts firsthand.)

As you can see in the following screenshot, Joey's Facebook Live broadcast showing him, Shelby Lewis and fellow Social Selling Warrior (and now fellow sales manager) Freddie Byerly taking his new Jeep Wrangler Unlimited through an automatic car wash with no doors or top enjoyed almost 8,000 views, 150 likes, 108 comments and 74 shares. That's the hallmark of a Social Selling Warrior!

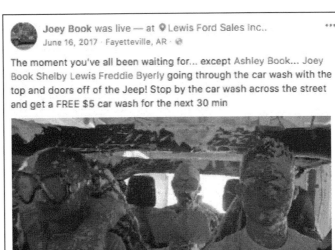

Joey Book was live — at ♥ Lewis Ford Sales Inc..

June 16, 2017 · Fayetteville, AR · 🌐

The moment you've all been waiting for... except Ashley Book... Joey Book Shelby Lewis Freddie Byerly going through the car wash with the top and doors off of the Jeep! Stop by the car wash across the street and get a FREE $5 car wash for the next 30 min

👍😮😡 150   108 Comments 74 Shares 7.7K Views

Joey Book is with Shelby Lewis and 10 others at Lewis Ford Sales Inc.

May 19, 2016 · Fayetteville, AR · 🌐

We are giving away 3 Yeti Ramblers on Monday Afternoon. To enter simply "Like" and "Share" the video. Be sure to tell your friends on Facebook where the best place is to buy their next new or preowned vehicle. #RedBull #Snickers

8.1K Views

👍 Like   💬 Comment   ↪ Share

👍❤️😮 Joanna Falkner, Freddie Byerly and 159 others

371 Shares   18 Comments

While cool stunts like driving your Jeep through a car wash are expected to garner attention, just telling a good story on Facebook (and asking for some likes and shares for a simple contest) is often enough (as the last screenshot shows with 8,100 views, 161 likes, 18 comments and a whopping 371 shares!)

To become a true Social Selling Warrior, I recommend following other Social Selling Warriors, like Joey, on Facebook. You don't have to friend them, just follow them and you'll see their public posts in your news feed. Watch their progress and note which posts generate the most engagement; then, emulate this (where you can remain genuine) in your feed.

Some Final Thoughts on Social Selling

Before diving headfirst into social selling, you'll want to consider a few final thoughts:

- Facebook first – As of this writing, the return on your time investment is too miniscule to spend much effort on any social network besides Facebook. That said, if you have linked social accounts (for example, Instagram and Facebook), feel free to manage both profiles and allow a post on one site to populate the other.
- It's your personal profile – Because of the way Facebook's current algorithms work, social selling is just not practical with a business page. Page posts (as of this writing) receive little to no interaction because no one sees them. Facebook buries these (they say) to improve the user experience. Of course, Facebook would gladly let you pay to boost your page's posts into anyone's news feed. This means you'll need to use your personal profile if you want to become a Social Selling Warrior. Doing this brings up a few things to consider:
  - o No more drunk posts. When your personal profile is doubling as your business page, you're basically always at the dealership. So, act like it on Facebook. If you go out for a few beers after work, refrain from posting anything until you're sober. It doesn't take much to outrage the online public today.
  - o Avoid controversy. There are a few issues where we can all agree. For example, I think we can all agree that childhood cancer sucks. Feel free to get involved with these

types of issues but try to avoid anything controversial. Even showing your support for a controversial new road on your Facebook page stands the chance of alienating a potential future customer. Besides, no one is going to wonder "Why didn't Steve speak up on his Facebook page about that new road?"

o   Be sensitive. Gone are the days when you can publicly dress like a Native American and mimic their ceremonies. This extends to all cultures, colors, races, creeds and religions. Understand this and find something else to dress as this year for Halloween.

o   Make everything public. Since you're often going to friend your customers, you'll want to be sure that everything you post is intended to be posted for all to see. When you limit your posts by setting them to anything but the "Public" setting, you're not only keeping those who follow you and friends of friends from seeing what you post, you're also eliminating the chance for a post to go viral.

o   There is a limit. As of this writing, Facebook has a 5,000-friend limit on personal profiles. While not a big deal when you're just starting out, for Social Selling Warriors this can cause a problem. You'll want to encourage other salespeople, vendors and anyone outside your market to follow you so that you can friend as many locals as possible.

o   No contests. Despite what Joey Book was able to accomplish in his 2016 posts, when you use a personal profile, you're not allowed to run contests on Facebook like you can with a business page. If you find the need to run contests, start a business page, then market the contest via your personal posts.

•   Calls-to-action. Be sure to include calls-to-action in your posts, and especially on your Facebook Live events. This means you'll want to tell your audience what you want them to do. (Some people need that before they'll engage.) So, ask them to share, like, comment, call you, download your app, and send you referrals. Those are all good calls-to-action to include. Of course, don't overdo it, you'll want to limit these to about one or two calls-to-action per post.

•   Buy a good selfie stick. When posting pics with new buyers or doing a Facebook Live event, you can either have someone else hold your smartphone and film you, or you can use a selfie stick. Since you don't want to have to always depend on others, invest a few dollars in a good selfie stick. If you're serious about using live videos to drive your social selling, spend a few more bucks and buy a selfie stick that doubles as a video stabilizer (this is sometimes called a gimbal).

- Play to your audience. So, you have the Batmobile for sale at your dealership; but, it's an $85,000 Demon and you know that 99.9% of your Facebook audience can't afford something so expensive. This doesn't mean they don't want to see it, they do. However, you'll want to include some content that will encourage them to buy what they can afford from you, so pan over to the used Challenger that's $15,000 during your Facebook Live event about the Demon, and tell them why the $15,000 version is also cool.

- Buy a drone? This one is up to you (and depends on the current laws), but drone footage of a super sale or offsite event can generate a lot of engagement. Additionally, offering to shoot drone footage for the clubs and organizations you joined in your old-fashioned networking will help you become more involved (which helps you generate more business from these activities).

- Celebrity status. A very strange thing will happen after you've done a few Facebook Live events that generate engagement: you'll become a local celebrity! Be prepared. People will walk up to you in restaurants and ask, "Are you Joey? I just love your videos." This is when you know you've reached the status of Social Selling Warrior. Be genuine and authentic (just as you are online) when asked these questions; and be sure to ask for their business (I mean, they already like you, right?).

- It's about referrals. Never forget your goals when you're engaged in social selling; it's about generating sales, and sales from social will come mainly from referrals. So, ask for referrals; and if your state allows you to pay bird dog fees, then advertise and celebrate this in your posts, where appropriate. Without paying for referrals, your social audience will be somewhat smaller, because people won't be working for you. Your network will share more of your information if there are dollars involved.

- It's your brand. Be friendly, be approachable, be funny, be self-deprecating and be honest. Your social profile (who you are online) is your personal brand and only you get to decide what that is.

10

THE INBOUND PHONE CALL

Chapter Note: *Just a quick reminder on the direction and verbiage for calls anywhere in this book: the same basic structure and goals apply whether these conversations are via phone, text, chat, email or Messenger. All two-way communications are treated the same and have the same overriding goal: an appointment that shows.*

The phone is ringing. It's a sales prospect. They're not calling to chat. They found your vehicle on the internet and (by calling you) they've already proven value and relevancy. Now, they just need someone to sell it to them!

By the way, I hate phone training; I really do. I hate it because the kind of phone training that dealerships pay thousands for every year is a waste of time and money. Dealers would be better off spending that money on bus bench billboards than on phone training that doesn't get their team any closer to answering the phone correctly. Whether the lessons come via interactive online phone training videos or phone mystery shops or some outdated DVDs, most dealers are just throwing their money away.

While it's true that I am in the business of training and consulting with dealerships, groups and even OEMs on everything from digital marketing to (you guessed it) how to dominate on the phones, I am indeed advocating that most dealerships eliminate the expense of phone training.

I advocate this because, very simply, it's not working. The average dealership's team is getting no better on the phones. They're not doing a better job of overcoming objections on the phone. Dealership turnover has not improved despite spending all this money to train the sales teams. The average dealer's sales from phone activities (Phone Ups and outbound calls) have not increased. Continuing to do the same thing over and over, while expecting a different result, is the definition of insanity.

Tell me if this true story sounds familiar:

Five years ago, the owner of a small group was complaining to me that his sales teams "stunk" on the phones. So, he hired an outsourced training company to provide online phone training, monthly phone mystery shops, and one-on-one reviews for his salespeople.

For the next five years, he used this outside company to train his salespeople on how to sell more cars by winning on the phones; paying more than $100,000 in the process.

Today? He complains that his teams "stink" on the phones. Rinse. Lather. Repeat.

After decades of expensive phone training, salespeople today only ask for an appointment on about one-third of the Phone Ups they take. In fact, about 90% of Phone Ups still end without a scheduled appointment.

One of the reasons phone training doesn't stick is that you're taught unnatural word tracks and expected to regurgitate them as if they're your own words. But… they're not your own words, are they? In fact, sometimes the words don't even make sense. The problem is you're taught what to say and how to say it, when you should be taught why.

The Biggest Why

The processes and word tracks I teach in real life and in this book spring from one premise: today's prospect is a ready buyer just looking for someone to help them buy. When you understand and internalize this, the word tracks will come more naturally, and you'll more firmly embrace Assumptive Selling.

The caller is a ready buyer looking for help; don't blow it using old-school word tracks. Today's Phone Up is different than the one just a few years ago. Every phone call is an order, not an inquiry. Everyone is a buyer because in today's world, they complete their research before the call. They're just looking for someone to sell them; but, they don't want to be sold.

Phone Ups are Phone Ups primarily because of two factors: (1) they fear sales pressure; and (2) they don't want to waste their time driving from dealership to dealership. Let's remember these two as we explore the best ways to pull the prospect through the phone and into your dealership.

Your Only Goal

To be clear right from the start: When you have a prospect on the phone you have just one goal, and that is an appointment that shows. Period. End of story. Your goal is not to sell them a car (that will come later). Additionally, your goal is not to sell the dealership or yourself (your authenticity will do that for you).

If you're using an old-school Phone Up Card you're going to lose more often than you win with today's Ups because these tools (while they worked great a decade ago) are a grind to the Phone Ups you get today. Today's buyers don't like the old-school processes, and they want to be treated as a buyer. Assumptive Selling does this, while the old-school Phone Up Cards simply do not. There are multiple reasons why those tactics fail with today's Phone Ups; let me show you why.

Old-school Phone Up Cards generally want you to follow steps like these when you're speaking with a prospect on the phone:

1. Introduce Yourself
2. Acknowledge the Customer
3. Get Customer Information
4. Build Rapport
5. Interview the Customer
6. Uncover Likes & Dislikes
7. Offer Alternatives
8. Ask About Current Vehicle
9. Check Availability
10. Set the Appointment

Let's start with how redundant/irrelevant the first two steps are. While we're certainly going to introduce ourselves when we answer the phone ("Hi, thank you for calling ABC Motors; this is Steve Stauning, how can I help you today?"), there is no need to go into a deeper introduction and no need to formally put this as an action item on the Phone Up Card.

As far as the second step, simply answering the phone and asking, "How can I help you today?" is all the acknowledgement today's customer wants or needs. They want someone to help them buy the car they just found, and they're going to tell you this with their response:

Phone Up: "I'm looking at this 2017 Ford Explorer you've got on your website…"

Guess what? They found value and relevancy in that Explorer; now, they just want you to help them buy it with no hassles. Unfortunately, virtually everything that follows on this Phone Up Card is a hassle.

Before you've provided the prospect anything of value to them, the old-school method wants you to get their information in the third step. This is often seen as an intrusion to today's buyers. They don't want to tell you who they are just yet; they first want to see if you're authentic. That is, can they trust you? Can they trust your dealership? Are you going to try to take advantage of them? Are you going to answer their damn question?

Asking them for their information too early in the call (before it's even necessary in their mind) is a great way to tell them you're not authentic.

In the fourth step of this old-school Phone Up Card, you're expected to build rapport with the caller. What does this even mean? You know nothing about them and now you're going to ask them an insincere question about the weather, last night's game or worse: you're going to start selling yourself and the dealership! Ugh.

If you haven't already done so, the fifth, sixth and seventh steps will help you prove to them that you're wholly inauthentic; all because this Phone Up Card wants you ask them silly questions like:

- Have you bought from ABC Motors before?
- What is it you like about the Explorer; is it body style or pricing?
- What equipment were you hoping for?
- Do you have to buy it today?
- Is it just Explorers you're looking at, or would you consider any large SUV?

This is a vehicle they found to have value and relevancy; and now you're making them question why in the world they called you in the first place! (By the way, I love the question, "Do you have to buy it today?" when you have a Lot Up, as this removes sales pressure. When you ask this of a Phone Up, you're removing all urgency from the purchase.)

By the eighth step this is starting to feel like an interrogation. Furthermore, questioning them about their current vehicle at this stage is unnecessary and will sometimes get them to reconsider replacing this vehicle. Questions like the following make them second guess the need to buy something different:

- What do you like about your current vehicle?
- Have you had your vehicle professionally appraised?
- Do you have a loan on that vehicle? If so, what is the payoff amount?

Checking the availability (the ninth step) can only lose you appointments. You should review your inventory every morning and there should be no need to stop the call to check your current stock. Plus, since most sales calls you get today are asking about availability, if you wait until after you've completed your interrogation to answer this question, you've demonstrated that you're inauthentic.

It isn't until we get to the tenth step in this Phone Up process that we ask for the appointment! Today, this is the ONLY GOAL we have when we have a prospect on the phone – everything else is inauthentic fluff. They called to buy a vehicle they believed was a good value and was relevant to their needs; and because we failed to provide authenticity, we appear to lack transparency. Moreover, we've removed any urgency or excitement they had for this purchase. This is why the dealers I've worked with were only closing about 8-10% of their Phone Ups before they enacted an Assumptive Selling process. Their old-school Phone Up Card was helping buyers eliminate them.

To be clear, I understand that explaining why the old-school Phone Up Cards don't work today is akin to negative coaching (something I try to avoid in my training); however, it's important to dissect what you've probably been taught in the past before we look at the best way to handle today's buyers on the phone.

When you employ Assumptive Selling with your Phone Ups, your expectations should be that every call is a buyer trying to place an order; that every buyer wants to buy your vehicle; and that every buyer wants to buy today. When you use Assumptive Selling on the phone, you should reasonably expect to sell 40% of your Phone Ups within 24 hours. (Yes, that's probably four to five times more Phone Ups than you're selling today.)

Assumptive Selling is Simple

Today's buyer wants candid, honest and transparent dialog with you. They're tired of the old-school runaround, and they'll gladly eliminate your dealership when they feel you have an integrity problem on the phone.

The key, as you'll notice throughout this chapter, is that handling a Phone Up is not science or selling or anything complicated. It's just answering questions and setting appointments (often in the same breath). It's taking charge, it's being direct, and it's providing guidance.

Whether you become an assumptive seller or you prefer to continue to stick to old-school word tracks, one of the first rules of sales is to stay in agreement with the prospect (especially when you disagree). When you stay in agreement with a Phone Up, your guidance will be more readily accepted and appreciated. Let's look at a quick example where the customer is 100% wrong, but we stay in agreement to set the appointment:

Phone Up: "The other Chevy dealer told me there's a $9,000 factory rebate on the Impala. Will you guys honor that rebate, as well?"

Salesperson: "You can rest assured that Chevrolet makes all rebates available to all dealers in this market; and my managers are the best at finding every Chevy dollar they can for our clients. So, let's do this, let's test drive the Impala and then get you a firm written offer with every rebate you qualify for included. Does this make sense?"

It does you no good to tell this prospect he's wrong or that the other dealer lied to him. Most customers take this as an insult and they'll drive to the other dealership to prove you wrong. Plus, because you don't know if the customer made up the wrong information or if the other dealer lied to them, trying to correct the customer might feel like an accusation to them. It's always best to stay in agreement and move them through your process.

You may notice that proper Assumptive Selling often requires you ask for the appointment each time you answer a question. However, there are some questions that are clearly objections, where asking for their agreement before you move to asking for the appointment is more important. Therefore, I ended the previous response with, "Does this make sense?" Once the prospect responds in the affirmative, I'll reply with:

Salesperson: "Great! We've got two test drives open on that Impala this afternoon, we've got a 12:15 and a 12:45; which one of these works best for you?"

The Phone Up Fears You

No offense – and primarily due to the sins of the past – car salespeople don't rank very highly on the list of the most honest and ethical professions (as perceived by the public). In fact, each year that Gallup releases their survey asking Americans, "Please tell me how you would rate the honesty and ethical standards of people in these different fields – very high, high, average, low, or very low?" car salespeople rank near the bottom.[9]

In the most recent such Gallup survey released before this book was published, car salespeople were stuck right between Members of Congress and lobbyists. Yikes; this should tell you exactly what the prospect on the other end of the phone is thinking when they call your dealership.

By the way, this isn't your fault; but, it is your problem. Today's buyer fears you. They believe you're going to pressure them into buying and they expect a hassle when they start the car shopping process. Your job is to make them not fear you. Your job is to make them trust you. Old-school phone scripts were often meant to confuse the prospect; to get them to forget their original objection. These were also often very successful.

Not any longer. Today's Phone Up knows virtually everything they need to know about the vehicle they want; they just don't know how the buying process works. They want to buy a car, but they don't want it to be a five-hour grind like the last time. When you employ old-school phone tactics, you reveal to the prospect that you're untrustworthy. Their belief is that someone who cannot answer a simple question cannot be trusted.

What They're Really Saying

Once you understand what the Phone Up is really saying you'll more easily answer their questions with an Assumptive Selling response – one that assumes they want to buy from you today (because, of course, they do).

The most common type of inbound sales call you'll encounter today is about availability. In fact, the average dealer sees more availability calls than all other inbound sales calls combined. In these instances, the Phone Up will ask something like, "Is it in stock?"

Why do you think they're asking this? Are they just taking a poll? Are they calling every dealer in town about their inventory ensuring their online listings are accurate? No! They found the car they want and they're checking to see if it's still on your lot so that they can buy it. You hear:

> Phone Up: "I see you have a yellow 2017 Camaro on your website, is it still in stock?"

But, what they're really saying is:

> Phone Up: "I see you have a yellow 2017 Camaro on your website, is it still in stock *because I've been searching online forever, and this is the exact car I want to buy, so I'm hoping you'll sell it to me without taking advantage of me, so I hope it's still in stock, is it?*"

The reason they don't tell you any of the stuff in italics is because they don't trust you; they're afraid that you'll use their enthusiasm for this Camaro against them somehow. Nevertheless, once you understand what they're really saying, you can respond in a way that helps them buy "the exact car" they want without the inauthentic word tracks of the past. Here's your response:

> Salesperson: "I saw that Camaro this morning, but at the price we have it listed for it will likely not make it to the weekend. Now, we do have two test drives open on that Camaro this morning. We've got a 10:45 and an 11:15. Which one works better for you?"

To be clear, there is never a reason to lie to a prospect and no place for it in Assumptive Selling. When asked if a vehicle is in stock, you can honestly respond that you "saw that vehicle this morning" if you'll spend a few minutes at the start of your day reviewing your dealership's online inventory. (We'll deal with the proper processes and word tracks if it turns out that Camaro was sold when we explore The Perfect Appointment.)

Your response, by the way, created a sense of urgency in the prospect's mind with two lines:

- "... at the price we have it listed for it will likely not make it to the weekend."
- "... we do have two test drives open on that Camaro this morning."

The first line gets the prospect away from the belief that car buying is only a weekend endeavor. If you received that call on a Monday and asked, "When would you like to come in?" the average prospect would respond with "this weekend" or "Saturday."

Today is Monday; a lot can happen between Monday and Saturday. If you think they'll still have new car fever in five days, you're taking a huge gamble. Moreover, if you think they won't start shopping somewhere else before Saturday, you're delusional. Get them off the weekend and onto today!

The second line indicates there may be others interested in the Camaro (I mean, people must be lining up to test drive it, right?). This creates additional urgency that will encourage most people to rearrange their schedules to come in as soon as possible.

Okay, let's look at another example of what they're really saying. You hear:

Phone Up: "Does it have third-row seats?"

But, what they're really saying is:

Phone Up: "Does it have third-row seats *because I really want to buy it & I thought if I asked you a question where I already know the answer, I can create a smokescreen while also testing to see how authentic you are, so does it?*"

Again, they can't tell you any of the stuff in italics because they don't trust you. Provided you know the correct answer to their question, here's your response:

Salesperson: "Yes, that vehicle does have third row seats, and at the price we have it listed for it likely won't make it through to the weekend. Now, we do have two test drives open on that vehicle this afternoon, we have a 3:15 and a 3:45. Which one works better for you?"

Before we continue with what they're really saying, we should look at how old-school phone trainers would want you to handle the question, "Does it have third-row seats?" Here are a few inauthentic responses I've been taught over the years:

- "Besides third-row seats, is there any other feature that's a must have on your next vehicle?"
- "How many people do you expect to be transporting with this vehicle?"
- "Are third-row seats important to you?"

If you want to prove to a Phone Up that you're not ready to help them, feel free to fall back on an old-school word track instead of answering their question. Today's buyer needs authenticity, and your response won't come across as authentic unless they mirror what you might say to a friend; and, you'd never ask a friend, "Are third-row seats important to you?"

Alright, here's our final example of what they're really saying. You hear:

Phone Up: "Is that you're best price?"

But, what they're really saying is:

Phone Up: "Is that your best price *because it's actually already a great price & I just want to be sure you're not trying to trick me somehow; so, if that is your best price, I'll drop everything & come down right now to buy it, so is it?*"

Understanding what they're really saying allows you manage this as a question instead of an objection. When your inventory is priced-to-market, you get price questions that are truly just questions. The prospect found value and they want to be sure that there are no tricks or traps with that price. Treating this like the question that it is allows you to fashion a response that defends the online price, builds trust and drives appointments:

Salesperson: "If you've been shopping online, then you know we price all of our vehicles competitively right from the beginning. We would never dream of insulting our customers by showing you our second-best price and then making you jump through a bunch of hoops to find some hidden best price. That pre-owned Camry is priced to sell at $15,399 and it will likely not be on our lot much longer at that price. Now, I do have two test drives open on that Camry this morning, I have a 10:15 and a 10:45, which one of those works better for you?"

Let's compare this response to an old-school word track I once taught in response to the question/objection "Is that your best price?" (before vehicles were priced online at or near their selling price):

Old-School Salesperson: "No, that's not our best price. We reserve our best price for customers who've selected and test-driven a vehicle. It does neither of us any good to work up a price if it's not the perfect fit for you. Now, your presence in our dealership is your leverage, and if you'll schedule and keep an appointment with me, I guarantee that once you've selected and test-driven a vehicle, I will get you the very best price on that vehicle. Now, I have two test drives open on that Camry this morning, I have a 10:15 and a 10:45, which one of those works better for you?"

Which of these two word tracks would give the prospect confidence in you and your dealership? Conversely, which one would make you sound like you have something to hide or that you're dishonest?

Today's Phone Up fears you – don't let your words give them a reason to.

Market-Based Pricing Triple Discount

When you fail to defend your online price with the Assumptive Selling word track, you invite what I call the *Market-Based Pricing Triple Discount*. Let me explain how this works. Your used car manager priced a trade-in at $16,300 online because that's what his pricing software said was a good price in your market.

That's discount number one. If there was no internet, your manager would've marked up this trade to something like $21,000; expecting to come down a little from there to make the deal. Today, he or she must price used vehicles close to or at their actual selling price to get anyone interested in it.

A prospect calls and asks, "Is that your best price?" If you know that your manager will usually take $200-300 off the online price to make a deal with a difficult customer, your inclination is to explain this to the prospect in some attempt to endear yourself to them. You might respond with a very weak, "Well, I'm not allowed to tell you this, but my manager often takes $200 to $300 off most vehicles in order to make the deal. And, your presence in our dealership is your leverage; so, if you'll come by and ask for me, I'll fight to get you that discount."

That's discount number two. Congratulations, your lame attempt to build rapport just cost your dealership a minimum $300. That's, of course, assuming the prospect will show. You might find this hard to believe, but when you waver on price like I just did, you see fewer shows and fewer sales from Phone Ups than when you defend the price.

Remember: They're not calling you until after they've found value and relevancy. When you waffle on the price like that, you prove you're inauthentic. You prove your dealership is an old-fashioned grinder. You prove you cannot be trusted.

They would never have called if you were overpriced. They felt your price was fair and only asked the question about best price because that's what we've trained buyers to do for 100 years. We've trained them that the price is never the price. Only today, it is.

Plus, for the few prospects who do show up to see this vehicle (because you caved a little on the selling price over the phone), you've set the expectation that you're willing to negotiate. So, if the online price was $16,300, you knocked it down to $16,000 when you wavered. Where do you think the prospect expects to be if they buy?

$16,300? Nope.

$16,000? Nope.

When they walk into your dealership, the $16,000 you basically told them on the phone is like the MSRP of a new car. It's a suggested price; it's the idiot price; a price only an idiot would pay. The average customer now fully expects to pay about $15,000 (or less) for the vehicle because you failed to defend the already good online price.

But, since your manager really doesn't have that kind of room on this vehicle, they will probably settle near $15,800. That is, if they can even reach a deal. (Had you just defended the price, there would be no back-and-forth on pricing at the dealership. They'd take first pencil, wouldn't they?)

So, instead of selling the vehicle for $16,300 (which is exactly what happens when you defend the price); you sold it for $15,800 (the third discount) after you unnecessarily gave up $500 in gross! If you're a traditional commissioned salesperson earning 25% of the gross, you gave the buyer $125 out of your pocket and turned this deal into a mini.

When your vehicles are priced-to-market, there's never a need to even hint at an additional discount. A good price is a good price; and when you defend the online price over the phone, the resulting appointment is a slam-dunk sale because you've already agreed on price, haven't you?

But, We're Not Priced-to-Market!

Some shortsighted dealerships still refuse to price most of their used units to market; and many dealerships (either on their own or because of OEM marketing restrictions) don't price their new vehicles at or near their expected selling price. Therefore, some readers will want to know how to handle the "Is that your best price?" or "What's your best price?" questions in these instances. Let's tackle both of these situations if your dealership will not allow you to give a competitive price over the phone or via email:

Used Car Priced Above It's Selling Price

Phone Up: "What is your best price?"

Salesperson: "We price all of our pre-owned vehicles competitively, but your presence in our dealership is your leverage. After you've test-driven the Corolla and are certain it's the vehicle you want to own, my manager will be happy to give you a great price. We've never lost a deal over a few dollars and we're not going to start now. Now, we have two test drives open on that Corolla this afternoon, we have a 12:15 and a 12:45; which one of these works best for you?"

Alternatively, if they ask, "Is that your best price?" you can go with an answer that sounds even more like the old-school word track we learned earlier:

Salesperson: "No, that's not our best price. We reserve our best price for customers who've selected and test-driven a vehicle. Now, your presence in our dealership is your best leverage, and if you'll schedule and keep an appointment with me, I guarantee that once you've test-driven the Corolla, I will get you our very best price in writing. Now, we have two test drives open on that Corolla this afternoon, we have a 12:15 and a 12:45; which one of these works best for you?"

New Car Priced at MSRP (or above the expected selling price)

Phone Up: "What is your best price?"

Salesperson: "ABC Motors has been selling cars in the Dallas area since 1968, and we would not have lasted over 50 years if we were not always competitive on price. We will never lose any deal over price. This means if we cannot meet or beat any of our competitors' valid offers on an in-stock unit, we'll fill your tank with gas and give you a $100 gift card to the Olive Garden. Once you've selected and test-driven a vehicle, we'll gladly provide you with a firm written offer. So, if you're ready to test drive the Accord, we've got two test drives open on that Accord this morning, we have a 10:15 and a 10:45; which one of those works better for you?"

These three responses, of course, are old-school and not very transparent; and they'll result in far fewer sales than if your vehicles were priced-to-market and you employed an Assumptive Selling approach. However, unless or until your dealership begins to trust the process and allows you to quote the market price for your vehicles, you'll have to resort to old-school word tracks if you want to set any appointments that show.

Phone Training 101

I would be remiss if I didn't touch on the very basics of phone skills for salespeople somewhere in this book, so let's tackle these here. (We'll explore some additional requirements for phone handling in the "Making Outbound Calls" chapter.)

There are six basic elements to a good phone call that have nothing to do with salesmanship; but, using these on every call can make a good salesperson great and a great salesperson a true superstar on the phones.

1. Smile. Believe it or not, customers can hear the difference in your voice when you smile. If you're smiling during the call, you'll be friendlier, and you'll project more energy and enthusiasm for helping them find the right vehicle – and they'll sense this! So, how can you be sure you're always smiling? Position a small mirror near you to look at while you speak with prospects on the phone.

2.   Stand, if possible. If not, sit upright with exaggeratedly-good posture. This opens your airways and lungs; and like smiling, gives you more energy and enthusiasm when speaking on the phone.

3.   Always answer the phone quickly. The customer's enthusiasm for buying from you decreases a little each and every second the phone remains unanswered. When you answer quickly (and with some confidence that we'll discuss later), the customer is reassured that they made the right move in calling you for help in buying their next vehicle.

4.   Limit hold times. While I would like to advise you to never put someone on hold, I understand that this is sometimes a necessity. Therefore, when you must put someone on hold, make sure you limit the amount of time they need to wait before someone reengages them. Thirty seconds on hold can feel like five minutes to a customer; while five minutes can feel like an hour. Limit your hold times if you want the prospect to still be on the phone when you pick up.

5.   Take your time. Once you're speaking with the Phone Up, relax and take your time. There's no rush; so, speak clearly (enunciate) and speak deliberately. It's more important that the prospect hear and understand what you're saying than to try reciting this entire chapter to them in one breath.

6.   Be positive. This is an exciting time in your prospect's life; so, be excited for them and remain positive. Slugs believe everyone is a tire-kicker until they prove themselves worthy of buying. That's negative thinking; and your caller can feel this over the phone! Being positive also includes the use of positive words over negative words that we touched on in an earlier chapter. Eliminate negative words like "can't" and find positive ways that express the same thing.

Using a Call Guide

Now that we've covered the basics, let's circle back to the old-school Phone Up Card we discussed in the beginning of this chapter. If you recall, the call guide I described had appointment setting as the tenth step. Thinking about all you've learned so far about today's prospects, I'm hopeful the thought of putting appointments so far down the list of priorities now sounds ludicrous to you – it does to me.

Although you may feel like you have a grasp on how to get a Phone Up to show for an appointment, I never recommend "winging it" when it comes to handling Phone Ups. As we'll learn later in this book, Phone

Ups are different than an outbound call prospect primarily because we can and should fully prepare for the outbound call. We cannot fully prepare for a Phone Up because we simply don't know what that next caller is going to reply when we say, "Thank you for calling ABC Motors, this is Steve. How may I help you today?"

Using a call guide or Phone Up Card is critical to keeping the call on track and keeping you focused on your goal of an appointment that shows. Therefore, whether you use the Assumptive Selling Phone Up Card at the end of this chapter or create your own call guide is up to you; as long as you know using one is not an option for 30+ sellers.

When creating your own call guide, be sure to understand your goals when handling a Phone Up. For example, do you care how much your prospect owes on their current vehicle? While this information would be great to know, the fact is that if you ask too many inauthentic questions over the phone, you'll lose today's prospect.

Today's buyers see those questions as an interrogation, so avoid any questions that don't bring you closer to an appointment that shows – they're unnecessary. Certainly, if a prospect offers information, you should jot it down, but your call guide should do just that: guide the call; guide the call to your goal of an appointment that shows.

The essential elements of any good call guide (in no particular order) include:

- Caller's information (name, email, phone)
- Vehicle(s) of interest
- Appointment date and time
- Call date and time
- Section for call notes

Optional elements of a good call guide include:

- Trade-in information
- Advertising source
- Appointment recap verbiage

You might be thinking that I've listed far too few elements to make an effective call guide. Well, you'd be wrong. The only goal when you have a prospect on the phone is an appointment that shows; and unnecessary greetings and the exchange of irrelevant information do not get you closer to that goal. Moreover, because Assumptive Selling tells us everyone is a buyer and they want to buy from you today, your call guide should reflect this. (The old-school Phone Up Card assumes everyone is a suspect who needs to be interrogated until they prove they're a buyer. This thinking worked more than a decade ago; not so much today.)

For your call guide to be effective, you should lay out the elements in a logical order. For example, putting the customer's name, email and phone across the top doesn't make sense because you're going to get these later in the call, not as soon as you answer. As you'll see in my example at the end of the chapter, I place the date, time and ad source across the top. If I'm manning the phones, I'll have today's date written at the top of the first Phone Up Card in my stack.

I can complete the time after the call or while the customer responds to my greeting. I include the ad source at the top in case the caller identifies where they saw your vehicle; if they do, they'll generally do so early in the call. For example:

Phone Up: "I saw your 2016 Camry on UsedCars.com and I wanted to know if that's your best price."

I recommend leaving out the sticky sweet introductions and phony attempts at rapport building. These are unnecessary. Besides, you should have a standard greeting that you use with every Phone Up; so, there's no need to write this down on a call guide.

I like to include the vehicle of interest on the second line of the Phone Up Card because today's caller generally gives you this information right away (as in the example above). I include the stock number in this line, though I don't expect the caller to provide it; I'll complete that blank either during or immediately after the call.

My Phone Up Card, by the way, is designed to handle the most common type of Phone Up you'll receive today; generally, a VIN-specific inquiry:

Phone Up: "... is it in-stock?"
Phone Up: "... what's your best price?"
Phone Up: "... does it have third-row seats?"

When you have the rare inquiries that don't include a specific vehicle or Year/Make/Model, you'll want to focus your responses to those questions in a way that drives an appointment that shows. However, trying to include every possible customer phone inquiry on your call guide will cause most salespeople to lose focus and get confused during the call. I recommend limiting your Phone Up Card to only the most common types of inbound calls; and our research shows that vehicle-specific inquiries account for about 90% of the sales calls your dealership will receive.

Anything beyond the basics on a Phone Up Card is just clutter; so, avoid trying to fit everything on the card or guide you use.

Once the vehicle of interest has been identified, you will want to create a sense of urgency (using one of the word tracks we introduced in this chapter) and set the appointment. I don't recommend including all of the word tracks on your Phone Up Card, however, because this will encourage most salespeople to read these to the prospect. You should internalize this verbiage and make it your own; otherwise, you may sound robotic to the prospect.

Once the appointment is set, we can gather the customer's information. (Hint: They'll freely give this to you once they've set the appointment.)

Finally, you'll want to recap the appointment to gain a commitment from the prospect to show. (We'll review the reason for and the word tracks to use for "The Recap" in a later chapter.)

The Assumptive Selling Phone Up Card

On the following page, you'll find the current Phone Up Card I recommend. Of course, it's a little hard to see everything that's included, so I rewrote what's included on this card below.

However, I strongly recommend you use this as a guide only and create a Phone Up Card that you'll use and that's most effective for you (FYI: I include "The Recap" and the "Keep Your Promises" sections on my Phone Up Card so that these critical elements are never skipped):

Today's Date: __/__/___ Time of Call: _____ Ad Source: _____

STOCK #: _____ YEAR: ____ MAKE: _____
MODEL: _____

USED/NEW (Specific Vehicle): Create Urgency and Set Appointment:

STEVE STAUNING'S
ASSUMPTIVE SELLING PHONE UP CARD

Today's Date: ____/____/_____ Time of Call: _____ Ad Source: _____

STOCK #: _____ YEAR: _____ MAKE: _____ MODEL: _____

USED/NEW (Specific Vehicle): Create Urgency and Set Appointment:

"That's a great choice! In fact, we've received a lot of calls about that _____. At that price, it's probably not going make it through to the weekend. Now, I do have two test drives open on that _____ this morning / afternoon / evening. I have one at _____ and one at _____. Which one of those works better for you?"

NEW (Model or Trim Only): Create Urgency and Set Appointment:

"That's a great choice. The incentives on the _____ expire soon and we're not sure what (OEM) is going to do, as the inventories are coming down fast. Now, I have two test drives open on _____s this morning / afternoon / evening. I have one at _____:15 and one at _____:45. Which one of these works better for you?"

AFTER THE APPOINTMENT IS SET: Get their information

"Great. I look forward to seeing you at _____. I am _____, if I could get your name and number I would be happy to lock down that test drive for you."

Name: _____ Number: _____

"Excellent, thank you. If I could get your email address, I will send you the details of our appointment and some information about the _____."

Email Address: _____

RECAP:

"Outstanding. Just to recap: we're going to see you _____ at _____ to test drive the _____. Now, (Customer Name), we're going to get that _____ cleaned, gassed and parked out front and ready to go, so that when you arrive for your _____ appointment, we will get you in and out and on your test drive within 5 minutes. Now... if anything happens to us or your _____ we're going to call you well in advance so that you don't waste a trip down here. All I would ask from you is that you show me the same courtesy.

So, can I count on you for _____?"

KEEP YOUR PROMISES!

If for some reason their specified vehicle is no longer available for sale, you should find two alternates and call them ASAP with the following:

"_____ I have some great news and some bad news. Unfortunately, the _____ was sold as of this morning, though I do have two alternates that are actually better values. I have a _____ and a _____ and I'll have both of these cleaned, gassed and parked out front for your _____ test drive. So, can I still count on seeing you at _____?"

"That's a great choice! In fact, we've received a lot of calls about that _____. At that price, it's probably not going make it through to the weekend. Now, I do have two test drives open on that _____ this morning / afternoon / evening. I have one at _____ and one at _____. Which one of those works better for you?"

NEW (Model or Trim Only): Create Urgency and Set Appointment:

"That's a great choice. The incentives on the _____ expire soon and we're not sure what (OEM) is going to do, as the inventories are coming down fast. Now, I have two test drives open on _____s this morning / afternoon / evening. I have one at _____:15 and one at _____:45. Which one of these works better for you?"

AFTER THE APPOINTMENT IS SET: Get their information
"Great. I look forward to seeing you at _____. I am _____, if I could get your name and number I would be happy to lock down that test drive for you."
Name: _____ Number: _____
"Excellent, thank you. If I could get your email address, I will send you the details of our appointment and some information about the _____."
Email Address: _____

RECAP:
"Outstanding. Just to recap: we're going to see you _____ at _____ to test drive the _____.
Now, (Customer Name), we're going to get that _____ cleaned, gassed and parked out front and ready to go, so that when you arrive for your _____ appointment, we will get you in and out and on your test drive within 5 minutes. Now… if anything happens to us or your _____ we're going to call you well in advance so that you don't waste a trip down here. All I would ask from you is that you show me the same courtesy.
So, can I count on you for _____?"

KEEP YOUR PROMISES!
If for some reason their specified vehicle is no longer available for sale, you should find two alternates and call them ASAP with the following:
"I have some great news and some bad news. Unfortunately, the _____ was sold as of this morning, though I do have two alternates that are actually better values. I have a _____ and a _____ and I'll have both of these cleaned, gassed and parked out front for your _____ test drive. So, can I still count on seeing you at _____?"

11

OVERCOMING OBJECTIONS ON THE PHONE

Beyond the in-stock, equipment-check and pricing questions we've already tackled, there are certainly other questions and objections you're going to get over the phone that require an Assumptive Selling response in order to schedule an appointment that shows. (Which, I'm hopeful you agree, is our only goal when we have a prospect on the phone.)

For all objections you receive over the phone, you're going to want to frame the next steps in the process in a way that overcomes the objection. This keeps the prospect moving through your process instead of getting you caught up in too much back-and-forth.

Your Competitor is Cheaper

It's important when dealing with competitive price objections on the phone to realize that you're often being played. The prospect could be lying (or is being lied to); they could've been quoted a price on a vehicle the competition doesn't have in stock; or they could be comparing apples and oranges. Keep this in mind, remember your goal, and remember that you cannot sell an empty seat.

Phone Up: "Bob's Subaru quoted me $500 below your price. Can you beat their price?"

Salesperson: "Well, Mr. Jones, I can assure you that here at ABC Motors, we are never going to be beat on price. In fact, if we cannot meet or beat any valid written offer on an in-stock unit, we'll fill your tank with gas and give you a $100 gift card to the Olive Garden. Now, I have two test drives open on that vehicle this morning: I have a 10:15 and a 10:45. Which one of these works better for you?"

The key here is that I didn't get stuck in a no-win back-and-forth. I didn't give him a lower price because, if I did, he'd thank me and hang up the phone. I would've just given him ammunition to go back to Bob's Subaru. You cannot sell an empty seat.

He'd call Bob's Subaru and say, "Hey, ABC Motors just said they can do $31,000 even." At some point you've got to stop this back-and-forth madness and get the customer in for an appointment that shows. Unless you have a good online buying tool where you can send him to complete the deal, the best way to get him to show for an appointment is to overcome the objection by moving him away from the negotiation and assuring him with word tracks like these:

- "We're not going to be beat on price"
- "We've been in business for 45 years"
- "We'll meet or beat any valid competitive offer"

We'll learn later that this technique is called "bury the dead," and it's often the only way to win these deals; as trying to negotiate over the phone results in fewer total sales at lower margins.

You'll want to use the "bury the dead" technique when either you can't give your lowest price over the phone or you're already at your lowest price. But, rest assured, only about one in eight buyers are strictly motivated by price. The others just want a fair deal from a trustworthy dealership – this is where authenticity matters most.

Make no mistake, you are going to lose many of the pure price buyers in this exchange; but, that's okay. These are often loser deals that result in a poor OEM survey. You will, however, win more than your share of those who want a competitive price and a good buying experience. This is where your "Why Buy" messaging will help, as well. By inserting one of your "Why Buy" messages during these over-the-phone negotiations, you'll improve your chances with all but the pure price buyers.

I Can't Afford It

While this is an objection you'll hear on the lot more often than on the phone, you should be prepared to overcome it for those rare instances where someone will utter this on a call with one of the following statements:

Phone Up: "I can't afford a new Silverado."

Phone Up: "That's way outside my budget."

Phone Up: "That payment is too high."

In these cases, it's important to never lower your price over the phone. If you do, you'll often find yourself in a no-win negotiation call – something you should try to avoid. After all, when you have someone on the phone you have just one goal: An appointment that shows.

It's also important to avoid trying to find them a lower-priced alternative at this stage. They're on the phone, not on the lot. Trying to work the deal now will (for most prospects) greatly reduce your chances of getting an appointment that shows. We've got to get them into the dealership to work the deal. So, when someone tells us they can't afford the selected vehicle, our response must move them to the next step in our process, not bring them back to the beginning of their search:

Salesperson: "Well, you'd be surprised Mr. Jones at how hard my manager is willing to work to make a car deal. Now, with today's incentives and with the right loan terms, I'm certain we can find the perfect vehicle for you that will fit into your budget. Let's do this, let's look at the options and work the numbers to get you the best deal. We've got two appointments open with our product specialists this afternoon: I've got a 12:15 and a 1:45. Which one of those works better for you?"

Moving from the phone to the showroom is what we need to do with every objection, every question, every time we're on the phone with a prospect.

I Can be There on Saturday

You've asked for the appointment and the prospect gives you a clear buying signal like this:

Phone Up: "Well, I can be there on Saturday; what time do you open?"

If you hear this on any other day other than Friday, you need to treat this question as an objection. As we learned in the last chapter, a lot can happen between today and Saturday. Your goal of getting an appointment that shows should also drive you to work to set your appointments for today or tomorrow only. Since, of course, these will show at higher rates than appointments set for a few days from now. Therefore, even though you tried for an appointment today with your earlier response of, "We've got two test drives open on that vehicle this afternoon, we've got a …" you need to give this one more attempt.

Salesperson: "That's great Mr. Jones, we'd love to see you on Saturday. Of course, around here, Saturdays can be a little hectic. I think we'll be better able to serve you and get you an offer more quickly if you have some time in the evening to swing by and test drive it. Now, we also have priority test drives open on that vehicle tonight at 5:15 or 6:15. Would either of those work better for you?"

Certainly, if your prospect is adamant about Saturday (or if they work outside the market and simply can't make it until then), then go ahead and set the appointment for Saturday. Be prepared, however, to do a good job confirming the appointment between now and then. (We'll tackle appointment confirmations in "The Perfect Appointment" chapter.)

I Want That in Writing!

There are a lot of dealerships that still refuse to give their very best price in writing. They are willing to give a price on the phone, but they're not willing to put it in writing. If this describes your situation, then you should be prepared to overcome this, as it will be a common objection you hear:

Phone Up: "Listen, I want that price in writing!"

Salesperson: "Mr. Jones, that makes complete sense to me. However, because we are never undersold here at ABC Motors, our competitors often mystery shop us, and we've found that providing our very best price in writing only gives them ammunition to hurt our sales without the customer actually getting a better deal. There's a lot that goes into the final numbers and many competitors will claim they can beat our price, but they do so by adding in hidden charges. That said, you have my word that we are absolutely going to honor this price if you will set and keep an appointment with us. Now, we have two priority test drives open on that vehicle this afternoon. We have a 1:15 and a 1:45. Which of those works better for you?"

The key, again, is to frame the next step in the process (an appointment) as you work to overcome the objection.

I'm Not Ready to Buy

One of the most frustrating objections you can hear from a Phone Up happens after you've given them information; you've been helpful; yet, when you attempt to schedule the test drive you hear one of the following:

Phone Up: "I'm not ready to buy."
Phone Up: "I just started my research."
Phone Up: "I'm still a couple of months out."

Only... they are ready to buy; they didn't just start their research; they're not a couple of months out. They're afraid of you! They fear sales pressure, so they want to find an easy way to buy. (It's also possible, if they know the expected selling price, that they don't think they can afford the vehicle right now.) Assumptive Selling demands that you assume they're a buyer who wants to buy today. Anything less will result in a lost deal; therefore, your response must be a positive acknowledgement that gives them a reason to come in today:

Salesperson: (New Cars) "Hey, that sounds great, Mr. Jones. I'm glad I could provide you with today's information. Now, since you've been shopping online, you know that Ford has some of the best incentives and offers we've seen in a long time, and those will certainly expire by the time you are ready to buy. What I recommend you do is test drive the F-150 and take a look at how these current incentives might make a difference. We'll be happy to give you some quick numbers that you can take home, and then decide when you're ready. Now, we've got two test drives open on the F-150 this afternoon. We've got a 12:45 and a 1:15. Which one works better for you?"

Salesperson: (Used Cars) "Hey, that sounds great, Mr. Jones. I'm glad I could provide you with information about the Camaro. Of course, at that price, it won't be in our inventory when you're ready to own it.

What I recommend you do is test drive the Camaro and let me give you some quick numbers that you can take home, and then decide when you're ready. Now, we've got two test drives open on that Camaro this afternoon. We've got a 12:45 and a 1:15. Which one works better for you?"

If the prospect was concerned that the vehicle price was too high, they'll often indicate that here. If they do, of course, work to overcome their "I can't afford it" objection using the appropriate word tracks.

I'm Interested in Leasing

Phone Ups will often give us clear buying signals in the questions they use. They do this because they may actually want a little more information, or they may just want you to sell them a car. It's important when you're using Assumptive Selling to treat these buying-signal questions like objections; that is, if you expect to set an appointment that shows.

When you treat questions like questions, the natural response is to provide an answer… and nothing more. This practice, of course, creates the pre-visit, back-and-forth information exchange you need to avoid if you want to successfully handle your Phone Ups.

When the questions move toward incentives, payments or leasing, you'll want to move your prospect quickly away from the details and focus them on test driving the vehicle. You want to do this not because you're trying to hide information, but because the answers to these questions can often be very complex – and highly dependent on the prospect's credit worthiness.

You simply want to stay out of the weeds. Here are just a few ways the prospect can give you buying signals with their lease questions:

Phone Up: "What are your best lease deals on the 3-Series?
Phone Up: "Does BMW have any lease specials right now?"
Phone Up: "I'm interested in leasing. Can you give me some information?"

If you allow yourself to get pulled into very detailed responses here about rates and residual values, you stand a very good chance of confusing the prospect and losing the deal. So, instead of trying to answer their question with a specific, complete answer and lots of information; you're better off treating these like objections and framing the next steps.

Phone Up: "What are your best lease deals on the C-Class?

Salesperson: "Right now, Mercedes has some of the very best leasing deals we've seen in a long time; including $389 for a 36-month lease on the C-Class. Our next step will be to schedule a priority test drive on the C-Class and then work up the very best deal on your lease based on your unique situation. Now, we've got two test drives open on the C-Class this morning; we've got a 10:15 and a 10:45. Which one of these works better for you?"

Phone Up: "Does Mercedes have any lease specials right now?"

Salesperson: "Absolutely! Right now, Mercedes has some of the very best leasing deals we've seen in a long time. Our next step will be to schedule a priority test drive for you and then work up the very best lease deal for your unique situation. Was there a particular Mercedes-Benz you are interested in driving?"

Phone Up: "I'm interested in leasing. Can you give me some information?"

Salesperson: "Absolutely! Right now, Mercedes has some of the very best leasing deals we've seen in a long time; and there are plenty of great reasons to lease rather than buy, including lower monthly payments and a lower down payment. Another great reason is you will be driving a new car every two or three years, and, finally, there are little to no out-of-pocket costs for repairs when you lease. Now, what I'd like to do is schedule a priority test drive for you with one of our leasing specialists. Was there a particular Mercedes-Benz you are interested in driving?"

Because this is a Phone Up, we may know very little about the specific vehicle or trim the customer is interested in leasing. However, not knowing which vehicle a prospect wants does not stop the assumptive seller from moving them towards the appointment. Once the Phone Up identifies a Model, it's time to ask for the appointment. You can narrow down their preferences once they understand you're trying to provide a hassle-free way for them to demo their new car.

I Want my Out-The-Door Number!

When a Phone Up is demanding they need everything – tax, title, license, etc. – before they'll commit to a purchase, your dealership's policies will dictate your response. For example, if you're a One-Price Dealer, then you likely have all you need at your fingertips to provide this (assuming you also ask for the appointment in the same breath). Additionally, if your dealership website includes fully-automated online buying capabilities, you can direct the customer to use that application (with your help, of course).

However, if your dealership is unwilling/unable to share the final out-the-door numbers, then you're going to have to move this customer to the appointment using an old-school word track before you can sell them a car:

> Phone Up: "I'm not coming in until you give me my out-the-door number."

> Salesperson: "I agree, Mr. Jones, most people want to know all of the elements of the car deal before they arrive. However, we do reserve our very best price for people who've selected and test-driven a vehicle, and your presence in our dealership is your leverage. Now, I have two priority test drives open on that vehicle this afternoon: I've got a 1:15 and a 2:45. Which one of those works best for you?"

This is very old-school, and for the pure price buyer, this will likely fail more often than it succeeds. Therefore, moving to a version of the bury the dead word track might be necessary:

> Salesperson: "I agree, Mr. Jones. It sounds like you want the very best price available on your next CX-9. Is that correct?"

> Phone Up: "Of course. What do you think we're talking about here?"

> Salesperson: "Excellent. Because we will never be undersold here at ABC Motors, I can guarantee you're going to get the very best price on a new CX-9. What I need you to do is schedule a priority test drive

with me on the CX-9. After we've worked up the deal, just present us with your very best written offer. If we cannot meet or beat a valid written offer on an in-stock unit, we're going to give you a $100 gift card to the Olive Garden and we're going to fill your tank with gas. Now, we have two priority test drives open on that CX-9 this afternoon. We have a 1:15 and a 1:45. Which one of those works better for you?"

Can You Send Me Some Pictures?

Salespeople still receive this question today (usually only on new cars with stock images or used cars you just took in trade); though it's mostly a smokescreen designed to feel out the dealership. The Phone Up fears sales pressure and doesn't want to come right out and say, "the vehicle is just what I want, and the price is right; so, will you sell it to me?"

When you hear questions about images or other non-price concerns over the phone, you also must assume the prospect is trying to eliminate you; the more information you give them, the easier you make it for them to do this. Unless it's an exotic or hard-to-find vehicle, there is no need to send them pictures right away – your goal, after all, is to generate an appointment that shows, not to get bogged down in lots of back-and-forth. For used cars, I recommend the following:

Phone Up: "I'm looking at that 2017 Honda Odyssey that you've got on your website. Can you send me some pictures of that?"

Salesperson: "Actually that vehicle is brand new to our inventory and it's currently going through reconditioning; so, it would be hard for me to get you some great pictures right now. However, we've already had a lot of interest in that Odyssey, and we have two test drives open on that Odyssey later this afternoon when it comes out of recon. We have a 3:45 and a 4:15. Which one of those works better for you?"

Of course, you must know your inventory and you must be certain the vehicle will be available and fully reconditioned in time for the demo drive appointment. For new cars with stock images, I recommend the following:

Phone Up: "Can you send me some actual pictures of that new Enclave?"

Salesperson: "Absolutely! It will be my pleasure. Can I get a good email address for you so that I can take a few pictures and send them to you?"

Phone Up: "Sure. My email address is..."

Salesperson: "Great! Thank you; I'll get those pictures to you shortly. Of course, the best way to see this Enclave is in person. So, what I'd like to do is to also schedule a priority test drive for you on the Enclave. If we schedule this, we'll have that Enclave cleaned, gassed and parked right out front, so that when you arrive, you'll be able to get the keys and get out on a test drive in just a few minutes with no hassles. Now, we do have two test drives open on that Enclave later this afternoon. We have a 3:45 and a 4:15. Would one of those work for you?"

As with answers to any questions over the phone, you must always circle back to your goal of an appointment that shows.

What's My Trade-in Worth?

This question is more of an objection because the prospect is indicating to us that they're not coming in to test drive the vehicle they want until they know what you'll give them for their trade. For most dealers, trade value is something you should never give over the phone or in an email. Let me repeat that so there's no misunderstanding here: for most dealers, trade value is something you should never give over the phone or in an email.

When you give a trade value to someone sitting at home – even if it's just a ballpark figure – you're either going to eliminate yourself with a low number or lock yourself in (in the prospect's mind) to honor that amount regardless of condition. Additionally, you're inviting them to take your trade value to a competitor; where the competitor will get the opportunity to sell them a vehicle. And, of course, you won't.

Trade values via online forms are fine, as we will be able to overcome the prospect's objection to a lowball number given by "a computer." (You'll learn these word tracks in the "Assumptive Selling Your Internet Leads" chapter.) If you give a value over the phone, any objection to a low number is harder to overcome.

In these instances, you've likely already tried for the appointment on their vehicle of interest, and they may or may not have set one. However, before they'll fully commit, the prospect will ask you something like:

Phone Up: "I'm driving a 2015 Corolla; can you give me an idea on the trade-in value?"

If you start digging into their vehicle by asking a lot of questions around equipment, mileage and condition; you're setting yourself up to lose. They will expect a value from you! So, the best advice is to nix this idea early and to go for the appointment:

Salesperson: "Great, you've got a 2015 Corolla. I know my used car manager would love to add a clean Corolla to our inventory; but, of course, only a trained appraiser knows what your vehicle is worth, and it would be irresponsible for anyone to give you that information over the phone sight unseen. Now, I do have two appointments open with my appraiser this afternoon; I have a 12:15 and a 12:45. Which one of those works better for you?"

Alternatively, you can use an old-school AIM tactic to answer this objection. AIM is a great way to overcome new objections or objections you're simply not prepared for. AIM stands for Acknowledge, Ignore and Move On (to your goal). In this case, our goal is an appointment that shows, so let's break down an AIM response here:

Acknowledge the Objection: "Mr. Jones, I can appreciate that it would be great to know what your Corolla is worth before you drive down here..."

Ignore (or Redirect the Objection): "... however, only a trained appraiser knows what your vehicle is worth, and it would be irresponsible for anyone to give you that information over the phone."

Move On to your Goal: "Now, I do have two appointments open with my appraiser this afternoon; I have a 12:15 and a 12:45. Which one of those works better for you?"

When you use AIM to overcome objections, your prospect often believes their objection was adequately addressed just by your acknowledgement.

In this case, let's say this prospect already received a value from a competitor. You just told them that, "it would be irresponsible for a dealer to give you this information over the phone;" so, they're either thinking you're lying or your competitor is irresponsible. If it's the former, you'll often here this:

Phone Up: "But, Bob's Motors gave me a price for my Corolla!"

Salesperson: "Mr. Jones, there are only two things a dealer can do to you when they give you a trade value sight unseen. They can lowball you or they can lie to you; because only a trained appraiser knows what your vehicle is worth, and it would be irresponsible for anyone to give you that information over the phone. Now, I do have two appointments open with my appraiser this afternoon; I have a 12:15 and a 12:45. Which one of those works better for you?"

I wrote in the second sentence of this section "*For most dealers, trade value is something you should never give over the phone…*" because there are instances where dealers with a great in-store process can and do give trade values over the phone. When you employ a solid trade walk and write-up in your dealership, you can successfully give a trade value over the phone or via an email in instances like this:

- You're involved in a competitive situation on a new vehicle that's available at virtually any other dealer selling your brand;
- The buyer is relatively far from your location; and
- You're competitive on the new vehicle, but the buyer wants a firm trade value before they'll drive to come see you.

If you ballpark or lowball their trade, the dealer closest to their home will just beat your price and you'll lose the deal. You have two choices: you can either refuse to give them a number or you can value their trade as if it's in mint condition with a caveat that your final value is dependent on a thorough in-dealership inspection.

If you're competitive on the new vehicle and your trade value is high enough, their local dealer will not be able to match your deal. This means the buyer can either accept what they feel is a lousy number locally, or drive to see you in hopes of getting more for their trade. This is where a great trade walk and write-up come in.

During the trade walk, you'll want to be thorough as you "show" them everything that's wrong with their trade vehicle – this way, they'll be prepared for a lower value in the write-up. During the write-up, you'll need to be ready to defend your now-lower value by starting with what you offered them over the phone, and then explaining the reality of their vehicle. This is best accomplished with a quick, back-of-the-worksheet calculation:

$16,500 - Original Offer
-900 - New Tires
-300 - Detailing
-1,200 - Other Reconditioning
$14,100 - Actual Value

Since they've already driven all this way to see you and this new lower value is defensible (and likely about what their local dealer offered them), you're going to be able to make a car deal.

Will You Take $_____?

Handling customer offers on your vehicles, especially lowball offers, can be tricky when the customer isn't sitting across from you. In these cases, the prospect is giving you a clear buying sign and looking to see how low you'll really go before they make the drive down to your dealership. But, remember: you cannot sell an empty seat. Plus, accepting a customer offer over the phone indicates to the prospect that you may have even more room to give on the price; putting you in a negotiation situation if they do arrive.

The best way to handle offers (if you're priced-to-market or have already provided the customer with a competitive price) is to defend your price. Your instincts may tell you that the right thing to do is to reply to a lowball offer with something like, "My manager's been making some crazy deals this month... why don't you come down and let me see what I can do for you?" But, that's a losing strategy that will kill more deals today and tomorrow than defending a good price.

When you try to just "get 'em in" in the face of a lowball offer, you give the prospect false hope that backfires more often than it succeeds. You've just told someone that, in effect, their $25,000 offer on a vehicle that's priced-to-sell at $32,000 has a chance and will be considered.

It has no chance, and it won't be considered.

You might think that defending the price goes against the goal of an appointment that shows, but it does not. When you're priced-to-market, today's prospect knows this. Most often, Phone Ups use the lowball offer because they've been taught for decades that the price is never the price… only today, it is. So, defend the price:

Phone Up: "Will you take $25,000?"

Salesperson: "While we appreciate the offer, if you've been shopping online, then you know we have an extremely competitive price on that vehicle. Additionally, we would never dream of playing games with our customers by giving you our second-best price and then making you jump through a bunch of hoops to find some hidden best price. At $32,320 that Santa Fe is priced to sell and likely won't be on our lot much longer. Now, we have two test drives open on that Santa Fe this afternoon, we have a 12:15 and a 12:45; which one of these works best for you?"

Certainly, if your dealership will not allow you to quote a price at or near the expected selling price, then an old-school word track (still focused on the appointment) is all you can use at this point (not recommended unless absolutely necessary, of course):

Salesperson: "Wow, it sounds like you don't want me to put my kids through college! Listen, while I certainly can't accept a lowball offer over the phone, I can tell you that my manager has been making some crazy deals all month, and your presence in our dealership is your leverage. So, let's do this, let's schedule a priority test drive on the Santa Fe where I can get you in and out on the test drive in a few minutes. After we know that you want to own the Santa Fe, I will take your offer to my manager and do my best. Now, we have two test drives open on that Santa Fe this afternoon, we have a 12:15 and a 12:45; which one of these works best for you?"

Does It Come with a Warranty?

When you receive warranty questions on the phone – as with all questions – you should answer them truthfully and circle back to your goal:

Phone Up: "Does this vehicle come with a warranty?"

Salesperson: "That's a great question. All of our pre-owned vehicles come with either the balance of the original factory warranty, a factory certified warranty or an extended dealership warranty for up to two years. That Accord is certified, so it's covered by the Honda Certified Warranty, and as I said, we have two test drives open on that Accord this afternoon. We have a 1:15 and a 1:45, which one of those works better for you?"

This question is a buying signal, so treat it as fairly routine (and a good thing) when you answer it. If the prospect pushes back and wants to know more about the warranty details, you should provide a little bit of information and then circle back to your goal:

Phone Up: "What does the Honda Certified Warranty cover?"

Salesperson: "The Honda Certified Warranty provides great coverage. For example, it includes a 7-year, 100,000-mile powertrain warranty. Now, as I said, we have two test drives open on that Accord this afternoon. We have a 1:15 and a 1:45, which one of those works better for you?"

I Don't Want to Set an Appointment

I get it. Making an appointment to test drive a car sounds foreign to most buyers; and many simply won't understand why you're "making" them do this just to see the car they want. Of course, we're not making anyone do anything they don't want to do. However, because we know that appointments create a better experience for today's customers – and because we're lucky if we sell a car to someone unwilling to set and keep an appointment – successful assumptive sellers keep trying for the appointment until it's clear the customer has no intention of setting one:

Phone Up: "Why do I have to set an appointment? Can't I just come in?"

Salesperson: "Absolutely. You're free to come in anytime you wish. However, my customers have told me they don't like to waste five hours on a Saturday trying to buy a car. They've found that when they set and keep a test drive appointment with me, I'll have their vehicle cleaned, gassed and parked right out front so that when they arrive we can get on the road in minutes. Now, we do have two priority test drives open on that A4 this morning, we have a 9:15 and 9:45. Which one of those works better for you?"

12

ASSUMPTIVE SELLING AND YOUR INTERNET LEADS

When the first internet sales leads started spewing from dealers' fax machines in the late 1990s (yes, fax machines), the prospect who initiated the request was usually months away from purchasing. They were an early online browser who was curious to see how much a new vehicle actually cost; and they had about as much information as someone reading the newspaper back then… not much.

This was an internet inquiry and the salesperson who received the fax paper from the sales manager was told to "get 'em in!" The prospect was not yet ready to buy; and the dealership was twenty years from giving them a price over the phone. That was then, and this is now.

Lately, much has been written about the drop in the number of electronic sales leads dealers receive – not coincidentally, of course, most often by those wishing to sell more of their own brand of marketing to these same dealers – and while the decline is not steep, it is genuine for some dealers. Internet sales leads to dealers have declined relative to the number of online automotive shoppers over the past decade. However, my experience shows the driving force of this downturn – and what dealers should do about it – is greatly misunderstood.

I've heard the arguments that "consumers are smarter;" that they're "wary of sharing their information online." If either of these were a primary cause of the decline, then I suspect other industries' lead-generation efforts would suffer, as well. More specifically, if consumers were suddenly skittish about sharing their email addresses and phone numbers when shopping for vehicles, how would this correlate with the rise in lead-driven services like AutoWeb, TrueCar, or even CarGurus' ability to generate solid lead counts for their dealers?

I have a different thought. Previous studies that detailed the motivations of those who submitted online requests for information showed overwhelmingly – often at or above 90% of those intending to purchase – that these consumers did so to receive pricing information.

On the surface, then, it's no wonder internet sales leads are down as a percentage of online shoppers. Given that the primary reason for submitting an online request was to gain pricing information, the almost staggering availability of transaction or near-transaction prices online should (I suspect) remove the need for consumers to share personal information to simply gain an e-price. This is actually good news for dealers, as today's internet sales leads are better and more qualified than they were when pricing was still a question.

Today's internet inquiry is an offer to buy; an order, if you will. It is the culmination of sometimes months of online research. It's an indication that the prospect may have visited dozens of websites, viewed hundreds of vehicles, read vehicle and dealership reviews, and verified your pricing as competitive. They've found value and relevancy; and now they just need someone to sell them the car.

But, Don't Sell Them the Car!

Before you dive right into your road-to-the-sale with an internet prospect, it's important to remember you cannot sell an empty seat. While your internet prospect is still sitting comfortably at home, your goals should never include selling the vehicle or your dealership or yourself. If you're using Assumptive Selling, your goals in the internet sales process are determined by the type of communication:

- Auto-Response. The goal is to set the stage for what comes next.
- Email. The goal is to drive a phone call.
- Voicemail. The goal is to drive a return call.
- Initial Text. The goal is to drive a two-way communication.
- Phone Call (and any Two-Way Communication). The goal is to drive an appointment that shows.

Don't overthink your goals! The internet prospect is looking for authenticity (and help buying a car), but they used a form online to communicate with you because they're afraid of you; they fear sales pressure. Most of these prospects expect that buying a car is going to be a hassle. Given this, let's design an internet sales process that removes these hassles and reassures the prospect that you're a good person trying to help with the second-most expensive purchase many of these people will ever make.

The internet sales process is designed to move your prospect through your goals and into the driver's seat, so be sure you remain focused on these:

- The first step is to drive a reconnection.
- The second step is to set an appointment that shows.

That's it. Notice how none of the steps or goals introduced so far include "provide the prospect with all the information they need to make an informed decision." They already have all the information! This is the essence of Assumptive Selling. They've found the vehicle they want; they believe it is a good value. They don't need more information; they need someone to provide an easy, hassle-free way to buy. If you'll properly follow the steps in an Assumptive Selling process, you'll help them buy the car today.

A Quick Word on Process

You will read more than once in this book that a bad process is better than no process; and it is, hands down. Whether you start with my process or something your OEM's overpaid consultant told you to use doesn't matter. What matters is where you go with that process.

All processes should be continuously measured and improved. I've already explained this is called continuous process improvement. Without continuously improving your internet sales process, you'll find yourself using something that worked great ten years ago, but today closes fewer than 5% of the internet leads you receive. Additionally, when you freelance (that is, you try to wing it with every prospect), you have nothing to improve. You cannot measure freelancing; and if you cannot measure something, you cannot improve it.

So, start with the worst process ever; it doesn't matter. Just be ready to measure the steps, track your results, and make small improvements until you perfect it. Then… keep measuring and improving.

Today's Connected Customer

We already know that today's buyer has all the information; therefore, that lead you received is actually an order. Despite the questions they'll throw at you, they're not looking for more information; so, don't fall for that. Instead, assume the sale. They selected your car and your dealership from among the millions of cars for sale and the tens of thousands of dealerships online. They said to you when they submitted that lead, "Hey, your vehicle has value, and it's relevant to me. Right now, I'm looking for authenticity."

You can show them authenticity by pulling them through a process that makes sense. Your first goal, then, is to get reconnected with the prospect. This usually means getting them on the phone, though it could also mean generating a two-way communication via email or text. Remember this when you write your process emails to (or leave voicemails for) these non-responsive prospects.

Before we dive into these, let's review my current internet sales process for non-responsive prospects. This is the catch-all process that assumes they've provided a phone number and a vehicle of interest in the lead. Later, we'll look at processes for credit application leads, no-phone leads, and trade-in leads.

My current internet process is 45 days long, contains only 9 call attempts and asks you to make no calls after 15 days. (Remember, this is a non-responsive prospect. Once a prospect responds to any of your communication attempts – that is, you start a two-way communication – you're no longer going to complete any of the activities in this process. You're going to move them to a connected status and work to drive an appointment that shows.)

Stauning's 45-Day Traditional Internet Sales Process

The Traditional Internet Sales Process is the basic process recommended for most vehicle inquiries where the prospect has provided a working phone number. For credit application leads, trade-in leads, and leads with no phone numbers (or bad phone numbers), please refer to the respective process written for each of these. In 2006, this process was 180 days long and asked you to make calls through Day 60. Since then, the world has changed, and prospects are much lower in the sales funnel when they submit a lead.

The old-school rules to follow up until they "buy or die" are ineffective and have a negative impact on your desire to sell more cars; specifically:

- Emails sent after the first ten days are rarely opened by previously non-responsive prospects; and those that are opened must provide extremely compelling reasons to drive a reconnection in order to have any impact on prospects.

- Recent studies reveal that more than nine phone call attempts to non-responsive prospects provides no meaningful return on effort.
- Sending emails after the first four weeks greatly increases a dealer's chance of being labeled a spammer (without generating enough necessary reconnections to offset this risk).
- Virtually no salespeople successfully complied with the aggressive call schedules in our earlier processes.
- Our internal data shows that sending the pricing email before your competitors greatly increases your chances of reconnecting with and closing the prospect.
- Including a Request-to-Text on Day 1 and on Day 3 increases your connection percentage. (*Dealers should consult their legal counsel before texting any prospect that has not expressly opted-in to receive SMS messages.*)

These changes increase your chances of driving a reconnection, while reducing the amount of perceived spam a prospect will receive from you. Moreover, this updated process more closely matches the most current consumer buying timelines.

DEALERS SHOULD CHECK WITH THEIR OWN LEGAL COUNSEL BEFORE IMPLEMENTING ANY PART OF THIS PROCESS TO ENSURE THEY REMAIN COMPLIANT WITH ALL LAWS AND REGULATIONS, INCLUDING THE CAN SPAM ACT AND THE TCPA.

- Day 1 – Lead arrives in CRM; Auto-Response fires
  - o Review the lead completely
- Day 1 – Phone Call(s) – the first call should be made as soon as you've read and understood the customer's needs (with a goal of 5 minutes and a maximum acceptable time of 15 minutes). If the lead arrives early enough in the day, at least one additional phone call (utilizing a DIFFERENT voicemail message) should be made. Successful dealers will make up to 3 calls in the first day, when possible
- Day 1 – MANUAL email – Manually send Day 1 email template – include hand-typed answers to any questions asked from comments and/or vehicle pricing

- Day 1 – Request to Text – Sent from the CRM, & TCPA compliant
- Day 2 – Phone Call(s) – At least one, but up to two – especially if only one call was made on Day 1
- Day 2 – AUTOMATED email
- Day 3 – Phone Call
- Day 3 – Request to Text – Sent from the CRM, & TCPA compliant
- Day 4 – AUTOMATED email
- Day 4 – Phone Call
- Day 5 – Phone Call
- Day 7 – Manager Phone Call
- Day 8 – AUTOMATED email
- Day 10 – Phone Call
- Day 14 – AUTOMATED email
- Day 15 – Phone Call
- Day 20 – AUTOMATED email
- Day 28 – AUTOMATED email
- Day 34 – AUTOMATED email
- Day 45 – AUTOMATED email

After 45 days, Non-Responsive Prospects should either be moved to "Lost" and no more communications sent to them (recommended) or moved to an "Active Broadcast" status, meaning they will receive no more than one email each month with a sales call-to-action including specials and special offers. To minimize the likelihood of being labeled a spammer, no additional communications should be sent to this group. They're not your customers, they're just someone who tried to buy a vehicle from you; they don't want to read your e-newsletters!

I'm going to provide a few of the current email and voicemail templates from this and other processes in this book; though if you'd like my complete internet sales processes – including all email templates and voicemail scripts – visit SteveStauning.com and contact me through that site. I'll gladly share my current processes and templates with anyone who asks.

The Dreaded Auto-Response

It really is time to stop overthinking the Auto-Response in automotive. I've heard OEMs and third-party classified providers tell their dealers to stop sending automated responses to new leads, only to see the same OEM and third-party classified providers send an automated response on all leads submitted through their own websites.

Always send an Auto-Response. Always. To every new lead. Always. (Are we clear?)

Unfortunately, many car dealers listened to a bit too much outside advice and jettisoned the Auto-Response from their internet sales processes. Whether it was some well-meaning, though misguided internet trainer or a new sales manager with all the answers, someone convinced them that their team should be responding quickly enough by phone and email that they shouldn't need to have the CRM send an Auto-Response.

Even if this were true – that is, that your team was always responding within a few minutes – every dealer should be sending an Auto-Response to every new lead they receive. Let me give you three quick reasons why:

- First, the prospect may not have paid attention to which dealers received their information (as can be the case with third-party leads). Your Auto-Response, in this instance, let's them know to expect future communications from your dealership.
- Second, the Auto-Response is not spam to a consumer. It's actually a welcomed confirmation that their information was received. Just as consumers are happy to see the order confirmation email from Amazon.com, they're equally happy to receive your confirmation of their request.
- Finally, a properly worded Auto-Response can either drive an immediate reconnection (giving you the advantage over the competition) or set the stage for what comes next – ensuring they'll take your call when the phone rings.

Like all steps to all processes, let's not overthink this one. Here's my current Auto-Response to a traditional internet lead:

```
Thank you for contacting ABC Motors. This is
an automated response to let you know we've
received your online request for the 2019 F-
150; and an appointment coordinator will
contact you shortly.
```

We're genuinely excited to help you in your vehicle search. At ABC Motors, we're well known for providing a true no-hassle buying experience every time.

If you're ready to schedule your Priority Test Drive now, please respond to this email.

Otherwise, we will call you (if you provided a phone number) to help you schedule this. If you'd prefer, you may call us at any time at 555-555-1212. We look forward to assisting you!

This example lets the prospect know which dealer received their information and it sets the stage for what will happen next. Moreover, it will also drive reconnections for those customers ready to schedule their test drives immediately. Given that the goal of all process emails is to drive a reconnection, we told the prospect about this reconnection four times in the Auto-Response:

- "... an appointment coordinator will contact you shortly ..."
- "If you're ready ... please respond to this email ..."
- "Otherwise, we will call you ..."
- "If you'd prefer, you may call us ..."

Do you think it sounds like we want to reconnect with the prospect? If you were the prospect and received this email immediately after submitting a request, what would you think? Would you be offended? Would you feel spammed?

Nope. You'd do exactly as our research shows: you'd reconnect more quickly with this dealer than the one who failed to send an Auto-Response. Given that our primary goal of the entire internet sales process is to drive a reconnection, always sending a well-written Auto-Response should pretty much be a no-brainer.

[How to handle the phone call (or text or email) when the prospect does reconnect is covered in the respective chapters "The Inbound Phone Call" and "Making Outbound Calls."]

If You're Not First...

There are plenty of studies (some old, some more recent, some in automotive, some in other industries) that show dramatic differences in sales results when you're the first company to connect with a prospect versus just being second. Rather than regurgitate the data here, let's agree that your goal in reconnecting with a new lead should include that you want to be the first dealer to do so. (Our internal studies with our clients over the years show that the dealer who connects first is more than twice as likely to sell a car than the one who connects second.)

This means our goal of a reconnection is not enough; we must be the first dealer to reconnect if we expect to control and close the majority of our sales leads. Plus, your first reconnection attempt should be by phone or text, not email. This gives you a chance at an immediate two-way communication (allowing you to set an appointment that shows).

Unfortunately, too many dealerships rely on the first personal email as a way to "stop the clock." They do this because someone (most likely their OEM) has made response time a priority (which is good), but they only count email responses (which is foolish). Your goal is not to stop the clock; your goal is to drive a reconnection, and your chances of reconnecting increase exponentially when you call or text as your first personal response. Moreover, when you can do this within five minutes of receiving the lead, your chances of selling the prospect more than quadruple versus connecting in over an hour.

Why Only 9 Calls?

When we reduced our process to 45 days and asked that salespeople and BDC agents make no more than nine calls to a non-responsive prospect, some dealers questioned this as not being aggressive enough. Of course, the fact is (and our mystery shop data proves) the average internet salesperson is making fewer than two calls to any new prospect. So, instead of questioning why this process *only* includes nine calls, perhaps you should be questioning why it includes so many. Even top dealers struggle to get their teams to make more than five calls to any non-responsive prospect. Therefore, if you told me your process only requires five or six calls, I'd likely say that's plenty (provided they all occurred in the first week).

In fact, six calls might be the better target than the nine my process requires. A study by Velocify shows it takes six attempts to reach 93% of prospects who will convert into a sale; after nine calls, we've reached 97% of these people.[10] This means there is basically zero ROI in making more than nine call attempts to a new lead.

In the process provided earlier in the chapter, you'll see that the ninth call is scheduled for Day 15. Please don't take this literally. If your process requires two calls each on Days 1, 2, and 3; then one call each on Days 5, 7, and 10; you've reached your nine calls by Day 10, and you should make no more calls to this non-responsive prospect. As I wrote, there is basically zero ROI in making any calls beyond nine. Focusing your calling efforts on the fresh leads will provide a greater return on your efforts than trying to reach someone after you've already left nine voicemails.

On a side note, a friend recently sent me his OEM's brand-new (2018) internet sales process that required fifteen phone calls, including calls on Days 30, 45, 60, and 90 to non-responsive prospects. While this would be a terrible waste of time to make these calls this long after a lead has been submitted, the good news is that no one is doing this. There are virtually no salespeople making calls to non-responsive prospects months after the lead arrived. (Heck, most salespeople aren't making any calls after Day 1 regardless of what their process requires.)

Voicemail Best Practices

Since you're going to be leaving a lot of voicemails for your Internet Ups, this is as good a place as any to introduce some best practices for these:

- Always leave a message. Always.
- Sound like a human who is genuinely trying to help them buy a car. Too often, I listen to dealership voicemails that sound like a robot reading a script. Instead of reading from a piece of paper, you should memorize, personalize and internalize the voicemail scripts you like. Then, just use the script as a guide, and not something you plan to recite verbatim.
- Highlight your persistence in each message. ("… and, if you can't reach me right away, don't worry, I'll try you again later.")
- Keep voicemails short and to the point; preferably under 30 seconds. If you leave the prospect just one voicemail longer than a minute, they'll likely delete future voicemails without listening.

- Voicemails should be varied – that is, don't leave the same message every time. If they didn't call you back last time, what makes you think leaving the same message again is going to work this time?
- Use day-specific scripts, but never sound like you're reading.
- Never try to sell anything over voicemail. Not the car; not the appointment; not anything. The only goal of the voicemail is to drive a call back.
- Give the prospect a reason to call you back. Each voicemail should contain some WIIFM (What's In It For Me?) for the prospect.
- Always use a clear call-to-action that drives a call back: "Please call me back today at (number)."
- Never tell them to stop in and ask for you. The chances that they remember your name are slim; and without an appointment, your closing percentage is likely around 20% (versus 50-80% with an appointment).
- Never tell them what time you close or when you'll be at the dealership. Your goal is not to have the prospect arrive unannounced – you need a return call in order to set the appointment.

Once you've exhausted your nine calls and left your nine voicemails, your CRM should be 100% in control. In my processes, all emails to a non-responsive prospect should be automated, except for the first personal response email sent on Day 1. Just as there is no ROI in making more than nine calls chasing these leads, there is no ROI in hand-typing an email to a non-responsive prospect after the first day. In fact, the only reason the first personal email isn't automated is because you'll want to make sure you verify the pricing information and answer any questions the prospect has before hitting "send."

If you're immediately thinking, "But Steve, we want our emails to look personal!" I would say to write a personal-sounding email, make it a template by replacing the variable information with the proper merge codes for your CRM, and then add it to your automated rotation. Virtually no one is reading most of your emails anyway; so, spend your time on the phones and let the emails take care of themselves.

Email Best Practices

There are some very specific best practices that I encourage you to adopt when it comes to the process emails you send, for example:

- Your emails should be short and to the point. Do you want your emails to be read? Great, then quit trying to send *War and Peace* to your prospects and get to the point. Most emails are read on a smartphone and long emails are often trashed immediately.

- Your emails should be text only. I know your dealer principal loves that big, beautiful image header in your emails that includes your logo and lots of links to your various departments, but the truth is that emails with images and multiple links are often sent straight to spam. Additionally, if your prospect is trying to read your email on their phone, there is a good chance your big, beautiful header doesn't even render properly (or worse, it shrinks your text). Finally, think about the emails you receive from friends and/or coworkers. Do any of these emails contain giant email image headers or do they just contain simple text that gets to the point?

- Every email should include a single call-to-action like, "Call me at (number)." You never want to encourage the prospect to reply to your email or to "stop by and ask for me."

- Except for the Auto-Response, all emails should appear personal in nature. That is, each email should appear as if you just wrote it this morning specifically for that prospect.

- Check your email formatting. The same font and size should be used throughout the entire email; and avoid trying to be too cute with colors, bold and non-standard fonts.

- Emails should be varied – never send the same email twice to the same prospect.

- No typos. If your CRM doesn't check for these issues, use a program like Microsoft Word to check for spelling and grammar; but be careful to paste "as plain text" when moving your emails from Word back into your CRM.

- Remember your goal. The goal of every email you send is to drive a phone call (a reconnection). Do your email templates reflect this or do they contain lots of worthless fluff like:
    o   Store hours?
    o   Link to directions?
    o   Link to Facebook?
    o   Link to Twitter?
    o   Link to YouTube?
    o   Links to your online reviews?

- o Links to Service & Parts?
- o Link to Specials?

Some of you are reading the list above and thinking all or most of this is necessary to include in your emails. Let me cut to the chase: none of it is necessary in a process email to a non-responsive prospect. It's all fluff that could potentially land you in spam; and none of this fluff takes you any closer to driving a return call. I'll dissect these one-by-one:

- Store hours — Your goal is to drive a phone call, not encourage an Internet Up to turn into a Traditional Up and just bop on down to the dealership when they feel like it. Without setting a firm appointment that shows, you'll have no way to prepare for this visit. Leave the store hours for Google and your website; and stick to your goal.
- Link to directions — Ditto for directions.
- Link to Facebook — How much does Facebook pay you to remind your Internet Ups that there's this really fun site to go get lost in for the next 30 minutes? Ugh, this is an email to a buyer who wants to buy today; why on earth are you giving them a link to your Facebook page? Do you think this will make them want to buy from you more? They already selected you; now, just get them on the phone!
- Link to Twitter — Ditto for Twitter.
- Link to YouTube — Ditto for YouTube.
- Links to your online reviews — If you wanted to make an argument that emails to prospects generated from third-party websites should include links to great online reviews, I could be convinced to include these links sparingly in a few important emails. However, some dealers have these links as part of their footer in every email. Enough! The buyer chose your dealership already, so stop trying to screw it up! (As you'll read later in this chapter, including links to great reviews is a good way to build trust; though again, do this sparingly and remember your goal.)
- Links to Service & Parts? I'm trying to buy a car and you're providing me a link to your Service Department? Why? Do you expect the car to break down that quickly? Parts — I understand is an afterthought; but, again, why?

- Link to Specials? I've selected my vehicle; I believe it has both value and relevancy; I'm verifying that it's still in stock, and you send me a link to your "Clearance Corral?" What are you thinking? The last thing you want to do to any Up is have them go back to the beginning of their search. Stop sending links to specials or inventory. They are trying to buy the vehicle they selected from you; and they'll buy it today if you don't confuse them.

They're Ready to Buy; But...

Given all the available information online, an internet lead today represents an order. The prospect who takes the time to share their personal information with a car dealer is serious and they're ready to buy; but, you cannot sell an empty seat!

Staying focused on the goals of each step will help you maximize your units sold, grosses and CSI because all Assumptive Selling processes are designed to provide a great customer experience while pulling the prospect through your abbreviated road-to-the-sale. Trying to jump ahead a few steps might seem like a good thing for the internet customer sitting at home, but it guarantees you'll sell fewer cars and all for less money.

In the "Solving Dealership Turnover" chapter, I introduced an internet salesperson named Ray. Ray was a cherry picker who vomited the lowest price on every Internet Up and then waited at the dealership for a small percentage of them to show up and buy. As far as Ray was concerned, this was a smart move. He received about 450 leads a month and sold about 30 of these without having to make a single phone call. It was good for Ray while it lasted...

Your internet sales efforts, if you wish to have continued success, must be more efficient than Ray's; and just vomiting all the information on every internet prospect does not produce maximum results – just the opposite, in fact.

Another example of information vomiting I encountered happened with a BDC that was managing more than 1,800 leads per month. The workload was so massive that the agents asked for and received permission to desk their internet deals in advance and pass a worksheet to the prospect via email. The idea was to separate the tire-kickers from the buyers, and then deal with the buyers.

So, without ever having conversations with prospects, the BDC agents began responding to every vehicle lead they received with a PDF worksheet that included the dealership's lowest price as well as payment options (including lease payments) at the average interest rate. (To be clear, they were sending prospects the actual desking worksheet that most dealers would never let an in-store customer leave with, let alone send one in advance of a visit.)

Oh, and if the agent happened to communicate with the prospect, they'd include the trade and down payment in a revised worksheet and then send that off.

While on the surface this seems like a very transparent and customer-friendly way to do business, anyone with any time in the car business knows this is complete madness. Sure, the more than 1,000 prospects each month who received more information than they requested liked seeing these PDFs, but almost none of them ended up buying a vehicle from this dealer!

Why? Because they had all the information and they didn't need to come into the dealership!

In this case, the dealership's sales managers and I analyzed more than 1,000 of these worksheets sent to internet prospects over the course of a few months and found that the dealership closed just 6.2% of these deals – and this was a dealer who was known as the area's low-price leader.

You cannot sell an empty seat; and you're not going to make someone like you enough to buy from you when you vomit the entire deal into their lap before they ever visit your lot or test drive the vehicle. Of course, since today's customers claim to want transparency and authenticity, you might be wondering why the low-price leader didn't close the other 938 out of every 1,000 prospects who received these PDFs? There are several reasons; here are the top three:

- They chased the buyer out of the market. If a buyer currently enjoys a $399/month payment and you just sent them a worksheet showing a $599/month payment, you're convincing them that they can't afford a new car. They need to wait.
- They encouraged them to shop the competition. Even if you were their only choice when they began their vehicle search, by giving them the entire deal now (and in writing), you've encouraged them to shop your deal with others selling the same Make. Somewhere along the way they ran into a salesman.
- Apples and Oranges. Let's say you quoted a new Nissan Altima in your worksheet. Because so many consumers cross-shop among multiple brands during their online research, many of those receiving

your numbers took them over to the Honda and/or Toyota dealers and asked them to beat it. They, of course, gladly beat your best deal on an apple with their orange.

So, yes, your internet prospects are ready to buy, and they'd love to buy today. But, there is an internet sales process for a reason. Each step of this process is designed to guide the prospect into the dealership for an on-time appointment. Stick to the process and remember the goals of each step – you'll sell way more cars.

Internet Sales Buckets

The easiest way to manage the multiple processes that top dealers use for their various internet leads is to imagine each process as a bucket. The idea is to put the lead into the right bucket so that the prospect receives the correct correspondence in the right order.

For example, if you received a trade-in lead from a prospect, should you send them email templates that focus on current factory rebates? Of course not! You may have no idea what vehicle the prospect wants to buy – or even if they want to buy at all. Your email templates to trade-in prospects, then, should focus on buying their vehicle. This lead should go into your trade leads' bucket.

The first two buckets to consider are the Connected and Not Connected buckets. Thinking of your prospects in terms of connected and not connected helps some managers and salespeople understand the difference between an appointment-setting process (something we'll learn later) and an internet sales process (which this chapter teaches).

The internet sales process focuses on those prospects with whom we have not yet reconnected (also known as non-responsive prospects); because, of course, once we connect with them, our goals change based on the next steps. Our goal will initially be to set an appointment that shows; though we may discover the prospect bought elsewhere (so, we'll move them into a Bought Elsewhere or Lost bucket).

There are four basic buckets that I recommend you create in your CRM for non-responsive prospects (those in your Not Connected bucket). It's important to have at least these four, because the lead types that go into each bucket are sometimes vastly different and need communication that's focused on a specific buyer's needs:

- Traditional Internet Lead Bucket – This is the process we've already introduced in this chapter. This is a vehicle lead with a phone number.

- No-Phone Internet Lead Bucket – This is a vehicle lead with a bad or no phone number. The reason these leads require a separate process is we will not be making any calls to these prospects. Plus, we want our email templates to focus on gaining the prospect's phone number so that we can call and text.

- Trade-In Lead Bucket – These are leads that originated from a "value your trade" form (usually on your dealership's website).

- Credit Application Lead Bucket – Self-explanatory, of course. Handled properly, you have almost a 100% chance of getting the prospect who completed a credit application to show for an appointment today.

Dealers with robust CRM tools often have a dozen or more buckets to handle every potential lead source and type. For example, over the years I've seen specific follow-up processes (including customized email templates) for all of the following lead sources and types:

- Used car leads
- New car leads from outside our PMA (with a different process for leads from within the PMA)
- Truck leads (some even down to the trim level)
- Performance vehicle leads (a dealer I worked with that has a well-known performance shop correctly treats these leads differently)
- TrueCar leads (and sub-buckets for the various affiliates like USAA, American Express, etc.)
- Autotrader leads
- Cars.com leads
- CarGurus leads
- Costco leads
- Lease leads (when the lead form resides on a lease specials page)
- AutoWeb leads (formerly Autobytel)
- Kelley Blue Book leads (with sub-buckets for Instant Cash Offer, traditional website trade form, and KBB.com)
- Car & Driver leads
- Carfax.com leads

- Craigslist leads
- eBay Motors leads
- Dealer website leads
- OEM leads

Certainly, you do not have to get this granular to be successful; but there is an advantage in sending a response, for example, to a TrueCar USAA lead that reads in part "I'm Steve from the USAA desk at ABC Motors..."

On a final note, a great CRM can parse most leads into the correct buckets automatically (based on lead source, vehicle type, etc.). Be sure to ask your CRM provider if this is possible for your dealership.

FUSSE Lead Response

FUSSE is an acronym I use to test whether an email template or voicemail script is going to compel the prospect to call us back. FUSSE is pronounced like "fussy" and stands for Fear, Urgency, Scarcity, Shame and Excitement. The idea is that your communications to non-responsive prospects should contain at least one of these elements. I'll explain:

- Fear. Some prospects might be motivated by a fear of loss. For example, a traditional lead might be from a buyer who is afraid of missing out on a good deal. While a trade-in lead could be motivated to reconnect if they had a fear of a potentially large repair on their out-of-warranty vehicle.
- Urgency. Given that you assume every lead is an order from someone who wants to buy, it's important to create a sense of urgency in your communications. It does you no good to remove the urgency from this purchase by sending an email on Monday asking if they'd like to come test drive on Saturday. A lot can happen between Monday and Saturday; your prospect could buy elsewhere or decide they don't need to buy at all. Either way, you're more likely to sell a prospect by connecting on the day the lead arrives than you are a week later.
- Scarcity. Every used car lead you receive has a built-in scarcity factor. That is, there is only one of these vehicles and once it's gone, it's gone. So, try to build a sense of scarcity where it makes sense in your email templates and voicemail scripts.

- Shame. Shame emails and voicemails are great when used correctly with a non-responsive prospect. Remember, the goal is a reconnection; so, if you've left four voicemails and sent three emails over the past five days, leaving a voicemail that shames the prospect into calling you back can be very effective.

- Excitement. If you sell 25 cars a month and have been doing so for a few years, the car-buying process is probably not that exciting to you. You sell 300 cars a year, so what's another lead? For the prospect, however, this is a very exciting time for them – even if they're buying a pre-owned vehicle – so be sure to keep them excited with your communications. For example, "You are going to absolutely love this 2017 Accord. It's one of the cleanest trade-ins we've ever offered for sale."

Here are some quick examples of FUSSE emails you can include in your processes:

Fear

```
SUBJECT: Repairing is nearly always more
expensive than replacing

Hi Mr. Jones,

I wanted to take another shot at connecting
with you; and to give you some info that
might help you make a decision on whether to
trade-in now or not.

The average driver puts almost 15,000 miles
each year on their vehicle. If your car is
out-of-warranty, those 15,000 miles might
lead to costly repairs. That's why most
experts say it's usually better to replace
your used car with a new or certified vehicle
covered by a manufacturer's warranty than to
get hit with expensive repairs. (Especially
since the next big repair bill could come at
any time.)
```

We've got a great selection of vehicles under warranty and can even help you get the best finance rates available. Just call me at 555-555-1212 today to schedule a time to come in for a no-hassle, priority appraisal. (We're paying above the book price for a lot of good, clean trades these days.)

Urgency

SUBJECT: We need your Pontiac Aztek

Hi Mr. Jones,

I was speaking with our used car manager about your Pontiac Aztek; and he told me you have what is known as a "high-demand vehicle." And because it is, he would like to see if he can offer you more than book price for it.

We just need to see your Aztek for a quick final inspection and firm offer. We still have a few appraisal openings available today and would love to get a look at your vehicle.

Can you call me today at 555-555-1212? If it's more convenient for you, please give me a time to call you.

Thank you in advance for your courteous response – I look forward to assisting you!

Scarcity

SUBJECT: Requested Pricing for your 2019 Chevy Blazer from ABC Motors

Hi Robert,

I would personally like to thank you for contacting ABC Motors – I cannot wait to help you with your vehicle search! Your information request indicated you were interested in the 2019 Chevy Blazer:

2019 Chevrolet Blazer RS: Stock Number 12345; MSRP: $36,350; ABC PRICE: $33,900

You are absolutely going to love this SUV! Of course, with our Lowest Price Guarantee you are always assured of the best deal when you buy from us.

At this price, the Blazer won't be on our lot for very long, so I am anxious to schedule your Priority Test Drive at our state-of-the-art facility. Please call me today at 555-555-1212 and I promise to get you in and out in no time.

Shame

SUBJECT: My apologies, Robert

Dear Robert,

I'm sure you're busy, and I feel like I'm being a pest since I've left several messages and sent several emails but haven't heard back from you. Can you tell me if you're still in the market for a Blazer?

Also, if there is something I've done to offend you, please let me know and I will hand your folder over to another coordinator who can help. I definitely don't want to be the reason you don't buy from us.

Please call and let me know either way. My number is 555-555-1212.

Excitement

```
SUBJECT:  ABC Motors Performance Team

Hi Robert,

I would personally like to thank you for
contacting the ABC Motors Performance Team -
I cannot wait to help you with your new Roush
Mustang!

I know you are absolutely going to love it!
Before we can get to work on your new
vehicle, we'll need to hop on a quick call to
exchange some information. Please call me at
555-555-1212 as soon as you have a moment.
```

Beyond being FUSSE, you also want your communications to non-responsive prospects to build some much-needed trust in the process, in the dealership, and in you. You should assume that any lead you received was also sent to your competitors, so building trust will help them choose you first.

Regardless of the templates and scripts you use, you should track and measure to determine which ones do a good job of driving a reconnection and which ones do not. Move those that do a good job of creating reconnections earlier in your process and rewrite or discard those that do not.

Limit Choice

While your dealership marketing might include lines like "We've got over 100 Silverados in stock for you to choose from!" your communications should not include notes about your "huge inventory." Doing so removes all urgency from the car-buying process. Think about it; if you have over 100 new trucks in stock, then I can take my time before coming in and making a final decision, right?

Additionally, when buyers are faced with too many choices, they chose nothing. There's a great study on choice by psychologists Sheena Iyengar and Mark Lepper that showed when consumers were presented just six different varieties of jam in a supermarket, they purchased jam ten times more often than when faced with 24 varieties.[11]

Assumptive Selling tells you this prospect chose this vehicle and your dealership. They've done all their research and they're ready to buy today… if you let them. Presenting them with too many options before they arrive can restart their search as they begin to second guess their original choice. So, treat every lead like it's an order.

Of course, this does not mean you should never offer alternative vehicles in your email responses. For example, if you're not the low-price leader in your market (and we assume your prospect is shopping the low-price leader, as well), offering alternate choices via your price response can often move your prospect away from price and drive a reconnection. Here's an email template that's worked great as a first personal response in these instances:

SUBJECT: Requested Pricing for your 2019 Jeep Cherokee Trailhawk from ABC Motors

Hi Jeff,

I would personally like to thank you for contacting ABC Motors - I cannot wait to help you with your vehicle search! Your information request indicated you were interested in the 2019 Cherokee Trailhawk:

- 2019 Jeep Cherokee Trailhawk; Stock #12345; MSRP: $36,060; Sale Price: $32,190

You are absolutely going to love this Jeep! Of course, with our Lowest Price Guarantee you are always assured of the best deal with no hassles when you buy from us. (For your convenience, I also attached the window sticker for this Cherokee.)

I took a quick look at our inventory for you and found a couple of other options that might also meet your needs:

- New 2019 Jeep Cherokee Latitude; Stock #23456; MSRP: $25,885; Sale Price: $19,950

- Pre-Owned 2017 Jeep Grand Cherokee Limited; Stock #34567; Book Price: $35,499; Sale Price: $29,800

I am anxious to schedule your Priority Test Drive at our state-of-the-art facility. Please call me today at 555-555-1212 and I promise to get you in and out in no time.

There's a strategy to offering alternate choices that should be clear to you if you choose to include these in your lead responses. That is, the alternates are always less expensive than the vehicle of interest. In the email above, I offered a lower trim level of the 2019 Cherokee and a better-equipped pre-owned Grand Cherokee Limited to accomplish two goals:

- Move the prospect away from the price of the vehicle of interest (we're at $32,190 and the low-price leader probably shot them a price of $31,500); and
- Build trust by down-selling them on lower-priced alternatives rather than trying to up-sell them.

Because building trust will help you reconnect more quickly with your prospects, I recommend adding elements of this to your emails with one caveat: Don't overuse trust messaging by trying to cram everything into every email. This is where the "Why Buy From Me / Why Buy From Us" messages we discussed in the "Communicating with Today's Ups" chapter come in.

Sprinkling in one of your "Why Buy" messages into your emails is smart; though I recommend using different "Why Buy" messages in each email. Regurgitating the same "Family-owned and operated for 65 years" in every email makes this sound like an advertising slogan instead of a message that can build trust with the prospect. Finally, linking to your great Google reviews (if done sparingly) can also be effective at building trust.

The Trade Lead Internet Sales Process

We know buyers are often suspicious of the trade values your team provides in-person; but, what happens when your online trade-in tool provides consumers a value? How can you both reinforce this unbiased, third-party number and keep a prospect engaged (when they may feel lowballed by the online offer)?

For most dealers, your online trade-in tool is primarily a lead-driver. That is, it's key function is to entice website visitors – both sales and service – to exchange their personal information for a value on their current vehicle. Consumers don't take these steps because they're bored; they're somewhere in the sales funnel, and completing your trade-in lead form could bring them closer to buying sooner rather than later.

But... then they learn the book value. They owe $16,000 and your online trade tool just told them their vehicle is worth $12,000. For most consumers, this is all they need to know: in their minds they can't buy today. Perhaps in a year, but not right now.

The problem for you, of course, is that the prospect is sitting at home – not at the dealership – so defending the value or focusing on their vehicle of interest or payments just aren't options. They're not taking your calls or returning your emails. Moreover, they're not buying today.

It's important to note that trade leads are website leads. That is, they are most often generated from a form on your dealership's own site. Dealers with good internet sales processes routinely close their website sales leads (ePrice, Instant Retargeting, Credit Application, etc.) more than 20% of the time. Website leads, after all, are first-party leads and the prospects are generally lower in the sales funnel than with almost any other lead type. Given this, why is it most dealers close their trade leads about 6-8% of the time? These *are* website leads, aren't they?

Yes, these are website leads; though, because the prospect may not be happy with the value provided, they're not likely to engage with your team when you follow a traditional internet sales process. Trade-in leads are not traditional leads. They're different and they require a different process – one that focuses on the trade vehicle and not on their vehicle of interest. (Many of the trade-in leads generated on your website come from service customers who would be interested in buying if the value for their current vehicle proved high enough.)

Given that some prospects may feel lowballed by the value your online tool provided them, a good trade-in internet sales process is almost like taking someone through the five stages of grief: getting them from denial and anger, on to bargaining, perhaps a little depression and finally acceptance.

When dealers treat trade leads like traditional sales leads, they struggle to reconnect with prospects. This means they set fewer appointments, which means they sell fewer cars. There are great reasons for treating trade leads differently, and I'll give you two: first, most prospects were simply trying to value their trade and may not be sold on the selected vehicle of interest. Second, even if they do want the selected vehicle of interest, when you focus on the vehicle of interest you become the seller. Conversely, by focusing on their trade, you become the buyer. It's a different dynamic at play and focusing on their trade makes the prospect more receptive to your messages.

My current trade-in lead handling process is 60 days long – 15 days longer than the traditional lead handling process. The rationale is that the trade-in prospect could very well be a service customer just looking to see what their current vehicle is worth A service customer like this, of course, is often higher in the sales funnel than someone who submits a traditional sales lead.

As with all lead handling processes, the first goal is to reconnect with the prospect. That is, to get them on the phone, get them to text you, or to respond to your emails. And, the best processes don't ask your team to make unnecessary calls, but rather to focus on the right amount of calls and emails that drive the reconnection. Once you've connected, you focus on your new goal, which is setting an appointment that shows.

Calls-to-action are the key to driving a reconnection, and the best call-to-action in our emails and voicemails to non-responsive trade customers is like other internet sales processes – that is, "please call me back today at ..." However, the real issue is that the trade prospect probably doesn't like the value given. Therefore, your focus needs to include some messaging about the need to physically inspect their vehicle to perhaps get them more money.

Assumptive Selling in these instances means to assume that every trade lead prospect feels as if they got lowballed – and that their vehicle of interest was more of a placeholder. When you do this, your word tracks will be more effective at driving that reconnection:

- "We're excited to see your trade."
- "Let's schedule a quick appraisal so we can get you the most money."

- "Only a trained appraiser knows what your vehicle is really worth."
- "We'll buy your car even if you don't buy ours."

These messages help drive the reconnection better than simply asking trade prospects to call you back.

Stauning's 60-Day Trade Lead Internet Sales Process

Recently, I lengthened the Trade Lead Internet Sales Process from 30 days to 60 days. This, because our A/B testing showed many of these prospects were higher in the sales funnel than originally suspected. This 60-day process can now apply to multiple consumer buying timelines.

DEALERS SHOULD CHECK WITH THEIR OWN LEGAL COUNSEL BEFORE IMPLEMENTING ANY PART OF THIS PROCESS TO ENSURE THEY REMAIN COMPLIANT WITH ALL LAWS AND REGULATIONS, INCLUDING THE CAN SPAM ACT AND THE TCPA.

- Day 1 – Lead arrives in CRM; Auto-Response fires.
  - Review the lead completely
- Day 1 – Phone Call(s) – the first call should be made as soon as you've read and understood the customer's needs (with a goal of 5 minutes and a maximum acceptable time of 15 minutes). If the lead arrives early enough in the day, at least one additional phone call (utilizing a DIFFERENT voicemail message) should be made. Successful dealers will make up to 3 calls in the first day, when possible
- Day 1 – MANUAL email – Manually send Day 1 email template – include hand-typed answers to any questions asked from comments
- Day 1 – Request to Text – Sent from the CRM & TCPA compliant
- Day 2 – Phone Call(s) – At least one, but up to two – especially if only one call was made on Day 1
- Day 2 – AUTOMATED email
- Day 3 – Manager Phone Call
- Day 3 – Request to Text – Sent from the CRM & TCPA compliant

- Day 4 – AUTOMATED email
- Day 4 – Phone Call
- Day 5 – Phone Call
- Day 7 – Phone Call
- Day 8 – AUTOMATED email
- Day 10 – Phone Call
- Day 14 – AUTOMATED email
- Day 15 – Phone Call
- Day 20 – AUTOMATED email
- Day 28 – AUTOMATED email
- Day 34 – AUTOMATED email
- Day 45 – AUTOMATED email
- Day 60 – AUTOMATED email

After 60 days, Non-Responsive Trade-In Prospects can be moved to an "Active Broadcast" status, meaning they will receive up to one email each month with a sales call-to-action, or they can be simply marked as "Lost" to reduce the chances that the dealership will be labeled as a spammer.

Where possible, your messages to the non-responsive trade prospect should encourage them to have their vehicle professionally appraised by you. Here's the first personal email response in my current trade lead process:

```
SUBJECT:   Trade-In Information from ABC
Motors

Hi Robert,

I would personally like to thank you for
contacting ABC Motors - I cannot wait to help
you trade-in or sell your Dodge Charger.

Unlike other dealers, we specialize in
providing the highest value on all trades. In
fact, our Used Car Manager can often offer
more than the online computer appraisal you
received. We are currently in need of good
```

used vehicles to offer for sale and would
like to see your Charger right away so that
we may give you a firm written offer.

Please call me at 555-555-1212 so that I can
schedule your Priority Appraisal at our
state-of-the-art facility. I promise to get
you in and out in no time.

Additionally, your voicemails should support this and attempt to build
excitement in the prospect's mind. Here's the second voicemail in my
current process:

"Hello again Robert, this is Steve Stauning calling back from ABC
Motors and I wanted you to know my manager is very excited about
getting a look at your Charger. He's pretty sure he has a buyer lined up
for it and he just needs a few minutes to verify its condition.

"Is it possible for you to call me back today? As a reminder, my
number is 555-555-1212. Once again that's 555-555-1212. Don't
worry Robert if you don't reach me right away, as I will call you back.
Thank you and talk to you soon."

Did you notice that neither the email nor the voicemail contained a lot of
fluff? We didn't go into a long dissertation about how we're the #1
Dodge dealer in the area or how large our selection is or how we've won
the President's Award for the last 29 years running. We got to the point
and asked for the reconnection. That's Assumptive Selling: they found us
and want to do business with us; so, let's help them do that.

The No-Phone Internet Sales Process

When a lead arrives without a phone number (or a bad number), you're
left with emails as your only chance to drive a reconnection; and sending
these prospects emails that include messages like "… I'll call you later if I
don't hear back …" or "… I've left several messages …" are
disingenuous (aka inauthentic). Your CRM needs a No-Phone bucket so
that you can deliver unique messages to these prospects designed to drive
a reconnection.

Additionally, this process (because it lacks phone calls and requests to text) must include more email messages than the Traditional Internet Sales Process.

Stauning's 45-Day No-Phone Internet Sales Process

DEALERS SHOULD CHECK WITH THEIR OWN LEGAL COUNSEL BEFORE IMPLEMENTING ANY PART OF THIS PROCESS TO ENSURE THEY REMAIN COMPLIANT WITH ALL LAWS AND REGULATIONS, INCLUDING THE CAN SPAM ACT AND THE TCPA.

- Day 1 – Lead arrives in CRM; Auto-Response fires
  o Review lead completely
- Manually send Day 1 email template – include hand-typed answers to any questions asked from comments
- Day 2 – AUTOMATED email
- Day 3 – AUTOMATED email
- Day 4 – AUTOMATED email
- Day 5 – Sales Manager AUTOMATED email
- Day 7 – AUTOMATED email
- Day 9 – General Manager or Owner AUTOMATED email
- Day 11 – AUTOMATED email
- Day 14 – AUTOMATED email
- Day 17 – AUTOMATED email
- Day 21 – AUTOMATED email
- Day 28 – AUTOMATED email
- Day 35 – AUTOMATED email
- Day 45 – AUTOMATED email

After 45 days, Non-Responsive Prospects may be moved to an "Active Broadcast" status, meaning they will receive up to one broadcast email each month with a sales call-to-action; or they may be considered "Lost" and receive no additional communication.

Some of the emails in this process are very similar to what you'll send in the traditional process, though most include subtle differences; for example:

SUBJECT: Test Drive Confirmation

Hi Debbie,

My apologies that I haven't been able to reach you to schedule a Priority Test Drive for the 2019 Tundra, but I realized I don't have a valid phone number for you.

I've reserved today at 2:35 PM for you to come in and inspect the Tundra you asked about. If this is not convenient for you, please call me as soon as possible at 555-555-1212 or provide me with your number so that we can block out something that works better for you.

And:

SUBJECT: Quick Question

Hi Jamal,

My apologies; although I've tried to reach you over the last few days, I haven't been able to because I don't have a valid phone number for you.

I have some news about the 2018 Land Rover Discovery you asked about. Can you call me today at 555-555-1212; or can you give me a number and time to call you?

Today's buyer appreciates emails that are short and straightforward; so, please don't overthink these. Including your typical dealer fluff gets you no closer to selling a car.

The Credit Application Internet Sales Process

When a consumer visits your website and completes a credit application – and this is the first and only form they complete – they're not only telling you they're ready to buy, but that qualifying for financing is more important to them than the vehicle they ultimately purchase. They want your help; and they're proving this by providing lots of non-public information (for example, their social security number).

Even if your online credit application is a short form that only does a soft pull of their credit worthiness, the leads it generates are the lowest funnel sales leads you'll receive. This is because people don't start thinking about financing until they're ready to buy.

Primarily, you'll notice that those who complete these forms are credit challenged. This means your attempts to reconnect should provide some hope and generate some enthusiasm. You should come across as excited to help them; as many of these prospects may have been turned down for financing in the past.

Because credit applications indicate a strong desire to buy today, my credit application process is only 30 days long; and you'll notice that it's heavily front-loaded. Chances are with credit application prospects, you're going to reconnect by the second or third call, so they won't receive the first week barrage that you'll see in the process below.

Stauning's 30-Day Credit Application Internet Sales Process

DEALERS SHOULD CHECK WITH THEIR OWN LEGAL COUNSEL BEFORE IMPLEMENTING ANY PART OF THIS PROCESS TO ENSURE THEY REMAIN COMPLIANT WITH ALL LAWS AND REGULATIONS, INCLUDING THE CAN SPAM ACT AND THE TCPA.

- Day 1 – Lead arrives in CRM; Auto-Response fires
  - Review the lead completely
- Phone Call – this call should be made as soon as you've read and understood the customer's needs
- Manually send Day 1 email template – include hand-typed answers to any questions asked from comments
- TCPA Compliant Request to Text sent from the CRM
- If the lead arrives early enough in the day, up to 2 additional phone calls (utilizing DIFFERENT voicemail messages) should be made, and 1 additional email can be sent.
- Day 2 – AUTOMATED email
- Day 2 – Phone Calls (up to 2)

- Day 3 – Phone Call
- Day 3 – AUTOMATED email
- Day 4 – AUTOMATED email
- Day 5 – Phone Call
- Day 5 –AUTOMATED email
- Day 6 – Manager Phone Call
- Day 6 – Manager AUTOMATED email
- Day 7 – Phone Call
- Day 7 – AUTOMATED email
- Day 10 – General Manager or Owner AUTOMATED email
- Day 14 – AUTOMATED email
- Day 18 – AUTOMATED email
- Day 21 – AUTOMATED email
- Day 24 – AUTOMATED email
- Day 27 – AUTOMATED email
- Day 30 – AUTOMATED email

After 30 days, Non-Responsive Prospects should be moved to an "Active Broadcast" status, meaning they will receive no more than one broadcast email each month with a sales call-to-action; or, they could be marked as "Lost" and receive no more communication.

The email templates and voicemail scripts in this process should be even more direct than other processes because the typical credit application prospect needs this directness; they appreciate the guidance that you're going to offer. Let's look at three sample emails to give you an idea what I mean:

SUBJECT: Great News from ABC Motors

Hi George,

I would personally like to thank you for contacting ABC Motors – I cannot wait to help you with your vehicle search!

I wanted to let you know that I've got some great news regarding our no-hassle financing options. Please call me ASAP at 555-555-1212 so that I can share this with you.

And...

SUBJECT: Can You Take It Home Today?

Hi Maggie,

I was looking at our inventory this morning and realized we've got a few more cars than my general manager wants us to keep on the lot. Is there any way you can take one of these home today?

We work with more than 27 banks and credit unions, and we offer no-hassle guaranteed financing.

Can you call me ASAP at 555-555-1212 so that I can set up a time for you to come in and take something home today? If it's more convenient for you, please give me a time to call you.

Thank you in advance for your courteous response - I look forward to assisting you!

And...

SUBJECT: Car Shopping Stinks

Dear Brett,

I'm not sure why we've been unable to connect these past few weeks - as I'm sure you got bombarded by emails from everyone in the car business - but I wanted to let you know we're still here and we're still very excited about helping you.

If you're looking to be treated with dignity;
if you're looking for a dealership that
values your time; if you're looking for
someone who can help you navigate the
normally murky waters of car buying, please
give me and ABC Motors a chance.

Please call me today at 555-555-1212 and
allow me to schedule a no-hassle, no-haggle
priority appointment for you.

I truly look forward to serving you.

To be clear, it doesn't matter if you write your own email templates and voicemail scripts, or if you contact me at SteveStauning.com to get my current processes complete with these; because whatever you use will need to be constantly measured and improved if you want to always reconnect with the maximum number of prospects. Over time, your continuous process improvement efforts will ensure this.

Online/Offline Hybrid Sales

Dealers now find themselves in the age of digital retailing; and many have yet to see a decent ROI from their efforts on this front. Digital retailing, to be clear, is the overused and wildly incorrect moniker adopted by many vendors in the space of online car sales. They don't want to call it online car sales, because (as of this writing) relatively few deals have been fully consummated online. Calling it online car sales would, I suppose, give dealers the idea that they'll be selling lots of cars this way.

They're not... yet. The progressive dealers, however, are properly leveraging their digital retailing tools to bridge the online and offline processes in something called the online-offline hybrid sale. This is where a customer begins in one space and closes the deal in another.

For example, someone may begin building their deal online using a dealer's digital retailing plugin, and then visit the dealership to test drive the vehicle and complete the last few steps on their own tablet while still in the store. Likewise, a Traditional Up might complete everything except signing the purchase agreement and completing the F&I process; then ask that she be emailed a link to her deal, so she can finish it on her own time at home.

Handled properly, I believe these online-offline hybrid sales will be more prevalent than fully online purchases for the foreseeable future. The good news for salespeople is that the dealer and the customer don't need your help for the deals completed fully online; they do, of course, need you for the hybrid purchases.

Internet sales have been a form of this online-offline hybrid for years. When dealers allowed those buyers that started the process online to seamlessly flow into the next step offline, they enjoyed higher close rates. Conversely, dealers who routinely made internet customers restart the entire process once they arrived at the store saw closing rates often below those of Traditional Ups. (For example, when they required a complete in-person credit application from someone who'd already completed it online.)

Today's buyers see no difference between your online and your offline personas. They expect (as they do with any business that has an online presence) that what they do with you online will translate into their offline interactions, and vice versa.

When a consumer purchases a plane ticket at Southwest.com, they expect it will be honored when they arrive at the airport. When they order the wrong size shoes at Macys.com, they expect they'll be able to exchange these at a Macy's physical location. When they provide you with their desired vehicle, their trade-in and their personal information online, they expect they won't have to regurgitate all this to your team when they arrive at the dealership.

Often, they do. For dealers who embrace the concepts in this book, however, this is where many of you can enjoy a competitive advantage. It's time to start treating your online presence as an extension of your physical dealership. This means, when a consumer gives you information before their visit (or begins to build their deal online), you should allow this to flow as a seamless process when they arrive.

This is why your only goal when you're involved in two-way communication with an internet prospect is to set an appointment that shows. When they show, you're ready for them. You can take them directly to the next step in your process. This saves the customer time and removes many of the hassles of buying a car. In exchange for this, you'll be rewarded with higher closing percentages, better grosses and improved CSI.

Today, your only online-offline hybrid sales are likely sales leads, trade leads and credit applications that become shown appointments. Though eventually, you'll begin to see customers who self-desked their deal online and then scheduled a test drive with you.

When they arrive, the vehicle had better be cleaned, gassed and parked right out front so they can get on with their test drive without delay. Additionally, their deal should already be loaded at the desk and you should be prepared to give them a firm value on their trade by the time they return from the demo drive.

This is what today's customer expects; and the dealers who can deliver this will enjoy more sales, higher grosses, more referrals, and better reviews and CSI that will be hard for average dealers to overcome.

13

MAKING OUTBOUND CALLS

Chapter Note: *Just a quick reminder on the direction and verbiage for calls anywhere in this book: the same basic structure and goals apply whether these conversations are via phone, text, chat, email or Messenger. All two-way communications are treated the same and have the same overriding goal: an appointment that shows.*

Before we get too deep into making outbound calls in an Assumptive Selling environment, I want to discuss the multitude of studies that examine when it's best to make sales calls. These studies dissect the time of the month, the day of the week and even the time of the day where salespeople have the most success in reaching and selling a prospect.

Some of you may even have a poster from one of these studies hanging in your BDC. If you do, please rip it off the wall and throw it away. It's garbage; and it does not apply to you.

Our biggest problem in automotive retail is not that we're making calls on the wrong days or at the wrong times, but that we're not making calls! Showing salespeople that the best time to reach a prospect is between 2 and 4 p.m. on a Wednesday just gives them an excuse for why they're not making any calls on Tuesday.

The best advice I can give to anyone who wants to succeed with outbound calls in any sales environment – whether Assumptive or old-school – is to just make the calls. Make the calls. Make the calls. Make the damn calls. But, limit your outbound calls to money calls only.

"What's a money call," you ask? A money call is any outbound call where a successful outcome eventually means money in your pocket. All calls need to be money calls. Your time is money and not unlimited. Wasting time on calls that cannot make you money is silly; so, use your time wisely. Your customer's time is money and not unlimited. Wasting their time on a non-money call reduces the likelihood they'll take your next call.

Let me give you an example of a non-money call that many CRMs include in their default processes. The call is usually scheduled 3-7 months after a customer has purchased, sometimes titled as "Touch Base," and the accompanying script goes something like this:

"Hi Mrs. Jones, it's Steve over at ABC Motors and I just wanted to touch base with you to make sure you still love everything about your new Impala."

Ugh. Customers hate receiving this worthless call. Salespeople hate making this worthless call. So, why are you wasting your time making this worthless call? Because someone who never sold a car in their life designed a CRM that included this call as part of their default processes. Yikes, that's a terrible reason to do anything in this business.

This is not a money call; and if you're a manager and you require your salespeople to make these calls (that is, you don't load your own effective post-sale follow-up processes into the CRM), you can sleep well knowing they'll never actually make these calls. They will click to complete the task; make a quick note in the CRM like "loves the car;" and then move on to fake the next assigned task.

Every call should be a money call.

The Math of Outbound Calls

There's been a fairly reliable formula for salespeople making money calls from their dealership. Over at least the last few decades, the math on outbound calls has consistently shown that every 1,000 quality calls made equals about 30 units sold.

To be clear, I'm not talking about speaking with 1,000 people; I'm talking about making 1,000 quality outbound calls in a month (which includes voicemails); and doing so, should net you about 30 units sold. Provided, of course, that these are money calls and you're using the right word tracks.

For some of you, this might mean calling your 120 inbound internet leads an average of eight times each. (The eight calls will be a mix of voicemails to non-responsive prospects, live calls with prospects, appointment confirmation calls, missed appointment calls, and Be-Back calls.) For others, it could mean calling an orphan owner database of 250 people an average of four times each during the month (reaching voicemail 800 times and speaking with 200 of these customers).

Wherever the calls are generated, as long as they're money calls, dialing the phone 1,000 times in a month should get you to 30 units sold, on average.

"But Steve," you exclaim, "I don't have time to make 1,000 calls each month!"

Yes. Yes, you do. If you're an average salesperson, then you have at least two hours each day where you stand around doing nothing. Perhaps it's between 8:30 and 10:30 each morning or it's four scattered half-hour blocks throughout the day; but the average salesperson has more than two hours to spare in their workday.

It only takes about two hours to dial 50 prospects, leave 40 voicemails and speak to 10 people when you're using Assumptive Selling. Your voicemails will be about 30 seconds each (that's 20 minutes) and your conversations (when you use Assumptive Selling) should last no more than 3 minutes each (that's 30 minutes). This leaves you 70 minutes to make all the CRM notes you need for your 50 calls. That's plenty of time.

Do this each day for 20 workdays in the month and you'll easily get your 1,000 calls completed.

Assumptive Selling and the Outbound Call

Assumptive Selling during the outbound call begins before you even pick up the phone. It starts when you see the prospect's name in the CRM. You know (because they submitted a lead or because they're a previous buyer with a three-year-old car) they're going to buy; and they're going to buy today. If they're not, then it's probably not a money call.

If you'll assume you're calling someone who will buy today, your tone and energy on the call will change and the prospect will notice. Moreover, because you're treating them as a buyer, you'll relax and concentrate less on saying the right things and more on listening to the prospect and responding accordingly.

Think about it: during which of the following two calls would a salesperson have the most confidence:

- Cold-calling a Chevy Silverado owner from a list of names your manager bought, and trying to pitch him on a new F-150; or
- Calling a prospect who just submitted a stock-check lead on your website for a new F-150?

Clearly, you'd be more confident making the second call. Of course, if you've been in the sales field for very long, you know that when you're sure someone is not a buyer, you're always right. It's only when you believe you'll close every deal that you'll maximize your success in sales.

The 3 Cs of Phone Skills Mastery

Okay, you want to be confident when you're calling prospects and customers, but you're not sure how to ensure this is always the case. In this section, I'll share what it takes to have enough confidence (one of the 3 Cs you'll learn) to achieve phone skills mastery.

Phone skills mastery, interestingly, is most often the result of individual effort in automotive retail. One of the dirty little secrets in this industry is that most sales managers will not reinforce the expensive phone training your dealer paid for; so, if you want to master the phones, you've got to tackle this yourself. As you'll learn in this section, phone skills mastery is not about reading, memorizing and regurgitating a lot of word tracks. It's about having the competence, confidence and control necessary to pull your prospect through the phone and into your dealership.

The 3 Cs, of course, are Competence (knowing what to say), speaking with Confidence (because you know your prospect is buying today) and always remaining in Control of the call.

With the 3 Cs, it doesn't matter what your actual word tracks are. If you can attack the phone as a competent speaker, with confidence in your abilities, and keep control of the call, you'll win most of the phone "battles" you enter.

Let's start with competence. Competence is the first and the most important of the 3 Cs because it describes how well you know your material. Without strong product knowledge, having a handle on your store's inventory, or knowing the word tracks you want to use, you'll struggle to build enough confidence to keep control during the call.

Competence, you see, drives the other 2 Cs. Just like a public speaker who doesn't know his subject matter, trying to proceed on the phones without competence will make you sound nervous and/or forced – and your customers will hear this in your voice.

Therefore, learn your product, watch your inventory and internalize the word tracks you like and/or have been successful with. Whether these word tracks are provided by a phone skills trainer or something you've developed by yourself over time, you'll want to get good enough to repeat these verbatim at a moment's notice. If you struggle to repeat these when role-playing in the mirror, for example, what will happen if you're put under pressure by a rude prospect? Will you be able to remember and regurgitate the right responses every time? In other words, do you know the material backwards and forwards? That's competence.

This takes practice and there are no shortcuts. There are no pills or magic beans to give you competence. The key to learning the material – and gaining the necessary competence – is practice. Lots and lots of practice. Now, just like an actor learning his lines, you need to practice saying the words over and over again; until they roll off your tongue in your natural voice.

The best way to practice any word tracks you plan to use with prospects is to role play; and to role play every day. I'm not talking about the awkward, semi-formalized and most often worthless role playing that occurs at training classes or in a Saturday morning sales meeting. Those are sometimes too embarrassing to do anything but sink your confidence.

Your role playing will only be effective if it occurs in an environment of your choosing and under your control. It's only in these situations that you'll be attentive and relaxed enough to hear the nuances in the material and to learn to deliver it naturally. For most people, your best role-playing environment is usually one or more of the following:

- With the help of your children. If you have children who are old enough to read, write every possible objection and buying signal a prospect might give you during a call onto note cards; then hand these to your son or daughter. Ask him or her to quiz you with a few of these at around the same time each night (before dinner, after they finish their homework, whatever). You'll be under no pressure to answer correctly every time; no one will be judging you, and you'll have a little fun.

- With the help of a significant other. No kids of reading age? No problem. Just ask your spouse, boyfriend, girlfriend, roommate or parent (if you're still living at home) to try and stump you with the same cards. This audience will be a little tougher on you than a small child, but you'll still be under no pressure. More importantly, you'll start internalizing the word tracks and make them sound like you.

- With the help of your bathroom mirror. Instead of note cards, write buyer objections and questions on sticky notes and frame your mirror with them. Every morning while shaving, brushing your teeth or putting on makeup, read one of these aloud and then respond.

Once you feel you've mastered that objection, take down the sticky note and save it to a pile. After the mirror is completely clear of sticky notes, put them all back up and start over.

The key to competence with product knowledge is to study and experience all the bells and whistles your vehicles offer; the key to competence with your inventory is to walk it every day (or review it online if you're in an offsite BDC); and the key to competence with your word tracks is repetition. Even when you think you have the word tracks memorized, saying them out loud again and again is the only way you'll sound like you on the phone and not like a robot reading a script.

A great thing happens, by the way, when you're competent with the material: You gain confidence

The second of the 3 Cs of phone skills mastery is confidence; though, confidence goes beyond just knowing the material. It's also about understanding that you provide a needed service. Understanding that you are an important part of the buying process and understanding that you are selling a great brand for a great company. Of course, confidence also comes from knowing you're speaking with a buyer who wants to buy from you today.

Moreover, confidence comes from not caring how the customer is going to react when you properly use the word tracks; and from not caring when you occasionally make a mistake. In so many ways, confidence is about not caring what others think of you.

Of course, this doesn't mean that you should become some self-absorbed, egomaniacal jerk or that you should show up for work unshaven, or unbathed in dirty, wrinkled clothes. That's just silly. That's not confidence. See, "not caring" leading to confidence means that you are in control of you and that you're fearless in the knowledge that no one else's actions or opinions are going to dictate how you feel, and no one else's opinions or actions are going to alter your talent.

That is confidence; and without it, your phone calls will fall flat.

The third and final C of phone skills mastery is control. Control can only come after you have a mastery of the material (competence), and a solid belief in your abilities (confidence). To say this point clearly – you cannot stay in control of a phone call unless you know precisely what you are going to say, and you feel good about saying it.

Without the first two Cs, prospects will continue to take you off message as they bleed you for just enough information to eliminate you from their car-buying process. When the prospect keeps control of the call, they can manipulate the salesperson or BDC agent into helping them eliminate your company or product from their consideration set. For the prospect on the phone, this means one less dealer; one less salesperson. When you don't stay in control of the call, you make it easy for buyers to eliminate you and your company.

Conversely, when you keep control of the phone call you are able to guide the prospect down an abbreviated road-to-the-sale that starts with setting a firm appointment that shows. When you are in control, your successful phone calls generally last no longer than three minutes. Your calls should be short; and they will be short when you are in control.

Why Short Phone Calls?

When the bulk of your calls last less than two or three minutes, you'll find most end in an appointment that shows. This, of course, is because you were in control, you proved authenticity and you moved the prospect through your process.

When a dealer hires me to improve their team's phone skills, one of the first things I do is listen to their 11-minute and longer recorded calls in their call management tool. These are the calls that went astray; these are the calls where the salesperson lost control; these are the calls that almost never end in an appointment that shows.

Make no mistake, the prospect is usually quite happy during these calls. Why wouldn't they be? They're getting all their smokescreen questions answered by a very helpful salesperson or BDC agent. In fact, because the salesperson almost never asks for the appointment, the prospect never feels any pressure to act... so they don't. They say, "Thank you; I'll probably stop by on Saturday to see it." Then they hang up and buy somewhere else.

The prospect was in control of the call and you didn't sell a thing. Perhaps your dealership should call the competitor who ended up with the sale and ask if they'll split the deal with you since you did all the work answering the prospect's questions!

When you get into an information exchange on the phone, you're just giving the prospect lots of reasons to eliminate you. This is why you should stay focused on the singular goal of an appointment that shows. Doing so will help you circle back to your goal each time you answer a customer's question.

Maintaining control of the call is the only way to successfully set appointments that show; so, be sure to finish each statement with a word track that strongly asks for the appointment: "I have two test drives open on that vehicle this afternoon. I've got a 2:45 and a 3:15. Which one works better for you?" Failure to circle back to your goal ensures you'll be stuck in the never-ending tennis match of question-answer-question-answer...

You don't get paid for information; and, as I wrote earlier, you'll lose nearly every pre-visit information exchange you find yourself in. If you believe this, then take a moment and write "I don't get paid for information" on a sticky note and put this near your phone (lots of salespeople need this reminder today).

The 5 Types of Calls

With today's connected customer, there really are only a few types of outbound phone calls you will find yourself involved with. Gone are the days of cold-calling from the White Pages and asking, "Are you or any of your friends currently in the market for a new or pre-owned vehicle?"

Today's customer, whether a millennial or a baby boomer, has already done their research; they've completed their needs analysis; they've completed their product selection; they've completed their feature presentation. Now, they just need someone to sell them a car!

But, what they don't need is a salesman. Because the prospect who submitted a sales lead (we'll discuss outbound calls to our database customers in another chapter) already knows everything about your inventory, they're really just trying to find an easy way to buy. They don't want to be sold and they don't want to have to answer a lot of irrelevant questions. (They just want to get through this hassle called "car buying" with as few bruises as possible.)

Given this, let's look at the five most common types of calls you'll find yourself in when making outbound sales calls.

1: The Negotiation. Let's say you sell Nissans and you have a lead from a prospect located 60 miles away asking about your lowest price on a new, mid-level Altima. This, of course, is a vehicle he can get from any Nissan dealer in the county, including from any of the four other Nissan dealers closer to his home.

When you get him on the phone, he wants his "out-the-door number," which includes his payments, his interest rate and his trade-in value. He's willing to jump through all the hoops you need, including completing a credit application online. He just needs you to put the whole deal together, so he can decide if it's worth driving more than an hour to come buy from you.

Relax... because he's never buying from you. This is best handled as a "bury the dead" situation; I know, because I've seen this movie more than a few times.

This guy (we'll call him Bob) wants hard numbers from you so that he can hold his local Nissan dealer hostage. He wants you to do all the work, so he can reap the rewards of the lowest price. He has no intention of driving 60 miles to buy from you... ever.

Building his deal (assuming you don't just send him to your online buying application) can sometimes take 2+ man-hours. You're going to have to pull credit for someone who claims to be Bob and has Bob's Social Security Number. Your manager is going to put a firm number on a trade sight unseen. You're doing all the work and taking all the risk. And, you're doing all of this because Bob claims he wants to buy from you.

Remember: He's never going to buy from you.

"But, Steve," you exclaim, "We sold a guy like that just last month!"

Okay, perhaps never was too strong a word. Yes, you do occasionally sell this guy Bob a car – my estimation is dealers sell about one in every hundred. At 2 hours per deal, that's 200 hours of building deals to sell one car. Hmm, sounds like a colossal waste of time. What's more, is that the only reason you sold Bob last month was because the deal you built was such a complete loser that the other four Nissan dealers passed on it. So, answer these questions for me:

- Did the dealership make any money on the deal?
- Did you earn a good commission?
- Is this customer going to service with the dealership?
- Did the customer give you a perfect score on the OEM survey?

If, like me, you've seen this movie before, then you know how this one ends. The answers are no, no, no, and what do you think?

An important rule we learned earlier is that you cannot sell an empty seat. You will not win if the outbound call turns into an information exchange and you will not win if it turns into a negotiation. Your only goal when you have someone on the phone is an appointment that shows.

When you find yourself on the phone with a guy who wants to negotiate the entire deal before coming in, everyone involved needs to agree that he's probably never coming in. You need to agree that he's just using you as leverage against his local dealer. (Heck, he might even be calling you from that dealer's showroom.) The only way to get this customer in the door is to (A) be willing to lose way more money than your competitor; or (B) call his bluff (by burying the dead).

Understand this: if you're pricing your vehicles at or near the expected selling price, the guy who's still trying to negotiate the deal over the phone isn't planning to buy from you – he just wants to see if there's another $300 he can squeeze from your competition. You've given him a good price (or your online price already reflects this); your price is based on the market (it's competitive); and this guy still wants a few hundred dollars off that before he'll come buy it from you? Hmmm…

Again, he's never coming in to see you. If he was serious about buying the Altima, he could use your website's online buying application (if you have one) or go to any number of sites to get a firm price from any number of dealers. He's trying to get the perfect deal in writing, so he can force your competition to match it. Given this, I choose to (B) call his bluff over (A) be willing to lose way more money than our competitor.

You need to call his bluff with the "bury the dead" technique we learned earlier. With sales, when you bury the dead, you're moving on from a deal that you cannot win. Sometimes this might be a totally non-responsive prospect, or it might be Bob trying to squeeze you so he can squeeze your competition.

You know this guy isn't going to buy from you unless your price is so low that you lose more money than you can afford to lose. Then, he's going to crush you on CSI and he's never going to service with you! So, you need to stop negotiating over the phone.

To ensure you don't bury the dead too soon, you're going to ensure you give Bob your best price (one you can live with); but, when he wants a firm trade-in number, interest rate and the rest of the out-the-door numbers, it's time to call his bluff. It's time to say:

Salesperson: "Bob, I can guarantee you the very best deal on that new Altima and here's how. At ABC Motors we will never be beat on price. What I need you to do is get your best written offer locally. Then, I need you to call me and schedule an appointment. If you'll bring us a valid written offer that we cannot meet or beat on an in-stock unit, we'll fill your tank with gas and we'll give you a $100 gift card to the Olive Garden. How's that sound?"

The proof that he never intended to buy from you comes when he still tries for a written offer from you after you've called his bluff. Move on. Beyond saving you time with a non-buyer, when you bury the dead you drive more sales than when you capitulate and negotiate the deal over the phone. Why? Because the Bobs of the world will often want to call your bluff (after you bury the dead) and bring you their best local offer.

This is great news because someone else did all the work and all you have to do (provided it's a valid written offer and you have an in-stock unit) is match their deal. You'll never have to fill Bob's tank or give him an Olive Garden gift card.

There are, however, exceptions to my "no negotiations rule over the phone" that are important to note. The first exception is the trade value we already discussed on pages 158-159. The other exception is the Batmobile.

When you have a Batmobile – let's say a 10-year-old minivan with 53,000 miles on it – you're going to get calls from people 500 miles away because they just can't get a vehicle that nice, in that price range, in their local market. For these prospects, I will gladly work the deal over the phone, provided they give me a credit card deposit once we agree on the numbers. Why? Because there's only one Batmobile and I have it on my lot – and, I can ask for all the money.

2: Selling the Car. Just like negotiating the deal over the phone, trying to sell the car over the phone is a loser. What's worse, is that if you find yourself in this situation, it's because you put yourself there. Selling the car over the phone is a self-inflicted wound.

You called your prospect to schedule a VIP Appointment, the prospect asked a simple question and you went into full-on, ninja-warrior-salesman-of-the-year mode. You told them why this vehicle is a great car; why it's perfect for them; why it's a great deal; why it's smart to buy now; and why buying from you makes sense. You even asked them lots of old-school road-to-the-sale questions about body style, price, and colors. Ugh.

No customer today is hoping you will sell them over the phone. In fact, the primary reason they submitted a sales lead is they want to avoid sales pressure. Selling over the phone is a losing proposition with today's buyers. You cannot sell the car over the phone and no one wants you to.

The customer was just trying to buy the car, and they disguised it by acting as if they were looking for some more information (inquiring, see below) and you went into overdrive on them by asking them something completely ridiculous like, "Are there any colors you wouldn't consider?" You lost this one as soon as you started speaking, Champ.

You cannot sell an empty seat; so, never ever try to sell the car over the phone!

3: Inquiring. Often, prospects submitting sales leads to your dealership will indicate they're just looking for some information. When you get them on the phone, they'll say they have questions that need to be answered before they'll decide whether they'll buy this vehicle or something else. I call this an inquiring call; though for this type of call, you must understand that their inquiry is often a smokescreen. They found value and relevancy, and now they're looking for authenticity.

An inquiring call is an opportunity to sell a car. For the assumptive seller, an inquiring call is an opportunity to sell a car today.

Does it have third-row seats? Is it an automatic? Is that a tear I see in the picture of the back seat? They are ready to buy and all you need to do is answer their question in an authentic manner *and* ask for the appointment in the same breath:

Salesperson: "Yes, that vehicle does have third-row seats, and at the price we have it listed for, it will likely not make it through to the weekend. Now, I do have two test drives open on that vehicle this morning, I have a 10:15 and a 10:45; which of those works best for you?"

Handling your outbound calls is not rocket science. Answer the question and ask for the appointment.

4: Validation. There are two questions that might sound like an inquiry but are strong buying signals that I call validation calls. When your prospect is trying to validate either price or availability, they're telling you that they are ready to buy right now; so, please help them do this!

Your outbound calls often become validation calls when you're priced-to-market – they just want to be sure that's the real price and/or that the vehicle is really on your lot. There's no need for salesmanship here, just authenticity via an acceptable, affirmative answer that also asks for the appointment. Therefore, for the "Is that your best price?" validation question, you'll want to answer with something similar to what I introduced earlier:

Salesperson: "If you've been shopping online, then you know we price all of our vehicles competitively right from the beginning. We would never dream of insulting our customers by showing you our second-best price and then making you jump through a bunch of hoops to find some hidden best price. That pre-owned Camry is priced-to-sell at $15,399 and it will likely not be on our lot much longer at that price. Now, I do have two test drives open on that Camry this morning, I have a 10:15 and a 10:45, which one of those works better for you?"

To be very clear: almost no one submits a lead, calls or visits your dealership these days when you're overpriced. They want this vehicle at the price you have it listed for; you just need to be strong enough to defend the price and set the appointment.

5: Scheduling. This type of call is the proverbial "lay down" and the last thing you need here is to screw this up by showing off your salesmanship or trying to over-qualify a prospect before they ever set for on your lot. The scheduling call comes after they have all the information and now they just want a test drive that's convenient for them. They completed your "Schedule a Test Drive" form on your website, so this call is just a confirmation of that – do not fall for the temptation to try to gather as much info as possible; just confirm the appointment.

You'll win the scheduling call every time if you stick to the script. That is, if you simply confirm the vehicle and the date/time of the appointment. You can include a brief statement about what the customer might expect when they arrive; but, if you start interrogating them about this purchase over the phone, you will lose them. (We'll discuss appointment confirmations in more detail in the chapter covering "The Perfect Appointment.")

A prospect is trying to schedule a test drive; and, it's not important (at this time) to know if they have a trade. It's not important (at this time) to know their price range. It's not important (at this time) to know why they like your car. However, asking these questions on the phone of someone who used your online form to schedule a test drive could kill your deal before it ever even started. Instead, stick to a basic appointment confirmation word track on this call:

Salesperson: "This is Steve Stauning with ABC Motors and I wanted to call and thank you for considering us. I'm just confirming that we're going to have your Subaru Outback cleaned, gassed and parked out front so that when you arrive for your 3:30 test drive, you'll be in and out and on the road within five minutes. Now, if anything changes on our end, we're going to be sure and call you well in advance so that you don't waste a trip down here. I'm hopeful you can do the same for us. So, can we count on seeing you today at 3:30?"

That's it. No qualifying, no needs analysis, no rapport building. Just a to-the-point call – the kind today's customers want.

Connecting with Your Internet Leads

The most common type of outbound call originating from the average dealership is the call to an internet prospect. Most of these calls end in the voicemails we covered in the last chapter, though because you can expect to connect with 70-80% of these buyers eventually, you should be prepared with a strong word track that converts this prospect into an appointment that shows.

The key on this call – as with all two-way communications with customers and prospects – is to take charge, be direct and guide the prospect down your path. For example, imagine you're dialing a prospect who submitted a web lead on a 2019 Honda Ridgeline:

Prospect: "This is Barbara."

Salesperson: "Hi Barbara, this is Steve Stauning with ABC Motors. Did I catch you at a bad time?"

Let's stop and examine this call so far. Some readers will object to my saying, "Did I catch you at a bad time," because you want to avoid the word "bad" and ask, "Is now a good time?" That's your call; you should go with what makes you comfortable here because we're not going to listen to what our prospect says at this point anyway.

Just be sure to avoid unnecessary greetings when making this call. The buyer submitted a web lead because they want to buy a car, not talk about how they're feeling. Besides, they're feeling great! Why? Because they're buying a Ridgeline from you today, that's why!

Some readers will wonder why I didn't tell Barbara why I was calling, as their standard greeting to an internet prospect goes something like this:

Typical Salesperson: "Hi Barbara, this is Joe Salesman calling from ABC Motors, family-owned and operated for over 72 years and home of the lifetime free oil change. I'm calling about your internet inquiry on the 2019 Honda Ridgeline. Is now a good time to talk?"

If you're thinking, "What's wrong with that?" then you don't understand today's buyer. They want you to get to the point and they're not interested in hearing your store's entire history and resume. They found value and relevancy in that 2019 Ridgeline, and they're just trying to find an easy way to buy it. So far, you're proving this is not going to be easy.

"Well, at least we tell her why we're calling in the second example," you retort.

She already knows why you're calling! She "ordered" the 2019 Ridgeline from ABC Motors! Assumptive Selling gives you the confidence your buyer is looking for over the phone. She needs authenticity and someone to pull her through the phone and into a new Ridgeline. Treating her like a buyer from the very first encounter is the cornerstone of Assumptive Selling. Besides, if she doesn't know why you're calling, she'll ask you:

Prospect: "What is this about?"

Salesperson: "I'm just calling to schedule your priority test drive on the 2019 Honda Ridgeline you selected on our website. Now we have two priority test drives open on that truck this morning; we have a 10:15 and a 10:45, which one of these works better for you?"

You have one goal when you have a prospect on the phone, and that's an appointment that shows. Being direct, taking charge and guiding prospects toward the appointment immediately will more than double the average salesperson's total legitimate shows from their internet leads and calls.

"Okay, but what if it's not a good time to talk right now?" you ask.

Great question! First, let's walk through this conversation and handle it like a typical salesperson:

Typical Salesperson: "Hi Barbara, this is Joe Salesman calling from ABC Motors, family-owned and operated for over 72 years and home of the lifetime free oil change. I'm calling about your internet inquiry on the 2019 Honda Ridgeline. Is now a good time to talk?"

Prospect: "I'm headed to a meeting and can't talk right now."

Typical Salesperson: "Oh, I'm sorry Barbara; I didn't mean to bother you before a meeting. Is there a better time to call you back?"

Prospect: "Sure. Can you call me on Monday around this same time?"

Typical Salesperson: "Great. I'll call you Monday around 9:00 a.m. At this same number?"

Prospect: "Yes."

Typical Salesperson: "Great. I'll call you at this number around nine on Monday. Have a great weekend."

Prospect: "You too."

Ugh. Do you see how long this takes when you don't assume the sale? When you don't take charge? When you don't guide the prospect down your path? Your goal is not to get a better time to call her back; your goal is to set an appointment that shows!

Besides, when does this typical salesperson now have permission to call Barbara back? Yep, Monday at 9:00 a.m.

What's going to happen between now and Monday? Yep, she's going to buy from one of your competitors. Likely from a competitor who took charge, was direct and guided her through their buying process. Instead of being weak and getting a better time to call her back, stick to your goal of an appointment that shows:

Salesperson: "Hi Barbara, this is Steve Stauning with ABC Motors. Did I catch you at a bad time?"

Prospect: "I'm headed to a meeting and can't talk right now."

Salesperson: "Great, I understand. I'm just calling to schedule your priority test drive on the 2019 Honda Ridgeline you selected on our website. Now we have two priority test drives open on that truck this morning; we have a 10:15 and a 10:45, which one of these works better for you?"

Assumptive Selling takes much less time to inform the prospect of your goal than the weak talk tracks of the past. Though, I know what you're thinking. You're thinking, "She doesn't have time to talk right now!"

Although that's not your concern, the Assumptive Selling talk track took much less time than the weak talk track. Also, it's not that you don't care if she has the time to talk; it's that Assumptive Selling tells you she's a buyer who needs your help. Nearly every objection, question and delay tactic she uses is just a smokescreen. She's afraid of salespeople and needs your help to buy her new Ridgeline.

You will be absolutely shocked at how many prospects stay engaged at this point with responses like:

- "Do you have anything around lunchtime?"
- "I don't get off work until five."
- "I can't today; do you have something open tomorrow?"

It is rare that the internet prospect will simply disengage at this point, but let's examine what that might look like:

Prospect: "I'm headed to a meeting and can't talk right now."

Salesperson: "Great, I understand. I'm just calling to schedule your priority test drive on the 2019 Honda Ridgeline you selected on our website. Now we have two priority test drives open on that truck this morning…"

Prospect: "I said I can't talk!" (CLICK!)

When does this salesperson have permission to call the prospect back? Right away! (Though, I would give her an hour to get through her meeting before I called back.)

While the typical salesperson was given a better day and time to call back (and thus Barbara rewarded the sale to a competitor); those using Assumptive Selling may call back whenever they choose, take charge, be direct and guide the prospect in for an appointment that shows.

Don't be afraid of taking charge and being direct on your outbound sales calls; it's the authenticity today's buyer wants from you.

14

ASSUMPTIVE SELLING AND YOUR DATABASE

Chapter Note: *Just a quick reminder on the direction and verbiage for calls anywhere in this book: the same basic structure and goals apply whether these conversations are via phone, text, chat, email or Messenger. All two-way communications are treated the same and have the same overriding goal: an appointment that shows.*

There are plenty of names given to the efforts to sell to your database of customers, so I understand if you can be confused when someone discusses these in your dealership. The four most popular names for this effort are Database Marketing, Owner Marketing, Equity Mining, and Post-Sale Follow-Up; and all four mean pretty much the same thing: reengaging and selling to your previous customers. (In fact, I may use them interchangeably throughout this chapter.)

In this chapter, I'm going to teach you how using Assumptive Selling techniques will help you close more of these deals while also avoiding many of the pitfalls that traditional database selling efforts seem to encounter far too often.

For your dealership's database marketing efforts, you might be leveraging one of a plethora of third parties who provide software that helps identify potential in-market customers and scripts designed to get them to visit the store. If these efforts are genuinely successful for you over the medium and long term, then keep at it. However, if you're experiencing any of the following, you may want to rethink how you attack your database:

- Angry customers who tell your team to "stop calling or else!"
- Data from these calls entered in the third-party tool, but never in your CRM.
- Low number of appointment shows relative to the efforts exerted.

- Low number of closed deals relative to the number of shows.

Unfortunately, for most of the dealers I work with who are using third-party software in an effort to mine their database, the results are mixed, at best. The typical lifecycle of these efforts goes like this:

1. Equity mining software is installed, and it finds the low-hanging fruit.
2. The dealership enjoys a quick boost of great results because the best prospects are identified first.
3. After a few months, the results begin to lag; and the team has to work harder to produce less.
4. Your team starts making more calls, more often.
5. Customers begin hanging up on your team and/or demanding that they stop calling.
6. Your database of formally loyal customers is all but destroyed.

Your database, you see, is the proverbial goose that lays the golden eggs. Lopping it's head off and looking for all the eggs at once won't work. If you're beginning to see the previously great results fade, you may need to change course before you destroy your dealership's most valuable asset: your database of customers.

What's most interesting to me is that dealers pay a third party to identify prospective buyers in their database instead of following a simple post-sale follow-up process that prompts the salesperson to reengage a customer on a planned schedule. In fact, a free process I've taught for years prompts you to contact your database (via your CRM) on a schedule that doesn't feel like you're spamming everyone. Additionally, the talk tracks (which I'll include here) have a friendlier, less salesy feel than what many of the third parties provide you.

For nearly all dealers there is a need to change the thinking when it comes to database marketing. That is, we need a paradigm shift in automotive retail if we expect these efforts to be successful over the long term.

Currently, most dealers look at their database marketing activities as a way to "squeeze out some deals;" instead of thinking of these efforts as long-term owner loyalty drivers. As I wrote, your database is the proverbial goose that lays the golden eggs; so, if you want to enjoy long-term success from using it, then you have to treat it with care.

Your goal with your database and your equity mining should be to create loyal customers for life, not to just squeeze out some deals. Therefore, before you try Assumptive Selling your database, it's important to review your current database marketing efforts. This means taking an honest assessment of the results-to-date to determine whether or not these efforts have a goal beyond squeezing out a few deals.

Squeezing Out Some Deals

To be clear, when we talk about squeezing out some deals, there are some (initially) good results. This is what makes the sales pitch from the equity mining vendors seem so genuine. Your first few months at virtually any database marketing effort drives sales. You get immediate gains – which are welcomed – but your efforts usually turn desperate because your impact is generally short term, and you eventually exhaust the low-hanging fruit in your database. Then, your team starts to annoy once-loyal customers.

I listened to one customer call a dealership where they'd previously purchased five vehicles. The guy was angry, and he told the general manager, "If you ever call here again, I'm calling the police. This is harassment!"

Why would you do that to your customer base? Your goal has got to be to create customers for life.

Interestingly, when you follow the right processes, you still get immediate gains. However, because your efforts are purposeful and highly targeted (and sane), you can use the strategy forever because it's sustainable and it's appreciated by your database. The keywords in that last sentence are purposeful, highly targeted, strategy, sustainable and appreciated.

Whether you use the Assumptive Selling methods I'll share in this chapter or something your equity mining vendor suggests, you need to have a clear strategy that's purposeful (to you and your customers), highly targeted, sustainable over time and appreciated by your customers.

I quoted a study earlier in this book that revealed it costs companies five times more to acquire a new customer than to keep an existing one. This makes database marketing a critical component to holding market share without breaking the bank.

Database Loyalty Management

First, let's change the name of these efforts. Instead of equity mining or database marketing, let's call what you do in your dealership "Database Loyalty Management," or DLM for short. This will help define the strategy and limit the tactics your team employs to only those that drive long-term customer loyalty. Focusing on long-term loyalty eliminates the angry calls to your GM from frustrated former customers.

When writing the strategy for these efforts, you'll want to be sure that your team is only tasked with money calls and that everyone understands email is not free.

There is a misconception in some dealerships that blasting the entire database with a "buy now" message is somehow a free event. That it costs you nothing because… well, email is free. It's not. Sending an email to a prospect or customer that provides no value to the recipient can cost you dearly. The customer can unsubscribe from your emails – eliminating your chances of marketing to them via email in the future – or (as we learned earlier) they can simply put you in their junk folder.

When enough users of a given email service (like Gmail or Yahoo or Hotmail, etc.) put you into their spam or junk folders, that service tags all your emails as spam. This costs you when you're trying to communicate with a new lead or send important information to an existing customer.

I once sat in front of an executive with a large group who held eighteen emails a former customer printed and sent to him. The customer received all eighteen in a single month from one of the group's stores. Why did the store send eighteen emails in one month? There were a couple of reasons:

1. Everyone believed "emails are free."
2. Everyone believed they were the only ones sending blast emails.

During the month, this former customer received:

• Five emails from the internet manager, who was sending one email every Monday to all internet prospects, as well as sold and serviced customers in the database. These emails usually contained generic vehicle specials.

• Two emails from the GSM, who thought of himself as a digital marketing guru. The emails were sent every couple of weeks and contained a PDF of the dealership's newspaper ad.

• Six emails from the dealership's two service marketing vendors. To be clear, the dealership didn't realize they were paying two companies to do the same thing! That said, the four emails Vendor A sent provided the same value to this customer as the two emails from Vendor B: zero.

• One email that was a worthless newsletter that truly no customer cared about or read.

• Four emails from the dealership's primary ad agency. These were super slick pieces that would look great in a magazine but didn't render properly as an email on a mobile device. Moreover, they used a ton of ink when the former customer printed them to send to the group's executive.

While eighteen emails in a single month is an extreme example, it illustrates what can happen when departments and vendors don't communicate about their marketing efforts; and when everyone assumes email is free. The solution, of course, is to assign one manager to oversee all email marketing efforts. This person is the sole decider on what is sent in bulk to any portion of the database. The rule is simply written so that any email that is not a direct response to a customer or prospect, or not part of an existing CRM-driven process, must be pre-approved by this manager.

This eighteen-email example brings up an interesting debate about how many emails is too many. My answer is that even one email a month is too many if it doesn't provide value to the recipient.

Beyond ensuring your emails provide value, the manager in charge of these efforts should also ensure that any bulk emails she approves do not have the potential to overwhelm your team.

In the "Communicating with Today's Ups" chapter, I gave the example of sending 10,000 "we want your trade" emails all at once. If 300 customers responded to this offer, your team would be overwhelmed, and you'd turn a potentially lucrative situation into a bad customer experience for everyone. Therefore, whether it's a sales or service email, check for the respective team's capacity to manage the potential outcome before sending.

Finally, don't wait for your customers' loyalty to be tested. This is a mistake that some dealers commit when they don't conduct any targeted database marketing or equity mining. About half of those in your database don't know they can upgrade their vehicle before their loan is paid off or their lease expires; while most customers would upgrade about every three years if they knew they could. So, whether you use the Assumptive Selling methods for database loyalty management or you use an outside vendor for equity mining, it's critical that you do something to alert your customers that they can indeed trade-in ahead of lease or loan expirations.

Using DLM to Set & Sell Owner Marketing Appointments

With Assumptive Selling and a decent CRM, many dealers can properly target and attack their sold database in a way that provides value to the customer and increases their repeat business. The key is setting up a post-sale follow-up process filled with only money calls and purposeful emails. First, I have a few questions:

- Do you get paid for referrals? Great! We'll put in a couple of referral requests.
- Do you get paid for perfect surveys? Excellent! We'll make sure a message about the OEM survey is included in our process.
- Do you get paid to "touch base?" No? Okay then, no garbage activities like that will be included.
- Do you get paid when a repeat customer buys from you? Fantastic! We'll be sure to include activities that drive that.

Based on your answers to the above questions, I put together a quick post-sale follow-up process you can add to your CRM to improve your DLM efforts (and grow your sales from previous customers):

Stauning's Forever Post-Sale Follow-Up Process

This process has a few goals: Early on, the goals are to (1) gain referral business; (2) set the first Service Appointment (if the purchase was a new vehicle or a used vehicle your service team wants to service); and (3) ensure a Perfect CSI Survey (if the purchase was a new or certified pre-owned vehicle).

After 25 months, the goals are two-fold: (1) to make a reconnection; and (2) to set a firm appointment that shows. Once a reconnection is made, the automated and other future activities in the process should be discontinued, as the salesperson should manually create the next scheduled activity (appointment; call back; etc.).

To be clear, you should set the first "Can we buy back your vehicle" calls appropriately based on the situation. For example, if the customer paid cash for a used car, then you may want to begin this process 12 or

18 months after purchase. Conversely, if the customer took out an 84-month loan on a new car, then you may want to delay the start of these calls until 36 or 48 months after purchase.

If, during any of the calls, the customer indicates they sold or no longer own the vehicle they purchased from you, update the records and change the customer status and future process accordingly (bought elsewhere, etc.).

Each letter in the process can be replaced by an email where the dealership has the correct email address on file; however, don't discount the power of snail mail to cut through the clutter and drive a sale.

This process contains no text messages. Texting your prior customers without already establishing a reconnection (at least as of this writing) seems too intrusive for someone living in an Assumptive Selling environment.

Finally, this process is created to trigger the activities on the days since purchased. For example, where you read Day 1, this is the day after purchase; Day 365 is the anniversary of the purchase, etc. The process activities below are listed as "Day Required – Type of Activity – Who is Responsible – Message or Goal".

- Birthday – Physical Card – Salesperson – Happy Birthday!
- Holiday(s) – Physical Card – Salesperson – Happy Whatever! (Choose the holidays appropriate for your customer, your market or you.)
- Day 1 – Phone Call – Salesperson – Thank you; I'm here to serve you
- Day 2 – Physical Letter – Salesperson – Thank you and referral request
- Day 7 – Phone Call – Salesperson – CSI request
- Day 90 – Phone Call – Salesperson – Set first service appointment
- Day 120 – Physical Letter – Salesperson – Referral request with a reminder about referral bonus paid (if any)
- Day 180 – Phone Call – Salesperson – Anything else in the garage? Can we appraise it?
- Day 270 – Physical Letter – Salesperson – Anything else in the garage? Can we appraise it?
- Day 365 – Physical Card – Salesperson – Happy Anniversary! Can I be of assistance?

- Day 730 – Physical Card – Salesperson – Happy Anniversary! Can I be of assistance?
- Day 760 – Physical Letter – Salesperson – Can we buy back your vehicle?
- Day 762 – Phone Call – Salesperson – Can we buy back your vehicle? - If voicemail is reached, leave a message and schedule the following call
  - Day 764 – Phone Call – Salesperson – Can we buy back your vehicle? - If voicemail is reached, leave a message and schedule the following call
  - Day 766 – Phone Call – Salesperson – Can we buy back your vehicle? - If voicemail is reached, leave a message and schedule the following call
  - Day 768 – Phone Call – Salesperson – Can we buy back your vehicle? - If voicemail is reached, leave a message and schedule the following call
  - Day 770 – Phone Call – Salesperson – Can we buy back your vehicle? - If voicemail is reached, leave a final message. The next call should already be in the process scheduled for about six months later.
- Day 940 – Physical Letter – Salesperson – Can we buy back your vehicle?
- Day 942 – Phone Call – Salesperson – Can we buy back your vehicle? - If voicemail is reached, leave a message and schedule the following call
  - Day 944 – Phone Call – Salesperson – Can we buy back your vehicle? - If voicemail is reached, leave a message and schedule the following call
  - Day 946 – Phone Call – Salesperson – Can we buy back your vehicle? - If voicemail is reached, leave a message and schedule the following call
  - Day 948 – Phone Call – Salesperson – Can we buy back your vehicle? - If voicemail is reached, leave a message and schedule the following call
  - Day 950 – Phone Call – Salesperson – Can we buy back your vehicle? - If voicemail is reached, leave a final message. The next call should already be in the process scheduled for about six months later.

Rather than take this process through the next ten years, just do the math yourself to set all the appropriate birthday, holiday, anniversary and "Can we buy back your vehicle" reminders in your CRM.

To be clear, the reason the salesperson should want to set the first service appointment with the customer – even though it appears that it's not a money call – is to ensure the customer services their vehicle with you. When they do – provided they always have a good experience – they're more likely to purchase from you the next time.

I'll provide some of the templates and word tracks for this process later in the chapter; but, it's important to stress now that when you're calling to purchase a customer's vehicle, your goal is still an appointment that shows. It's not to sell them something new – not yet. You first need to get a butt in the seat in front of you if you expect to sell your previous customers a new vehicle.

Of course, the common pushback I get on this from seasoned salespeople is, "Why should I want appointments? Why can't I just encourage my previous customers to be sure and ask for me?"

Because they won't... not anymore. If you call your previous customers today; get them excited about trading in their vehicle on something new (but fail to set an appointment), chances are they'll want to shop around first. They'll shop your competition to simply "gather information;" then, they'll run into a salesman and they'll never get a chance to come see you. You must set a firm appointment that shows; because, as you know, you cannot sell an empty seat.

Plus, if the appointment you set is for today, you greatly reduce any chance they can shop around before coming to see you.

In the past, top sellers could count on many of their customers returning when it was time to upgrade their vehicle. Today, however, consumers have too many choices and too many places to gather information about competing brands. Additionally, brand loyalty has decreased over the years. This means dealership loyalty has decreased (as has salesperson loyalty). Consumers just aren't that loyal anymore.

Finally, even if they are brand loyal, this doesn't guarantee they won't shop online to find the best price first; and, if you're not the dealership with the lowest advertised prices, there's almost zero chance they're going to buy from you.

Unless, of course, you ask them to. Unless, of course, you ask them before they catch new car fever on their own. This is the reason owner marketing exists; it gives you a chance to inject your previous customers with new car fever long before they imagined replacing their current vehicle. Without a robust owner marketing (post-sale follow-up) process in place, you're at the mercy of your customers' whims, the market conditions and your competitors' pricing.

Appointments Are Everything

With your previous customers, appointments are everything. If you fail to get the appointment, you're lucky to get the sale. If you get nothing else out of this chapter, I want you to understand that relying on your previous customers to walk off the Up Bus and onto your lot all by themselves is a foolish wish for today's connected buyers: if you fail to get the appointment, you're lucky to get the sale.

Even if your previous customers are 100% loyal to only you, you cannot allow them to catch new car fever on their own. That is, not if you want to earn better grosses. When a customer catches new car fever, she visits sites like KBB.com (to find out what her trade-in is worth); she visits sites like TrueCar.com (to find out what she should pay for your car). She does all the pre-work that takes all of the gross (and sales commission) out of your deal. Some consumers even pre-arrange their financing; removing all the back-end gross your dealership was counting on to make a few bucks on the deal.

Appointments, you see, are everything. That said, even if the efforts in this process don't result in an appointment, don't fear. Given that all the communications are personalized to and have value for the customer, you'll likely be on the top of their minds when they do start the car-shopping process. This means you might still salvage a sale; though the grosses will be lower than if you were the one who injected them with new car fever and set an appointment that showed.

More than just better grosses, appointments that show on time close at higher rates than Traditional Ups. For the dealers I work with, a purposeful, targeted owner marketing campaign that nets an appointment sees that appointment close two to three times better than a Traditional Up. A previous customer who shows up without an appointment is, for all intents and purposes, a Traditional Up. They're a Traditional Up because you cannot prepare for their visit, you cannot guarantee they'll be greeted properly and by the right person, and you have no idea what prompted their visit.

If I was selling cars today, I wouldn't want to take Traditional Ups. Rather, I'd prefer to work a database of 2,000 to 3,000 orphaned owners and set owner marketing appointments with this group. I would be in control of my day. I could plan my week; and I would enjoy closing rates, grosses and CSI at rates much higher than those managing mostly Traditional Ups. Additionally, my deals would take less than 90 minutes from beginning to end, because I would employ The Perfect Appointment (something you'll learn in a later chapter) with each customer.

When a customer asked me on the phone what time we close, I'd say, "We close at nine, but our last appraisal time on trucks is 7:45. Now I have a 7:15 and a 7:45, which one of these works better for you?"

You see, while those handing mostly Traditional Ups might land a prospect at 8:45 and be at the dealership until midnight, I can ensure my owner marketing customers show up early enough for me to complete a deal before closing time. This is better for me, it's better for the managers, and it's better for the customer.

The beauty of owner marketing efforts is that they don't have to be your previous customers to be included in your targeted list. Lots of customers in every dealer's database bought their vehicles somewhere else (and they service with you); and still more bought from your dealership, though their salesperson has moved up or out. These are now orphaned owners; and in many dealerships, there are no salespeople actively working this lucrative database.

If you're relatively new to your dealership, I recommend you put this book down and walk up to the owner, general manager or sales manager and say, "I'd like to start making owner marketing calls, but I'll need a database of 4,000 to 5,000 orphaned owners moved into my name to do this. Can you help me with this?"

I would be surprised if the owner or manager who hears this doesn't get teary-eyed at the idea that one of his salespeople actually wants to make phone calls. He's heard about salespeople like you, but he always believed you were a myth created to give false hope to managers everywhere. He'll probably reach out and lightly touch your face just to make sure you're not a mirage.

In all seriousness, you can expect to get anywhere from 50 to 5,000 orphans in your name just by asking. (Some managers won't believe you'll make the calls from this chapter, so they'll want to start you off with 50 orphaned owners as a test. Once you show success with these, they'll move more customers into your database.)

The Biggest Secret to Setting Appointments

There is a secret to setting appointments that apparently most in the car business haven't heard. That is, you have to *ask* for the appointment. Today's prospects – including previous customers that we've just called out of the blue – need to be told what to do. No one knows you want them to set an appointment – or that an appointment represents a better way to buy a car – unless you ask them for this.

"But Steve," you exclaim, "I always ask for the appointment!"

No, you don't. If you're a typical salesperson or BDC agent, you say things like "When would you like to come in?" As we already learned, this removes all urgency from your efforts and, more importantly, greatly reduces the chance they'll show even if the prospect chooses a day and time.

Here's another secret about appointments: people are more likely to keep their appointments when you offer the date and time than when they choose their own. Why? Because when a business, including a car dealer, selects the date and time, it feels more like the strict definition of a real appointment to a customer. When a customer is allowed to pick their own date and time, they consider showing up as a courtesy, not a requirement.

Appointments that show, at least as of this writing, are easier to set over the phone than via text, chat or email. While overall text and chat appointment percentages (for sets and shows) are increasing, the phone is still king. When you're speaking with someone over the phone, you're better able to pick up on the tone of the customer and you're much less likely to make mistakes; and the prospect is much less likely to misinterpret your meaning.

Most of the Assumptive Selling word tracks used in this book are quite direct. Over text, these could be misinterpreted as being cold or uncaring. It's important, then, to adjust the phone responses you learn here to other mediums like text, chat and email in ways that properly convey your message. Again, this is why speaking with the prospect over the phone is king.

The best way to ensure success with your owner marketing efforts is to sit at your desk with your CRM open. Walking around outside on your mobile phone might feel freeing; however, having quick access to customer information keeps you better focused. Preferably, you're wearing a headset when talking to customers, as this allows your hands to be free to make notes directly into the customer's record in the CRM. (Hands-free calling is especially important for those of us who talk with our hands.)

The Basic Owner Marketing Word Track

If you know the customer's equity position and that you can keep them at the same or similar payment, you should lead with that. However, when you're unsure whether a customer is in a positive equity position with their current vehicle or if moving them to a new vehicle can keep them at or near their current payment, it's best to stick to a simple, proven word track. The basic Assumptive Selling word track for owner marketing calls is focused on a simple, "... I have a buyer and an immediate need..."

Here's a sample call:

Customer: "Hello?"

Salesperson: "Good morning. This is Steve with ABC Motors and I'm looking for Robert Jones?"

Customer: "This is he."

Salesperson: "Hi Mr. Jones, again I'm Steve with ABC Motors and this may sound a little strange, but my general manager wanted me to call you today because we have a buyer and an immediate need for a 2016 Cherokee configured like yours. Now, I don't know if you'd consider selling it or not, but we do have two appraisal times open on Cherokees this afternoon. We've got a 12:15 and a 12:45, would either of those work for you?"

Yes, this word track cuts right to the chase, doesn't it? That's the idea! Most of the customers today don't want lots of back-and-forth with someone at your dealership (no offense); moreover, our only goal when we have someone on the phone is an appointment that shows.

Let's quickly dissect the word track so you'll have a clear understanding of why I recommend this:

- "... this may sound a little strange..." – Calling a previous customer and asking them if they'll sell you their current vehicle does sound strange, so say this upfront.
- "... but my general manager wanted me to call you today..." – Ask your GM if she wants you to call customers today; I'll bet she does.

- "... because we have a buyer..." – We always have a buyer. For most dealerships, this is your used car manager.
- "... and an immediate need..." – There is no urgency if our need is not immediate. Additionally, we're basically asking the customer for a favor (which is easier and more productive than asking them to buy something).
- "... I don't know if you'd consider selling it or not..." – Clearly establishing that we are the buyers and Mr. Jones is the seller.
- "... but we do have two appraisal times open on Cherokees this afternoon..." – Indicating we may have a few more openings this evening, but there are folks just lining up to sell us their Cherokees.
- "We've got a 12:15 and a 12:45, would either of those work for you?" – I don't expect the majority of customers to choose a time right away, but I've set the stage for what I want and what I need them to do. Doing this increases my chances for a shown appointment.

Be prepared; some customers may actually choose one of the times offered immediately. They may have been thinking about selling their vehicle and you called at the right time; so, be ready to set the appointment. Of course, more often than not (even if they want to sell), they're going to ask some questions or throw up an objection. Because these are your store's existing customers, and because these efforts are intended to manage customer loyalty, when the customer indicates they're not interest in selling at this time, your job is not to push them to reconsider. Instead, wind the call down like this:

> Salesperson: "I understand, Mr. Jones; thank you for considering my offer to get you a written appraisal. Would you mind if I called you in a few months if we find ourselves needing another 2016 Cherokee like yours?"

It is rare for any customer to tell you something like, "Leave me and my family alone!" Most likely, your customer will tell you, "Sure." When this happens, make your notes in the CRM and verify there is a call scheduled for six months from today. And... this part is critical... move on! Too many dealers are destroying their database by hard selling their loyal customers.

The letter (or email) you send in advance of these calls also doesn't need to be elaborate. Again, if you know the equity position and are sure you can keep the customer at the same or similar payment, then lead with that. Otherwise, asking to buy their vehicle (and setting up your upcoming call) is all you need. Here's a sample:

October 21, 20XX

Mr. Robert Jones
1234 Any Street
Anytown, CA 90042

Dear Mr. Jones:

This note may sound strange, but Carol Smith, our general manager, asked me to write you because we would like to buy your 2016 Jeep Grand Cherokee back from you. We have a buyer and an immediate need for a Grand Cherokee like yours.

Unlike other dealers, we specialize in providing the highest value on all vehicles we buy. In fact, we are always willing to buy vehicles from the public even if they don't buy from us. We would like to see your Grand Cherokee as soon as possible so that we can give you a firm written offer.

I'll call you this week to schedule a Priority VIP Appraisal in our state-of-the-art facility; though, if you'd prefer to schedule this sooner, please call me at 555-555-1212. I promise to get you in and out in no time.

Best wishes,

Steve Stauning
555-555-1212

If you can't overcome an addiction to email (because, you believe email is free), and you want to incorporate a few emails into your owner marketing process, you'll want to keep them short and the focus on driving a phone call. This requires a clear call-to-action, like this email intended for an orphan owner:

SUBJECT: We need your Cherokee at ABC Motors

Hi Robert,

My name is Steve Stauning and I am a product specialist here at ABC Motors.

This may sound strange, but we would like to buy your 2016 Cherokee back from you. We are in desperate need for good used vehicles like yours and cannot find what we need at the auctions.

Unlike other dealers, we specialize in providing the highest value on all vehicles we buy. In fact, we are always willing to buy vehicles from the public even if they don't buy from us. We would like to see your Cherokee as soon as possible so that we can give you a firm written offer.

Please call me today at 555-555-1212 so that I can schedule your Priority VIP Appraisal at our state-of-the-art facility. I promise to get you in and out in no time.

If you're sure you can lower your customer's APR, then lead with that:

SUBJECT: We want to refinance your Patriot at ABC Motors

Hi Fred,

My name is Steve Stauning and I am a product specialist here at ABC Motors.

This may sound strange, but we would like to refinance your 2016 Patriot to get you a lower rate and reduce your monthly payments.

Since you purchased the Patriot, interest rates have come down significantly, and we want to get you a lower rate today. There's

nothing for you to buy and if I can schedule
an appointment for you, we will get you in
and out quickly.

Please call me today at 555-555-1212 so that
I can schedule your appointment ASAP.

Answering Owner Marketing Questions

When calling your owner database to buy back their vehicles, the questions you receive are usually buying signals. However, because your customer is not sitting in the seat in front of you, treating them as objections ensures you'll set more appointments that show.

The question you'll face most often is about the value of their vehicle. That is, the customer wants to know what you're going to pay for their vehicle before driving to the dealership. Give them a value over the phone and you'll never see them.

Nearly everyone believes their vehicle is worth more than a dealer offers. When you make this offer over the phone (or even provide a range of values), you'll almost never set an appointment that shows. This is best handled similarly to how we handle this objection with the internet customer:

Customer: "How much are you going to give me for it?"

Salesperson: "Well, Mr. Jones, I can appreciate that you'd want to know exactly what your vehicle is worth before driving down here; however, only a trained appraiser knows what your vehicle is worth, and it would be irresponsible for a dealer to give you that information over the phone. Now, I do have two appraisal times open on Cherokees this afternoon. I've got a 12:15 and a 12:45, which one of those works better for you?"

Always circling back to your goal when answering an objection or question keeps you in control of the call and directs your customer to agree to an appointment. Here's a big buying signal you should be prepared to answer:

Customer: "What am I supposed to drive home?"

Salesperson: "Well, Mr. Jones, Jeep has some of the best deals that they've had in a very long time going on right now. However, I have a buyer and an immediate need for your 2016 Jeep Cherokee and I have two appraisal times open on Cherokees this afternoon. I have a 12:15 and a 12:45. Which one works better for you?"

The key to winning when you hear this buying signal/objection is to be very careful how you answer. Vomiting all current incentives, rebates and lease specials on this customer ensures they'll never come in. Your goal is an appointment that shows. Therefore, generating a little excitement in the current offers and then immediately circling back to your goal is the best way to handle any buying signal like this. For example, here's another clear buying signal:

Customer: "What about my payments?"

Salesperson: "Mr. Jones, when we have a buyer for a customer's vehicle, we are often able to keep people at or near their current payment on a new vehicle; however, I do have an immediate need for your Cherokee, and I have two appraisal times open on Cherokees this afternoon. I have a 12:15 and a 12:45, which one of these works better for you?"

In the example above, your customer wants to buy; he may even be picturing himself in your new vehicle right now, but he's worried about his payments. Addressing his payments directly when we don't know all the facts can kill your deal before it ever even starts. Generate a little excitement and then circle back to your goal; because, as you know, you cannot sell an empty seat.

Customer: "I don't get off work till 5:00."

Salesperson: "That's great. We actually have a 5:15 and a 5:45, which one of those works better for you?"

There's a misconception among automotive salespeople and BDC agents that you have to learn the customer's availability first, and then narrow in on the appointment. Unfortunately, that leads to soft appointments (if they'll set one) and removes all urgency from your request. Your interested customer will tell you if both 12:15 and 12:45 (as in this example) are inconvenient; this allows you to give them the great news that you also have open appraisal times that are convenient to them.

Narrowing down the customer's availability might seem courteous, but it's only going to lead to fewer shown appointments and fewer sold units. You've just told him you have a buyer and immediate need; getting soft on the appointment setting means the need is not so immediate.

Customer: "I can be in on Saturday. What time do you open?"

Salesperson: "Oh, Mr. Jones, gosh, I'm sorry. I do have an immediate need for a 2016 Cherokee. Now, I have ten more Cherokee owners on my list to call today. If I can't get one of them to sell me their Cherokee tonight or tomorrow, I'll call you on Friday to schedule that Saturday appointment. How does that sound?"

This word track may run counterintuitive to everything you know about the car business. He wants to come in on Saturday and your response basically tells him you're not that interested in doing business with him. Relax and remember your goal. Your goal is not to get him to simply agree to an appointment; it's to generate an appointment that shows.

Assume that you're having this conversation with him on a Tuesday. You just gave him new car fever... and it's only Tuesday. He agrees to an appointment with you on Saturday; but, what would the average customer do between Tuesday and his Saturday appointment? He's going to go car shopping! He'll shop online, and he'll visit a few dealers between now and Saturday. Where will he not shop in that time? With you... because he has an appointment on Saturday.

You're never going to see him!

He's an honorable guy and a loyal customer; in fact, he's planning on buying from you on Saturday. He really is. He's going to walk into every dealership and say, "Hey, I'm just looking; I'm not buying." And, between Tuesday and Saturday, he's going to run into a salesperson and they're going to sell him a new vehicle. You'll see your formerly-loyal customer driving past your dealership in someone else's SUV.

It's important to actually tamp down his new car fever if he really can't come in until Saturday. In the word track above we're actually calling his bluff, if you will. We do this to find out how entrenched he is on waiting until Saturday. He'll respond in one of two ways:

Customer: "Oh, okay. Please call me on Friday either way."

This is rare; but, still okay. You'll make a note in the CRM to call him Friday evening after you respond with:

Salesperson: "Excellent. I'll call you Friday and let you know."

When you call him on Friday, you'll set a Saturday morning appointment and remove the opportunity for him to shop around in advance of that. The other, and more common response, is:

Customer: "Oh, I can be there tomorrow."

Salesperson: "Great, Mr. Jones. You just saved me ten calls; I really appreciate it. Tomorrow morning we've got a 9:15 and a 9:45 open, which one of those works better for you?"

Tamping down new car fever takes discipline (and guts), but it's the only way to ensure your customers will show. To be clear, however, this word track is for owner marketing calls only. While all appointments should be set for today or tomorrow, you're not going to completely shut down an internet prospect's attempt at a Saturday appointment on a Tuesday (like you can with an owner marketing customer).

Customer: "I don't know when I can get there, and I don't want to set an appointment!"

Salesperson: "That's fine; there's no requirement to schedule one. However, our appraiser does work primarily by appointment and if he's working with someone when you arrive, he won't be able to drop everything to help you. However, if you'll set and keep an appraisal appointment, he'll be able to get you a firm written offer on your vehicle more quickly. Now, we do have two appraisal times open on Cherokees this evening, we have a 5:45 and 6:15. Would either of those work better for you?"

While our goal is always an appointment that shows, not every customer is going to understand that appointments are better for them. Explaining this in a quick word track can help in most situations, but not all. Given that you're speaking to a loyal customer, you cannot afford to become entrenched and demand appointments only. Use your head and work hard to set the appointment; but, in the end, your efforts should be designed around increasing (not decreasing) customer loyalty.

When the customer does agree to an appointment, it's important to ensure they'll show. This means explaining how serious you and your team are about the scheduled time:

Salesperson: "That's great Mr. Jones! Nick, our used car manager, will be anticipating your arrival so that we can get started appraising your Cherokee right away. Now, if anything changes in Nick's schedule, we'll be sure to call you well in advance, so you don't waste a trip down here. I'm hopeful you'll let us know if anything changes on your end. So, can we count on seeing you today at 5:15?"

Owner Marketing Calls – The Schedule

As you learned in the last chapter, making 1,000 quality calls in a month equals about 30 units sold. This math has been fairly consistent for decades; and it's still true today. If your dealership is typical – that is, the bulk of your walk-in traffic shows up on the weekends – you're going to want to limit your owner marketing calls to a Monday through Thursday schedule. This focuses you on setting Monday through Friday appointments, leaving your Saturdays free to assist Traditional Ups.

If you'll dedicate just two hours each day to making these calls, you can expect to set a minimum of two appointments each day that will show. Using The Perfect Appointment (that you'll learn in the next chapter), you can expect to close 60-80% of these.

Assuming just a 60% close on your eight or more Monday-Friday appointments, you'll go into every Saturday with a minimum of five units already sold for the week!

Of course, making calls for two hours every Monday-Thursday takes discipline. You're sitting at your desk dialing away, and your co-workers are outside standing around the smoking circle having a great time. This is what separates the superstars from the slugs. Stick to your plan; stick to your processes; and you'll outsell everyone in the smoking circle combined!

15

THE PERFECT APPOINTMENT

All this appointment setting you've been learning will have zero impact on your results if the customer arrives on time only to discover that you're a typical salesperson. You're not ready for them. You ask them a lot of nonsensical road-to-the-sale questions. They want to start the test drive and you try to take them back to needs analysis and qualifying.

There are reasons most people dislike car dealers; and the customer experience is chief among these.

That's why I created The Perfect Appointment. You can call it a VIP Appointment to your customers, but you've got to treat it (internally, at least) as The Perfect Appointment. It's called The Perfect Appointment for a reason. That is, you cannot cheat, shortcut or shortchange any of the steps if you expect to enjoy legitimate 80%+ show rates and 80%+ close rates.

Plus, when you properly execute The Perfect Appointment, customers will gladly pay you more; they'll gladly give you a perfect survey; they'll gladly give you five stars on Google and Yelp; and they'll gladly refer their family and friends.

Dealers who properly execute The Perfect Appointment routinely tell me about customers who come out of the F&I office after completing a deal with great front and back grosses; look for the first manager they can find to shake her hand and tell her, "This is the best car-buying experience I've ever had... the absolute best car-buying experience I've ever had!"

Everyone, you see, wins when you properly execute The Perfect Appointment.

Why Do We Need Appointments?

When long-time sellers enter a session I'm teaching on The Perfect Appointment, I'll invariably hear one of them grumble, "Why do we need appointments, anyway?"

I love hearing this because now I know where to focus my training. If I can get the guy sitting in the back of the room with his arms folded to understand the importance of appointments with today's connected customers – if I can get him to become an advocate for The Perfect Appointment in his dealership – I can sway the entire group.

It usually takes about four minutes to get him there.

The average dealership closes about 20% of their Traditional Ups – that's one in five. These Ups take three to four hours to work a complete deal, even today. Most Traditional Ups buying a new car result in a mini. The OEM survey is a coinflip; and whether or not we can get a referral out of the Traditional Up is just as tenuous. Traditional Ups, in other words, are a lot of work for little (relative) return.

Conversely, dealerships who execute The Perfect Appointment close up to 80% of these customers – that's four in five. The average deal takes less than 90 minutes, including F&I. The grosses are always higher with these deals. These customers give you perfect CSI and will refer at least two future customers to you (when you ask), on average. The Perfect Appointment, in other words, is a lay down.

The arms unfold, the body leans forward, and the hand starts furiously taking notes. Another satisfied customer!

We've always heard that people buy cars from people they like; and, while there is a lot of truth to this saying, today's customer cannot like you if they never get a chance to meet you. You might be the friendliest salesperson in America – and customers might instantly like you – but, hoping the buyer you're speaking with on the phone will be on the next Up Bus is not a strategy; and if you fail to get a firm appointment that shows, you'll be lucky to get a sale. (That's because they have to meet you to like you.)

The Up Bus is almost empty if/when it arrives at most dealerships. This leaves appointments as the only way most salespeople have any shot at selling 30 or more units a month. Either embrace appointments or change professions; there's a dim future for salespeople who want nothing more than to stand out front waiting on the next Up.

In this chapter, I'm going to teach you everything I've learned in the nearly ten years since we first created and taught The Perfect Appointment. I'll teach you what works and what doesn't work, so you don't repeat the mistakes of the past. More than anything else, however, I have to stress again that it's called The Perfect Appointment for a reason. This means, let's do it my way and then you can improve it. You can't be successful if you try to pick and choose the parts you'll implement.

The Four Steps

Like every effective strategy you've ever implemented, The Perfect Appointment is simple. In fact, there are only four steps to follow it perfectly:

1. Strong Appointment Setting
2. Appropriate Appointment Confirmation
3. Pre-Appointment Preparation
4. In-Store VIP Treatment

Many of the dealers who have failed at this – and I've taught hundreds how to conduct The Perfect Appointment – have all tried to cut corners or change some of the "little things." Most, of course, failed because their managers treated The Perfect Appointment like another in a long list of "programs" their dealer principal or OEM tried to shove down their throats. These managers knew that two or three weeks into this "program," the dealer principal would focus on something else and they could just check a box for a few months until it was completely forgotten.

"Yeah," they'll tell their dealer, "That perfect appointment thing didn't really work for us."

Rinse. Lather. Repeat.

The Perfect Appointment is not a "program," it's a culture. It's the processes you employ when your dealership has adopted a true appointment culture. Instilling this culture in your dealership (from the top down) ensures everyone understands that appointments are important... so important, in fact, that they drive the store's culture. An appointment culture replaces the longstanding seat-of-the-pants-end-of-the-month culture that describes so many dealers struggling to maintain market share. It's a culture of putting the customer first, all while earning great grosses and perfect CSI for doing so.

STEP 1: Strong Appointment Setting

The first step to The Perfect Appointment is strong appointment setting; and without it, you cannot execute the others. For example, if you set a weak or soft appointment – one that could arrive hours before or after the scheduled time – then there's no way to properly provide the in-store VIP treatment (Step 4), since we cannot prepare for the buyer's visit.

Salespeople who set weak appointments enjoy, of course, a lower show rate; but, it's worse than that. Those prospects who do show up at your dealership close at rates well below average. Why? Two reasons: first, the buyer didn't realize they even had an appointment; and second, as I already said, you can't give them a VIP experience when you're not even sure if/when they're going to show.

You can only conduct The Perfect Appointment when the customer arrives on time. The customer will only arrive on time if they clearly understand they have a real appointment. They will only understand they have a real appointment when you practice strong appointment setting.

Are we clear?

Setting a strong appointment requires a belief that your only goal when you have someone on the phone is an appointment that shows. This is important, as those salespeople and BDC agents who believe their job is to build value in the dealership, themselves and the vehicle will struggle to set firm appointments that show. Likewise, those who treat customer calls as an information-gathering activity fail when compared to reps focused on the singular goal of an appointment that shows.

Additionally, if you believe your goal is to build rapport – especially if "build rapport" is written on your call guide – you're going to come off as inauthentic to your prospect. You simply cannot build rapport over the phone by *trying* to build rapport. Rapport is only built through a genuine human contact.

So, while it is possible to build rapport over the phone, it must happen naturally. Smiling, being direct, taking charge and guiding the prospect by helping them set an appointment will build more genuine rapport than uttering something nonsensical like, "How about that weather we've been having?" Ugh.

When your only goal is an appointment that shows, you'll be able to easily circle back to your goal after each question and objection. Always circling back to your goal takes discipline; a discipline that many salespeople will have to build over time through trial and error.

Weak Appointment Setting

The best way to teach what strong appointment setting looks like is actually to give you a few examples of what it *doesn't* look like. Weak appointment setting is what happens most often in dealerships today; but, it's not your fault.

OEMs and even some phone trainers have been teaching for years that salespeople should set weak appointments. They don't call them this, of course, it's just the result of the processes they endorse. For example, one OEM recently shared their appointment-setting strategy with their dealerships' salespeople and BDC agents in a colorful training pamphlet that used a "V" as the guide to setting appointments.

The "V" represents, according to the training materials, the narrowing of the prospect's choices until you can agree on an appointment date and time. (I'm paraphrasing here, as I don't want to embarrass the OEM who spent money on printing and distributing these pamphlets.) The word tracks basically go like this:

Salesperson: "Would you prefer to test drive this vehicle during the week or on the weekend?"

Prospect: "The weekend works best for me."

Salesperson: "Great, would you prefer Saturday or Sunday?"

Prospect: "Saturday, please."

Salesperson: "Excellent. Would you prefer morning or afternoon on Saturday?"

Prospect: "I think something in the morning would work."

Salesperson: "Fine, we open at 9:00 a.m. on Saturday, and we have a 9 o'clock or a 10 o'clock available. Which one of these works best for you?"

Prospect: "Ten o'clock is good."

Salesperson: "Great; I look forward to seeing you at 10:00 a.m. to test drive the…"

This is weak appointment setting 101! The salesperson removed all the urgency from the purchase and pushed an appointment that likely could've been set for today to Saturday! Additionally, the customer may have made a verbal commitment to the appointment, but not a mental one. In other words, this prospect is more likely to skip the appointment than she is to reschedule it if something changes in her schedule. The appointment just feels soft to the prospect... because it is.

The most common word track used that creates weak appointments is the dreaded "When would you like to come in?" Lots of phone trainers are still teaching salespeople to ask this right after they've conducted a needless needs analysis over the phone. As you already learned from this book, when you ask, "When would you like to come in?" you're telling the prospect:

- "There's no rush."
- "We're never busy."
- "We don't care when you buy."
- "That car is going to be here forever."

Again, this removes the urgency from the purchase and makes whatever time the prospect chooses fairly tentative in their mind.

Finally, I've read phone guides that task the salesperson with asking one more question after an appointment is set: "Can I answer any more questions for you?"

This, of course, is lunacy. They're trying to buy a car from you; you got them to agree to a date and time; and now you're going to reopen the Q&A? At this stage, anything beyond a strong recap of the appointment (coming soon in this chapter) will just further soften what is already a soft appointment.

Strong appointment setting requires you stay in control of the call. When you invite more questions or ask, "When would you like to come in?" you're ceding control of the call to the caller. Since most people dislike the car-buying process, giving up control of the call allows buyers to throw up a big enough smokescreen to eliminate you from their consideration set.

Remember: This is Assumptive Selling. We're assuming they know what they want and that they're ready to buy today. Stay in control and you maintain the best chance of setting an appointment that shows.

Appointment show rates, not surprisingly, increase the closer these are set to the time of the call. This means your best chance for a 100% show rate is to set the appointment for today. In fact, data from my clients collected for nearly a decade reveals that the probability any appointment will show drops about 10% with each passing day. In general terms, if today is Monday, appointments set for:

- Today will show over 80% of the time;
- Tomorrow will show over 70% of the time;
- Wednesday will show about 60% of the time;
- Thursday will show about 50% of the time;
- Friday and beyond will show less than 40% of the time.

There are a number of reasons for this drop, though often the customer just loses their new car fever. They started to think long and hard about buying a new vehicle and they decided they'd better wait. If you had set the appointment for today – when they were hot to buy – you'd likely be congratulating them on their new purchase and asking for a referral three or four days later; instead, you find yourself calling to find out why they missed their appointment.

Strong appointments, therefore are those that are set for today or tomorrow only – and this takes discipline. Setting the appointment beyond that horizon gives your prospect too many opportunities to get buyer's remorse (before they even buy) or to be sold elsewhere.

In order to be considered a strong appointment, you and the prospect must agree on a specific date and time. Therefore, none of the following is a strong appointment:

- "After 5:00"
- "Before 9:00"
- "Around lunchtime"
- "Saturday morning"

A specific date and time leaves no room for interpretation. 5:15 p.m. is 5:15 p.m.; while "after 5:00" could mean 5:30 to you and 7:45 to your prospect. This is why The Perfect Appointment dictates you set a firm appointment for a specific date and time; this is a requirement for strong appointment setting.

While this sometimes goes without saying, your prospect must have a clear and specific goal in their mind for the appointment or they'll probably skip it. The most likely goals are test drives and appraisals; though their goal could be to find out if they qualify for financing or to compare two different vehicles. Whatever their goal for the appointment, you need to be sure it's clear and specific; and that both you and the prospect are aware of it.

Finally, to be considered a strong appointment, you must get not just a verbal commitment by the prospect, but also a mental commitment. You get this mental commitment and you nail down the specific date, time and goal all with something called The Recap.

The Recap

Once your prospect has given you their verbal commitment to an appointment for a specific date, a specific time and a specific goal; you must gain a mental commitment to have the best chance of getting them to actually show and to show on time. You achieve this mental commitment when you complete The Recap.

As I've likely written more than a dozen times in this book already, your only goal when you have someone on the phone is an appointment that shows. Just because your prospect said "yes" to your request for an appointment doesn't mean they're going to show... not without The Recap. Your goal, then, is not to get off the phone quickly – it's an appointment that shows. Given this, avoid using this or similar word tracks when your prospect agrees to come in at 5:15 today:

Prospect: "Sure, 5:15 works for me."

Typical Salesperson: "Great. I'll see you at 5:15. Be sure to ask for Steve!"

Even though you received a verbal commitment to your 5:15 appointment request ("Sure, 5:15 works for me"), your prospect has likely not yet committed mentally to the appointment. They need to know you're serious about it and that if they no-show they'll be causing you to do unnecessary work. Only once they understand this and say "yes" to your appointment request do you have a firm appointment. You get them to understand this, by the way, through The Recap. Let's look at an earlier appointment-setting word track with The Recap included:

Salesperson: "Hi Barbara, this is Steve Stauning with ABC Motors. Did I catch you at a bad time?"

Prospect: "I've got a few minutes."

Salesperson: "Great. I'm just calling to schedule your priority test drive on the 2019 Honda Ridgeline you selected on our website. Now we have two priority test drives open on that truck this morning; we have a 10:15 and a 10:45, which one of these works better for you?"

Prospect: "Well, I don't get off work until five."

Salesperson: "Excellent; we've also got a 5:15 and a 5:45 available. Which one of these works better for you?"

Prospect: "5:45 is perfect."

Salesperson: "Great; I'll lock in 5:45 for your priority test drive. Now, just to recap, we're going to see you tonight at 5:45 to test drive that 2019 Honda Ridgeline. Barbara, between now and then, I'm going to ensure your Ridgeline is cleaned, gassed and parked right out front so that when you arrive for your 5:45 test drive, you will be in and out and on the road within five minutes. I'll be sure to call you well in advance if anything changes on our end; and I'm hopeful you can do the same for me. So, can I count on seeing you tonight at 5:45?"

Prospect: "Yes; I'll see you then."

It's only after The Recap that the prospect gains the necessary mental commitment to the appointment. Prior to this, they looked at your 5:45 request as more of a placeholder than a firm time commitment for you and for them.

Do not shortcut The Recap. I know there are a lot of words you must say in order to gain the mental commitment, but salespeople who skip The Recap see their appointments show only about 40% of the time, with most of these showing up more than 30 minutes early or late.

When you regularly use The Recap, you'll see higher show rates; and most of those that show will show up within ten minutes of the scheduled appointment time. Ensuring your prospects show up on time makes a huge difference when you're trying to conduct The Perfect Appointment. You simply cannot provide an in-store VIP treatment, for example, to someone who walks in an hour early or an hour late.

If you're a manager and want to know whether or not your team is regularly using The Recap, take a look at the following stats for their appointments:

- Set appointments
- Shown appointments
- No-show appointments
- Canceled/rescheduled appointments

When your team properly uses The Recap, they make buyers feel guilty if they no-show. This means you'll have prospects call you in advance to cancel or reschedule their appointments. Without The Recap – as is true with all weak appointments – prospects will simply no-show.

Your salespeople with 40-50% show rates and no cancelations are setting weak appointments. Conversely, those with 60%+ show rates and prospects calling to cancel or reschedule are clearly using The Recap; as their prospects have made mental commitments to their appointments. Simply put: if those who miss their appointments are not calling in advance, then you're not making it clear this is a real appointment and not gaining the necessary mental commitment.

If you plan to text a confirmation to your prospects, be sure to alert them on this call; though, if they've not yet officially opted-in to receiving your texts, let them know you'll need this opt-in first:

Salesperson: "Great; do you mind if I send you a quick opt-in text message? This will allow me to send your test drive reminders via text."

Prospect: "Sure, that's fine."

Salesperson: "Excellent. Please reply with the letter A when you see my text; and we'll see you tonight at 5:45."

Sending the opt-in text right away is good idea, since your buyer is expecting it.

> ABC Motors is confirming a request to send messages. Reply A to allow, S to stop, H for help. Message and data rates apply.

Subtle Differences Matter

This book contains many word tracks that I don't actually want you to memorize; rather, I want you to internalize them and make them your own. More than learning the words, I want you to understand the spirit of what Assumptive Selling is trying to convey to the prospect. Instead of focusing on what to say, I want you to understand why we say it this way with Assumptive Selling.

With Assumptive Selling, little differences in the word tracks matter; and, when you understand the why, you'll quickly hear yourself when what you're saying isn't exactly what you want to convey. For example, let's look at a few of the recommended Assumptive Selling word tracks and alternatives that may sound the same to you, but convey a different meaning to your buyer:

Test Drives:

Recommended: "… We do have two test drives open on that Taurus this morning. We have a 10:15 and a 10:45, which one of those works better for you?"

Not Recommended: "… I have two test drives open today. I have a 10:15 and a 10:45, which one of those works better for you?"

In the recommended word track above, the appointment is clearly for the vehicle "we have" and because the open times offered are called out as being "… this morning," the prospect can surmise that there are likely later appointments available if these two choices are inconvenient.

Conversely, when the salesperson says, "I have two test drives open today," they're indicating to some prospects that the appointment is with the salesperson (not the vehicle) and only those two times are open with no flexibility on the part of the salesperson.

Finally, the recommended word track shows the salesperson to be helpful, while the other can make the salesperson seem entrenched and almost "too busy" for the prospect. The differences are subtle, but they indeed matter.

Owner Marketing:

Recommended: "… we have a buyer and an immediate need for a Mustang like yours …"

Not Recommended: "… we're always looking for good used cars and trucks …"

The first word track directly references our need for the customer's vehicle. This indicates we might be willing to pay more because we're in a bind, and this makes the customer more likely to agree to an appraisal appointment. The second word track removes all urgency and does nothing to drive an appointment; as the customer doesn't feel their vehicle is special or will earn a higher value with you.

By the way, don't assume that if you learn to say the recommended word track, that you won't eventually get lazy and start using the one not recommended. This example came from a dealership I trained on Assumptive Selling and The Perfect Appointment. A couple of months after the initial training, I returned to find half their salespeople underperforming with setting appointments from their owner marketing efforts. It took just a couple of minutes listening to their calls to understand right away why customers weren't setting appointments: it was the lazy word track they had unknowingly begun using.

In another example where understanding the spirit of the Assumptive Selling word tracks matters, how you verbalize your dealership's policy on giving a trade value over the phone can make all the difference. Look for the differences in these two responses to a prospect who indicates they won't set an appointment with you until you tell them what their trade is worth:

What's My Trade Worth?

Recommended: "… only a trained appraiser knows what your vehicle is worth, and it would be irresponsible for any dealer to …"

Not Recommended: "… it's our policy not to give trade values over the phone …"

I know you're thinking that you would never utter the second word track; but, it's exactly what I heard a BDC agent say on the fifth day of training during a live call. Over the previous four days, I trained a brand-new centralized BDC and their manager to say the first word track when a buyer demanded to know what their trade was worth. However, when the live calls started, one agent said, "I'm sorry, it's not our policy to give trade numbers over the phone; you'll have to come in for an appointment."

My head nearly exploded when I heard that!

I'm certain you can see the differences between these two; though in case you cannot, let me help you. The recommended word track is honest and helpful. It tells the consumer that we want to get them a fair value for their trade and that any dealer who gives them a number over the phone is somehow not trustworthy.

The other word track tells the consumer we should not be trusted, that we have something to hide, and that our policies are meant to deceive the public. Not very authentic, is it?

Finally, when setting appointments, it's good to avoid overusing the word "appointment." Instead, use the term that describes what the appointment will accomplish like "priority test drive" or "VIP appraisal."

STEP 2: Appropriate Appointment Confirmation

Just like in the first step of The Perfect Appointment, your only goal in this step is an appointment that shows. And, because not every appointment is the same, your confirmations must vary to stay true to your goal of an appointment that shows.

For example, an internet sales appointment for a test drive on a new Tundra for next Saturday (ten days away) might include most or all of the following confirmation attempts:

- An immediate confirmation email with directions and calendar links;
- An immediate text opt-in for appointment reminders;
- A salesperson call or email on the Tuesday before the appointment ("We have an unexpected opening this evening");
- A confirmation email sent two days before the scheduled appointment with a PDF boarding pass;
- A manager phone call approximately four business hours before the appointment; and
- A text reminder approximately one hour before the appointment.

Conversely, if a buyer called from your competitor's lot fifteen minutes from your dealership and you set an appointment for twenty minutes from now, your confirmations may only include a quick email or text with the store's address (if that). You see, the goal is an appointment that shows, and a buyer who is literally on their way does not need a manager calling them in a few minutes to confirm the appointment. That's inauthentic and will often cause your slam-dunk appointment to reconsider visiting your dealership.

This is why Step 2 is called *appropriate* appointment confirmation – there is no one-size-fits-all when it comes to appointment confirmations. Your goal is all that matters here; so, act accordingly.

Given the goal and the examples provided, it should be clear that not all appointments even require a confirmation. Appointment confirmations, like all four steps of The Perfect Appointment, are not an exercise in box-checking. (Save that for the next program the OEM forces upon you.) Let the goal of each step guide how you should act.

To uncover soft appointments and save these from becoming no-shows, managers should make the confirmation calls. If you rely on the same person who set the appointment to confirm it, you'll experience a couple of common issues: (1) they won't even make the confirmation calls (because they're the one who set the appointment and they're certain they did it right); or (2) the customer who lied about coming in when the appointment was set will lie when the same person calls to confirm.

With a manager making the calls, you have a real opportunity to uncover and overcome potential no-show appointments before it's too late. Properly done, a manager confirmation call not only improves the show rates, but also the closing rates of those who show.

For most appointments, the first confirmation you'll send is an email with both a calendar link and a directions link. The reason for links instead of simply including the date, time and address in your email is that a consumer reading your email can click the calendar link to add the appointment to their own calendar. Likewise, they can click the directions link to open their smartphone's mapping application with your dealership's address as the destination. (Check with your CRM provider to learn how to properly create these links in your appointment confirmation emails.) Here's a quick example (with the links simulated, of course):

```
SUBJECT:  ABC Motors Priority Test Drive
Confirmation
```

Hi Mr. Jones,

We're excited to have you visit ABC Motors for your Priority Test Drive on the 2018 Camaro. Here are the details of our appointment:

- Date and Time: <u>Thursday, 5:45 p.m.</u>

- <u>Click for Directions to ABC Motors</u>

As I said on the phone, we promise to have your Camaro cleaned, gassed and ready to go when you arrive. This will allow you to start your test drive as quickly as possible with no hassles.

We also promise to notify you promptly if anything changes at ABC Motors that would affect your Priority Test Drive. We would appreciate it if you could extend us the same courtesy. If there is any reason you need to reschedule your Priority Test Drive, please call me as soon as possible at 555-555-1212.

I look forward to meeting you this evening – thank you again for your interest in ABC Motors!

I call this email the "thank you email with appointment particulars;" and it's appropriate for nearly all appointments – even those where the prospect has indicated they are on their way (because of the directions link).

If your prospect has opted-in to receive text messages, feel free to substitute a text with your dealership's address as the only confirmation to those buyers who are on their way.

> Thank you for considering ABC Motors.
> We'll see you at 2345 Any Street,
> Anytown, at 5:45pm for your test drive.

Appointment Confirmation Calls

My rule of thumb on appointment confirmation calls is to include one where the appointment is set for at least four business hours away. This does not mean to never call to confirm appointments set for three hours from now or to always call to confirm appointments set for five hours from now. This is merely a guideline and managers should use their own good judgement on whether or not to make the call when it's close to my four-hour guideline.

The goal, if you recall, is an appointment that shows; and if an appointment set for three hours from now feels tentative (based on the notes in the CRM or on what your BDC agent just said), then the manager should definitely call to confirm.

Confirming a test drive appointment for a $40,000 vehicle is not like confirming a $40 oil change. The appointment confirmation call (whether you speak to the prospect or leave a voicemail) requires more energy and excitement than an oil change confirmation. Additionally, the manager should use recap-like language that makes the prospect feel guilty if they no-show. Here's an example of an effective confirmation voicemail:

"Hi Mr. Jones, this is Steve Stauning, I'm the sales manager here at ABC Motors; and I just wanted to thank you for considering us for your next vehicle purchase.

"As Carla may have told you, she will have your new Tundra cleaned, gassed and parked out front so that when you arrive for your 5:45 test drive, you'll be in and out and on the road within five minutes. Now, if anything happens to us or your Tundra, Carla will be sure to call you well in advance, so you don't waste a trip down here. All I would ask from you Mr. Jones is that you show Carla the same courtesy.

"I look forward to meeting you at 5:45. If for any reason you need to reschedule, please call me back at 555-555-1212. Once again that number is 555-555-1212. Thank you and see you soon."

Effective, however, is relative. My clients' results show that leaving a voicemail confirmation is just slightly more effective than not making the confirmation call in the first place. Where dealers see the best results (as reflected in their appointment show rates) is when the manager speaks to the prospect.

When you do speak to the prospect, the verbiage is essentially the same as the voicemail above. It's direct and to the point. Don't fall for the temptation to start qualifying the prospect over the phone or inviting more questions at this point. Your only goal is an appointment that shows; therefore, ensure they know you're excited to help them and that your team is doing a lot to prepare for this VIP experience. Here's a quick example of one of these calls:

Manager: "Hi, Mr. Jones; this is Steve, I'm the sales manager over at ABC, and I wanted to call and thank you for considering us; and to let you know that Carla will have your Tundra cleaned, gassed, parked out front and ready for your 5:45 test drive."

Prospect: "Sounds good."

Manager: "As Carla may have told you, if anything happens to us or your Tundra, we're going to be sure and call you well in advance so that you don't waste a trip down here. All I would ask is that you show Carla the same courtesy and give me a quick call if you're running late."

Prospect: "Will do."

Manager: "Great; and thanks again. We'll see you at 5:45."

If the salesperson completed The Recap and the manager ensured the prospect was aware of all that the team was doing in advance of the appointment, the prospect will likely feel guilty if they miss this appointment, right? This is why, as part of the appropriate appointment confirmation, all no-shows should be called at the scheduled appointment time.

If Mr. Jones has an appointment for 5:45, and it's 5:45 and he's not here, then he's late. While most dealers will wait an hour before they call missed appointments, some dealers don't call their no-shows until the next day. This is lunacy! Assumptive Selling tells us that he's a ready buyer; and unless you know why he's late, you must assume he's sitting in the dealership across the street about to go into the box.

Call your no-shows at the scheduled appointment time! This is a real appointment (just like at the dentist office) and if they bop in unannounced an hour late, you cannot provide them with the in-store VIP experience. Call your no-shows at the scheduled appointment time:

Salesperson: "Hi Mr. Jones, it's Steve over at ABC Motors. I just wanted to be sure you were able to find our facility."

He'll tell you he forgot (you'll reschedule); he'll tell you he's running late (you'll move the appointment); he'll tell you he's pulling in now (you'll go outside to greet him); he'll tell you he's over at the Nissan store (you'll remind him you're waiting with a cleaned and gassed Tundra); he'll tell you he arrived 30 minutes ago and your buddy Bob is helping him (you're being skated!).

Waiting an hour might be too late; and because you and your manager correctly made him feel guilty to no-show, calling him tomorrow will likely put you directly into voicemail (as he's embarrassed that you went to all that trouble and he simply forgot about the appointment).

Call your no-shows at the scheduled appointment time!

While I generally recommend only one confirmation call in the process, I've already alluded to an earlier confirmation call that I recommend for some appointments. When you've set a weak appointment for too many days from today – for example, setting a Saturday appointment on a Monday – you can add what feels like a confirmation call to your process, but is really an attempt to set a better appointment (one more likely to show).

In the case of a Saturday appointment set on a Monday, you'll want to add a task to your Wednesday list of activities. This task is usually a phone call but can be an email or text if one of those is more appropriate. The call goes something like this:

Salesperson: "Hi Mr. Jones, this is Steve from ABC Motors and I was calling about your Saturday test drive."

Prospect: "Uh huh."

Salesperson: "We actually have some flexibility in our schedule and have a couple of priority test drives open on the Tundra this evening. I was curious if your schedule had changed and if you'd like to come in today to test drive that Tundra?"

Then wait. If they want to change their test drive to today, great! If they want to keep Saturday, just reremind them of the appointment time and all you plan to do to get ready for them (a mini version of The Recap, if you will).

The Boarding Pass

When you're really good at confirming your appointments, you may want to add some pizzazz that can set you apart from your competition. For some of the dealers I've worked with, the addition of a boarding pass can create added legitimacy in their appointments. More importantly, it can improve their show rates.

Creating these is a manual process, though worth it if you're already doing all you can to confirm your appointments and not yet at a 100% show rate. Most of my dealers who've used boarding passes create them in PowerPoint and change the particulars with each appointment. Then, you can save the boarding pass as an image or PDF to send off to your prospect via email or text. Check out this quick, albeit black-and-white, example:

Your prospect will have no doubt they have a scheduled test drive appointment with you when they receive their boarding pass.

Confirming the Oddball Appointment

Remember, this step is called *appropriate* appointment confirmation, so you just might find yourself winging it when it comes to confirming the occasional oddball appointment. Let me give you an example of one of these appointments and how the salesperson was able to ensure the prospect showed and bought by using some out-of-the-box thinking.

The prospect was a soldier stationed overseas who was rotating back to the states the following month. He'd saved up enough to make a sizeable down payment on the Dodge Charger he'd always wanted; so, he visited the website for the Dodge dealer nearest his home and completed their Contact Us form.

The salesperson worked with him via email to understand what he was looking for and when he was expected back into town. Rather than simply instructing the soldier to call him when he was ready, the salesperson took the extra step of setting a firm test drive appointment on Chargers for the soldier. He emailed a confirmation, though the appointment was still a month away and the salesperson wanted to be sure the soldier would keep the appointment and not start shopping one of the neighboring dealers. He told the soldier that he'd like to send him a brochure on the Charger and asked for his overseas mailing address.

Then, the salesperson visited his store's parts department and purchased a Charger hat and t-shirt (with his own money), grabbed a Charger brochure and put these in a box with a letter similar to the following (that he had the owner sign):

February 12, 20XX

Corporal William T. Jones
PSC 123, Box 12345
APO AE 09204-1234

Dear Corporal Jones:

I wanted to send you a quick note to thank you for your service to our great country! It's because of the sacrifices you and your fellow soldiers make that the rest of us are able to live free.

I understand you'll be visiting with Jeff Johnson next month to test drive a new Charger – I look forward to personally shaking your hand when you do.

In the meantime, we thought the enclosed hat and t-shirt might hold you over until you have time to get behind the wheel here at ABC Motors. See you soon – by the way, you're going to absolutely love your new Charger!

Best wishes,

Robert Smith
Owner, ABC Motors
555-555-1212

Do you think this soldier kept his appointment! You bet he did. He was so appreciative of the swag he received that he never thought of shopping with anyone else. (Oh, and yes, the owner reimbursed the salesperson for the hat and t-shirt as soon as he saw the letter the salesperson asked him to sign.)

The goal, after all, of your appointment confirmation is an appointment that shows. In the case above, the quick-thinking salesperson ensured an appointment set for a month away was a slam dunk to show. He remembered his goal and understood that this step is called *appropriate* appointment confirmation.

But the Vehicle Was Sold!

You learned a word track earlier for setting appointments when someone calls about a vehicle's availability. In this exchange, you said something like this:

Salesperson: "I saw that Camaro this morning, but at the price we have it listed for it will likely not make it to the weekend. Now, we do have two test drives open on that Camaro this morning. We've got a 10:45 and an 11:15. Which one works better for you?"

After the customer agrees to one of these times, you provide The Recap where you promise to let them know if anything changes. What happens if you're about to prepare this Camaro for the appointment and discover it's no longer available for sale? What do you do?

You keep your word!

In The Recap, you told the prospect you'd call them well in advance if anything changes and you will... right after you find two alternate vehicles. Let's assume they're both new Camaros like the one the prospect inquired about and in the same or similar color, but with more features. If this is the case, here is the call I recommend:

Salesperson: "Hi Mr. Jones, this is Steve over at ABC Motors and I've got some bad news and some great news for you. The bad news is, yes, that Camaro was sold as of this morning; but the great news is that I have two better-equipped Camaros cleaned, gassed and parked out front waiting for your 11:15 test drive. Can we still count on seeing you at 11:15?"

If he says yes, you'll likely close him 90% of the time (because you kept your word); but, if he says no and cancels his appointment, that's okay. He wasn't going to buy one of the alternates anyway.

If you try to treat this like an old-school "just get 'em in" situation, you're going to spend two hours pulling Mr. Jones off the ceiling as he loudly accuses you of "bait and switch," goes home to give you multiple one-star reviews online, and perhaps even calls General Motors and the owner of your dealership to complain.

You do not need this kind of brain damage. With Assumptive Selling you always keep your word... always.

STEP 3: Pre-Appointment Preparation

If you think of the final step of The Perfect Appointment (in-store VIP treatment) as a show you're going to put on for the buyer, then it makes the importance of the pre-appointment preparation much clearer. The pre-appointment preparation includes all the behind-the-scenes stuff that makes a great show great. Without preparing for the appointment, there is no way to provide a VIP experience every time. Think about it, would the buyer feel like a VIP...

- ... if the vehicle didn't start and needed to be jumped before the test drive?
- ... if the vehicle was out of gas?
- ... if the vehicle was filthy?
- ... if the managers had no idea who the buyers were?

Without the pre-appointment preparation, it is simply not possible to create a true VIP experience in the final step. Interestingly, when dealers fail at The Perfect Appointment, it's because they don't believe in or enforce the pre-appointment preparation.

Some managers think they can flip every customer, so why get a car ready? I mean, they're just going to put the customer in something else, right? Wrong! Their closing rate for VIP appointments is around 20%!

Others believe they should complete a thorough needs analysis with every customer first (even with those who've already found value and relevancy online); so, they decide there's no need to get the car ready until they're sure the customer is on the right vehicle. This makes sense, right? Wrong! Their closing rate for VIP appointments is around 20%!

Still others believe that "tying up all that inventory" by having it cleaned and parked out front is a waste. I mean, salespeople can just walk the Camry customer out to the Camrys when they get here, right? Wrong! Their closing rate for VIP appointments is around 20%!

Of course, I think most managers who don't enforce the pre-appointment preparation just look at this step as work. Moreover, they see it as unnecessary work that's mostly cosmetic; so, it can't really affect closing rates, right? Wrong! Their closing rate for VIP appointments is around 20%!

I already wrote that you cannot shortcut or shortchange any of the steps to The Perfect Appointment if you expect to enjoy 80%+ close rates, and this includes the pre-appointment preparation. We're putting on a show in the final step, and that show requires preparation; the impact of which cannot be underestimated.

Cleaned, Gassed, Parked Out Front...

About an hour before the prospect is scheduled to arrive, you should begin preparing the vehicle for the appointment. This means making sure it will start. While you and I know that a vehicle sitting for 45 days likely needs a jump to get going; your prospect will picture themselves broken down in traffic with your "lemon" if they see you using the jumper box on their vehicle.

This also means making sure the vehicle is more than "dealer clean." Dealer clean describes how most vehicles look on the average lot right now. They've got some dust; but they're not filthy. There are a couple of unnecessary labels and stickers left on the new cars; but they're not in the way of anything important. Perhaps there's some glass paint on the windshield touting monthly payments; but you can still see well enough to drive.

That's dealer clean. And, to a prospect arriving for a VIP appointment, these vehicles aren't ready to be owned or driven home. You're going to close at low rates and never understand why.

With Assumptive Selling and The Perfect Appointment, you should always assume the sale. You should assume that every appointment is a delivery; and, if you do this right, you'll deliver more than 80% of the vehicles you prep. Of course, if you treat the appointment like a typical test drive, then you'll deliver somewhere closer to 20%.

This means you should ensure your appointment vehicles are as close to "delivery clean" as possible. Ensure everything is spotless and, except for the stickers required by law, there is nothing on the windows. If the vehicle is brand new, you'll want to put the floor mats in the truck (or be certain they are stowed away). Buyers will not take mental ownership of a dirty or cluttered vehicle.

Having enough gas in the vehicle is essential to an enjoyable, stress-free test drive. While you don't need to top off every tank before the demo drive, you do want to ensure the fuel warning light does not illuminate while your prospect is behind the wheel. Any warning lights, even just the one showing you need gas, can cause unnecessary stress for the buyer. (This is, after all, the second biggest purchase they will likely make in their lifetime.)

When helping implement The Perfect Appointment in dealerships, I like to ensure the dealership has both a prominent and fairly segregated place to park the appointment vehicles prior to the customers' arrival. While you might say a vehicle will be "out front" to your prospect on the phone, the truth is the vehicle can be anywhere close to the showroom, backed in and ready to go.

Of course, you want to also ensure that the parking place is away from similar vehicles. This is so your prospect doesn't get car drunk. As I wrote in an earlier chapter, giving customers too many choices often results in no decision; plus, you want the customer to take ownership of the vehicle they've selected for the test drive.

Including the right signage on the parking space can also help the customer take mental ownership. I like a simple "SOLD VEHICLES ONLY" sign, similar to what was prominent in the 1980s when many dealerships employed a "sold row." (We'll talk more about the sold row in the next chapter.)

Don't overthink this sign. The idea is to have the customer arrive for their test drive, see their vehicle, see the sign, and think they already bought the car. That's it. So, while I've taught "SOLD VEHICLES ONLY," I've often found dealerships chose to create signs that they felt were more creative (if wholly ineffective). Signs like:

- VIP APPOINTMENT PARKING
- VIP RESERVED PARKING
- APPOINTMENT VEHICLE PARKING

- VIP DELIVERY AREA

Contrast what you believe the customer is thinking when they read one of these signs with a simple "SOLD VEHICLES ONLY" sign like this one:

Once the vehicle is cleaned, gassed and backed in on your sold row; you'll want to include a hang tag (printed in color) that reserves this vehicle for your customer. Again, don't overthink this. The idea is to have the customer look at the hang tag, see their name, and feel better about their purchase. Here's a sample hang tag with a simple logo:

You can use your logo or your OEM's (if it's a new car); just don't (as I've said already) overthink this! It's a hang tag meant to help drive mental ownership. Don't put tons of details on the hang tag. The customer's name, the letters VIP and "reserved for" are about all you'll ever want to include. I've seen dealers put the year, make, model, stock number and salesperson's name on these; leaving little room for the customer's name!

Finally, you'll want to create a deal jacket (VIP folder) with VIP in large letters, put the appointment details in the jacket, attach the keys to the jacket, and store the jacket at your sales tower. We're keeping this folder at the sales desk for a few reasons:

1.   Managers need to memorize as many details as possible about every appointment. This is critical when it comes to the fourth step.
2.   Managers will want to see at a glance that appointment vehicles are prepped and ready to go.
3.   Managers must meet the prospect before the test drive, and the least awkward way to do this is to have the vehicle's keys at the tower and then funnel the customer there before the test drive.

The VIP folder is a critical component to The Perfect Appointment. Done right, you'll actually have some customers ask if they can keep their folder after the sale; you'll have customers tell your team, "I've never been a VIP before." Again, don't overthink this. Here's a simple folder we've taught for years:

In this example, the letters VIP are in red and everything else is in black (unless your logo has color). These can be printed in advance at a print shop, with the CUSTOMER NAME and APPOINTMENT DATE/TIME areas left blank. Then, when creating these for a specific appointment, the blank areas can be printed in black using any standard ink jet or laser printer.

Of course, even though we taught the simple folder on the previous page, some dealers created their own version when they overthought this whole VIP folder thing:

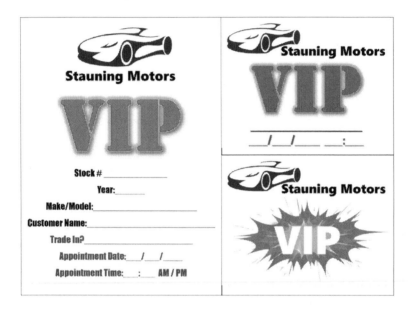

The example on the left was completed in pen and the customers couldn't even see their own names. The one on the top right was completed by the salesperson using a Sharpie (regardless of whether or not the salesperson could write legibly). And my favorite (bad) VIP folder cover was just like the one on the bottom right. In this instance, the dealer didn't want to waste 12¢ for every color copy, so he had his team reuse these folders and just put the customer's information inside.

Do any of these seem like a VIP experience to you? People like their own names and they want to be called a VIP; however, this shouldn't be done as an afterthought (like the examples where you handwrite the customer's name) or feel contrived (like a generic VIP folder cover reused for every customer). Don't overthink the VIP folder and don't be cheap. Done perfectly, these appointments will close 80% of the time at higher grosses and with perfect CSI. Perhaps that's worth twelve cents per folder...

The final task in this step is for everyone to memorize as many details from the VIP folder as possible. If a sales BDC set the appointment, then the managers and assigned salesperson should memorize the details. If a salesperson set the appointment, then the managers should also memorize the details. You're doing this to ensure you can provide a true in-store VIP experience when the customer arrives.

STEP 4: In-Store VIP Treatment

Before we hit all the important points in the final step of The Perfect Appointment, let's understand what is supposed to transpire in the mind of our prospect. Their experience in buying this car should be a complete "wow" for them – something they've never experienced at a dealership before. To be clear, the final step of The Perfect Appointment is all about the experience; and this includes an abbreviated road-to-the-sale. Additionally, an in-store VIP treatment includes lots of price and process transparency.

Your VIP customer should already know the price of the vehicle they're coming to test drive. If they're an internet prospect, they've got your price and that's the final price. There's no reason to change it since they didn't contact you in the first place because you were overpriced. The only reason there will be any negotiation on the price for your vehicle is if your sales manager tries to get cute and presents a first pencil showing MSRP to a VIP appointment. Congratulations, you just guaranteed a 20% close rate... oh, and because they already have a price from the internet, you're not going to end up making additional gross on any of the few deals you do happen to close.

Price transparency for the VIP appointment comes after the trade walk (and before the demo drive) when you can show your prospect a third-party wholesale value for their vehicle. By completing this step with your prospect on a kiosk or tablet, you build trust by removing the mystery over why this number is so low.

The process transparency is about keeping the VIP customer informed during every step; letting them know what you're doing, what you're going to do, and why you're doing these things. For example, when your manager says something like, "When you get back from the test drive, we'll go ahead and do the numbers" he's letting them know what to expect (and delivering a nice assumptive close for the write-up).

Part of this wow experience is driven by the entire team acting human and treating the customer like a prospect and not a suspect. When you assume the sale, you stop speaking to your top tier credit customers like they can't buy; you stop interrogating everyone. It remains a wow experience because you keep them engaged. That means you keep your VIP customers with the salesperson the entire time; and you manage their expectations.

Finally, you're able to make it a wow experience by moving the prospect through a road-to-the-sale that makes sense to them. They arrived for the demo drive and that's the step you're going to move them to soon after they arrive (instead of trying to take them back to a needs analysis).

There are some important guidelines to follow to ensure you stay focused during the in-store portion of The Perfect Appointment. I'll share these first, then walk you through an example customer as she's guided through this process:

- Greet and treat the customer like a VIP. Attacking her car as she circles the parking lot is not a VIP experience; neither is making her answer a lot of nonsensical (anti-skating) questions like "Have you been to ABC Motors before?" and "Do you remember who you worked with the last time you were here?" (If you memorized the appointment details, you already know all you need to about the buyer. Plus, if you implemented the protected prospect rules I recommended in the "Solving Dealership Turnover" chapter, you never again have to ask anyone who they worked with before; it's irrelevant.)

- It's preferable that a manager greet the customer; though, if this is not possible, walking the customer to get the keys (which are at the desk) allows your manager to shake her hand and thank her for coming in.

- The attitude of everyone who comes in contact with the VIP customer is that this is a done deal. It's as if she already bought the car online and you're just taking care of the "pesky details" like the test drive and the paperwork.

- Treat every appointment as if it was a delivery. Assume the sale unless/until the customer stops you.

- Limit your old-school road-to-the-sale questions to just those where you really need an answer, or that act as trial closes.

- The VIP folder is part of the show you're putting on in this fourth step. Make sure (without being obvious) that the folder is prominent throughout the appointment. Hold it in front of you as you speak to her; place it face up on the table when you do the write-up; etc. (People love their own name, and when your customer sees hers under the letters VIP, it will resonate. As I wrote earlier, some VIP customers will even ask if they can keep their folder after the sale.)
- Keep the customer engaged throughout the visit. This means someone is by her side at all times; keeping her busy and informed.
- Your goal should be to have the entire deal completed, including F&I, in under an hour. (For those who think this is impossible, there are dealers routinely completing these deals in under 45 minutes.)

Got it? Great, let's walk through what you and your buyer can expect when your team strictly follows the steps of The Perfect Appointment.

A Perfect Appointment

During the third step of The Perfect Appointment, you memorized the VIP folder for a woman named Barbara Jones. You discovered she's scheduled to test drive a new Camry at 5:15 today and she owns a 2017 Ford Escape. You have the keys at the sales tower, and you see her Camry properly cleaned and parked in the sold row.

At 5:08 p.m. a woman pulls into your lot driving a Ford Escape. Let's take a chance that this is Barbara Jones and get outside to open her vehicle's door after she's parked.

Sales Manager: "Are you Barbara Jones?"

Barbara Jones: "I am."

Sales Manager: "Hi Barbara. It's great to meet you. I'm the sales manager, Steve. Welcome to ABC Motors. Gosh, we're glad you're here; come on, let's go get the keys to your new Camry."

You extend your elbow and she grabs on as you head inside to the sales tower to retrieve her keys for the test drive. As you do this, Barbara is already thinking, "My God! This is the best car-buying experience I've ever had!"

Your general manager sees you coming and she picks up the VIP folder and grabs the keys. The salesperson you assigned to this appointment heads to the desk to meet you, as well. The GM smiles as you approach, holds the VIP folder so everyone can read Barbara's name, and reaches out to shake Barbara's hand.

General Manager: "You must be Barbara; I'm Gwen, the general manager. We're so glad you're here; you are going to absolutely love that new Camry!"

The salesperson approaches.

Sales Manager: "Barbara, this is Jeff, he's our product specialist on the Camry. He'll help you with your test drive and answer any questions you might have. Of course, Gwen and I will be available at all times, as well."

After a few pleasantries, some necessary qualification questions, a license scan and a couple of small trial (assumptive) closes, the GM hands the folder and keys to the product specialist; and just before Barbara and Jeff leave for the test drive, the GM adds:

General Manager: "Enjoy the Camry, Barbara. When you get back from the test drive, we'll have all the payment options calculated for you. See you soon."

What does our customer, Barbara, think about the experience so far? What do you think she believes is going to happen when she returns from the test drive? Do you think this is still the best car-buying experience Barbara has ever had?

Since she's trading in her Escape, your team will want to put together her value while she's on the test drive. This allows you to present the write-up immediately when she returns. The salesperson asks Barbara to take a quick detour with him to allow him to "gather just a little information" about her trade.

She's not getting into the Camry just yet, but this can still be a VIP experience. Keeping Barbara engaged as the salesperson walks the trade is important. Of course, Barbara wants to hop in the new Camry right away; though unfortunately, you cannot routinely buy vehicles profitably if you don't devalue the trade vehicle during a trade walk.

Since devaluing a customer's trade can sometimes be a bit of a downer, it's important to complete this before the test drive. Your buyer is at their highest point – they are most likely to buy – as they return from the test drive and park in your sold row. Because of this, you don't want any steps required between the demo drive and the write up. (In a best-case scenario, the salesperson is using a tablet during the trade walk and asking Barbara to help complete the steps. Once completed, he can show Barbara the wholesale value for her vehicle before the test drive. Anything you offer above this amount during the write-up will seem generous to her.)

After walking the trade, the salesperson takes Barbara over to the sold row. She sees her Camry backed in; she sees the hang tag that reads "Reserved for Barbara Jones;" she sees the SOLD VEHICLES ONLY sign… and, guess what? She thinks she bought the car!

As Barbara admires the Camry, one of the managers comes out to retrieve the trade sheet from the salesperson (if you're still using paper in your dealership; otherwise, all the trade data is transferred from the salesperson's tablet directly into the desking tool). Valuing the trade and completing a soft-pull on Barbara's credit during the demo drive will allow the manager to have a write-up waiting for Barbara when she returns.

The salesperson shows Barbara a couple of cool features about the Camry but does not complete an entire feature presentation. Why? Because with Assumptive Selling, and especially during The Perfect Appointment, we understand that our buyers have already completed most of this step on their own. Moreover, no one gives a crap that the polymer in the headlamps is made of the same substance that they used on the space shuttle! Show off the cool stuff and move on.

Our done-deal attitude helps us move Barbara through the steps efficiently, without skipping anything important. Unlike the last time Barbara bought a car, this visit won't get bogged down and she won't have to give up her entire Saturday trying to buy a car. Plus, the done-deal attitude helps you hold to the price that Barbara has already been presented online.

During the demo drive, the salesperson should listen more than he talks; though if there are important questions that still need to be asked, then asking a few of them here is okay. For example, do we know if Barbara is planning to finance this purchase or pay cash? Has she ever leased a vehicle before? But – and this is critical – the salesperson must keep his talking to an absolute minimum! During the final half of the test drive, he'll want to take Barbara's temperature to be sure the Camry is everything she dreamed it would be.

> Salesperson: "So, Barbara, what is it you like the most about your Camry?"

This is an old-school assumptive trial close that gets the customer talking and allows the salesperson to listen for clues as he watches the buyer's body language. Assumptive closes help the prospect imagine ownership and are less clumsy today than the more heavy-handed closes required in the past. (Because price isn't the great unknown that it was a decade ago, pulling prospects through The Perfect Appointment and assuming the sale throughout gets your customer in an "owning" mindset early.)

While Barbara and the salesperson are enjoying the test drive, one of the sales managers is busy putting together the write-up complete with trade value, leasing options and a variety of payment options. When the salesperson and buyer return from the demo drive, the move to the write-up will be seamless and easy. Unless she hates the vehicle, or the salesperson couldn't shut up during the demo drive, you can expect that once she returns the Camry to the sold row, she'll follow the salesperson into the dealership.

More often than not, The Perfect Appointment is a first-pencil event for your team. As long as there are no surprises (for example, trying to start back at MSRP after Barbara has already been presented with invoice pricing in an email), you can expect the write-up to take just a few minutes as the VIP buyer selects a payment and moves on to the F&I office.

To keep the appointment perfect, you need to keep the customer engaged and their expectations managed. If there's a two-hour wait to get into F&I, don't tell the customer, "it will just be a few minutes." Explain to Barbara that the business manager is backed up and that it's going to be some time before she gets in there.

In the meantime, fill her time by completing any paperwork that can be done in advance, present the menu options she'll see in the business office (if your salespeople are trained to do this), present the most common accessory options for her Camry, complete the service walk, set her first service appointment and begin the vehicle delivery (set the radio, pair the Bluetooth, etc.). The key is to keep her engaged and manage her expectations. Doing so will ensure a higher back-end gross and perfect CSI.

As I wrote earlier, if The Perfect Appointment is properly executed, expect to see Barbara come out of the F&I office and look for the first manager she can find, shake his hand and announce, "This is the best car-buying experience I've ever had... the absolute best car-buying experience I've ever had!"

It's because the entire process was efficient from beginning to end; it's because every step in the process made sense to Barbara; it's because you treated Barbara like a qualified buyer throughout; and it's because you listened to everything she said as you walked her through your buying process. You managed her expectations and kept her informed. Moreover, you kept your word:

- The vehicle was cleaned, gassed and parked out front;
- Your first pencil matched the online price;
- Your trade offer was "fair" (it matched or beat the wholesale book price you helped Barbara compute before the demo drive).

But... The Price!

It's true that for today's buyers, it's still about getting a good deal. However, when the experience is truly a "wow" for them and they're paying what they believe is a fair price, they won't feel like they have to grind you for every dollar (because you're not grinding them). If you defend the price before they arrive, and you present the previously agreed upon price during the first pencil, this will most often be your only pencil. I call this a "fair pencil." The buyer sees this as fair because it matches everything discussed to this point.

It's no surprise that top dealers, top managers and top salespeople excel at The Perfect Appointment better than their peers. This is because they always see everyone as a buyer; though, they know they can't win them all. They understand that sales is a numbers game; so, they don't fall in love with any trade, any buyer, or any vehicle. And, they would never change their proven processes just to fit one customer.

They stick to their processes, like The Perfect Appointment, because they know process outsells the opposite. They know that however smart they are, they're not as smart as the process. If they can close 80% of the appointments that show, they're more than satisfied, as they know they'll sell the other 20% at some point. Everyone, after all, is a buyer.

Old-School Manager Warning

When I entered the car business, the used car manager would never even look at a customer's trade until we'd already agreed on a vehicle and a price. Then and only then would he begin the slow grind on their trade vehicle. We could do this because customers had no information back then. There was no internet, so their knowledge of the car deal was limited to what we advertised in the paper. If they didn't like the trade number, our manager could easily defend his offer by showing the customer the book he used to compute it (the wholesale book prices before the internet were very "dealer friendly.")

Today, most dealers will buy consumer vehicles even if the consumer doesn't want to buy anything from them. Smart dealers know they can acquire these vehicles for less than it costs to buy them at auction, pay the auction fees and ship them to the dealership. Despite this, I still run into plenty of old-school sales managers who flat out refuse to even consider looking at a customer's trade until they've agreed on a price for your vehicle.

This is lunacy; and it results in more lost deals than almost any other antiquated process still in practice today.

Given that customers are at the height of new car fever the second they pull back into the sold row, dealers who delay the trade walk and appraisal until after the demo drive risk losing deals for no reason other than the customer started overthinking their purchase as the salesperson fumbles to devalue their trade. Plus, when the trade value is computed during the test drive, the salesperson and the manager stand a better chance of getting the customer to come inside after the test drive. For example:

Customer: "The Camry was okay, but I think we're going to look at something else."

Salesperson: "I understand; that makes perfect sense. Let's do this: my manager wants to give you a firm written offer on your Escape because we simply can't get vehicles that clean at auction. Let's go inside and get that offer so that you'll have something to compare when you look elsewhere. Does that make sense?"

If you haven't completed the trade walk yet and the manager has no value to present, the prospect will likely leave. However, if you offer to buy their vehicle whether or not they buy yours, you can uncover their Camry objections and move them to something else in your inventory.

To achieve an 80% close rate of appointments that show, you've got to achieve 100% write-ups. You can't present numbers to 100% of your prospects if you delay the trade value until after you've agreed on a vehicle and a price. Besides, your customers arriving for The Perfect Appointment already agreed on a vehicle and a price, didn't they? (They did if you're practicing true Assumptive Selling.)

The Perfect Appointment: Owner Marketing

Remember those owner marketing calls you learned earlier? The ones where you told your customer, "I've got a buyer and immediate need for your ..." Your goal for those calls was to set an appointment that showed; but, what do you do once they agree to an appointment? How do you conduct the pre-appointment preparation and the in-store VIP treatment when they're coming in to have you potentially buy their vehicle?

Typically, when you work from a targeted list, dealers close about half of their owner marketing appointments. If you're closing fewer than that, you're likely either lowballing everyone or you're calling customers who are too upside down in their loans to trade. There has to be a WIIFM (What's In It For Me) for your customers to agree to sell you their vehicles. (Of course, the goal when they arrive is not to just buy their vehicle, but to get them into a brand-new vehicle as well.)

You can and should conduct The Perfect Appointment for your owner marketing appointments – doing so will earn you closing rates closer to 80% for these customers. For the purposes of this section, we're going to assume you've already successfully completed the first two steps (strong appointment setting and appropriate appointment confirmation), and now it's time for the pre-appointment preparation.

Just as with all other instances of The Perfect Appointment, your pre-appointment preparation is intended to set the stage for the show you plan to put on during the final step. This step should not be discounted, as proper preparation will give your customer the same wow that others enjoy during The Perfect Appointment.

Pre-Appointment Preparation: Owner Marketing

When preparing for an owner marketing appointment, you're still going to get a vehicle cleaned, gassed, parked out front, and ready to go about an hour before they're scheduled to arrive. Of course, unlike a traditional appointment, you're probably not clear on what vehicle you should prep. Like all areas of Assumptive Selling, don't overthink this; the idea is to inject the customer with new car fever when they arrive; and they cannot catch new car fever lest they get in a new car, right?

Choose something close to what they're currently driving. If they're in a five-year-old crew cab truck, don't prepare a two-door coupe. Instead, find a nicer-equipped truck in a similar color and have it ready to go. (You don't want to choose the same color vehicle as what they're driving now because their neighbors need to know they got a new vehicle; so, the color must be different.)

Prepare the VIP folder and place it with the keys to the new vehicle at the sales tower. And, just like other appointments, the salesperson and managers should memorize as much as they can about the customer and the appointment before they arrive.

In-Store VIP Treatment: Owner Marketing

Get ready; your customer is likely going to come in with his keys in hand and his arm extended:

Customer: "My truck's out there; I've got five minutes. Give me a price."

Take their keys and throw them on the roof!

Just kidding! I wanted to be sure you're paying attention because this is critical. If you take their keys and give them a value in five minutes, you'll never sell a thing. Unlike other appointments, it's important to slow down your owner marketing customers. It's important to take enough time for your customer to find value and relevancy in the new vehicle; enough time for them to catch new car fever.

Because you're conducting The Perfect Appointment, you'll want to anticipate your customer's arrival. In this case, let's assume customer Mike Jones is scheduled to arrive in his grey 2016 Silverado at 12:45. At 12:47, a grey Silverado pulls into the customer parking area; our pre-appointment preparation tells us this is Mike Jones; so, let's alert the sales manager, grab the folder (yes, in advance of him meeting the manager this time) and greet him as he exits his truck:

Salesperson: "Hi Mike, I'm Jeff Johnson. It's great to see you again."

Mike Jones: "Here's the truck; here are the keys; I've got five minutes. Give me a price."

Gladly accept his keys.

Salesperson: "Great, Mike; though in order to get you the most money for your Silverado, our appraiser is going to need it for about 30 to 45 minutes. In the meantime, you're free to wait in our lounge, browse the lot, or if you prefer, I have the keys for this new Silverado you can take for a spin."

This is the vehicle you prepared. It's backed into the sold row, it has a hang tag that reads "Reserved for Mike Jones;" it's how he is going to catch new car fever. If it's the wrong vehicle for him, he'll tell you. However, without having a vehicle prepared in advance, the visit does not feel as special to the customer.

If he is interested in driving the Silverado you selected, walk him to the vehicle and begin pointing out what has changed from his current vehicle. Also, be sure to ask questions about what he likes and doesn't like about his current truck. Unlike a traditional appointment, you must conduct a needs analysis with your owner marketing customers.

As with any questions you ask buyers, be sure to let him do most of the talking. This will make you sound smarter and more caring.

Your manager should be outside by now. If so, she should greet Mike as if they're longtime friends:

General Manager: "Hi Mike, I'm Gwen the general manager. It's great to see you again. It looks like you've taken good care of your Silverado; we're excited to buy it back from you."

Once a suitable vehicle is selected by the customer to demo, the remainder of the appointment continues just like a traditional appointment. If for some reason Mr. Jones doesn't want to look at the new truck and just wants an appraisal, you'll walk him to the sales tower so that he can meet the sales manager there:

Salesperson: "That makes perfect sense; let's go get the appraisal started."

A best practice in this case is to give the customer's keys to the sales manager; and after some pleasantries are exchanged, the salesperson should work with the customer and review the trade-in vehicle on a tablet or kiosk to calculate the wholesale book value with him. This will give credence to the offer your manager is going to give you to present in 30 minutes.

After the book value is calculated and the salesperson reaffirms the customer's equity position, a further needs analysis will likely uncover a desire to upgrade the vehicle (where the customer was just being standoffish earlier). In other words, just because the customer said they only wanted a value for their current vehicle does not mean you waste the next 30 minutes doing nothing. We're using Assumptive Selling here; so, we assume he wants to buy, and he's going to buy today.

Like all instances of The Perfect Appointment (regardless of the direction this appointment takes), the experience is vastly different from how the average customer is treated on car lots today. The key is to treat owner marketing appointments as if the deals were already done (just like traditional appointments). Assume he has a great truck to sell us and that he'll accept our offer – and treat him this way. Assume he's a qualified buyer who can't wait to upgrade – and treat him this way. Even if you're unsuccessful at buying Mr. Jones' truck, he was greeted and treated like a true VIP; and his expectations were set early and met.

Everyone who steps foot on your lot wants to be treated like a qualified buyer. They want to be treated with the respect their $5,000 or $50,000 purchase demands. The Perfect Appointment helps you accomplish this by creating a truly memorable buying experience for your customer using some very simple tools (like the VIP folder, the hang tag and the old-fashioned sold row) and an Assumptive Selling mentality that treats every appointment like it's a delivery.

16

ASSUMPTIVE SELLING AND THE UP BUS

Assumptive Selling is not an entirely new way to handle Traditional Ups. In fact, it's actually been used for years by successful salespeople without anyone in the industry putting a name to the approach. Let me give you three quick examples:

1.   Top sellers often turn and start walking into the showroom – just assuming that the prospect will follow them in. It's a bold move that confident salespeople have used for decades and many still use today.

2.   Unsuccessful salespeople believe it when they hear a customer say, "I'm just looking;" while successful salespeople actually hear, "I'm buying today and I'm buying from you."

3.   When a slug sees someone getting out of a clunker on the lot, they assume he's just a tire-kicker; while the superstar sees a ready buyer who definitely needs an upgrade.

These three examples use the techniques of Assumptive Selling to close more Traditional Ups based on nothing more than assuming that everyone is a buyer… and then treating them as such.

Let me be clear: Everyone. Is. A. Buyer.

This, more than anything else, is what separates the top from the bottom. When you know everyone is a buyer, you have more confidence, you like your job more, you love your customers, and you couldn't imagine doing anything else with your life. (Why would you? Everyone is a buyer, dammit!) This is the essence of assumptively selling your Traditional Ups.

There's an old story that's been told so many times with so many different characters playing the customer that I'm not sure if it's true. That said, there is a valuable lesson in the story that makes it worth retelling (despite its dubious provenance). The version I've heard most often goes something like this:

Two salespeople are sitting in an air-conditioned showroom as they watch an old guy parking a rusted-out, dirty pickup truck in front of the dealership on a particularly hot day. (There's an old hunting dog in the passenger seat in a few versions of this story.)

The old guy gets out and starts wandering around the new truck inventory. The more senior of the two salesmen says to the other, "You go out and help that guy, Green Pea; you're up."

"I thought you were up," says the Green Pea.

Just then, the sales manager gets on the intercom with the standard "Joe Cook to new trucks." (Code for "there's an unattended customer looking at new trucks.")

The old car dog gives the Green Pea a stare and says, "Get out there, boy! I'm not telling you again."

As the Green Pea reluctantly walks out and starts talking to the Up, the sales manager and the old car dog laugh at how he's wasting his time with that old tire-kicker.

"That old boy couldn't buy a new truck if his hunting dog was made of gold," jokes the old car dog.

After spending nearly an hour with the old guy reviewing nearly every feature and benefit of nearly every truck, the Green Pea walks back into the dealership and introduces the customer to the sales manager. "Bob," the Green Pea says proudly, "I'd like you to meet Mr. Sam Walton. He runs a company called Wal-Mart and he'd like to order a few dozen trucks today if that's okay."

Like I wrote, the story has been told so many times and in so many versions that I'm not sure if it's true; though it does make for a nice lesson. The lesson here is that you can't qualify your customer through the glass. Moreover, when you plan to fully adopt Assumptive Selling, you have to assume everyone is a qualified buyer and they're buying today... unless they stop you.

By the way, why is it that so many Green Peas seem to do so well in their first couple of months? In my experience, I see the same three traits in all successful Green Peas:

1. They follow steps (because they're told to)
2. They don't talk too much (because they don't know too much)
3. They assume everyone is a buyer (because they don't know any better)

Oh, and everyone is a buyer. Study after study shows that consumers are now buying cars after visiting fewer than two lots on average. Gone are the days when most Traditional Ups stopped to see you and four or five other dealers before going home "to make an informed decision." They're showing up armed with information and ready to buy. They're ready to buy if you'll let them.

The reason the average buyer is visiting two or fewer lots before they buy is not because salespeople are doing a better job, it's because customers are doing a better job. They're doing their own needs analysis, product selection and feature presentation long before they set foot in their first dealership. They already know enough "to make an informed decision;" and if you treat them like a buyer (and assume the sale) you'll close them before they get a chance to visit dealership number two.

Or… you can keep treating everyone like a suspect and make them prove to you they're worthy of getting your attention for the next hour or so. Keep doing that and you'll continue to enjoy 20% closing rates, low-grossing deals, and terrible CSI.

Instead of continuing to languish as a below-average performer, remember these three little rules about Ups:

1. People with great credit scores want to be treated like serious buyers.
2. People with crappy credit scores want to be treated like serious buyers.
3. No one objects when you treat them like a VIP.

In the end, it doesn't cost you anything to assume everyone is a qualified buyer and everyone is buying today. However, I know some of you are ready to tell me about that guy who came in to see that $50,000 SUV and he wasted your time for 25 minutes until you realized he couldn't buy a $5.00 toy car! Oh, the humanity!

You mean you treated someone like a qualified buyer for a whole 25 minutes and then found out he couldn't buy?!?! Dear God, I'm hopeful you've been able to recover from this tragedy! The nerve of some people!

Acting like he can buy; earning your respect! Ugh! Now you know better, of course! Now you interrogate everyone for 20 minutes to separate the deadbeats from the real deals! Now you're able to sniff out the real buyers. Now you're able to close just that 20% of the Ups who pass your smell test!

Congratulations; every Up is now guilty until proven innocent, and the possible tragedy of treating anyone as a qualified buyer for less than half an hour has been avoided. This, of course, is one of the many reasons you're not selling 30 or more units each month.

To be clear, a tragedy is three kids trapped in a well. Spending 25 minutes with an Up only to discover he couldn't buy is an inconvenience. Though, if you continued to treat him with respect even after you found out he had no credit – and if you did your best to get him approved but couldn't – chances are he'll come back to see you when he can buy. Plus – and this is a big plus that assumptive sellers understand – just because you couldn't sell him doesn't mean you can't ask him for a referral (especially if you pay a bird dog fee).

Everyone on the Up Bus is a buyer. Everyone.

Everyone on the Up Bus likes to be treated like a VIP. Everyone.

Managers & Assumptive Selling

Looking at data from the dealers I've worked with over the past decade, it's clear that when a sales manager meets the prospect before the test drive, the store closes at more than twice the rate of the average dealership. These are not traditional T.O.s; these are proactive meetings where a sales manager simply greets the customer, thanks them for coming in, hands them a business card and assures them they are in good hands.

Of course, the sales manager is also looking at body language and taking the customer's temperature. If they sense an issue, they might linger a little longer and assist the salesperson in the buying process. Adding a trial close to this manager meet & greet can help your Up move to the write-up stage after the demo drive. Something as simple as, "I think you're going to love the new Tacoma. When you get back from your test drive, we'll have the numbers ready for you to review."

Demo drive percentages more than double; write-ups more than double; and closed deals more than double. So, why isn't every manager doing this?

Great question!

Some sales managers will tell you they don't have time; that they are too busy desking deals and putting out fires. They also say that they can't afford to waste time on non-buyers. They want to sit back until the customer has selected and test-driven a vehicle and is ready to negotiate. Of course, by then it's too late. They think they can swoop in and "close anybody." The truth is they cannot.

Great closing techniques have almost no impact at the end of a lousy road-to-the-sale. Studies in and out of automotive retail have proven that what you do during the first third of your buying process has more impact on your closing ratios than what you do in the final third. Meeting the customer early and treating them like a qualified buyer – with a done-deal attitude – reduces the number of pencils you'll have to present and doubles your store's closing percentage of Traditional Ups. (Yes, more deals at higher grosses!)

If your managers are converts to Assumptive Selling, they'll have plenty of time and no problem meeting every Up within minutes of their arrival. Why? Because everyone is a buyer!

However, if they simply cannot find the time, your dealership should consider adding another sales manager to the ranks. Although, this one should never sit behind the desk. Her job is simply to meet & greet all Ups before the demo drive.

But, let's be clear: I hate adding headcount; so, figure it out. Top dealers have no issues getting a manager to meet & greet every Up before the demo drive; even those with higher Up counts per manager than those who claim their sales managers have no time.

My advice – if your managers believe they have no time to complete this simple task – is to offer to hire an additional manager and divide the current sales manager pay among all. This means, if you currently pay four desk managers a total $X (with each earning approximately one-fourth of X), you'll now have five managers with the pot split five ways. It's amazing how quickly your four desk managers will find the time to meet & greet everyone before the demo drive!

The 10-Foot Rule

Because so many corporations have some version of the 10-foot rule – including Ritz-Carlton, Walmart, and the Rick Case Automotive Group – it's not possible to credit any one company with creating this customer-experience driver. So, let's just agree that it works.

Today's Ups – just like yesterday's Ups – aren't unhappy when your team acknowledges them; they're unhappy when no one acknowledges them. So, let's put in a 10-foot rule or a 12-foot rule or a 20-foot rule in place for your dealership. The rule is very simple:

> When anyone (and I mean anyone) on your team is within X feet of anyone else (and I mean anyone else) they should make eye contact, smile and say, "Welcome to ABC Motors; we're glad you're here. Do you have all the help you need?"

This includes the UPS guy, the Autotrader rep, the cleaning crew and fellow employees. When you instruct your team to greet everyone they see, your dealership quickly transforms into a fun place to visit, to work for, and to do business with.

You'll quickly begin to break down much of the built-in animosity your Traditional Ups feel at the average dealership each time someone on your team looks them in the eye, smiles and says, "Welcome to ABC Motors; we're glad you're here!"

But, as much as these mandated customer-first policies like the 10-foot rule can work, nothing works as well as a motivated team who likes selling cars and likes working for you. Therefore, if sales team turnover is still an issue for you, I recommend you reread and internalize the "Solving Dealership Turnover" chapter.

The Traditional Up

Appointments are great – if you can get them. However, not every buyer is going to connect with you in advance and give you the chance to set an appointment. In fact, about six out of ten buyers are going to have no previous contact with your dealership before they show up and buy.

These are your Traditional Ups, but there's nothing traditional about them. As we see in the data, today's Up (unlike the Up from just a few years ago) knows what they want, and they have a really good idea what they're going to pay. This does not mean you cannot hold gross with today's Up, it just means you need to be disciplined in your approach to do so; and treating everyone like a buyer is the first step to earning better grosses on every deal. That's because it's about the experience.

For the average dealer, today's Up is ready for the test drive, yet your road-to-the-sale puts the demo drive in Step 5 or 6. This traditional road-to-the-sale – which buyers absolutely hate – is inauthentic, long and clunky to most consumers. Moreover, this road-to-the-sale often blows out potential buyers before you ever have a chance to present the write-up. Some even take themselves out of the market because your needs analysis feels like an interrogation and your unwillingness to provide process and pricing transparency in your dealership puts them in a defensive position.

Yes, the ones you win, you crush on gross and steal their trades. The trouble is you are only winning one in five. It's time to improve the experience. Working to create a better offline car-buying experience is no longer an option. It's no longer an option if you have any interest in gaining actual market share while holding gross and creating customers for life. Today's buyers have too much information and too many places where they can buy their next vehicle to continue to reward those dealers providing the long, combative, five-hour road-to-the-sale.

Improving your buying process matters because every Silicon Valley startup that plans to "revolutionize" the way Americans buy cars is attacking you on the old-fashioned car-buying experience. The sad part for traditional dealers is that it's not that hard to improve the buying experience. Moreover, when you do make the necessary adjustments, everyone's job becomes a little easier and you start to make more money immediately.

To achieve the improved offline car-buying experience – that is, create a great customer experience – only requires a couple of changes. It requires a shorted road-to-the-sale and the addition of something called process transparency. Just implementing these two seemingly small changes makes for a great experience.

Not sure you agree? Let's look at two buying experiences: one that mirrors a typical road-to-the-sale today and one using a shortened process that includes transparency. Which one do you think your customers would prefer?

SCENARIO A: This one is a four-hour grind where everything is hidden from the buyer throughout. In this process, your sales rep started by taking them through every step of the road-to-the-sale before they began their test drive 38 minutes after arriving.

Once back at the dealership, your salesperson leaves your customer at a table by themselves while he goes to the desk a few times. The customer doesn't really know what's going on and spends the time looking around or using his smartphone to shop your competition.

Later, assuming they've agreed to your fourth pencil, they now have no idea why they're waiting 45+ minutes to get into the business office to give you their money. In their mind, they've already bought the car, yet you're making them wait for whatever reason.

SCENARIO B: In this process you asked the customer what vehicle they wanted to see and had them on their test drive within 15 minutes. You did a quick trade walk with them before the demo drive so that your manager could put together the deal before you returned.

As soon as you returned, your manager had the first pencil ready, including a defensible value for their trade. You handed them a tablet and they self-desked the deal by determining the payment terms they wanted.

While waiting for F&I, they used your tablet to learn about some of the F&I add-ons that your finance manager was going to present in a few minutes. Throughout the entire process, your salesperson never left their side, and they were in and out in 90 minutes.

Obviously, the first scenario is not a great experience for your customers or your sales team. Your customers want speed, they want efficiency, and they prefer to be kept informed throughout the process.

This is exactly what you provided in the latter scenario: a shortened road-to-the-sale that seemed efficient to the customer and that provided process transparency throughout. Not surprising, but dealers employing versions of the second process close their Traditional Ups at a much higher rate. What might be surprising, is that they earn average grosses equal to or better than dealers who grind out a four-hour nightmare known as the traditional road-to-the-sale.

But, They Said They Were "Just Looking"

During a traditional meet & greet, everyone claims they're "just looking." In fact, buyers have been "just looking" for about as long as there've been car dealers. Forty years ago, "just looking" often meant something like, "We're in the market for something good on gas, and we want to see what you have on the lot."

They were, in fact, just looking. They were potentially high in the sales funnel and just starting their research. A great experience where the salesperson took control could close them that day; though these visits most often resulted in be-back situations.

Today when you hear, "We're just looking," it's important to understand the customer is likely saying something like, "I'm here to buy that white 2017 Civic that you have online with stock number…" They're ready to buy today; though they're afraid to tell you this. They fear sales pressure, and they believe the best way to avoid this is to simply tell you they're "just looking" or "just gathering information" or that you're their "first stop." If they're really afraid of you, you might hear all three!

When you treat today's Ups more like buyers, they act more like buyers. Conversely, when you treat them more like tire-kickers, they act more like tire-kickers. And, treating everyone like a suspect – where you assume no one is a qualified buyer until they prove otherwise – ensures you drive away qualified buyers, leaving you with your self-fulfilling prophecy that "everyone's a deadbeat." (Because only deadbeats remain; the 800 Beacons won't put up with these shenanigans.)

As much as Assumptive Selling on the lot is about assuming the sale, it's also about ignoring the "no." That is, you're not going to listen to the prospect.

Everyone tells you some version of "no." Everyone is lying, of course. You are not their first stop; they are not just looking; and yes, they will buy today… you just have to assume that's what they planned from the moment they left their house and headed to your dealership. Assuming the sale, by the way, creates a great experience for the customer because you're not taking them down a road-to-the-sale filled with lots of unnecessary (in their mind) steps and questions.

Using an old-school road-to-the-sale today frustrates buyers. They arrived on your lot ready for your Step 6 (demo drive) and you're taking them back to "why" they think this is the car for them (needs analysis)! In their mind, you're almost demanding that they prove they're worthy of buying your vehicle from you.

To get you to understand why this creates a bad customer experience today (when buyers arrive after conducting extensive online research), let's apply a traditional car dealer road-to-the-sale to a few other retail situations:

- You're ordering at the counter at McDonald's and before the cashier will agree to enter anything in her register, she asks you, "What is it you like about the Big Mac? Is it just a Big Mac you're considering, or will you also consider a Quarter Pounder?"
- You're at the appliance store looking at their collection of expensive Sub-Zero refrigerators. You're ready to buy one that runs

about $9,000 when the salesman asks you, "Have you ever owned a Sub-Zero before? May I ask you why you're thinking about buying a Sub-Zero?"

- You walk into Macy's and a clerk stops you and asks, "Welcome to Macy's; have you ever shopped with us before? Did you work with anyone in particular?"

You're pretty sure you know what you want in the above instances and you're just trying to conduct some business. If those situations would put you in a foul mood, what makes you think similar qualifying questions and roadblocks don't leave today's car buyers feeling similarly uncomfortable?

Today's buyers know what they want, and they'll most often buy at the first place they shop. Provided, of course, that they have a good experience, they find authenticity in the salesperson and dealership, and they're presented with what they consider to be a fair deal. An assumptive buying process provides all of this by keeping the salesperson focused on remembering just two things:

1. Everyone is a buyer who is buying today; and
2. What's my next goal?

Instead of having to remember and follow a nonsensical twelve-step antiquated road-to-the-sale, you only have to focus on the next goal (one of only three) in an assumptive buying process: demo drive; write-up; F&I. While there are a few more steps in the actual process, there are only three distinct goals. Though the steps in the process are important, they exist only to further the next goal.

Unlike the old-fashioned road-to-the-sale – where every step held equal importance – the road-to-the-sale in the assumptive buying process recognizes that the achievements of the demo drive, the write-up and F&I are the milestones that most often lead to a sold unit.

In a traditional road-to-the-sale, the needs analysis and qualifying steps hold as much importance as the demo drive or write-up. This helps explain why the average salesperson gets fewer than half their Traditional Ups to take a test drive. They're so busy interrogating Ups during needs analysis and qualifying that their prospects decide they don't really want to buy today after all.

There are plenty of controllable reasons why you didn't sell a ready buyer, but the most common in my experience are (in no particular order):

- The encounter felt like an interrogation to the prospect (thus, no rapport was established);
- The prospect arrived ready to test drive and you asked them a bunch of questions instead (thus, they believed you weren't listening);
- You showed off your vast product knowledge before and during the test drive (thus, they felt like they were being sold);
- You offered multiple alternatives to their original choice (thus, they couldn't decide);
- The first pencil started at MSRP+++ despite a lower online price (thus, you broke trust with the buyer);
- You often left the prospect sitting alone without keeping them informed (thus, there was no process transparency)

If you could eliminate these gaffes (and all the times you never asked for the business), you'd find yourself closing nearly every Up that can buy. Of course, if you knew you had an informed, ready buyer in front of you, none of this would have happened. You would've simply walked them through the demo drive to the write-up to F&I... and, you'd have sold a vehicle.

By focusing on the next goal of the assumptive buying process, you'll find yourself pulling them through to the next step with ease. For example:

- They just arrived? Great, let's get them on the test drive?
- On the test drive? Great, let's trial close them with something like, "If everything checks out during the test drive, we'll run the numbers when we get back to the dealership."
- Presenting the deal? Great, let's have the F&I manager come out to meet them to let the buyers know she's going to help them, "complete the paperwork" once they're ready.

You walk them through your process; stay in control one step at a time and assume the sale throughout. It's not about slowing down or speeding up; it's about a road-to-the-sale that feels like a natural progression to the buyer. It's more of a closing process, if you will. They're here to buy a car. Our job is to help them buy. That's all it is.

A Better Customer Experience

For dealers who've successfully conducted business the same way for decades, I can understand that (A) some of you still don't buy-in to the whole "better customer experience" thing; or (B) those who do buy-in may have no idea how or where to start creating this better experience.

If you still don't buy-in, all I can say is good luck. Enjoy rising or falling with the market. Enjoy the sales team turnover that you've enjoyed for decades. Enjoy tightening margins and the 4+ hour "grind-fests" you and your customers loathe. You will still make money (as you always have) for the near term, you just won't be growing share or making as much as you could by providing a better experience.

For those ready to change, but who just don't know where or how to start, let's begin by getting beyond the built-in roadblocks your managers will throw at the notion of a great buying experience. Things like, "But, statistics from this old-school sales trainer taught us that if we take three or more hours to close a deal, we close more deals."

This data (which still gets shared today on sites like LinkedIn) was relevant in the pre-internet days; when the customer leaned on the dealership to provide value and relevancy; when they needed (and appreciated) a needs analysis; when they wanted help with product selection; when your full feature presentation meant something.

As you've already read numerous times in this book, today's Up completed their own needs analysis, product selection and feature presentation... now, they just want someone to sell them a vehicle. Today's Up wants the deal done in under an hour (and they overwhelmingly hate the typical road-to-the-sale).

Of course, some old-school sales managers will tell you "If we shortcut the road-to-the-sale, we'll shortcut our profits." Clever. Even true... if a shortened road-to-the-sale was actually a shortcut; it's not. Shortening the road-to-the-sale is merely about creating an efficient process that customers will love. Of course, the reason that we need an abbreviated road-to-the-sale is that the buyer already has all of the information, and they most often arrive ready to test drive.

Moreover, shortening the road-to-the-sale allows your team to assist more customers per salesperson. Assuming prospects are just lined up in need of help, the dealership where the entire deal takes 90 minutes can assist twice as many customers as the one where it takes 3 hours to complete a sale. Of course, that's perfect math, but the premise is still a valid one. That is, when deals can be completed efficiently, salespeople have more time available to assist others (or to complete their assigned activities, like phone calls to their sold database).

Everyone's Online; So Why Fix Our Offline Processes?

Virtually all shoppers are virtual, right? Virtually everyone hates the dealership experience, right? Absolutely! But, they still want to shop... so let's make them want to shop with you.

As already stated, industry data shows that roughly six of every ten buyers make no contact with dealerships before they arrive to buy today. No contact, despite all the opportunities they've been presented to submit a lead or pick up the phone or chat with your team.

Surely, as great online car buying options continue to grow, the percentage of buyers who begin as Traditional Ups is going to be reduced; but to what? 50%? 40%? Whatever happens with online buying over the next several years, the 100% in-store experience is still going to be an important chunk of every dealer's business. That's precisely why you want to fix this and provide a great customer experience to everyone getting off the Up Bus.

Your final road-to-the-sale – whether you create your own or use the one I'll present later in this chapter – must be efficient; it must make sense to the prospect; it must value their time; and it must assume they are a ready buyer who wants to buy today.

Before we look at an efficient road-to-the-sale, let's talk about what today's Ups dislike about the traditional variety:

- It takes too long;
- It repeats steps; and
- It lacks transparency.

Even dealers who feel like they've squeezed all the unnecessary steps from their road-to-the-sale still spend about three hours on the average sold Up. Most consumers say they want this entire process to take less than an hour; and no one wants to give up their entire Saturday to buy a car. Yet, old-school trainers are still telling your team to slow down.

An efficient road-to-the-sale may still take a couple of hours from beginning to end, but it doesn't seem that long to the prospect. This is because the steps make sense and the prospect is engaged in the process. Think about it, what feels longer: Sitting quietly for 30 minutes or watching a 30-minute sitcom? Keeping the customer engaged throughout the process makes it feel more efficient.

The buying process feels most efficient when a prospect can start at your dealership where they left off online. This is easy when they connect with you in advance because you can conduct The Perfect Appointment. Unfortunately, with a Traditional Up, you often don't know where they left off in their research, and you don't know which websites they explored or what inspired them to visit your dealership today.

This causes you to repeat steps the prospect has already completed and reduces your closing percentages. An efficient buying process – in the prospect's mind – starts on the next step the prospect needs in order to complete the purchase; though without skipping any steps your team must take in order to close the deal. Because the average Up's answer to your meet & greet is often, "We're just looking; you're our first stop," you either need to employ mind readers or take every Up back to the first step in your road-to-the-sale.

Frustrating, I know. However, before we dive into a simple meet & greet question that will help you uncover where most buyers actually are in the process, let's look at some simple changes you can make to your existing road-to-the-sale to make it seem like a better experience for the prospect who's unwilling to share that information upfront:

Reduce Unnecessary Paperwork: Before smartphones, tablets, scanners, etc., sales managers often needed lots of handwritten documentation completed by the salesperson before they would begin to work a deal. Some of this was required to formulate the first pencil and some of this was just busy work sales managers would heap on their sellers.

Today, everything a sales manager needs can and should be collected and shared electronically. However, some sales managers still insist their salespeople manually complete certain forms. For example, some require handwritten trade-in forms (that include the VIN and other important and easy-to-screw-up data) before they'll put a number on a trade. This needlessly slows down the buying process even when the salesperson correctly records all 17 digits of the VIN.

Additionally, some dealers still require a paper credit application be completed even though all other entities in the transaction – like the bank – are good with the electronic version your customer completed before they arrived. If this describes your dealership, find a way to get to the 21st century with the rest of the industry and get rid of these customer timewasters.

Reorder the Steps: Today, most dealers will buy vehicles from consumers even if the consumer does not buy from them. Despite having that policy in place, many used car managers still refuse to put a value on a trade until the customer has selected and test-driven a vehicle. (Some won't even look at the trade until the Up has also agreed on the purchase price of the replacement vehicle.) Of course, this process was designed to help managers find additional gross in the trade that may have been given up in the purchase.

However, with the plethora of trade tools available for consumers, this practice is no longer as effective at generating any more gross than valuing the trade earlier in the process. (In fact, more gross can be gained by doing a proper trade walk with the Up before the test drive than by delaying the appraisal.) Plus, when you consider that prospects are most likely to buy the minute they return from the demo drive than at any other time in the process, you're hurting your closing percentages by slowing down the deal at this point.

By appraising the trade while the buyer is on the test drive, you can present a complete deal as soon as they return; when they're most likely to buy.

Provide Process Transparency: Some of the frustration that today's Ups have with the car-buying process stems from not knowing what's going on at all times. This is where process transparency comes in.

Process transparency can be as simple as telling your Up what you and your team are doing now and what you're going to do. For example, once they understand that the F&I manager needs 30 minutes to load the deal and prepare the paperwork before the buyer can enter, they'll be more patient as they wait. Without this process transparency, they sit staring at the business office wondering why it's empty and they can't go in now.

Keep Them Engaged: You're waiting on the F&I office with your prospect. They know why they're waiting, but nothing is actually happening. To help shorten the perceived wait time, keep your prospect engaged and involved in something at all times. During this expected downtime, some salespeople:

- Complete the service walk, and set the first service appointment;

- Begin a mini-delivery with the customer;
- Demonstrate some of the available accessories;
- Introduce F&I products using either a tablet or simple, laminated sheets.

By keeping the buyer engaged, you shorten the perceived wait time and complete necessary steps more efficiently and/or improve your back-end grosses by introducing products and services in advance of the business office visit.

Provide Pricing Transparency: There is a fear that if we're as transparent with our pricing in the store as we are online, we'll lose all the gross with the Traditional Up. Hint: They were already online and they're carrying a smartphone! Providing pricing transparency in the store does not reduce gross, it reduces friction.

Being transparent with pricing doesn't mean we show the prospect what we paid for a given vehicle; rather, we make sure they're informed about important values and prices as soon as possible in the process. For example, pricing transparency includes:

- Allowing an Up to value their own trade on your tablet or theirs;
- Introducing and defending the addendum immediately prior to a test drive;
- Presenting multiple payment options and the ability to self-select terms (again, with your tablet or theirs); and
- Reviewing F&I add-ons (with pricing) before entering the business office.

When the buyer is informed early about an addendum or a low trade value (that they helped calculate), they can process this and justify it before the write-up. This reduces friction and helps you close more deals for more money.

Involve the Prospect: If you're all-in on keeping them engaged and providing both pricing and process transparency, then you're probably already going to involve the prospect every step of the way. There is, however, a step that I still see fewer than half of salespeople take that helps dealers buy trades cheaper and keeps the prospect engaged and informed. It's sometimes called a silent walkaround or the trade walk.

This is the trade walk you learned about in the last chapter and should not be confused with the other trade walk (see the glossary to figure out what this all means).

These few simple changes not only deliver the prospect a more efficient process, but they also go a long way to reducing the friction that's built into the typical road-to-the-sale.

Let's Remove (Not Reduce) The Friction

Newsflash: Regardless of what you and your team believe, customers perceive multiple points of friction in the car-buying process. Friction, by the way, that has today's buyer seeking ways to avoid the dealership experience while working overtime to ensure you make no money on their deal.

Given this, how your buyers view your buying process is all that matters; and you need to accept this because of two unrelenting truisms:

- Perception is reality; and
- The customer is not always right, but they are always the customer.

Understanding these allows you to move beyond the debate over whether there is friction that needs to be removed; and simply get to the task of removing it. For dealers truly interested in removing friction, the task begins by uncovering the causes of the most damaging friction and making the necessary changes to rectify these.

Of course, we've already uncovered and addressed most of the primary catalysts of friction in your current road-to-the-sale:

- A lack of price transparency
- A lack of process transparency
- Paperwork
- Waiting

When you add in the repeated sales steps a traditional road-to-the-sale forces on today's Ups, you should have a clear vision of what your buying process should become. By focusing on these few causes, it becomes easier to spot where friction is most likely to occur in the traditional process, for example:

- A lack of price transparency – Throughout most in-store processes, but especially during the trade appraisal and desking.
- A lack of process transparency – Again, throughout most in-store processes.
- Paperwork – Excessive (in the minds of the buyers) paperwork occurs most often in the business office, and during some trade appraisals.
- Waiting – Most needless waiting occurs during desking (the back-and-forth) and prior to getting into the business office.
- Repeating sales steps – Generally at the beginning of the Road-to-the-Sale (needs analysis, qualifying, product selection).

Any of these instances of friction can make the entire process feel like a grind to most customers; and taken together, they likely explain why the typical dealer still closes just 20-30% of their Traditional Ups, despite the average buyer visiting fewer than two lots today. Removing friction can not only improve close rates, but also front and back grosses, and (of course) CSI. We'll look at some radical and not-so-radical solutions some dealers are using today to remove friction entirely from the process.

One of the easiest steps to implement – once you get over the fear that you'll lose control of the deal – is the concept of self desking. Whether you're ready to admit it or not, the future of desking involves a tablet and a customer... and no desk manager. Moreover, giving the customer a tablet and the ability to self-select their lender (which they can do today online or offline with some third-party tools), the ability to play with the length of the loan, and to decide on a payment, moves the discussion away from price and onto terms.

This is the epitome of process transparency and provides just enough price transparency (in the form of a self-selected interest rate, for example, where the dealer still earns their reserves) to give the consumer the required confidence to buy today... all without the friction (or waiting) that comes standard with traditional desking.

Yes, this is a radical move; but many one-price dealers have been doing a version of self-desking for years... they just may not have called it that. When a single person works with the customer from beginning to end, the desking process can be a cooperative exercise. That is, the customer participates in the final selections.

Moving from buyers participating in the process (as is done at many one-price stores) to handing the customer a tablet and helping them go through the steps is an easy transition that builds trust, eliminates unnecessary waiting, and, above all else, removes friction.

The next, and more radical, approach is sometimes called DIY F&I. Today's old car dogs will surely react with utter disdain and perhaps even great vengeance and furious anger when they read that I not only believe Do-It-Yourself F&I is the future, but that dealers who fail to embrace this trend will find themselves struggling to create a buying experience that customers love (and are willing to pay extra for).

Of course, I find this misdirected anger a little humorous when you consider it was the old car dogs from forty years ago who railed against the very idea of adding an F&I manager in the first place. (Similar to the old car dogs in the last two decades who railed against the internet, used car stocking/pricing tools and putting vehicle prices online.)

Big changes always seem to occur gradually and then all at once. Today, DIY F&I and even self-desking might seem like implausible dreams, but they're successfully being adopted gradually. One day, they're going to come all at once. That's how big changes happen in automotive retail. They happen gradually and then all at once. That is, just when it looks like predicted big changes will never really come to pass, we blink, and we see they already happened.

Of course, if you're now thinking, "What the heck? How am I supposed to make any back-end gross without a trained killer in the F&I manager's chair?" you wouldn't be in the minority, nor would you be naïve. It's a great question.

So, instead of trying to wrap your head around something too difficult to comprehend (and that may still be on the distant horizon for your dealership), just open your mind enough to explore ways you can (A) improve the car-buying experience and (B) grow your back-end grosses at the same time. For example, empirical data shows that pre-presenting F&I products to consumers grows their willingness to purchase these once they reach the business office.

This means educating them (or allowing them to educate themselves with a tablet) about those items included in the menus you're about to present. You see, the better they understand products like GAP, LoJack and vehicle service contracts, the more likely they are to buy these.

While you're not ready to move to a full DIY F&I; incorporating a tablet into your process – where buyers can learn about the benefits of the products they'll be presented – reduces the education load on your

F&I managers, while making the time your buyers wait for the business office seem much shorter.

The friction points that surround the F&I process (including the waiting, the hard selling, and the tons of paperwork) can all be removed with just a little technology. We already explored how employing a tool that allows for buyers to self-present F&I add-ons – whether online or on a tablet in-store – removes the friction associated with waiting and hard selling; now the goal is to reduce the need for so much paperwork (or at least the perception of so much paperwork) where possible.

Moving some of this paperwork out of the F&I office and into the hands of the salesperson is one way to reduce that perception. Moreover, removing the friction doesn't have to mean reducing your profits. As we know from looking at online vehicle sales, the back-end grosses of those purchases (where the buyer fully self-presents the add-ons and completes nearly all of the paperwork before they arrive) is about equal to the average F&I manager presenting these in-store.

So, while there's no need to get rid of your F&I department today, there should also be no need to panic about allowing your in-store buyers to self-present your F&I products while they wait on your trained killer F&I manager. Today's connected customers want speed, they want efficiency and they want to reduce the friction. You're not going to lose your F&I grosses if you help them achieve that speed and efficiency while you remove the friction.

If you're thinking, "Okay, I'm in, but how do we get there?" You're not alone. It can be mindboggling to think about how to get from your current road-to-the-sale to doing it all on a tablet. Just keep in mind that you can't get there overnight; but you should be working toward making buying with you a great experience. Ultimately, this major change will happen; it will happen gradually and then all at once.

Gradual Change

If you're indeed ready to create a great buying experience in your dealership (or, if you're a salesperson who plans to go it alone on this whole customer experience thing), you're probably wondering what steps you need to take to make this happen. That's understandable, because although you agree change is necessary, we all know that change (especially in automotive retail) can be disruptive.

Therefore, your goal should be to figure out how to make buying from you a great experience without driving away any truly productive employees or managers. Also, you and your team should agree on one unmistakable truth: You cannot create and maintain a great buying experience without simple, repeatable sales processes. Any meaningful improvements will require a strict process. Process, after all, is what ultimately sells cars.

Over the medium term (i.e., one month to a year) and the long term (i.e., more than a year), processes – even bad processes – outsell and out-gross and out-everything the opposite. This is true because the opposite of process is no process. In other words, everything is seat-of-the-pants and on-the-fly and ad-libbed. And, while your managers and salespeople might argue that they always say and do the right things to close every deal and make the most money, the truth is that without simple, repeatable processes that are strictly followed, you're losing deals and leaving gross on the table.

Have you ever noticed that no one ever talks about the deals their fly-by-night style lost for the dealership?

Simply put, lousy buying experiences (devoid of process) actually cause some consumers to take themselves out of the market. Moreover, a lack of sales process is why you have 8-Car Alans and 30-Car Theos on the same team; all receiving the same number of opportunities after being provided the exact same training. (It's also why average F&I managers gross so much less than what F&I superstars deliver.)

Even if your processes are bad, at least they can be improved (provided they are strictly enforced). When everyone just sort of does their own thing, there is no path to improvement, because the holes and the weaknesses (other than a lack of process) cannot be identified (as they can with even a bad process).

Some dealers lean on technology to drive their processes; though frankly, you really shouldn't need fancy or even simple software (including your CRM) to help you manage sales processes that you believe in. You and your management team should be so convinced that adherence to your processes makes for a great buying experience – one that delivers more sold units at higher grosses – that managing your processes is second nature, so much so that it doesn't seem like work.

Of course, that's in a perfect world and you live in the real world. Leveraging the tools that are available (especially your CRM) does indeed make it easier for you to create, manage and improve your sales processes. Given this, let's look at the basic first steps for creating, managing and improving a sales process:

1. Write a shortened sales process that covers all the steps you absolutely need, and ensure the steps are in the order that make sense to a connected customer.
2. Now, make it shorter (or seem shorter by involving the prospect as much as possible in the steps).
3. Review the process with your sales team and ask them to (A) poke holes in it, (B) tell you why they cannot follow it 100% of the time, and (C) whether this will be more enjoyable to the average buyer than the current road-to-the-sale.
4. Make changes based on their feedback.
5. Commit the process to written form and have all managers and employees sign off on it.
6. Get with your CRM provider to ensure the sales process steps are built into the CRM as required checkpoints. (This means your team must complete "A" before moving to "B" and so on.)
7. Announce a date when this process will be strictly enforced and stick to that date. (In the meantime, your leadership team should begin managing all sales through this process and providing constructive feedback to those who struggle to adhere to the steps during this grace period.)
8. Make improvements to your process over time, but only if they make sense and help you sell more vehicles at higher grosses.

It's important to note, of course, that tools like your CRM have limitations. They are only as good as the data you or your team input, and only as effective as the level of enforcement your managers choose to employ. For example, if your process requires someone to scan a license before they can get the keys for a test drive, then your managers can never allow anyone to get keys for a test drive without first scanning a license.

This seems simple enough, but this is precisely the kind of step that breaks down when your sales managers are "busy." If you allow even a single exception to your written process, you no longer have a process.

Beyond just using a CRM, there are successful dealers using tablets and/or kiosks today to help their teams stay on track with great processes. With the right process baked into a tablet, your salespeople are "forced" to follow your steps in a way that makes sense to the prospect. Moreover, with a tablet or kiosk, your prospect can more easily participate in the process – making it seem efficient and transparent.

The right tablet (or kiosk) software, configured correctly, simply won't allow your team to merely "check boxes" or skip steps. Instead, these tools can hold your team to the exact process you dictate. This makes your sales process repeatable and strictly enforced; and to be considered great, processes merely need to be simple, repeatable and strictly enforced.

If I were running your dealership group, the tablet/kiosk sales process I'd put in place would begin where the customer wants to start and would include them in every step. For example, a simple road-to-the-sale that feels more like a buying process would look something like this:

1. Meet & Greet
2. License Scan
3. Select Test Drive Vehicle(s)
4. Trade Keys
5. Evaluate Trade
6. Demo Drive
7. Write-Up
8. Service Walk
9. F&I Add-Ons
10. F&I
11. Delivery

While this buying process shows eleven steps and technically has the demo drive sixth on the list, keeping the prospect engaged the entire time, simultaneously completing steps and allowing every step to occur on the same tablet, makes this feel like just a few steps to the customer. From the buyer's perspective:

Step 1: Scanned my license, selected a vehicle to test drive, entered some information about my trade and discovered the wholesale book value.

Step 2: Gave my keys to the product specialist so his/her manager could provide a firm offer, then got in my new vehicle to test drive.

Step 3: Returned to the dealership, did the paperwork, learned about their service department, and learned about GAP Insurance, LoJack and an extended warranty.

Step 4: Finished the paperwork with their business manager and then drove home.

During this entire process, the salesperson never needs to leave their side (unless you are still using a traditional F&I manager). Additionally, the write-up and any steps involving F&I product education can (and probably should by now) be completed by the salesperson sitting side-by-side with the prospect

Of course, if you want to go all-in on a great experience, just turn the tablet around and allow the guest to enter/explore everything from their trade value to lenders to terms to F&I. This experience not only keeps the prospect engaged but creates tremendous process and pricing transparency that builds trust. Additionally, with the right tool powering this, the customer will take ownership sooner in the process and your closing rates and (believe it or not) grosses will improve.

Allowing the customer to complete desking and F&I steps on their own (with your team sitting by their side, of course) via a tablet that also manages your new simple, repeatable and strictly enforced process is actually part of a natural progression from "no process" to creating a buying experience that customers love; whether they're 100% offline buyers or an online/offline hybrid.

The Common Denominators of a Great Experience

The good news about trying to create a great car buying experience is that there are similarities among all great dealership experiences that can be studied and adopted. Understanding what these are and why they make for a great buying experience allows you to easily include them in all your store's sales processes:

Take Control: Although this may sound counterintuitive, all great car buying experiences are controlled. Primarily, this is due to the complexity of the vehicle purchase and the fact that the average consumer has no idea how the process works today – all they know is that they really didn't like the process the last time they bought.

By taking control of the process and guiding the customer through your steps in order, you can keep the purchase on track and you'll close at a much higher rate. Conversely, when you cede control to the prospect, you allow confusion and doubt to overtake their desire to purchase today, and your closing rates decline.

Make Sense: When you take steps that don't appear to get the prospect any closer to the actual purchase, you begin to build unnecessary friction and anxiety. All great buying experiences make sense to the customer. More specifically, the steps you guide them through follow in a logical order in the prospect's mind.

One way to ensure the process makes sense to the customer is to let them know what you're doing and why you're doing it during each step. This way you'll ensure they understand the need for a particular step; and you'll head off any confusion or anxiety before it occurs.

Engage Them: All great buying experiences seem shorter or more efficient than they really are because the customer is involved throughout. Contrast this to the typical road-to-the-sale where the customer is often left alone while the salesperson goes back-and-forth to the sales desk.

Does their time spent waiting feel efficient to them? Does the whole process feel shorter or longer than it is? Keep the customer engaged in the entire process, so that no matter how long the process takes, it will feel much shorter than it really is.

Buying, Not Selling: All great customer experiences employ a buying process. This means the customer feels like they're buying and not being sold. With a proper buying process in place, the customer will feel like your equal. You are still in control, but the steps seem logical and they are headed towards the purchase.

When the customer is buying, you need to overcome fewer objections, because you simply move them through a process that makes sense. After all, they came to buy today, didn't they?

It's Not Complicated: That's really all that's required to create a great car buying experience: You're in control; the process makes sense; you keep them engaged (often with a tablet or kiosk); and you allow them to feel like they're buying instead of being sold.

Assumptive Selling: Finally, you can improve our chances of closing customers that you take through your great buying experience when you also assume the sale throughout. This means from the moment their vehicle pulls onto your lot, you should assume they're here to buy and that they're here to buy today. Doing so will help you avoid treating your prospects like suspects and will ensure you take them through each step of your shortened road-to-the-sale.

The Road-to-the-Assumptive-Sale

Deals are not won in the write-up as much as they're won before the demo drive. We already know that most of today's Traditional Ups arrive on your lot only after they've selected a vehicle they feel has value and relevancy – they're just looking for an authentic person to sell them the car. If you're inauthentic at the beginning of your road-to-the-sale, the best closers in the business will struggle to save your deals.

Given this, it's critical to focus solely on "the next step" during your buying process:

- Customer is exiting their vehicle? My focus is on understanding why they're here.
- They identify a vehicle of interest? My focus is on the demo drive.
- On the demo drive? My focus is on the write-up.
- We're presenting a deal? My focus is on closing.

With Assumptive Selling, you don't need to focus on the close the moment they drive on your lot because you already know you're going to sell them a car. They're here to buy and they're going to buy today. You just need to follow some logical steps (one at a time) to make this a great buying experience that earns you great grosses today and referral business tomorrow.

Most often, the salespeople who fail to close today, failed early in their process. They were so busy closing the sale (or trying to sniff out the deadbeats) that they didn't listen to the Up. To be clear, I'm going to give you contradictory instructions in this book when it comes to listening. In this paragraph I'm saying they didn't listen to the Up and that's one reason they failed; though, the truth is you should never listen to the Up. Let me explain the difference.

You should always *hear* what the Up is saying (and not saying). You should always *consider* what the Up is saying (and not saying). But, and this is key, you should never let what they're saying make you doubt that you have a ready buyer in front of you. You are the only one who can decide that; not the Up.

The best example I can provide is that nearly every Up tells you, "We're just looking; we're not buying today." If you believed this, you'd never sell another car. This is what I meant when I wrote *you should never listen to the Up*. Hear what they're saying; acknowledge it; then move on to your goal (which is always the next step in your road-to-the-sale).

When dealing with a Traditional Up, three of the four communication rules explained earlier in this book apply; these are take charge, be direct and provide guidance. Additionally, today's buyer appreciates when you speak to them like a fellow human – just as you would if you were selling to one of your friends – so avoid asking the nonsensical questions that don't resonate with prospects. For example, if you wouldn't ask a friend, "Are there any colors you wouldn't consider," then don't pose this same question to your Ups.

It's about being human. Speaking to them like a human using active language and telling them what to do. It's about having a one-goal strategy, which is to wow them at every step. Whatever step we're on in the road-to-the-sale we want to make certain it's the best experience that they've ever had at a dealership.

Today's connected customer needs you to take charge the moment they get out of their car; if you don't, you'll likely never sell them a vehicle. They want you to be direct with them (it's more honest) and they appreciate your guidance (that's why they stopped in rather than called you or used a web form). You must control the entire experience from beginning to end; and if you do, you're going to win way more often than you lose.

It's not possible, of course, to control the buying experience if you're not following a process. In this case, your process is your simple, repeatable and strictly-followed road-to-the-sale. Controlling the buying experience means you're going to pull them (gently and happily) through your process.

Three Hours is Unrealistic

As you build your road-to-the-sale, focus first on a goal of less than 60 minutes from beginning to end. (Yes, this includes F&I!) You'll still occasionally encounter an Up that chews up five hours of a Saturday, but one hour can become your norm if you design it this way from the beginning and enforce its use.

Slower is not better – despite the old-school stats that show longer in-store times equal higher close rates. When you employ Assumptive Selling, you can move your buyer through an efficient process – one that does not skip steps, does not feel rushed and is not careless. Today's Up is arriving ready for the demo drive, so taking them back to needs analysis is inauthentic – it's also not how you would sell to a friend.

Efficiency starts with the meet & greet. If you're still using a traditional greeting that encourages the prospect to lie to you, expect to take everyone back to the first step of an old-fashioned road-to-the-sale.

If you're hearing some version of "just looking" from nearly every Up, then you're asking the wrong questions in the meet & greet. We can certainly overcome "just looking," but it requires taking them back into needs analysis instead of into the demo drive:

Customer: "Oh, we're just looking; we're not ready to buy."

Salesperson: "Excellent; that takes all the pressure off me. Let's make today all about gathering information. Does that sound okay?"

Congratulations, because you asked them the wrong question in the meet & greet, you allowed them to tell you they were "just looking" and you added at least 30 minutes to this deal... if you close them.

When a customer is ready for a demo drive, taking them back to needs analysis is inauthentic and it kills your deal. I've actually heard a salesperson blow a sale using this exchange:

Customer: "We're here to test drive that blue minivan you have on your website."

Salesperson: "Great! So, is it just minivans you're looking at or are you also considering mid-sized SUVs?"

Yikes! They found value and relevancy in your used minivan. They're here to buy it, but you're making them question their choice in vehicles and dealerships! It's not authentic to reply to a request for a test drive with a needs analysis or qualifying question.

Instead of answering like a robot who doesn't understand that this prospect wants to buy your minivan, consider how you would reply if a friend walked on the lot and said the same thing:

Friend: "We're here to test drive that blue minivan you have on your website."

Salesperson: "Great; let's get your license scanned, get the keys and take it out for a quick test drive!"

Do you recognize the difference? When you treat today's Up like a qualified buyer who's already completed many of the steps to a traditional road-to-the-sale, you'll more easily focus on the step of your buying process that's most important (that is, the next one).

The road-to-the-sale I'm going to recommend is the one I introduced earlier in this chapter:

1. Meet & Greet
2. License Scan
3. Select Test Drive Vehicle(s)
4. Trade Keys
5. Evaluate Trade
6. Demo Drive
7. Write-Up
8. Service Walk
9. F&I Add-Ons
10. F&I
11. Delivery

However, you should think of the above process more like this:

1. Meet & Greet
   a. License Scan
   b. Select Test Drive Vehicle(s)
   c. Trade Keys
   d. Evaluate Trade
2. Demo Drive
3. Write-Up
   a. Service Walk
   b. F&I Add-Ons
4. F&I
5. Delivery

Looking at the road-to-the-sale as written above helps you understand the actual steps that represent your goals versus the sub-steps that have value but should never be your next overriding goal. For example, when you're involved in the meet & greet, your primary goal should be moving to the demo drive.

First, I'll present the above road-to-the-sale as if your buyer does everything you ask (and many will!); and then we'll use the next chapter to help you overcome objections on the lot.

But, before you walk out to meet your next sale, it's critical that you turn your phone to silent mode and ignore incoming calls and texts. The person getting out of their car on your lot is a qualified buyer who is going to buy today. There is no call or text that you'll receive during this encounter that is more important than the ready buyer in front of you.

The Meet & Greet

The goal of the meet & greet is to move to the demo drive. Period.

While using the Assumptive Selling meet & greet, you will still maintain a secondary goal of building a relationship and finding common ground (as was true with any successful road-to-the-sale); however, this should not be your primary goal. Yes, people buy cars from people they like, but they won't like you if you're inauthentic – and you certainly won't be able to find any common ground if you dive into needs analysis and qualifying right away.

When you approach the Up, make and maintain eye contact. If there are others with her, make eye contact with everyone – including the kids – as you shake the hand of each person (assuming they're open to a hand shake). Women, you may know, make the bulk of the car-buying decisions, so do yourself a favor and assume she is the qualified buyer when you're upping a couple or family that includes a man and a woman.

If you're a sales*man*, be attentive, but not flirty to the female buyers. Don't ignore the man when dealing with a couple; though be certain no one feels you're ignoring her. Likewise, if you're a sales*woman*, be attentive, but not flirty to the male buyers. Regardless of your gender, the majority of your attention should be focused on the female buyer when dealing with a couple.

To be clear, when I say, "majority of your attention," I'm implying a 51/49 split with 51% of your attention focused on the female buyer. Our ultimate goal is to sell a vehicle, and you'll sell very few if anyone feels ignored by you when there are multiple buyers.

As you greet the Up and her family, your Assumptive Selling greeting is simple and meant to imply they are buyers who've already done their research:

Salesperson: "Good afternoon and welcome to ABC Motors. My name is Steve Stauning. What vehicle did you folks come to test drive today?"

We don't know their name, we don't know if they've been here before, and we don't know what other vehicles they've been looking at. Moreover, we don't need any of this information just yet. With our Assumptive Selling meet & greet we have just one primary goal: to get them into the demo drive.

This Assumptive Selling greeting is authentic in the minds of most every buyer. They've done their needs analysis, their product selection and their feature presentation. They feel like a qualified buyer who is ready for the test drive... and you just treated them like a qualified buyer who is ready for the test drive.

While most buyers will announce their vehicle of interest now, we'll handle that in moment. First, let's talk about what to do when the Up answers with a traditional smokescreen response:

Prospect: "Oh, we're just looking."

When this happens, you're going to pivot to a more old-school road-to-the-sale. You see, we tried to respect the prospect's time and get them into the test drive right away, but they chose to lie to us. That's okay, we'll just resort to some old-fashioned meet & greet questions like:

Salesperson: "Just looking? That's great to hear, then you must be here for our big sale."

And, then move them through the longer, old-school road-to-the-sale you learned on your first day in the car business.

It will shock you at first, but most Ups will honestly answer your "what vehicle did you come to test drive today" question with something specific like one of the following:

Prospect: "Actually, we were looking at the blue 2017 Civic you've got on your website." Or

Prospect: "We're here to look at your Explorers." Or

Prospect: "We're here to look at your trucks."

Your response when using Assumptive Selling is simply:

> Salesperson: "Great. Let me get your license scanned so I can get you the keys and you can take that Civic out for a test drive."

They are ready buyers who are here to buy today. They already told you what they came to test drive, so you don't need to ask them to take this step. In fact, you told them to take this step, didn't you? You took charge, you were direct, and now you're guiding them through your process.

Most prospects will appreciate this, since most people arrive on your lot today ready for the demo drive. They'll hand over their license as you walk them to the license scanner, kiosk or copy machine. (For the remainder of this process, I'm going to assume you're using a kiosk and have the ability to switch seamlessly to a tablet throughout your road-to-the-sale.)

During the walk and while at the kiosk, you'll reintroduce yourself and ask a few important needs analysis and qualification questions; though, always assuming you are looking at a qualified buyer who is here to buy today.

That's it. It's simple. It's intuitive. It's seamless. It's transparent. It's efficient. Oh, and when done right, it doubles your demo drive percentage.

While at the kiosk you'll enter the Up in the CRM, add their vehicle of interest and ask about a trade:

> Salesperson: "Would you like me to also get you a written offer on your Taurus?" Or

> Salesperson: "Will you be trading-in your Ford Taurus?"

When the customer responds in the affirmative, you're going to ask to trade keys and then ask for their help:

> Salesperson: "Outstanding; it looks like it's in great shape. Can you help me gather the information from your Taurus? This way, my manager can appraise it during the test drive."

You're now entering a new step called the trade walk (noted as "evaluate trade" on our road-to-the-sale); and you want the buyer to remain by your side the entire time you're gathering information from their trade-in.

It's important that they help (and, if possible, that they enter the data into a tablet or kiosk), as we need to let them tell us everything that's wrong with their trade and expose them to a wholesale book number that sets their expectations.

They won't like the wholesale number and that's okay; we're not going to fully address that objection until the write-up. However, if they seem completely flipped out by the low number, a simple reassuring response will get them back on track without giving them false hope that we'll be paying retail for their trade:

> Salesperson: "Yeah, that does seem low. Of course, that's the price we could expect to get if we sold this vehicle at auction. That's why my manager wants to complete a thorough appraisal; to ensure we didn't miss any options and to be sure he can get you the most money for it."

Now move on to the demo drive! (Don't worry, they'll follow you.)

The Demo Drive

The goal of the demo drive is to move to the write-up. Period.

Of course, if you're following an Assumptive Selling process, you may not feel 100% comfortable with your customer's ability to afford this gem you're about to demo. No worries, as we can and should ask a few qualifying questions before the actual test drive.

Because we got the Up registered in the CRM right away and secured the keys to the test drive, this already feels like a better experience to them. The buyer feels like we understand her needs and she's more relaxed because we didn't pepper her with old-school road-to-the-sale questions about the used Civic she wants to buy. For example, we didn't question her judgement with any of these outdated, inauthentic word tracks:

- "Do you plan to use the Civic primarily for business or pleasure?"
- "What features were you hoping for in your next vehicle?"
- "What is it you like most about the Civic, is it style or price?"

While we certainly would love for our buyer to talk, the questions we use to prompt this should make sense to a buyer who is ready to buy today.

Of course, some old-school managers see the first question as an assumptive trial close that will help the customer take mental ownership. While that could be true, it's not authentic to the buyer; plus, there are better assumptive trial closes we can ask that help the buyer take mental ownership. (We'll explore these later.)

The last two questions are part of an old-school needs analysis that could help you flip the prospect into a more profitable vehicle for the dealership. The only problem with these questions today is that you simply cannot flip buyers like you could in the past.

In my experience, dealers who try to flip most of their buyers today close fewer than half as many buyers as those who employ Assumptive Selling techniques. Plus, their average grosses are roughly equal to their Assumptive Selling peers. (The whole reason you would try to flip a prospect is to improve your front-end grosses, but with the availability of information today, those gross increases are muted. And, because the experience was typical of an old-school car-buying process, these dealers often earn less back-end gross and subpar CSI scores.)

Stop trying to flip today's Ups! They found value and relevancy; and now they just want you to sell them the car.

Okay, back to those few qualifying questions you can ask as you walk to and around the vehicle prior to the demo drive. Personally, I don't recommend most qualifying questions when using Assumptive Selling because they often sound like you assume the prospect *cannot* buy. When you assume the sale, you assume they are a qualified buyer; so, why would you ask traditional qualifying questions? You like to ask these, of course, because you were burned once by an Up who "wasted" 25 whole minutes of your day on a demo drive in a vehicle he could not afford; so, you swore "never again!"

Everyone who's been in the business more than a few months has taken that guy out for a test drive. The difference between a 30-Car Theo and an 8-Car Alan when it comes to this situation is the 30-Car Theos don't get angry. They know this guy will eventually buy and they're glad they treated him like a qualified buyer. They also don't mind asking this guy for a few referrals (because they know he needs the money).

The 8-Car Alans are so pissed about this guy wasting their time that they vow to never get taken again – and they proceed to treat their next hundred prospects like suspects.

If you insist on asking qualifying questions before the demo drive, here are a few that are less insulting than most:

- "Did you plan to finance your Civic or were you going to pay cash?"
- "You look very familiar. Do you work in the area?" (Diving down with follow-up questions like, "Oh, how long have you been there?" allows you to ask qualifying questions while you build some rapport.)
- "Is this your current address?" (You ask this after they've handed you their driver's license for scanning.)

Plus, and this is a big one, your manager can always run a soft pull of their credit once you've scanned their license and they've agreed to certain terms (including your privacy policy, for example). Now, you never have to ask another interrogation-sounding qualifying question again!

Interestingly, most subprime customers will self-identify way before you start the test drive. Usually, you'll hear the prospect volunteer something like:

Prospect: "I've only been at my current job about six months. Is that going to be a problem?"

This is one of the best buying signals you'll ever hear. What the prospect is really saying is, "If you can get me approved, I'll buy whatever you want me to buy at any price." In the industry, this prospect is known as a Get-Me-Done. It's perfectly okay (and even recommended) when your prospect self-identifies as credit challenged, that you slow down the process and pivot to the credit application by saying something like:

Salesperson: "Excellent; thank you sharing that. Let's do this to save some time. Let's get the credit application done now so my manager has time to look for all the best financing options while we're on the test drive. Does that sound okay?"

With that, you turn and walk the prospect to your desk or kiosk (wherever you plan to complete the credit application).

Feature Presentation

Traditionally (at least for those salespeople who followed their store's processes), the salesperson would complete an elaborate feature presentation before the demo drive. This would include butterflying the vehicle (opening all the doors, hood and trunk) and performing a championship-caliber walkaround that would highlight everything about this particular model. Including features which held no value to the buyer like:

Salesperson: "...and the polymer used in these headlights is the same as they used on the space shuttle."

Isn't that special? Not really. Today's customer sees this as a timewasting drag and some old-school ploy to sell them the car. Just point out the three coolest features about the vehicle, ensure the customer knows about any special safety information, and get ready to test drive.

But, before getting into the vehicle, you may need to defend the price – especially if you have an addendum to the original sticker attached. If you fail to defend the price before the demo drive, be prepared for multiple pencils when you're in the write-up. If you have no addendum and your online price is competitive, you may not need to defend the price unless your prospect hits you with something like:

Prospect: "Hey, you think your manager will take 25,000 for this?"

If you answer with something like, "I'll do my best," then you just killed any remaining gross in this sale and you likely killed your chance to close the sale later. Why? Because the customer now believes that $25,000 is the idiot price. (Only an idiot would pay $25,000.) That's where the customer decides they're going to start their negotiations because you didn't defend the price. Instead, defend the price with something like this:

Salesperson: "Since you were shopping online, you probably noticed that we always put our best price upfront. We wouldn't dream of insulting our customers by showing you our second-best price and making you jump through a bunch of hoops to find some hidden best price. At 26,759 this vehicle is priced-to-sell and it includes..."

"But Steve," you ask, "How do we know if the customer was online before they showed up?" Believe me, they were. Do you remember the meet & greet? Do you remember that we asked them what they came to test drive? If they already knew what they wanted to test drive, where do you think they saw it?

Some dealers are able to hold additional gross by including an addendum on every new and most used vehicles. Generally speaking, the addendum shows some combination of protection products like window tinting, paint protection and fabric protection; and usually runs between $599 and $799. Of course, if their salespeople fail to defend the addendum prior to the demo drive, they end up negotiating this out during the write-up – and, closing fewer overall deals.

You must proactively defend any addendum before the demo drive. This means pointing it out before the customer has a chance to ask about it. When you highlight and defend the addendum, you remove it as an objection for most buyers; and you're more often able to hold the additional gross it delivers. Here's a quick example some people call "planting the seed":

> Salesperson (pointing to the addendum): "As you know, the factory builds vehicles for the entire world; and what's good in Alaska isn't always best here in Texas. That's why we equip every vehicle with the Lone Star protection package. Now, this package includes ..."

By proactively defending the addendum, you've planted a seed in the buyer's mind that they need this package and that the price is non-negotiable. When your defense of the addendum (and the price) is strong, you'll be shocked at how easy this makes the write-up. This means, don't be afraid to set the stage as much as necessary with word tracks like this one:

> Salesperson: "As you may know, we're not a typical dealer that tries to lock you into a back-and-forth, tug-of-war hassle. Our customers have told us they want our best price upfront and that's exactly what we do every day."

Okay, we're ready to get the customer behind the wheel and driving their new car; but, there is a rule about demo drives that's critical to remember. The rule is simply: talk less; listen more. While likely not true, it feels like more deals have been lost because the salesperson just wouldn't shut up during the test drive than all other reasons combined.

This is the buyer's time to fall in love with their new vehicle; to smell the leather; to feel the seats and steering wheel; to check out the cool gadgets; and to picture themselves owning it. Your constant interruptions will often come across like fingernails on a chalkboard; so, keep your words to a minimum.

Your goal during the demo drive, if you recall, is to move to the write-up. Anything you do say should keep that goal in mind. That said, getting some prospects from the test drive to the write-up requires a bit more than just parking the vehicle in the sold row and walking inside.

If you're following an Assumptive Selling buying process, then you've been setting the stage for the write-up throughout, but just to be certain you're on the right track, it's important to ask a couple of questions during the demo drive that will help you gauge your prospect's interest in this vehicle. Questions like:

- "What do you like best about the Mustang so far?"
- "Is there anything about it that's different than what you imagined?"

You'll be able to determine the likelihood they're going to buy based on how they answer these simple questions. If their excitement has not waned, be ready to move to the write-up when you get back to the dealership. If they seem tentative now (more than before), it's time to ask a few needs analysis questions to be sure you've got them in the correct vehicle. Questions like:

- "What do you like most about your current vehicle?"
- "What is it you dislike most about your current vehicle?"
- "What is it you want most in your new vehicle?"

However, always subscribe to the "talk less; listen more" rule. Your questions should be brief and necessary; your goal is still to move to the write-up unless the buyer indicates they're on the wrong vehicle. Of course, if you've been practicing Assumptive Selling to this point, this is rare.

While you and your buyer are on the demo drive, your manager should be preparing the write-up, including the customer's trade. Assuming this is the right vehicle for them, they will be most likely to accept your first pencil if it's presented within minutes of the test drive; and, if all the numbers are defensible.

The Sold Row

As I wrote, many dealers in the past employed a sold row near the front of the dealership. Usually, this consisted of up to a dozen parking spaces with signs that read "Sold Vehicles Only." It was a simple, yet powerful way to get a prospect to take mental ownership of their new vehicle after the test drive.

I encourage your dealership to consider adding a sold row for both The Perfect Appointment and to help all Ups take mental ownership when they return from their demo drives. If you'll add these spaces, you can easily direct your buyer to park in the sold row as you return to the dealership from the test drive:

> Salesperson: "Let's park your Civic there so no one takes it while we work up the numbers."

After they park, let them keep the keys as you direct them inside. If you've been correctly applying the principles of Assumptive Selling, they should be expecting to "work the numbers" and should follow you without any additional effort on your part. We'll cover overcoming objections in the next chapter for those rare times that they will push back.

The Write-Up

The goal of the write-up is to move to F&I. Period.

To get here and then to F&I, the stage should've been set before now. Deals are not won in the write-up, they're won on the lot. However, getting the customer inside for the write-up should tell you you've been doing things right so far... perhaps even perfectly. If you'd like to stay perfect, here's what The Perfect Up looks like today:

> Within minutes of returning from the test drive, the deal, a pen and a beverage are presented to the customer. The first pencil is a fair pencil. The numbers presented support everything you've discussed. The numbers are defensible: you defended the selling price, you planted the seed on the addendum and they helped calculate the wholesale value of their trade.

Now… it's all about terms. The buyer selects a payment, and the hard part is done. Congratulations! You sold a car!

Of course, not every Up will be The Perfect Up; however, assuming the sale throughout every step and treating everyone like a qualified buyer will get you here more often than doing what you've been doing. Plus, as vehicle and pricing information become even more prevalent online, those practicing Assumptive Selling will see their close rates continue to rise.

Why? Because no one wants to visit two or more dealerships today. They've done their research and they're arriving on your lot ready to buy. Treat them like they're important and qualified, and they'll begin to see you as that authentic salesperson they were seeking.

To help you close more deals, let's review a few best practices that are helping salespeople create a better experience in the write-up that leads to higher grosses, closing percentages and CSI scores:

- Never leave them alone – keep them engaged. This makes the time seem to go by more quickly, which can help make this a fun process for the buyer. You don't want them getting buyer's remorse before they've even had a chance to buy the vehicle. You also don't want them surfing the web on their smartphone looking at your competitor's website.
- Using touch screens kiosks or tablets can make everything in the write-up seem simple, seamless, transparent, and even fun.
- There should be no table or other barriers between you and the customer. Sit alongside them (or in between them if they're a couple), as this will make the write-up feel less like a negotiation.
- Unless the deal is being transmitted back to the salesperson's tablet, the manager or closer should present the deal at this point (so the salesperson can stay with the customer). Because you believe in perfect data, everything the manager needs should be in the CRM, right?
- The manager should approach the customer as if the deal is done with a hearty, "Congratulations, Mr. and Mrs. Jones! All we need to do now is select a payment."
- The first pencil should be a fair pencil.
- The finance manager should make an appearance to meet & greet the buyers before they move to the business office. This is

sometimes called an "F&I Fly-By;" and it will help you drive higher back-end grosses by humanizing the finance manager. A simple, "Welcome; I'm Steve and I'm going to complete the financing and all the state paperwork with you when you've wrapped this up," creates some process transparency and goes a long way toward removing any anxiety the customer has about these last steps.

It will shock you (unless you're already doing The Perfect Appointment), but most prospects you close using Assumptive Selling will accept your first pencil. Of course, they will only accept the first pencil when it's a fair pencil.

A fair pencil is where we treat the customer like they have at least a small brain and the ability to recollect certain facts and experiences. We know they've been online and they've seen our online price, right? Bringing in a first pencil of MSRP+++ with today's connected buyer guarantees you'll be grinding for an hour on every deal. It also guarantees you'll close fewer deals (because you're breaking trust with the customer).

The silliest fact about those sales managers who still deliver an unconscionable first pencil is they can only remember the winners. They can only remember the one or two five-pounders they closed this month. They never recollect the dozens of qualified buyers who walked (and will never return because they don't trust you) or the buyers who ended up grinding you down *below* your online price (usually during the last week of the month). Moreover, while their average front-end grosses can sometimes be above what's typical in your market, their total gross and total units fall well short.

On top of that, they're expending so much unnecessary effort and taking so much time per deal that they have little time to train and lead their teams. The CRM in their store is a mess, as salespeople are either faking their outbound calls or have thousands of past due activities piled up. Most Ups aren't ever recorded in the CRM, and those who are might have multiple (duplicate) entries.

Imagine if every Up accepted your first pencil? How much time would that free up for your salespeople and (especially) your managers? How many more deals could you close? How much additional gross, repeat business, referrals and service business would you enjoy?

Of course, while every Up won't take your first pencil even when it's a fair pencil, many will. With your fair pencil, you're going to present the price that's already been agreed to (including the addendum you defended) and a defensible number on their trade. (Defensible, because they calculated their own wholesale book value and your offer is at or slightly above that amount.)

As you present the worksheet, you'll continue Assumptive Selling with a smile and a simple:

> Salesperson: "I've got great news for you Mr. & Mrs. Jones, we've been able to get you $599 a month with your trade and just $5,500 down. Now, I just need you to initial here and sign here. Oh, and I forgot to ask you, will you be titling your new F-150 in just one or both of your names?" (Or any question that seems appropriate here. You're attempting to move them away from the payment and price, and onto your last question in a way that assumes the sale.)

To be clear, every pencil you ever present to your prospect is a terrific deal... especially when it's not. Assumptive Selling doesn't take a different direction just because your sales manager likes to send you in with a terrible deal (that you just know the customer is going to hate). You always assume the sale. Always!

Yes, presenting a fair pencil is easier for you; however, you're not going to always get a fair pencil even when your managers buy-in to Assumptive Selling. If you present a bad deal to your prospects as if it's anything other than the greatest deal of all time, you will simply never close them. Assumptive Selling is about assuming the sale; not just about assuming the sale when all the stars are aligned.

I'm sure you've heard that if this job was easy anyone could do it.

Assumptive Closes

People love to shop, and they love to buy things. However, when the thing they're buying costs $35,000, they sometimes need help pulling the trigger. The fear of making a bad decision with some people is so great that they will make no decision if you let them. The key is to reinforce their decision to buy – and to buy today – throughout the process. If you didn't set the stage before the write-up, then it's probably too late; and the best closes in the world likely won't work.

When you assume the sale, you do a much better job with trial closes because you stop asking yes or no questions and instead ask questions that provide two affirmative choices (yes or yes). Here are a few quick examples:

- "Will you be paying cash or financing this purchase?"
- "Will you be titling your Mustang in one or both your names?"
- "Which one of you is getting the new car?"

Assumptive closes don't give the prospect the option of answering no. When you assume the sale, there's no reason to ask a yes or no question, because the sale is already a done deal, right? You're just gathering information at this point.

These yes/yes questions can work at any point in the process, but they're especially helpful when you're dealing with more than one buyer. In these instances, yes/yes questions help you get the customer to do what you want without having to ask them if they want to do it. For example:

- "Which one of you will be completing the credit application?"
- "Who's going to test drive first?"
- "Which one of you is going to help me gather some quick information about your trade?"

If you've done a good job assuming the sale through to the write-up, but your prospect doesn't take your fair pencil, you're either on the wrong vehicle or your defense of the vehicle pricing and/or trade value wasn't strong enough. I hate to tell you this, but you need to be ready to negotiate and move into using more traditional closes; something like:

Salesperson: "Barbara, let me ask you this. If I can get you the trunk tray and the floor mats at our cost, will you drive it home today?"

If the deal is lost, remember that it wasn't lost in the write-up; it was lost much earlier in the process. Learn from this loss and improve the execution of your processes earlier with your next Up.

But – and never forget this – everyone is a buyer. If you didn't close them today, that doesn't mean you won't close them tomorrow. It also doesn't mean they don't have friends or family who are in the market for a great vehicle at a great price. Before any unsold prospect leaves your lot make sure they know they have a friend in the car business. Give them a couple of extra business cards as you thank them for giving you a chance:

Salesperson: "Well, Robert, I feel terrible I wasn't able to help you today, but I want you to know that you always have a friend in the car business. Now, while I am definitely not going to give up trying to help you buy, I would consider it an honor if you'd pass my card to any family or friends looking to buy. If any of them do buy from me, I'll send you a check for $100 as my thank you."

When you understand that everyone is a buyer, you never stop making sure that people know they have a friend in the car business – even when they've just told you to shove your worksheet where the sun doesn't shine. (Which, by the way, almost never happens to assumptive sellers.)

F&I

The goal of F&I is to move to the delivery. Period.

Of course, any solid finance manager will tell you that the goal of F&I is to maximize back-end gross. And, while I don't disagree with this, I'll just add to the end of that sentence "for the long term." The goal, you see, should be to maximize back-end gross today and tomorrow. Burying the customer in a loan that will keep them upside down for the next six years means you'll likely not see that buyer again.

This doesn't mean you shouldn't expect high back-end grosses – you should. It also means that the long-term loyalty of a customer should always be the highest priority. To maximize both today's back-end gross and tomorrow's sales and service business, the F&I process needs to start before the customer sits down in the business office.

For most dealers, this means you should consider compensating your salespeople on some or all of the F&I products your business managers are able to sell. This will motivate your sellers to pre-present your F&I add-ons and accessories to their customers.

I've already written about the positive impacts this has on your back-end grosses and your customers' perception of time, so I won't regurgitate that now; but, dealers who are doing this enjoy better CSI and higher back-end grosses. Period; end of story. (Well, end of chapter, anyway.)

17

OVERCOMING OBJECTIONS ON THE LOT

Okay, we've walked through a shortened road-to-the-sale, though without the speed bumps of multiple objections. Even those practicing Assumptive Selling will hear objections, of course. However, these will come less often since we're treating everyone as a qualified buyer instead of a suspect. (Hint: Many of the objections traditional salespeople hear are a product of the old-school questions and antiquated processes that buyers hate.)

For nearly all objections (and objections disguised as questions), it's important to remember your goal. If you're in the meet & greet, then your goal is the demo drive; if you're on the demo drive, then your goal is the write-up, etc. This means you'll want to make sure that *addressing* the objection includes a move toward the next step in your process.

You cannot sell a car during the meet & greet; but, you can lose a sale there. You cannot sell a car during the demo drive, but you can lose a sale there, as well. That's why it's important to remember the goal of each step on your road to the sale. It's also important to keep in mind:

- You cannot sell a car until you do the numbers, right?
- You cannot do the numbers unless they come inside, right?
- You cannot do the numbers before they test drive, right?
- You cannot do the numbers without their trade info, right?
- You cannot do the numbers before they select a vehicle, right?

So, why are you trying to overcome objections before the write-up? Never listen to the customers – take them down your road to the sale (which should be to guide them to the next step). Keeping this in mind, let's work on addressing (not necessarily overcoming) some of the most common objections salespeople still face today.

Although I do not use the prospect's name in these examples, you should. When you know the customer's name and you use it to open your responses, you gain their full attention; plus, people like hearing their own name. For example:

Salesperson: "Barbara, what I'm hearing you say is…"

Salesperson: "Mr. Jones, thank you. I appreciate that you…"

Finally, the word tracks you use to address objections are less important than the goal of moving your buyer to the next step. As I've done here, the verbiage you use can be a mix of new-school and old-school language; provided it allows you to take charge, be direct and guide your prospect to the next step.

Just Looking

I'll first show you how to overcome this objection as if you're still using a traditional meet & greet interrogation instead of using the recommended Assumptive Selling question ("Which vehicle did you come to test drive today?").

Customer: "We're just looking."

Salesperson: "Excellent! Are you more looking or shopping? (Whatever they answer) Great! That's exactly how most of my customers start out. So, tell me, are we your first stop or have you already been to a few places?"

Customer: "You're our first stop."

Salesperson: "That's outstanding to hear, thank you for choosing us first, I really appreciate that. I'm hopeful I can save you from having to visit multiple stores. Now, which vehicles would you like to test drive today?"

Your goal here is to move them to the demo drive. If the test drive question was already your first question of the meet & greet and they answered they were just looking, your response would still be tailored to move them through your process:

Customer: "Oh, we're not ready to test drive yet; we're just looking."

Salesperson: "Excellent! Are you more looking or shopping? (Whatever they answer) Great! That's exactly how most of my customers start out. So, tell me, are we your first stop or have you already been to a few places?"

Customer: "You're our first stop."

Salesperson: "That's outstanding to hear, thank you for choosing us first, I really appreciate that. I'm hopeful I can save you from having to visit multiple stores. Now, when you are ready to buy, are you planning on trading in your Taurus?"

This will likely move them to the next step and give you a chance to appraise their trade (meaning they'll need to come inside for the write-up later). It will also keep you in the game and in control of the buying process. If they respond that they want to sell it themselves, we'll tackle that later in this chapter.

Alternatively, you can ask them why they chose you first. If you do this, their answer will reveal the reason they want to do business with you. Your job is to use that reason to help them buy from you. For example, they may already service with you or you have a vehicle they're interested in seeing. Whatever the reason, use it to move to the next step:

Customer: "You're the closest dealership to our house."

Salesperson: "Great; so, it sounds like you've probably got a full day ahead of you. Let me do this; let's get to the vehicles you want to see first and get you all the information. That way, you can leave here knowing all you need to know quickly. Does that sound fair?"

Assumptive Selling tells us that no one wants to visit two dealerships. They chose you first because they want to buy from you – even if you're simply the closest dealership to their home. We know that most everyone expects a hassle when they start the car shopping process, so let's remove the hassles right away and let them know we can help them gather the information they need quickly.

Our first goal is to get them to the demo drive, not to get them to buy our vehicle. Focusing on helping them gather information quickly will open them up to your next steps. If they answered your earlier question that they've already been to a few places, then you'll want to deep dive on that:

> Salesperson: "Great, most of my customers who've already visited a few places tell me they either can't find the right vehicle or the right price. Tell me, what's been your biggest headache so far?"

This is where knowing your inventory and understanding the unique benefits of your new vehicles comes into play. If you have decent product knowledge, you can begin asking questions to move them through your process and onto the test drive. For example, if they say they haven't found the right vehicle because they need something good on gas that's large enough for seven people and doesn't cost an arm and a leg, you might answer with:

> Salesperson: "Okay, it sounds like you're looking for a larger vehicle that's also efficient. If I've got a suitable alternative you love with the right rebates, I assume you're ready to stop this endless shopping and get the vehicle you're looking for. Let me do this. Let me show you some new Explorers with the EcoBoost engine. Then, I promise to put together all the information and pricing on the Explorer you like best. Does that sound like a plan?"

In this case, we're already teeing up the customer for the write-up even before we have a vehicle selected or a demo drive set. That's okay, because it's just a soft trial close on the write-up without vomiting all the information about our vehicle. Contrast that with a salesperson who just blathers on about how fuel efficient and affordable the Explorer is (which sounds like you're selling them instead of helping them buy). Once we find a suitable Explorer we'll assume the demo drive.

Conversely, if they just comment that one thing (like price, selection, salesperson, etc.) was the problem, they've given you everything you need to know to move them through your process.

> Customer: "The last dealer wasn't willing to budge on price."

Salesperson: "Okay, thank you; that helps. So, what I'm hearing is that if we can agree on a price you like, you'd like to own the Tundra today; is that right?"

This is a very traditional (and still very effective) closing technique sometimes called the Concession Close. You don't agree to the concession, you merely acknowledge it. If you agree to a concession, you end up inviting more customer demands throughout the rest of the buying process.

Not Buying Today

Customer: "We're not buying today."

Salesperson: "Excellent; you just took all the pressure off me because I don't want you to buy until you're ready. Tell me, if you were to buy today, would you be trading in your Taurus?"

Another way to answer this is to ask a yes/yes question:

Salesperson: "Excellent; you just took all the pressure off me because I don't want you to buy until you're ready. Tell me, are we lucky enough to be your first stop or have you already visited a few dealerships?"

If they answer that you're their first stop, take this as a compliment (because it is). No one wants to visit multiple dealerships before they buy. They chose you first for a reason; even if the reason is that you're the closest dealership to their home. Because, if you are the closest dealership to their home, they're telling you they want convenience and they want to save time. Respond as I outlined earlier under **Just Looking**.

If they answer that they've already been to a few places, then we need to find out what's been holding them back. Again, respond as I outlined earlier under **Just Looking**; their answers will tell you exactly how to sell to them.

Just Leave Us Alone

Occasionally, you'll encounter buyers who so greatly fear sales pressure and salespeople, that they'll tell you to just leave them alone.

Customer: "Look, can you just leave us alone and let us wander around by ourselves?"

Salesperson: "Absolutely. Take all the time you need; but, don't worry, I'm going to check back in with you every ten minutes or so; that way, you don't have to chase me down with questions. By the way, just so I'm clear, you don't have to buy today, do you?"

That last question is important, as it removes some of the sales pressure they fear. By asking a Lot Up, "you don't have to buy today, do you?" you're letting them know that you're not going to try to sell them. Rather, you're going to let them buy on their timeline.

Customer: "No, we're not even sure what we want yet."

Salesperson: "Okay, great; you just took a lot of pressure off me. If I can help point you in the right direction, please let me know. I want to be sure you leave here with all the information you need to make an informed decision. Does that sound fair?"

At this point, many standoffish buyers will open up and tell you what they're looking for. When they do, you can begin a basic needs analysis with typical questions like this:

Salesperson: "Okay, great to hear. It sounds like you're looking for a great deal on a full- or mid-size SUV. Is there any equipment you're absolutely hoping to have on your new SUV?"

Besides the fearful buyer, you'll also get this objection from the customer who really doesn't know what they want, and they genuinely want to spend some time perusing your lot:

Customer: "We're really not sure what we want. Is it okay if we just wander around by ourselves for a bit?"

Salesperson: "Absolutely, you're free to browse the lot all you want. I'll check in with you every ten minutes to be sure you're finding everything you need. Does that sound okay?"

Customer: "Sure."

Salesperson: "Oh, there is just one more thing... We have over 300 vehicles on the lot right now, including some that are currently being reconditioned. If you could let me know what you're most interested in seeing, I can point you in the right direction. Are you primarily looking for new or used?"

Then, continue into a traditional needs analysis as you guide them around the lot.

I Need to Talk it Over with My Spouse

When a buyer tells you, "I need to talk it over with my spouse," this may or may not be the case. There could be something wrong with the payments or this just isn't the vehicle they want to own. Additionally, they might be saying, "I'm scared. I need a salesman to help me buy a car. Will you be that salesman?"

Before sending them home to discuss the purchase with the spouse, you need to uncover the real objection:

Salesperson: "That makes perfect sense – you should talk it over with your wife first. Tell me, if she agrees with you, is there anything about the vehicle that's keeping you from owning it today?"

If this doesn't uncover objections about the price, the trade value or the vehicle, then they're either afraid to buy it or they truly cannot buy it without their spouse.

Salesperson: "Outstanding; this sounds like the vehicle you want to own. What do you think your wife will say about it?"

This may uncover an objection that you'll need to answer. However, if they're pretty sure their spouse will love it as much as they do, trying to close them is not a bad idea:

Salesperson: "That's great to hear. What do you think your wife would say if you surprised her with this new vehicle?"

If they say they'll likely get divorced, you're probably not closing this one without the spouse… but, don't let your buyer leave in his own vehicle. There's an opportunity here for you to make a Puppy Dog Close. This is where you let the customer take the puppy (vehicle) home to see if they like it – and everyone loves puppies, right?

You're going to let the buyer take your vehicle home to show the spouse (for an extended test drive). If you use this technique, be sure to suggest the buyer return with the spouse:

Salesperson: "Once your wife has a chance to drive it, bring her back with you so that I can address any concerns or questions she might have about your new Eclipse. Does that sound like a plan?"

That's a Lot of Money

This objection can occur on the lot or in the write-up. If it happens on the lot, it's important to note that a comment like "that's a lot of money" is a relative statement that could be driven by a few factors:

1. What the buyer is used to paying for a vehicle;
2. What the buyer wanted to pay for your vehicle; and/or
3. What the buyer thought your vehicle would cost.

However, this statement is almost never because of an actual comparison with another dealer's vehicle. (If that was the case, they'd tell you your competitor was cheaper.) It also doesn't mean they're not going to buy it today from you at your price. With Assumptive Selling, we know that everyone is a buyer and they're going to buy today, so let's address their statement with that in mind:

Customer: "Wow; that's a lot of money!"

Salesperson: "I understand; it is a beautiful car that's loaded with great features like (choose a feature that you believe is important to your buyer and do a quick FAB statement). Let's do this; let's take it for a quick test drive, make sure it's the vehicle you want to own, and then let's see how today's incentives and rebates might make it more affordable. Does that sound fair?"

I never like asking them what they were hoping to pay. I think that's a weak question that can invite an insane lowball offer today. Moreover, their lowball number could very well set a price in their mind that you likely cannot achieve.

When the buyer makes this statement during the write-up, it indicates you may not have done a good job of setting their expectations up to this point. This doesn't mean you've lost the sale, but it does mean (for many salespeople) that you may need a closer or manager to gain agreement with the buyer.

Customer: "Wow, that's a lot more than I expected to pay."

Salesperson: "I understand, it is a beautiful Wrangler with every available feature. If this is more about payment than owning the Wrangler you really want, we can certainly look at one without the hardtop. Does that sound fair?"

This technique is sometimes called the Take Away Close. The Take Away Close is most often used when your buyer is still on the fence about the vehicle because of price or payment; and it works because taking something away that they really love will often move them to act today on the original vehicle at the price you presented.

I Need to Think About It

When you hear this on the lot or during the demo drive, don't panic; you're in good shape. You still have a ready buyer in front of you. When you hear this in the middle of the write-up, you need to close them; and, you will only close them if you've done everything right to this point. (Remember: deals are not won during the write-up; they're won in the first third of your process.) Let's first tackle this objection when it occurs prior to the write-up:

Customer: "I need to think about it."

Salesperson: "That makes perfect sense; of course, you need to think about it. I haven't given you enough information to make an informed decision yet. Let's do this; let's take a few minutes so that I can give you a firm proposal. This way, you can have all the information and the final numbers before you leave. Does that sound fair?"

If your buyer is unwilling to come inside for the proposal, you're likely either on the wrong vehicle or they simply don't like you very much (no offense). Asking a quick question to help uncover the real objection is necessary here:

> Salesperson: "Okay, it sounds like I've done a poor job today helping you find the right vehicle. Can you tell me what it is you must have that this Camry is missing?"

If they answer that they love the car and won't share any other information, then you are likely the problem. Feel free to be frank with them and imply that someone else might be able to help:

> Salesperson: "Great, I'm glad to hear you like the Camry and I'd love for you to own it. It sounds like I might be getting in the way of that, so if you'll allow my manager to take three minutes to review the numbers with you, you can leave here with everything you need to make an informed decision. Does that sound fair?"

Now, let's tackle this objection when it occurs during the write-up. You've presented the customer with a fair pencil that includes a payment in the buyer's range, but they object with:

> Customer: "I need to think about it."

If they're on the right vehicle and you've done a good job of Assumptive Selling thus far, they're going to need to be closed. This is a big decision, and some people just need help making it. They need to know they're making a sound decision:

> Salesperson: "When my customers tell me they need to think about it just when we're ready to complete the purchase, I find there's usually something about the vehicle or deal they don't like. Tell me, what aspect of the vehicle or deal is it that you still need to think about?"

> Customer: "It's a big decision... I would just feel more comfortable waiting, that's all."

If it's a used vehicle or if you're at the end of the month (and the incentives are ending), you can and should employ a Scarcity Close here:

Salesperson: "That makes sense to me. Of course, we've had a lot of inquiries about this Challenger and I'd hate to see someone else buy it out from under you; I don't remember the last time we've had one this nice at such a low price. Is there anything else about the vehicle that's keeping you from owning it today?"

If the customer responds that there is nothing else holding them back, I recommend treating this just as you would someone who volunteers that they're not an impulse buyer (an objection we'll tackle in a few pages):

Customer: "No, I think it's perfect. I just need to think it over, that's all."

Salesperson: "Excellent, I'm glad this is the vehicle you want to own. Now, you may not know this, but most of my business comes from referrals from happy buyers. Can you tell me if there's anything I've done or said that would keep you from recommending me to your friends?"

Customer: "No, you've been great. I just need to think about it."

Salesperson: "Thank you for that. It's really important to me that you're happy with my service. In fact, I'd rather you buy from someone else if I've failed to assist you in every way possible."

Customer: "No; again, you've been great to work with."

Salesperson: "Fantastic. By the way, how long were you researching vehicles before you decided to stop in today?"

Customer: "A few weeks, I suppose."

Salesperson: "Well, you certainly did your homework before coming in. That's smart. Tell me, if you've been researching for weeks and this is the perfect vehicle at the right price, what is it that's really keeping you from owning it today?"

This may uncover a final hidden objection that you can address. Alternatively, this could earn you the sale at this point.

If you still can't get the buyer to sign, the Puppy Dog Close is most likely your last resort. Let the buyer leave in your vehicle so she can "be certain it's the one she wants to own." At the very least, she'll need to return it, giving you one more chance to close the deal.

Just Gathering Information

The buyer usually indicates this during your meet & greet. As always, let's hear them, but not listen to them. This means your goal is to move to the next step, which in this case is the demo drive.

Customer: "We're just gathering information."

Salesperson: "Excellent; then you don't have to buy today, is that correct?"

Customer: "That's correct. We just want to see what you have on the lot."

Salesperson; "That's great; that takes a lot of pressure off me. The last thing I'm going to do is ask you to buy today. Is that fair?"

The buyer will likely nod or give you some other agreement. Follow up with a response that takes you to the next step or begins some needs analysis:

Salesperson: "Great. Let's do this; let me get you all the information so that when you are ready to buy, you can make an informed decision. Will that be okay?"

Customer: "Sure."

Salesperson: "Okay, so help me understand how I can help you. Was there a specific vehicle or category that you were hoping to test drive today?"

The buyer will either tell you what they're really looking for or force you into a traditional needs analysis. Either way, your next steps should be very clear (and your goal, of course, is to move to the demo drive)..

Just Tell Me About the Rebates/Offers

You're presenting the vehicle they've selected for the test drive and the buyer blurts out that they just want to know about the rebates or offers:

Customer: "Just tell me about the rebates."

Your goal is to move into the demo drive, so this is not a good place to blather on about all the available incentives from the manufacturer. Instead, move them to your next step:

Salesperson: "I'm glad you asked about those. You may already know this, but Ford has some of the best rebates and incentives on trucks that they've offered in a very long time. Let's do this; let's take this F-150 out for a quick test drive and if this turns out to be the truck you want to own, let's take a few minutes to review the numbers and look for every available rebate and incentive you qualify for. Does that sound fair?"

I've Got 20 Minutes

Most car buyers, as I've written before, fear sales pressure and salespeople. One of the defense mechanisms that many of them will use is to tell you they have very little time. They're usually lying. They tell you this, because they're so afraid of being sold that they assume cutting the visit short will protect them from some "evil hypnosis trick" that car salespeople are apparently known for. Don't listen to them… take them through your process:

Customer: "I've only got twenty minutes; can you just give me a price?"

Salesperson: "That works for me; I'm happy to give you all the information you need to make an informed decision. In fact, once we've selected and test-driven a vehicle you want to own, it will take us less than five minutes to give you all the numbers you need. Does that sound fair?"

For most buyers, this will suffice to slow them down as you take them through your road-to-the-sale. However, there will be occasions when buyers are truly pressed for time. In those cases, it's important to save any details about the deal until they can return; otherwise they may never return:

Customer: "No, I'm just here during my lunch and I really don't have the time for all that."

Salesperson: "I completely understand. Let's do this; to save time, let's take the vehicle out for a quick test drive and if it's truly the vehicle you want to own, we'll have all the numbers ready for you when you come back later today. Does that sound okay?"

If this works for the customer, move to the demo drive, though expect to be able to keep some of them engaged longer than they indicated. When you use Assumptive Selling and pull them through your process, you'll often have buyers who were once pressed for time rearrange their schedules for you. When you return from the demo drive, direct them to the sold row and ask them if they have a few minutes to complete the write-up:

Salesperson: "Now I know you said you had to go, though if you have just ten more minutes we can review the numbers together. Does that sound okay?"

If they truly don't have the time, be sure to set a firm appointment for later today and use recap-like verbiage (from The Perfect Appointment) to ensure they know it's a real appointment. Of course, if your dealership allows extended test drives, you might prefer this response:

Salesperson: "That's perfectly okay; why don't you take your new Explorer with you back to work. It will give you a chance to show it off as you enjoy an extended test drive; does that sound okay?"

An extended test drive can also be used for the buyer who doesn't have time for the test drive and is just pushing you for the final numbers:

Salesperson: "It sounds like you're very busy. Let me know if you think this will work: We'll give you the keys to the vehicle you're interested in and you take it back to the office, back home, wherever. Later, give me a call and we'll schedule a time for you to return. In the meantime, my manager can fully appraise any trade-in you have so that when you do return, if you love the new vehicle, we can give you all the information you need to make an informed decision. How does that sound?"

I Just Want a Value for My Vehicle

If your dealership operates a buying center, be prepared for prospects to arrive expecting to get a value for their vehicle in just a few minutes. To be clear, if you give them a value right away, they will thank you and take your offer to the next dealer up the street. While buying their vehicle might be great for the dealership, you need to set the time and value expectations up front to give them a chance to catch new car fever:

Customer: "I just want a value for my SUV."

Salesperson: "Great, I can help you with that." (Get the keys.) "Now, just so you're aware, in order to get you the most money for your vehicle, our appraiser is going to complete a thorough inspection of it. Additionally, he may also need to call a couple of brokers to see if we can get a buyer for your SUV right away. Does that sound okay?"

Customer: "Okay; but how long is that going to take? I'm in a hurry."

Salesperson: "Understood. Just to be sure we can get you the most for your vehicle, that process could take up to 45 minutes. You're welcome to wait in our lounge or, if you'd like, I could let you take a couple of vehicles out for test drives. Were you planning to replace the vehicle we're appraising?"

At this point you'll move to a traditional needs analysis and work to get your buyer into a new vehicle as soon as possible. They cannot catch new car fever lest they get behind the wheel of a new car.

What are the Payments?

They're on the lot or on the demo drive, and all they care about are the payments. This is great news, because it sounds like they've found the right vehicle and they're telling you they'll buy it if the payments are in their range:

Customer: "What are the payments like on this Impala?"

Salesperson: "It sounds like you found the right car for you; that's great. Let's do this; when we get back from the test drive, we'll take a few minutes to put the numbers together and present you with multiple payment options so that you can own it today. Does that sound fair?"

If the buyer continues to push you for information you simply do not have while still on the lot or on the demo drive, feel free to let them know about your team's expertise with getting buyers the lowest payments available:

Customer: "Well, I can't go above $300 a month; so, can you do that?"

Salesperson: "I understand you want to own the Impala for less than $300 a month. The great news is our finance managers work with 27 banks and credit unions, and they are experts at finding you the lowest payments and rates available. As soon as we get back from the test drive, we'll need just a few minutes to get you all that information. Does that sound okay?"

You Don't Have What I Want / I Don't Like the Vehicle

When the buyer tells you that you don't have what they want or that they don't like the vehicle they've selected, some salespeople believe the visit is over. It's not; it's just going back to the beginning. Everyone wants a friend in the car business, and you can become this buyer's friend by not giving up; you can become their friend by helping them find just the right vehicle.

The key when answering these objections is not to try to force them into a vehicle they don't want or even to try to sell them a thing. Instead, begin a stronger (more old-school) needs analysis. If you work for a dealership group that allows you to sell across multiple brands, be sure to use this to your advantage:

Customer: "You don't have what I want."

Salesperson: "I understand. Tell me, do you have to buy today?"

Customer: "Not really."

Salesperson: "Great, that's going to take a lot of pressure off of me and allow me to help you find your next vehicle. As you may know, our dealership group offers six different new car brands and we stock over 2,000 vehicles, so I'm sure we can locate the perfect one for you. Tell me, what is the most important thing you're looking for in your next vehicle?"

There's no need to regurgitate all of the possible needs analysis questions here. Any salesperson with more than a few days under her belt has likely been provided a list of these from her manager.

The key with a needs analysis is that it cannot feel like an interrogation to your buyer. This is a conversation – just as if you were selling to a friend – so keep it lighthearted and fun for the buyer, and only ask the questions that provide the answers you really need to know to help them find the perfect fit.

I Just Want Your Best Price

Depending on the study you read, true "price buyers" make up between 12% and 20% of the Ups you'll see on the lot. Of course, because we've trained customers for a hundred years that they're supposed to negotiate with us, you'll likely get the "best price" question/objection more often than that.

If you're not a one-price store and you volunteer your best price (or even a range of prices) while on the lot, be prepared to watch most buyers drive away before the write-up. Why? Because you already gave them all the information they need to shop with your competition. Don't panic when presented with a buyer who blurts out:

Customer: "I don't want to take a test drive; I just want your best price!"

Salesperson: "Excellent; it sounds like you know what you want to own. Have you already driven the all-new Camry?"

Customer: "Yes; I drove one at XYZ Motors."

Salesperson: "Perfect. So, you already know how great it handles and you're familiar with the new features. Can you tell me why you didn't buy a Camry from XYZ?"

At this point, the buyer will tell you what you need to close them. Likely, because of their insistence on just getting to the final price, they want to compare your price to your competition's. This is great news, because you can make a deal if you can get them inside for the write-up.

Quick caveat: Most managers will not desk a deal until the customer has selected and test-driven a vehicle. While this is a good strategy, there are going to be times (especially when the customer has a written offer from another dealer) when you will simply have to walk them inside without the demo drive. Let's see how this could play out:

Customer: "Their price was good, but I want to see what you guys can do."

Salesperson: "Excellent, because at ABC Motors we will never lose a buyer over price. In fact, I don't want you to show me their price – just keep that in your pocket until we review what we can do. If their price is better, you can show it to me after we've worked the numbers. Does that sound fair?"

Customer: "Okay."

Salesperson: "Great. Now, just to be sure we're looking at an apples-to-apples comparison, let's find the Camry you want to own and then we'll take a few minutes to put together our best deal. Will that be okay?"

At this point your buyer will be more relaxed and open to working with you. When you do locate the right vehicle, make one more attempt at getting the buyer to take a test drive "just to be sure this is the one you want to own." If they still refuse, then walk them inside and begin the write-up. Be sure your manager is aware of the competitive situation and that the buyer has already test-driven the vehicle on XYZ's lot.

If the buyer indicates they haven't driven it yet, but that they "know how the Camry drives," be prepared to keep working toward the demo drive.

Salesperson: "Okay, that helps. When was the last time you drove a Camry?" (Unless they arrived in one, of course.)

Customer: "It's been a couple of years."

Salesperson: "Well, I'm glad you're here and ready to own one (or "upgrade to a new Camry" if they arrived in one). Of course, in the last couple of years, Toyota's made a lot of improvements to the handling and interior styling of the Camry. I think taking a minute to sit in the new Camry you want to own – and even taking it for a quick test drive – will help you know if these improvements change your opinion in any way. Does that sound fair?"

Certainly, your expectation should be that a quick demo drive sounds fair to the buyer. However, if they continue to push back and just want your best price, providing them this without a demo drive will likely not result in a sale.

Help them select the Camry they want to own, proceed into a small feature presentation (including presenting some features that they need to get behind the wheel to experience), then ask for the demo drive once more. If you're forced to move to the write-up stage, be certain your manager is aware that they haven't test-driven the vehicle.

Is That Your Best Price?

Let's look at a few different scenarios where you might get this question. First, let's look at how to handle this question when it's asked out on the lot, prior to the demo drive and when you are priced above the expected selling price.

Customer: "Is that your best price?"

Salesperson: "Great. It sounds like this is the perfect vehicle for you. I assume this means you're ready to buy today if the price fits your budget. Let's do this, let's grab the keys and take it for a quick test drive. Once we return, it will take just a few minutes to put together the numbers. Does that sound fair?"

If the question is posed after the demo drive, but before the write-up, you should be able to make an easy segue to the write-up:

Customer: "Is that your best price?"

Salesperson: "Excellent; it sounds like this is the vehicle you want to own. So, if I'm understanding you correctly, if we can come together on terms that meet your budget, this is the vehicle you plan to drive home today. Is that right?"

Customer: "Well, if the price is right."

Salesperson: "That's great. Let's take a few minutes to review the numbers and get you all the information you need. Does that sound fair?"

If your vehicle is priced at its expected selling price and you get this question, it's critical for you to defend the price no matter when the question is posed:

Customer: "Is that your best price."

Salesperson: "If you've been shopping, then you've probably noticed we price all of our vehicles competitively right from the beginning. We wouldn't dream of insulting our customers by showing you our second-best price and making you jump through a bunch of hoops to find some hidden best price. Now, this Elantra is priced at its selling price and it includes … (hit the three top features important to the prospect)."

Do You Think Your Manager Will Take $_____?

This is often a substitute for "Is that your best price" that's asked solely because the buyer feels like it's their duty to challenge your selling price. They've been taught their entire life that the price is never the price, so don't expect them all to just lay down and accept your online or on-the-lot price as the final selling price.

However, be sure to always defend the price. Some salespeople think they can gain favor with a prospect by answering this way:

Customer: "Do you think your manager will take $15,000?"

Typical Salesperson: "I don't know; but, I'll do my best."

This is an extremely weak talk track that either killed your chance for a deal (since the buyer now thinks they can get it for much less than $15,000) or killed your gross (since $15,000 is now at the top end if their negotiation consideration).

When your vehicle has already been discounted to a price that's at or near its expected selling price and the customer tries to see if there are additional discounts to be had early in the process (for example, before the test drive) or even during the write-up, defending your price helps you close more deals and all at higher grosses than any of the weak talk tracks from the past. These talk tracks have already been introduced a few times in this book, but they bear repeating:

Customer: "Do you think your manager will take $15,000?"

Salesperson: "Well, if you've been shopping online, then you know we price all of our vehicles competitively right from the beginning. We wouldn't dream of insulting our customers by showing you our second-best price and then making you jump through a bunch of hoops to find some hidden best price. Now, this RDX is priced at its selling price and it includes… (hit the top three features important to the prospect)."

Then, as always, move the buyer through to whatever step is next in your process.

I Want Your Price, But I'm Not Buying Today

While this happens less often today with so much information available online, you will sometimes run into customers who want you to work up the whole deal today (usually on a new car) even though they have no intention of buying today. They're so adamant about getting all the information so that they can make an informed decision, that they'll waste hours at dealerships just to get final deals that will likely change.

As with all of today's Ups, you need to take charge, be direct and provide guidance to these misguided buyers:

Customer: "I want the price and payments, but I'm not buying today."

Salesperson: "I understand; of course, since the manufacturer incentives can expire at any time, you know it does us no good to complete much of the paperwork and work up the deal if you're not planning on buying today. Plus, with the direction that interest rates are going, anything we give you today on payments could be vastly different tomorrow. That said, I'm happy to do the work necessary to show you everything you need to make an informed decision. Before I do, can we confirm this is the vehicle you want to own?"

Customer: "Yes; I really like the new Titan."

Salesperson: "Excellent. Yes, it's a great choice. Can you help me understand why – even if the deal we work up is perfect – that you're not buying today?"

At this point the buyer will most likely tell you they're just gathering information, or they need to think about it. Regardless of how they respond, just move to answer that objection as you continue to pull them through your process. Many buyers, you'll discover, need to be sold.

We Don't Want to Test Drive It

There are a couple of primary reasons you'll hear this objection. One is that they're on the wrong vehicle and the other is that they're simply afraid of being sold. I recommend a response that assumes the latter and probes for the former:

Customer: "We don't really want to test drive it today."

Salesperson: "Excellent, because it sounds to me like you don't have to buy today, is that correct?"

Customer: "Yes."

Salesperson: "Great, I'm glad to hear that. That takes all the pressure off me and allows me to spend some time helping you gather information so that when you are ready to buy, you'll have everything you need. Does that sound okay?"

Customer: "Sure."

At this point, you begin or circle back to your needs analysis; focusing on their likes and dislikes of their current vehicle and what they want in their next vehicle. Of course, your goal is to move them through your process, so this means working to move them back to the demo drive during your needs analysis. Take charge and be direct once you feel they're on the right vehicle:

Salesperson: "Great; it sounds like the A4 might be a fit for you. Let's do this; let's take it for a quick test drive just to be sure you like how it handles and how it feels behind the wheel. This way when you get home, you'll have everything you need to think about. Does that sound okay?"

As is true in most instances with Assumptive Selling, you're actually telling them what you need them to do, more than you are asking.

When you return from the demo drive, of course, you're going to move them to the write-up with a very similar word track:

Salesperson: "It sounds to me like when you're ready, the A4 is the vehicle you want to own. Let's do this; let's take just a few minutes to get you the rest of the information so that when you get home, you'll have everything you need to make an informed decision. Does that sound okay?"

Now walk them into the showroom.

I Want to Shop Around

If you encounter this objection before the write-up, then the buyer may not like the vehicle they selected. Probe this first:

Customer: "I think we want to shop around."

Salesperson: "That's great; it sounds like you don't have to buy today, is that correct?"

Customer: "That's right."

Salesperson: "Excellent. That takes a lot of pressure off me. Help me understand what it is you don't like about the Enclave."

If they give you reasons, then go back into a little needs analysis to find the right vehicle. If they tell you they love it, then move them to the next step in your process:

Salesperson: "Great. Let's do this; since this is the Enclave you want to own but you still want to shop around, let's take a few minutes to get you all the information so that when you leave here you'll have everything you need to make an informed decision. Does that sound fair?"

Now, walk them inside for the write-up.

I'm Not an Impulse Buyer

Hearing this statement before the write-up means you'll simply use the verbiage already introduced when answering the **Just Gathering Information** objection. Hearing this during the write-up means your buyer is afraid to make a decision that he'll regret. Letting him leave without your vehicle likely means you'll never see him again.

Customer: "I'm not an impulse buyer."

Salesperson: "Excellent; that makes a lot of sense. The last thing I want is for you to leave here in a vehicle you're unhappy with. Tell me, is there anything about your new vehicle that you wish was different?"

This will uncover any remaining objections they have about the vehicle; most often, of course, this is not the case.

Customer: "No, I think it's perfect. I'm just not going to buy it today."

Salesperson: "Great, thank you, I'm glad this is the vehicle you want to own. Now, you may not know this, but most of my business comes from referrals from happy buyers. Can you tell me if there's anything I've done or said that would keep you from recommending me to your friends?"

It's likely that even if they don't like you, they're not going to tell you this now.

Customer: "No, you've been great. I really appreciate the help."

Salesperson: "Thank you for that. It's really important to me that you're happy with my service. In fact, I'd rather you not buy if I've somehow failed to assist you in every way possible."

Customer: "No; again, you've been great to work with."

Salesperson: "Fantastic. By the way, how long were you researching vehicles before you decided to stop in today?"

Customer: "A few weeks, I suppose."

Salesperson: "Well, you certainly aren't like any impulse buyers I've worked with; you did your homework before coming in. That's smart. Tell me, is there anything else we can do that will help you own this vehicle today?"

This could uncover a final hidden objection that you can address. Alternatively, this could earn you the sale at this point.

If you still can't get him to sign, the Puppy Dog Close is most likely your last resort. Let him leave in your vehicle so he can "be certain it's the one he wants to own." At the very least, he'll need to return it, giving you one more chance to close the deal.

I Want to See the Invoice

Occasionally, you'll encounter a buyer that wants to show off their knowledge of the car-buying process by telling you they want to see the manufacturer's invoice for a particular vehicle. Of course, this is usually good news because it gives you a chance to make a profit on a new vehicle.

If this happens before the write-up, be sure you're moving them through your process properly:

Customer: "I want to see the invoice on this truck."

Salesperson: "Excellent; most customers don't even know what that is; it sounds like you've done this before. (Smile) We believe in being 100% transparent, and we'll always share the manufacturer's invoice on any new vehicle. So, if you're certain this is the vehicle you'd like to own, let's take a few minutes to review the numbers and get you that invoice. Does that sound fair?"

Customer: "Okay, that works."

Salesperson: "Great. If you don't mind my asking, how much above the invoice do you think is a fair profit for a dealership to make?"

You now have your minimum margin built into the deal. Of course, if the buyer's request comes during the write-up, then whether or not you share the invoice comes down to the gross you've already built into the deal. If you've presented a price well above invoice, you're not likely to want to share the invoice. However, if you're near or even below invoice on the vehicle, be sure to set up your buyer to be pleasantly surprised by providing this response:

Customer: "I want to see the invoice on this vehicle."

Salesperson: "Absolutely. We believe in being 100% transparent, and we'll always share the manufacturer's invoice on any new vehicle. Tell me, if you don't mind my asking, how much above the invoice do you think is a fair profit for a dealer to make?"

I'm Shopping for My Company

As in "I'm just looking," this could be a smokescreen or a real objection. Regardless, the idea is the same: Never listen to the prospect and move them to the next step of your process choosing your favorite verbiage.

Customer: "Oh, I'm not buying; I'm just shopping for my company."

Salesperson: "Excellent – I can help you get our fleet discount. What kind of vehicle were you looking for?"

Customer: "It's a company car that I'll be driving."

Salesperson: "That's great – does your company give you a car allowance or are they going to buy the vehicle outright?"

Customer: "It will be a lease, I think."

Salesperson: "Terrific; I'm glad you chose to shop with us. If I were to work out the fleet pricing for you, would you be the one making the final decision?"

Obviously, this could go into an almost infinite number of directions and the above example is just to keep you focused on the essence of Assumptive Selling. That is, everyone is a buyer and they're going to buy today. When required, feel free to take anyone down a traditional needs analysis. It's a great way to take charge, be direct and provide guidance.

Too often, I see salespeople give up when confronted with "I'm shopping for my company;" as if there was no chance to close the deal today. Everyone is a buyer and they're going to buy today... provided you pull them through your process.

Coincidentally, just before this book was published, I was working with a client's floor managers to help them implement Assumptive Selling. One of their salespeople caught an Up that arrived in a company van. She said she was shopping for her company, just gathering information and that her manager would make the final decision. Because the salesman had just been through my Assumptive Selling training, he treated her like a qualified buyer as he helped her gather information for her manager.

That evening, he sold her and her husband a new SUV; and the next day he sold her company a new van. Prior to arriving that day, she'd visited three other dealers and none of them treated her like a qualified buyer. They listened to her and loaded her up with information for her boss. No one assumed she was also a buyer.

Everyone is a buyer. Everyone.

We're Just Shopping Prices Right Now

While increasingly rare with today's connected customers, there are still buyers who use dealer lots to compare prices. Whether they've not been online, or they didn't believe everything they saw, these buyers fully intend to visit five or six stores before they go home with all the information so that they can make an informed decision.

Your job, as it is with every Up you meet, is to assume they are a ready buyer who is going to buy today. Assuming anything less ensures you send them to your competition to close the deal.

Generally, you'll hear this objection before the demo drive – sometimes even during an Assumptive Selling meet & greet:

Salesperson: "Good morning, welcome to ABC Motors. My name is Steve. Tell me, what vehicle did you come to test drive today?"

Customer: "Oh, we're just shopping prices."

Salesperson: "Outstanding; it definitely pays to do your homework. Did you have a specific vehicle in mind that you'd like to get the pricing for, or are you looking at a range of vehicles?"

(Customer response.)

Salesperson: "Great; well, I'm here to help you get the right vehicle at the best overall deal. Tell me, what kind of pricing were you interested in getting today? For example, are you looking for payment information, trade-in values, leasing, a cash price or all of the above?"

Whatever the answer, take charge, be direct and guide them through your process. If you get this objection during or immediately after the demo drive, your goal is to simply pull them through to the write-up:

Salesperson: "Great; it definitely pays to do your homework. Let's do this; if this is the vehicle you'd like to own, let's take just a few minutes so that I can put together some numbers for you and give you all the information you need to make an informed decision. Does that sound like a plan?"

If you receive this objection during the write-up (and you're certain the customer is on the correct vehicle):

Salesperson (New Car): "Outstanding; this makes perfect sense – it definitely pays to do your homework. Of course, I did want to make sure you were aware that the manufacturer incentives and rates can expire at any time, so the numbers we work up today may not be valid tomorrow. Is there anything that's keeping you from owning this vehicle today?"

Salesperson: (Used Car): "Outstanding; I understand – it definitely pays to do your homework. Of course, at this price, we've had a lot of interest in this vehicle. If this is definitely the vehicle you want to own, I'm not sure it makes sense to wait – the price will not come down and it's possible the next customer could be interested in buying today. Is there anything that's keeping you from owning this vehicle today?"

Your Competitor Has You Beat

Realize there are three possibilities with this objection: (A) it could be a bluff; (B) the buyer is relying on the word (and honesty) of your competition; or (C) they have a valid written offer from one of your competitors. If the reality is (C), and they present you the offer, then congratulate yourself because you've just won the business.

If you're still on the lot or on the demo drive, be aware that any actual comparison must be done inside at your closing desk/table; and only after you're certain the customer is on the right vehicle. The word track for answering this objection can be used at any time in the process prior to write-up:

Customer: "Your competition offered us a lower price."

Salesperson: "I can appreciate that, though the truth is that we've been in business at this location for over 40 years and we simply would not have lasted this long if we were ever beat on price. Let's do this; because so much goes into the final price of any vehicle, I want to be sure we're making a true apples-to-apples comparison. So, if this is the vehicle you'd like to own, let's take a few minutes to run a side-by-side comparison. Does that sound fair?"

When you are in the write-up and they share this objection – but don't have anything in writing to prove it – it is likely that either your buyer or the other dealer is lying. Additionally, if the dealer did offer a price below what you're presenting, then there could be multiple reasons they did not buy at the other dealership. Do not be afraid to defend your price and ask for all the money.

> Salesperson: "That's great news because we promise to meet or beat any valid written offer on an apples-to-apples comparison for an in-stock unit. Do you happen to have the other dealer's written offer?"

> Customer: "They wouldn't let me leave with the paperwork." (Or something similar.)

> Salesperson: "Oh, that's okay. We've found that dealers who are unwilling to put their best offer in writing are sometimes hiding additional costs or fees they'll spring on you in the financing department. Tell me, given that the pricing they presented was so good, what kept you from buying at XYZ Motors?"

This will begin to uncover their real reasons for not buying from your competition. This allows you to address each one and explain why buying from your dealership makes the most sense. Of course, if they have a valid written offer and you have a suitable in-stock unit to sell them, then you'll do the deal. No need for anything more than a quick close like this:

> Salesperson: "This is great. To be clear, if can meet or beat this offer, you'll own our vehicle today. Is that correct?"

TrueCar Says I Should Only Pay $_____

When buyers have been shopping online (as we know they all have), you can expect some of them to present prices from third-party websites like TrueCar, Edmunds and Autobytel. While this may feel like an objection that's going to make your remaining gross evaporate, the fact is that when handled correctly, this objection can help you close deals more quickly for roughly the same gross as your average deal.

This objection can occur at any step in the process, so let's first look at how to handle it prior to the write-up:

Customer: "TrueCar says I should only pay $38,500 for this vehicle."

Salesperson: "Excellent; I am so happy to be dealing with someone who's done their homework. I can't tell you how easy that makes my job. Of course, TrueCar doesn't buy or sell cars; so, their computers can only provide an estimate of what a vehicle is worth. What's more, with manufacturer incentives changing constantly, a price estimate based on data that's more than a couple of weeks old can be thousands of dollars off today. Let's do this. After we've completed the test drive and you're sure this is the vehicle you want to own, let's compare your new vehicle and the information you received online and make sure we're talking apples-to-apples. Does this sound fair?"

As always, continue pulling your buyer through your process. Now, let's answer this objection during the write-up:

Customer: "TrueCar says I should only pay $38,500 for this vehicle."

Salesperson: "Excellent; I am so happy to be dealing with someone who's done their homework. I can't tell you how easy that makes my job. Of course, TrueCar doesn't buy or sell cars; so, their computers can only provide an estimate of what a vehicle is worth. What's more, with manufacturer incentives changing constantly, a price estimate based on data that's more than a couple of weeks old can be thousands of dollars off today. Why don't you share your TrueCar paperwork with me and we'll compare it to your new vehicle to make sure we're talking apples-to-apples. Does this sound fair?"

As a worst-case scenario, you'll match the TrueCar price; though often you're able to defend your pricing by showing that the comparison is not apples-to-apples.

Customer Won't Come Inside

Occasionally, you'll encounter entrenched customers that simply will not come inside the dealership to complete the write-up. This is a problem only if you capitulate and do as they ask:

Customer: "I don't need to go inside; just call me with the details."

Agreeing to this and calling with your pricing, trade value and payments ensures you will lose the deal more often than you'll win it. Don't budge; you cannot complete the write-up on the lot. (Unless, of course, you can with a tablet while sitting in the passenger seat after the demo drive.) Instead, respond with:

> Salesperson: "I appreciate that you'd like me to call you with the details; though, that's just not how we do business here at ABC Motors. Given there is so much that goes into a car deal, it's just not responsible business for us to call customers with all the details. We've found that the dealers who are willing to share this information verbally, instead of in writing, often don't honor those terms when the customer shows up to purchase. Let's do this, let's take just a few minutes to review the numbers and get you all the information you need. Does that sound fair?"

If, after a few tries similar to the one above, your buyer still won't come inside, thank him for the opportunity and be sure to ask him to refer a friend or two. (Yes, you ask for referrals from everyone you meet! Buyers, non-buyers, cashiers, etc.)

We're Going to Hold Off for Now

When the buyer was on the wrong vehicle, doesn't like the price, was presented with too many choices or is simply too afraid to pull the trigger, they could indicate that they're going to hold off buying for now. The best way I know to get them back into the market right away is to restart a needs analysis that makes their fear of loss greater than their fear of commitment. Here's what that might look like:

> Customer: "We've decided to hold off for now; though, thank you for your help."

> Salesperson. "That makes perfect sense; I completely understand. I'm just glad you gave me a chance to help you today. Tell me… when you are ready to buy, do you think you'll be looking more at new or pre-owned vehicles?"

(Customer responds.)

Salesperson: "Great; and, will you still be focused on a (body style they test drove) or are you now going in another direction?"

(Customer responds.)

Salesperson. "That makes sense. Of all the Makes and Models you've seen, is there one you're leaning towards?"

(Customer responds.)

Salesperson. "Got it, thank you again. You know, if you really do want to own a _____, it's too bad you're not in the market right now."

Now, just be quiet and wait for the customer's response:

Customer: "Oh, why is that?"

Explain why it makes sense to buy today. This can be anything that you learned in your earlier interaction. For example, if they seemed to key in on rebates and incentives, your response could be:

Salesperson: "Well, Ford has some of the best rebates and incentives they've had in a long time and these could expire at any time. I'm not sure what they're going to do after that, as the inventories appear to be coming down. We should work up the numbers to see how today's incentives might make a difference. Does that sound fair?"

Likewise, if their hot button was on the trade value of their current vehicle, your response could be:

Salesperson: "Well, you've got a nice clean trade-in that's worth more today than it will be worth tomorrow. In fact, the average vehicle can lose about $100 each week in wholesale auction value, so trading early always gets you more money. Let's do this; allow my manager to appraise your trade now while we test drive the new Explorer. This way, we can take a few minutes to put together a deal that works for you. Does that sound fair?"

Does This Come in Red?

When a buyer asks about the availability of color, options or other vehicle features, they are providing you with a buying signal. They're basically telling you what it will take to get them to drive home in your vehicle today. Be sure to be strong in simply turning this around on your buyer and going for the close:

Customer: "Do you have a white one with the sunroof?"

Salesperson: "That's a great combination and very popular. Tell me, if I can get you a white one with the sunroof, will you drive it home today?"

Can I Get This for Under $___ Per Month?

When the buyer is asking about interest rates, payments or any other information that will be shared in the write-up – and their request seems doable – answer as we did when they asked about color, then direct them to the write-up (provided, of course, that you've already taken the demo drive):

Customer: "Can I get this for under $450 per month?"

Salesperson: "Wow, that's a very competitive payment. Tell me, if we're able to get your payments to $450 per month, will you drive it home today?"

Customer: "Sure."

Salesperson: "Outstanding, follow me and let's see if we can make this happen for you."

If they're requesting an unrealistic or unlikely interest rate or payment, deflect the answer and go for the write-up:

Customer: "Will I be able to get 0% on this one?"

Salesperson: "Our finance managers are experts at getting our customers the lowest rates available. Now, we work with 27 banks and credit unions, so we will get you the absolute best rates you qualify for. Let's do this; let's take a few minutes to review the numbers and get to work on that interest rate. Does that sound fair?"

I Need to See How This Impacts My Insurance

This could be a stalling tactic or a genuine concern for the buyer. Either way, an assumptive seller knows to move them through the process when addressing any objection:

Customer: "I need to see how this will impact my insurance."

Salesperson: "Outstanding; it sounds like we've got the vehicle you want to own at the right price. I'm sure we can get in touch with your agent and ask him or her about this Durango. Of course, with its safety rating, I can't imagine it negatively impacting your rates. Do you have your agent's information handy?"

Of course, there are times when the customer just doesn't realize that the new vehicle will be covered automatically (provided they had full coverage before). Learn your state's laws related to this and share that information with your buyer:

Salesperson: "If you want to be certain that you're covered, don't worry. Our finance manager will make sure of that before you finalize the paperwork. Of course, most insurance carriers give you at least ten days to alert them about any changes like this. Prior to that, you're automatically covered by your existing policy. That said, if you're ready to own today, let's call your agent just to be sure, okay?"

The Payment is Too High

Obviously, you'll only hear this objection in the write-up (unless you think you're slick and start needlessly quoting payments on the lot), so we're going to assume the customer likes you and the vehicle, but just doesn't think they can afford the payment.

We're also going to assume the vehicle price and trade value are fair in the customer's mind, and that you've already explored extending the length of the loan and getting more money down to reduce the payment. (Two things I recommend doing before moving to these steps.)

Customer: "That payment is too high."

Salesperson: "I understand; though as you know, the final payment is based many factors, including credit score, trade value, down payment and the length of the loan. Now, we work with 27 banks and credit unions and we will get you the absolute lowest interest rates you qualify for. But, before we get into the finance office, help me understand a little bit about the payment. If this is the vehicle that you want to own, let's see if there is anything we can do to get the payment closer to where you'd like it. Can you tell me where it is you think this payment should be, based on all the factors?"

Customer: "Well, I can only pay $400 a month."

Salesperson: "Okay, that's helpful to know. Now help me understand; so, if you had to – I mean only if there were no other alternatives – could you go as high as say $499 month?"

Customer: "Well, if I had to…"

Salesperson: "Outstanding; thank you for being flexible. Okay, to avoid a lot of the back-and-forth, if I get you the $499 per month, are you prepared to own this vehicle today?"

Alternatively, you can use the Take Away Close to bring the vehicle down to the payment they want. With this method, you'll either close them on the original payment for the original vehicle, or you'll close them on a lower trim level at the payment they want. Remember, with the Take Away Close, you need to start by taking away those things you know are important to the buyer:

Customer: "Well, I can only pay $400 a month."

Salesperson: "Okay, that's helpful to know; and I think we can get there if we move to a 4-cylinder Accord without the leather. Does that sound okay?"

The Vehicle I'm Trading Isn't Here

Whether people just aren't thinking or they're overthinking how to keep from being sold, some buyers will show up on your lot without the vehicle they plan to trade. In these instances, it's often better to complete the deal with a conditional offer on their trade before sending them home to get the vehicle.

Customer: "Well, the car I want to trade is at home."

Salesperson: "That's not a problem; what vehicle were you planning on trading in?"

Use your typical trade walk sheet to gather as much information as possible, and then move back to the next step in your process:

Salesperson: "Excellent; this is very helpful. I'm going to give this information to my manager, so he can work up a conditional value while we take your new A4 out for a quick test drive. Does that sound fair?"

Kelley Blue Book Says My Vehicle is Worth $_____

With all the available tools online, be prepared when presenting the write-up for buyers to challenge your trade value with one they found on their own. Of course, if you're using a tablet or kiosk to work up the value with the buyer, you'll either not get this objection or it will come before the demo drive (giving you time to address this before the write-up so that you can present a defensible number). Let's handle this as if it's during the write-up, given that this is still when it happens most often:

Customer: "But, Kelley Blue Book says my vehicle is worth $12,500."

Salesperson: "That's excellent to hear; I am so happy to be dealing with someone who's done their homework; I can't tell you how easy that makes my job. Of course, Kelley Blue Book doesn't buy or sell cars, so their computers can only provide estimates. As you know, only a trained appraiser knows what a vehicle is worth; and many trade-ins require thousands of dollars in reconditioning and repair before we can offer them for sale to the public. Let's do this. Let's review your vehicle and the information you received from KBB and make sure we're talking apples-to-apples. Does this sound fair?"

Generally speaking, the consumer was overly generous about the condition of their trade-in when generating an online quote. Additionally, you'll often discover that the buyer has no idea there is a different value quoted for a trade-in versus what a dealer might sell the same vehicle for at retail. Be prepared to walk the prospect through the reconditioning and inspection your team does to every trade before offering them for sale.

If necessary, creating a handwritten worksheet to justify your trade value (starting at retail and working backward) will often overcome this objection during the write-up. For example, let's say the buyer "knows" you'll be able to sell their trade for $17,000 when it's in your inventory and you just offered them $12,000:

Salesperson: "Okay, that's fair. In perfect condition, we could probably get $17,000 for your vehicle from a retail buyer. Tell me, what should the fair profit be for us when we sell it? What percentage sounds right to you?"

Buyer: "Eight or ten percent."

Salesperson: "Great, that works. But, let's cut that in half and use 5%; that's $850. Now, the average dealer spends about $600 per car in advertising, so let's take that out. Plus, your vehicle is going to require (list everything you would need to do to get the vehicle front-line ready) before it can be considered perfect."

Build the worksheet by subtracting items from the original $17,000 retail value. It won't take long to show them their vehicle is only worth $11,000 (when you include reconditioning, tires, brakes, detail, sales commission, etc.). They'll see that you're being more than generous with your $12,000 offer.

The Trade-In Value is Too Low / I Want More for My Trade-In

If you're valuing a customer's trade with their help at a kiosk or tablet before the demo drive, then you can get this objection out of the way before you return for the write-up. This is a good thing, as you'll now be able to present a defensible number in the write-up.

Regardless of where you hear the objection, a proper trade walk will set the expectation for the buyer before anyone on your team shares a value with them. This ensures that any objection you hear is often muted. If you haven't completed a proper trade walk, be prepared for some buyers to dig their heels in on their value.

We'll answer this objection using two examples; in the first one let's say the kiosk value came back as $10,200. The buyer previously valued their trade using a third-party website before they arrived, and they were expecting something closer to $12,500:

> Customer: "That's much too low; I need more for my trade-in than that."

> Salesperson: "I can understand that. Of course, the $10,200 is all we can hope to get for it in its current condition at a dealer auction. Luckily, you've kept your vehicle fairly clean, so my manager will probably want to add it to our pre-owned inventory after our service team inspects it and reconditions it for resell. Let's do this; let's wait for our appraiser to inspect your trade-in while we're on the test drive and then we can take a few minutes when we return to review the numbers. Does that sound fair?"

When you deliver the trade keys to the desk, be sure to let your manager know you received an objection about the kiosk value (usually MMR or some other wholesale book number). This will help them develop a defensible value for the write-up.

Most dealers, at least as of this writing, do not use a tablet or kiosk to pre-value a trade before the demo drive. This means they don't hear the trade value objection until the write-up. Of course, completing a proper trade walk (with or without a tablet) sets the proper expectations in the buyer's mind well before the write-up. If you're hearing objections to every trade value you present (and these values are defensible), then you're not doing the trade walk correctly.

For the second example, we need to build a strategy for handling the trade value objection when it happens during the write-up and you're discounting your vehicle. In this instance, we don't need a talk track as much as we need a game plan.

When you're already discounting your vehicle and there's little to no gross left in the deal, addressing the trade-in objection by itself should be your first attempt. However, at this point, you may need to resell the value of the entire deal and show them how it doesn't matter where the amount comes from; it's the overall final deal that matters. (And, when I say "you" in the sentence above, I probably mean your manager or closer.)

So, if they'd like another $1,000 for their trade, this amount has to come from somewhere, "as we are already discounting the new vehicle well below the invoice and there's just no more to give." If the customer must see that extra $1,000 on their side of the ledger, move it from the discount and get them to recommit to the offer. If the customer insists on getting more for their trade at this point and does not want the amount to come from the discount on your vehicle, then a stronger defense of the trade value is warranted – one that educates the buyer about dealership operations:

Manager: "I understand. Tell me, exactly how much do you think your vehicle is worth and where did you come up with this figure?"

Customer: "It's worth $12,500… I looked it up online."

Manager: "You are correct; your vehicle is worth $12,500… when a dealer is selling it on their lot. Unfortunately, since you're buying your new vehicle below our invoice, I just don't have any room to overpay for your trade-in. You may not know this, but the average trade-in requires about $2,000 to $2,500 in reconditioning and repair costs before we can sell it on our lot. This means I would need to sell it for $15,000 just to break even. Of course, we both agree it's only worth $12,500; so, I would be losing a lot of money if I sold it on the lot. Let's do this; let's see how much I can get for your trade at the dealer auction. Does that sound fair?"

At this point, you should turn your monitor around and show the customer as you work up the MMR or other wholesale book value of their vehicle. Be certain to always give them the benefit of the doubt (for example, move it up in condition and round down on the miles):

Manager: "We'll call the condition 'Very Good' even though it will need some reconditioning to get there… let's round down on the mileage to 90,000; this will give us a higher figure…"

This level of process transparency builds trust in the customer's mind and helps them accept the lower value for their trade. Don't be afraid to use transparency about the car business to your advantage. Most every buyer believes dealers are making thousands of dollars in profit on the front-end of every new car deal. Understand this when you're asking for all the money; it's likely much less than the customer believes you are making.

I Plan to Sell My Vehicle Myself

When you always conduct a trade walk prior to the demo drive, you force yourself to ask about trades. Doing this prior to the demo drive allows you to uncover the "I plan to sell my car myself" objection early enough in the process to address it. In this example, the objection comes as part of a mini needs analysis you're conducting as you enter the customer's information in your CRM (before the demo drive), and there is a tax advantage in your state when a customer trades in a vehicle:

Salesperson: "Great... and were you planning to trade in a vehicle?"

Customer: "I have a 3-Series, but I plan to sell it myself."

Salesperson: "Oh, that's a great car. In fact; it's one we'd love to have on our lot. Let's do this; let my manager look at it while we're taking the test drive and that way he can give you a written offer when we return. Does that sound okay?"

For most buyers, this is generally all it takes to move to the trade walk. During the trade walk, be prepared to continue to knowledgeably answer the objection:

Salesperson: "Yep, this is definitely a vehicle we'd like on our lot. Tell me, do you know about the sales tax savings you receive when you trade in a vehicle?"

Customer: "I think I do... yeah."

Salesperson: "It's actually like getting a discount on your new vehicle. For example, if your trade is valued at $10,000, then you'll get a discount on your sales tax of about $600 by trading it in versus selling it yourself."

Additionally, you should address the hassles the buyer will face when trying to sell it themselves:

Salesperson: "A friend of mine tried to sell a car on Craigslist recently and he got so many lowball offers from scammers and sketchy people who just wanted to negotiate that he vowed to never do that again. Be sure to only show your car at the police station or some other well-lit public place… and take someone with you."

Finally, make sure they know that trading in the vehicle removes all future hassles:

Salesperson: "You know, one of the things I like about trading in my vehicles instead of selling them by myself is that I walk away free and clear. If the engine seizes after we buy your vehicle, that's on us. When you sell it yourself, the buyer often wants you to pay for the repairs, don't they?"

The great part about addressing this concern before the write-up is you don't need to overcome the objection, just provide some context as you pull them through your process.

I'm Upside Down

When a customer understands their equity position and they've already valued their trade with an online tool, they'll often blurt out during a proper trade walk that they're upside down in the vehicle:

Customer: "I owe more than it's worth."

The keys here – as they are throughout the Assumptive Selling process – are to remain upbeat and positive, and to pull them through to your next step. After all, you have a qualified buyer in front of you who is going to buy today:

Salesperson: "That's actually not a problem; in fact, most of my buyers owed more than their vehicle was worth when they traded it in. Let's do this: let's find the right replacement vehicle for you and see if the current factory incentives don't more than make up for the difference. Does that sound okay?"

I Have Bad Credit

There is a worry that using Assumptive Selling and moving quickly to the demo drive will often put unqualified buyers into the seat of something well outside their range. Although I addressed that a couple of times already, let's look at the best way to handle those prospects who self-identify as credit challenged.

Usually, this comes as a statement about job history ("I've only been at my current job a few weeks") or concerns about qualifying for a loan ("My credit's a little dinged up"). Regardless of how the buyer self-identifies as credit challenged, your response is the same:

> Salesperson: "Thank you for sharing that, and no worries. Let's do this; let's save a little time and go inside, get a bottle of water and sit down and figure this out. I'm sure we can find a way to get you into a vehicle today."

As you walk inside, feel free to ask your stronger qualifying questions, as this buyer is comfortable answering these and will not look at this as an interrogation.

I Want to Take It to My Mechanic Before I Buy

While this is a fairly rare objection, older buyers (who may or may not have a mechanic in mind) will sometimes want to have a used vehicle checked out before they'll buy it. The key for you is to provide them with piece of mind about this purchase. If your dealership offers a return or vehicle exchange option, make sure they know this. Often, that's all you need to do to move to the next step.

We'll address this objection as if your dealership does not offer a return or exchange policy, and the objection is presented before the demo drive:

> Customer: "I want to take it to my mechanic before I buy it."

> Salesperson: "Outstanding; it sounds like this is the vehicle you want to own. Let's do this; let's take it to your mechanic during the test drive if that works for you."

More often than not your buyer will not want to go to his mechanic during the demo drive because your buyer probably didn't have a mechanic in mind. However, he now understands you won't object to this, which gives him peace of mind and builds his belief that you're offering a quality vehicle for sale.

When you hear this objection after the demo drive, you'll want to offer peace of mind in a couple of ways:

Customer: "I want to take it to my mechanic before I buy it."

Salesperson: "Outstanding; it sounds like this is the vehicle you want to own. When you do take it there, you may want to share our 165-point inspection with your mechanic. (Give the buyer your inspection checklist.) Before we offer any vehicle for sale, it's put through one of the most extensive inspection, reconditioning and repair processes in the industry. After that, if it doesn't pass our 165-point final inspection, we simply won't sell it. We send it to the auction where another dealer will buy it and offer it for sale."

Customer: "Okay... thanks."

Salesperson: "My pleasure. You know, on top of that, most of my pre-owned customers looking for that extra peace of mind will include a service contract in their payment that covers virtually anything that could go wrong with the vehicle. My business manager will be happy to show you our warranty options if that's what you're concerned about."

Moving to close the deal is your next step. However, if your buyer insists on showing the vehicle to his mechanic before the purchase, treat this as an extended test drive and expect him to fall even more in love with your vehicle as he drives it to and from his mechanic's service shop.

We Didn't Bring Our Checkbook

Sometimes a stall tactic and sometimes a genuine issue; you find yourself sitting in the write-up and the buyers tell you they left their checkbook at home. Never let this slow you down until everything is signed. Then, you can worry about getting their checkbook:

Customer: "Oh, crap; we left our checkbook at home."

Salesperson: "Oh, that's never a problem. Let's do this; let's complete the rest of the paperwork and I'll let the business manager work out the details on the down payment. Does that sound okay?"

As you complete the deal, ask questions about and suggest alternate ways to get the down payment done, for example:

Salesperson: "Oh, and there are other ways to make a down payment with us. For example, many buyers will use a credit card for some or all of the down payment. This way they can earn miles or points. Not that we need it right away, but do you have someone who can pick up the checkbook and bring it in while we complete the paperwork?"

Given that there is likely to be a wait between completing the write-up and getting your buyer into F&I, most salespeople will want to complete the write-up before sending the customer home to retrieve their checkbook. Just be sure to remain upbeat and positive when handling this or any issue your buyer raises.

Uncommon or Other Objections

We certainly can't cover every possible objection you're going to hear when selling cars; so, for those we missed, feel free to go old-school and AIM for your goal (as we learned earlier when we were overcoming a trade value objection over the phone):

A: Acknowledge the concern.
I: Ignore or redirect the concern.
M: Move on to your goal.

For example:

Customer: "I'm not ready to buy today, so I'll come back to do the numbers when I'm ready to make a decision."

Salesperson: Acknowledge the objection – "That sounds great, Mr. Jones; getting the numbers when you're ready makes a lot of sense."

Ignore the objection – "Of course, with the incentives on the vehicle expiring soon, it might make more sense to work these up now so that you have something to compare to when you're ready."

Move On from the objection – "So, let's take just a few minutes to get you all the information so that you can make an informed decision when you're ready. Does that sound fair?"

The Objection Close

Once the buyer is ready to own your vehicle at the fair price discussed, confident salespeople will often ask for an objection in a way that closes the deal. For example:

Salesperson: "Is there any reason why we shouldn't finish the paperwork and get you on the road in your new Silverado?"

This allows the buyer to raise any remaining real objections without saying no to the deal. Often, of course, you'll simply hear, "Nope, let's do this." The objection close is very powerful at the end of a buying process where you don't believe any more objections exist.

However, when you sense an objection anywhere in the process, the best way to handle it is to proactively drive it into the open. For example, if your buyer seems to be pressed for time, but hasn't indicated it yet, be proactive and get the objection off the table by addressing it first:

Salesperson: "I know your time is valuable and I appreciate you spending some of it here. However, I want to help you accomplish everything you want to do as efficiently as possible, can you let me know whether you're doing more shopping or researching today?"

Be careful not to overuse this technique. For example, a buyer might make mention to her co-buyer that the vehicle doesn't seem too powerful during the demo drive. If you try to proactively answer this objection, you could be hurting, not helping, yourself. Unless you know the context of your buyer's statements, it's better to leave these unaddressed.

The Final Word on Closing

If you recall from the first chapter, Assumptive Selling is not about closing; it's about leading. Leading the customer down your path. It's about taking charge, being direct and providing guidance; all while understanding that every Up wants to buy and wants to buy today. Assumptive selling is about believing everyone is a buyer... and knowing that the first time you believe someone is not, you'll be right.

Today's Lot Ups want to buy; they're just afraid of being sold. They arrive with all the information; they're ready for the demo drive, and they don't like being interrogated. Salespeople who win today are the ones who recognize this, speak to their customers like human beings, and then pull them through a buying process in an efficient manner that makes sense to the customer.

Instead of always trying to close everyone all the time, open your mind. Don't try to close the sale, just assume it. Assuming the sale allows you to stop working so hard to overcome objections. It focuses you on simply addressing the objections and moving the buyer to the next step in the sales process.

People want to buy from people they like... who also pull them through a process and sell them a car! People will like you more if you like them, treat them with respect, and treat them like a qualified buyer. No one objects to being treated well.

When you do this with enthusiasm (for your customer and the vehicle), energy and passion, people want to share in your enthusiasm, energy and passion. They will come along for the ride just because it seems like what the cool kids are doing. Assumptive Selling without this enthusiasm, energy and passion is not Assumptive Selling.

When you believe every Up is a buyer, you become more believable. This makes Assumptive Selling the most powerful selling strategy today – because, as you already know, you approach every opportunity as if it's already a done deal. You do this, after all, because everyone is a buyer.

Finally, when dealing with monetary questions (price, trade value, payments, down payment) don't ask your buyer where they want to be or need to be, tell them where you need them to be. Taking charge and being direct will help you sell more deals and hold more gross than asking a customer their idea on a good trade value and getting hit with a ridiculous number you'll never match.

18

THE PERFECT DELIVERY

You just sold a car... so, the real work is done, right?

Not even close. The customer experience expectations of today's buyer coupled with the complexities of today's technology means that no matter how happy the customer is with you to this point, if you blow the delivery, you're getting crushed on the OEM survey. Moreover, you'll receive no referrals and you'll be awarded a bad online review.

Yippee; this car sales stuff is fun!

As I wrote in the first sentence of this book, selling cars is not hard... it just takes work. For successful sellers, much of that work happens after the sale. In fact, for those who live off repeats and referrals, arguably all the work happens after the sale... and by "after the sale," I mean immediately after the write-up.

Because so much about Assumptive Selling is working on the goal of your current step, it's important to stress that the goal of the delivery is to ensure you earn a perfect survey and multiple referrals. Period.

Interestingly, the two steps in the road-to-the-sale where you can most easily tell the difference between the 8-Car Alans and the 30-Car Theos are the meet & greet and the delivery. During the other steps, it's sometimes hard to spot the difference because everyone is engaged with their buyers; but, during the meet & greet and during the delivery, 8-Car Alans have no energy. They don't like selling cars and it shows. During the meet & greet, they're certain the customer is a deadbeat; and they treat the delivery like some sort of punishment.

The delivery is not a punishment! The delivery is your best opportunity to earn repeat and referral business!

For the buyer, the delivery is like Christmas morning to a child. They've been waiting, and now they finally get to take home their new vehicle. This is an exciting time for them and your energy and excitement should be equal to or greater than theirs. You should be proud of and excited for them; because, if you are and it shows, they'll gladly send you those referrals you so desperately want.

During the delivery, be sure to complete all the steps necessary, so that when they drive off the lot they have no more questions about the vehicle; they're not fidgeting with the sound system or Bluetooth or trying to connect their phone to your OEM's version of "CoolNameConnect."

Even if (or, perhaps, especially if) they bought a $3,000 cash car, take their picture in front of their new vehicle. Then, have another salesman take a picture with you and your customers in front of their new vehicle. Promise to send them these pictures, but also ask if you can post the one with you in it to your Facebook profile.

Treat them like the biggest VIPs you've ever met and make sure they know how excited you are for them and that they can call you at any time with any questions:

> Salesperson: "Barbara, I want you to know that I'm not just your salesperson, I'm your friend in the car business. I want you to call me anytime with any questions you have about this car or any car you own. I'm truly here to help you and I'm hopeful you know that."

Now, hand her some additional business cards and ask her for referrals – right now – while she's still giddy about her great purchase:

> Salesperson: "You may not know this, but I work primarily from referrals. It's how I make my living; so, I would consider it an honor if you felt comfortable enough with me to share my card with any family or friends you have who might be looking for a new vehicle, but just haven't found the right salesperson yet. I promise you that I'll take great care of them and get them the best vehicle at the best price."

If your state allows you to pay a referral fee, make sure she's aware of that, as well.

Since you actually sold a vehicle, we can all assume that (at this point) the customer is happy, that they like you and they like the dealership. Great, let's keep it this way by remaining engaged with and attentive to the buyer through the entire delivery process.

While prior to this moment you've been successful by hearing but not listening to the buyer; ensuring you always have a satisfied customer requires you to now start listening closely to the buyer and changing your direction to meet their needs. You need to perform The Perfect Delivery.

As we discussed in an earlier chapter, the delivery often begins before your buyer even gets in the box. For example, taking care of some of the delivery functions while you and the buyer are waiting on F&I will make that wait seem shorter, and make the delivery and overall process seem more efficient.

Sometimes, both the buyer and the salesperson just want the visit to end quickly once the buyer comes out of the business office. You may have spent hours together, you're both exhausted and you just want to go your separate ways. When you succumb to the urge to speed through the delivery, however, you'll never provide The Perfect Delivery.

Instead, you'll eventually find yourself dealing with a now-angry buyer who can't pair his Bluetooth or can't get your service team to return his calls to schedule his We Owe appointment. Any chances you had for a referral and a great review are gone... all because you rushed the delivery.

Like The Perfect Appointment, The Perfect Delivery is called this for a reason. You need it to be perfect for your buyer; anything less can undue all the goodwill you've built to this point. Your focus with The Perfect Delivery is to know your buyer is driving away from your dealership in their new vehicle with:

- A clear idea of how the features work, with no lingering questions;
- Confidence that any We Owes are going to be efficiently resolved;
- All the necessary paperwork signed and delivered to the proper parties;
- Their first service appointment scheduled; and
- A few of your business cards that they plan to distribute to their friends and family.

Providing The Perfect Delivery is about doing things right the first time, since this takes less overall effort and pleases more people than the opposite. When you fail to do things right the first time, you break trust with your customers and you end up doing more work than if you'd just taken the time to do it correctly initially. Because time is almost always a factor in the buyer's mind, providing The Perfect Delivery requires you to use their time wisely.

Waiting on the Box

If you're new to the car business and you just finished your first successful write-up, then you have no idea the torture you're about to put your buyer through. An experience, by the way, that is seen as wholly unnecessary and absolutely hated by your customer. They've agreed to a deal with you; they have $40,000 they want to give you; and you're making them wait an hour or more to get into the business office. To the buyer, this makes no sense.

Because the next hour+ could kill your chances of earning any repeat or referral business from this currently-happy customer, let's make it productive for your buyer. At the same time, let's knock out the parts of The Perfect Delivery that make the most sense. If you look at the areas of focus identified above as the elements required for The Perfect Delivery and break these out into a checklist, you'll be better able to maximize everyone's time as your buyer waits on the business office:

1. Vehicle Features; Additional Questions
2. We Owe Scheduling
3. Paperwork
4. First Service Appointment
5. Request Referrals / Provide Business Cards

Just a quick glance at this list tells me items 2 and 3 should wait until after the F&I step is complete. While you might be able to schedule the We Owes promised during the write-up, the business manager might create new We Owes by selling accessories or F&I add-ons that must be ordered and/or installed. It's better to handle all your We Owes at once.

Unless the vehicle is in detail, you can and should use the time waiting on F&I to introduce your buyer to the vehicle's features. This includes pairing any of their devices to the vehicle and activating any subscription services that were included in the purchase. You'll also use this time to ensure you've answered all their current questions and to let them know that any future questions – regardless of how insignificant they might seem to the buyer – should be posed to you. You are more than their salesperson, after all, you are their friend in the car business.

One of the easiest delivery steps to take while waiting on the F&I office is to complete the service walk with the buyer and schedule their first service appointment. Every dealership approaches the service walk differently, so be sure you understand what your managers expect from you when it comes to this step. Some dealers want you to show the buyer everything from how easy it is to use the service kiosk to where to park when they drop off after hours to even showing them your super-clean, organized repair bays. While others just want you to complete a quick introduction to the service advisor. Whatever the steps, make certain you hit them all.

Finally, making sure your buyer knows you live off referrals should be part of your delivery – especially if you find yourself waiting on F&I.

Keep Them Engaged

Left alone, most consumers will use their mobile devices as in-store purchase assistants. This means, when you make the buyer wait by themselves, they're going to pull out their smartphone and begin shopping around – even if they've already bought the vehicle. During their smartphone shopping, it's possible they'll find the vehicle they just bought from you advertised for a lower price up the street or they'll read some horror story about extended warranties. Either way, allowing a buyer to sit unaccompanied for any length of time is not recommended.

This is where moving some of the delivery functions earlier in the process helps. It gets your buyer up and walking around; it keeps them focused and engaged.

However, if you have no delivery functions to complete (you've done all you can, or the vehicle is in detail) and you're still waiting on F&I, I recommend pre-presenting many of the F&I products and add-ons your buyer will see in the business office. If this is not an option at your dealership, I recommend asking your managers to consider adding this as an optional step for qualified salespeople as it helps grow your back-end grosses and makes the process feel more efficient to the buyer.

Online Car Sales & The Perfect Delivery

As more consumers complete their vehicle purchase entirely online, providing The Perfect Delivery becomes more important. Why? Because the delivery could be the only chance you have to make a great impression! It's certainly your best chance to ensure the customer will service with your dealership and your only chance to ask for referrals.

As of this writing, every state still requires some sort of wet (live, in-person) signature on one or more of the delivery documents. This gives you two options when delivering a sold unit to someone who purchased online and lives in your market: in-dealership pick-up or home delivery. Let's look at each of these in terms of providing The Perfect Delivery.

In-Dealership Pick-Up

In this instance, the consumer purchased their vehicle online and they used the application to schedule their pick-up at your dealership. (Similarly, this could be a subscription customer arriving to exchange their vehicle after scheduling this online.) An in-dealership delivery should be your preferred method of delivering vehicles purchased online; that is, when you're sure you can provide a great customer experience every time. This is because the buyer gets to see your store, meet your team, and you can complete a service walk.

Your buyer expects everything to be ready when they arrive – just as they expect everything to be ready with a rental car or hotel room they booked online. Anything less ensures this will not be a good experience for them. Customers do not differentiate between your online and offline storefronts. So, if they completed something online, they expect it to be carried over to their offline visit.

The problem for most dealers is they're not equipped for this sort of delivery. This means, when a customer arrives at the scheduled time, they often encounter something like this:

1. Customer is upped on the lot and explains they bought the car online.

2. Salesperson has no idea what they mean and begins a needs analysis; confusing the customer.

3. Customer shows the salesperson their online paperwork and the salesperson becomes confused.

4. Salesperson takes the customer to the desk where the desk manager is wolfing down a sandwich while penciling two deals.

5. Salesperson introduces the customer to the desk and explains, "this guy says he bought the car online and he's here to pick it up."

6. After what feels like an hour of back-and-forth nonsense and some verification, the desk manager determines the customer needs to complete the paperwork with one of the F&I managers.

7. The F&I manager assigned to this deal is off today, so another F&I manager will just have to figure it out.

8. Of course, this F&I manager has three deals ahead of the online buyer and decides (since the deal is already done) that there's no more back-end gross to be made. He puts them fourth on his list.

9. The online buyer is told they can either wait a couple of hours or come back at a pre-scheduled time.

10. The buyer is ready to blow a gasket at this point but agrees to come back in exactly two hours.

11. When the buyer returns, the paperwork still isn't ready. The F&I manager agrees to start working on it now as the buyer waits in his office.

12. After the final paperwork is signed, the F&I manager kicks everything back to the desk manager who assigns a salesperson to make the delivery. The salesperson is promised a mini deal, so he agrees.

13. When he and buyer find the vehicle on the lot, it's still dirty and still has the Monroney sticker attached.

14. After an hour in detail, the salesperson is finally able to deliver the car.

15. The buyer drives away… never to return.

While an extreme example, this is exactly what could happen to the first few online vehicles sold and delivered by many dealerships. Moreover, no one involved in the customer interaction would care because the customer didn't technically buy from them. The customers are treated like just an online buyer who will never set foot in the dealership again. Of course, given the way they were treated, why would they ever come back? Do you think the buyer in this scenario would ever recommend you or your dealership to their family or friends?

Instead of that experience, imagine what The Perfect Delivery could look like to the online buyer:

1. The vehicle is detailed, gassed and parked out front in the sold row a full hour before the scheduled arrival of the buyer.

2. The paperwork is completed and the five places where we need a wet signature are highlighted so they can be easily found during the delivery.

3. A concierge greets the customer when they arrive and directs them to a manager who is waiting at a table to complete the paperwork.

4. Five minutes later, a product specialist is walking them to meet the service advisor to schedule their first service visit.

5.   Within ten minutes, the product specialist is reviewing some of the most important vehicle features with the buyer, connecting any devices they have with vehicle, and activating any subscriptions.

6.   15 to 30 minutes after they arrived, the buyer is driving off in their new vehicle.

If you delivered an in-dealership experience like the one above, do you think buyers would be more or less likely to recommend you and your team to their friends and family?

Home Delivery

Because delivering a vehicle to a buyer's home is so much different from what a dealer is used to doing, when they find themselves involved in these – even for the very first time – it's usually a better experience for the customer. They simply try harder, and it helps improve the experience. That said, it's still possible to blow The Perfect Delivery when bringing a newly-purchased vehicle to a buyer's home or office if you take too much for granted.

For example, the paperwork should be triple-checked and all the necessary places pre-marked for the customer's signature before your delivery concierge or product specialist leaves with the vehicle. The smoother the transition at the buyer's home, the more likely they are to recommend you in the future.

For The Perfect Delivery – especially at the buyer's home – the vehicle should be in perfect condition. It's too late to run it back to detail if you arrive in a filthy vehicle. Additionally, the physical delivery (like the pairing of devices and activating subscription services) should be as or more thorough than what you provide at the dealership. Why? Because your buyer is going to listen to more of what you say in this instance, as they're not taking delivery after three grueling hours in your store.

All Deliveries

Regardless of how the buyer became your customer or where they're taking delivery, The Perfect Delivery dictates that you treat everyone like they're the most important and valuable customer the dealership has ever assisted. For example, I've never understood why some salespeople and managers treat credit-challenged customers trivially after the sale.

The guy spending $3,000 on a cash car would be the local jeweler's biggest customer of the day. The guy taking out an 18% loan on a $20,000 new car would be the jeweler's biggest customer of the month. The jeweler might serve wine and cheese to these buyers; treat them with respect and wait on them hand and foot.

Yes, the margins are better at the jewelry store than they are in the dealership, but to the customer spending $3,000 cash or financing $20,000, there is no difference. When you provide The Perfect Delivery and treat everyone like a VIP, you ensure that today's special finance customer becomes tomorrow's biggest referral driver... and a customer for life.

19

THE BE-BACK PROCESS

When dealers ask me to help their teams improve their Be-Back appointment rates, the first thing I say is, "call them." By that, I mean, "Pick up the damn phone and actually call a Be-Back for once in your ever-loving life!"

I'm not trying to be a jerk; it's just that I almost never see salespeople calling Be-Backs. Because almost no one is calling Be-Backs today, if you just call, you're ahead of the game. You don't need a great script or even a good process; you just need to pick up the phone and call them. Get voicemail? Leave a voicemail. Get a live person? Ask them to come back into the dealership. It's really not that hard. In other words: Just call; we can figure out what you're going to say later.

Of course, that's not really a process, is it? And, as I wrote earlier in this book, process outsells the opposite. Therefore, let's come up with a process the dealer, the managers and the salespeople can all live with that actually gets your Be-Backs to return.

Despite your best efforts, today's Up didn't buy… now what? Given that the average buyer visits fewer than two dealerships before they purchase, your chances of getting a Be-Back to return are greatly reduced with today's connected customers. Of course, this shouldn't stop you from implementing a strong Be-Back process; it just means you can't wait until tomorrow to start it.

Today's Be-Back processes that work include a same-day call within about an hour of the prospect leaving your lot. But, let's be clear, few dealers have any formal Be-Back process in place; and many of those who do, don't enforce it.

Often, they don't enforce this process because it's ineffective. It was written over a decade ago when Traditional Ups visited five or more dealerships and sometimes spent weeks actively shopping for cars before they bought. Employing a process that asks today's salespeople to make Be-Back calls two weeks after the prospect's visit will simply not be followed. These calls don't produce enough return on effort.

Just a few years ago (back when buyers visited more than two stores before they purchased), my Be-Back process lasted twenty days:

Stauning's 20-Day Be-Back Process (OUTDATED: DO NOT USE)

This process assumes the floor sales team is collecting email addresses and/or mailing addresses of Be-Backs. Where this is not the case, obviously disregard those related activities.

- Day 0 – Phone Call – Salesperson
- Day 0 – Email or Letter – Salesperson
- Day 1 – Phone Call – Salesperson
- Day 2 – Phone Call – Clerk/BDC rep (Different Voice – what did we do wrong?)
- Day 2 – AUTOMATED email or letter
- Day 3 – AUTOMATED email – Manager
- Day 3 – Manager Phone Call
- Day 4 – Phone Call – Salesperson
- Day 5 – AUTOMATED email
- Day 7 – Phone Call – Salesperson
- Day 10 – Phone Call – Salesperson
- Day 13 – Phone Call – Salesperson
- Day 14 – AUTOMATED email
- Day 20 – AUTOMATED email

After Day 20, non-responsive Be-Backs who've provided an email address should be placed in an Active Broadcast status, where they will receive one email each month showcasing the store's specials, special events, etc.

If this resembles your current Be-Back process, throw it away. Your team is not making Day 13 calls and your non-responsive Be-Backs are sending your emails to their spam folders.

With today's connected customers, your basic goal of a Be-Back process – to get the prospect to return and give you another shot at their business – will be relatively ineffective after more than five days without a contact. Move on; your time will be better spent completing one of your moneymakers rather than chasing a non-responsive Be-Back after Day 5.

And... before you announce, "But Steve! We once called a Be-Back after 90 days and he came in and bought!" let me be clear: your time is finite, and each day you call a non-responsive Be-Back after the day of the visit your chances of connecting (and selling) are lower than they were yesterday.

Instead of following what is now an insanely-long process, I recommend you add a quick customer experience survey that takes the temperature of all Be-Backs within about an hour of their visit. This allows you to customize the next steps for each prospect based on their survey responses.

Getting a Be-Back to Be Back

Before you begin building your team's Be-Back process, it's important to understand that not all Be-Backs are created equally. There are lots of reasons someone didn't buy today; some of these reasons are clearly known while others are unknown. When we have a clear reason why they didn't buy, the process is dictated by this reason. Here are two common examples:

- Can't buy today. For example, your buyer needs his mother to cosign the loan and she is out of town until Saturday.
- Can't buy for a long time. Your buyer has terrible credit and you could not get him bought. He has no cosigner, no trade and no money to put down.

These reasons are concrete, and no amount of salesmanship could have overcome them during the initial visit. The Be-Back follow-up process will be different for each customer with a concrete reason for not buying based on their respective situation.

For example, if your Tuesday buyer needs a cosigner and his mother can do that on Saturday, then your follow-up process is written for you. Perhaps you'll speak to him on Wednesday to ensure everything is still a go, followed by a Friday email and a Saturday morning text reminder. The point is that you decide the next steps based on the concrete reason your buyer did not initially buy.

To be consistent, only a sales manager should be allowed to assign a known reason to an unsold prospect – all others should have notes in the

CRM detailing why a salesperson felt the customer did not buy, but the reason should be listed as unknown without a sales manager sign-off. This rule helps the salesperson by limiting the excuses, and it keeps the salesperson focused on driving a return visit. (Salespeople are often too close to the deal to uncover the real reason a prospect did not buy today.)

Prospects will provide plenty of reasons why they're not buying today, though – and I know this will shock you – they could be telling you a half-truth (or worse). Here are a few common reasons a customer might give you:

- Not enough for my trade.
- Vehicle price was too much.
- Payments were too high.
- Wanted a different color.
- Etc.

These should be considered smokescreens, because good salesmanship often overcomes these objections and sells a vehicle. Allowing salespeople to use these excuses as a crutch might not uncover the real reason why they're not closing deals at an acceptable rate. A good Be-Back process can and should uncover the real reason; until then, mark it as unknown and follow the process.

If you believe the prospect, for example, who claimed you weren't offering them enough for their trade, your follow-up could be misguided. If you make a call that focuses on the wrong reason, you'll fail to get them to return. Perhaps they just had a fear of committing to the deal or just wanted to shop around a bit (and you were unable to uncover this during the initial visit). A call urging them to return so your manager can get a better look at their trade would likely do nothing to move them.

The solution is to treat all Be-Backs (those that do not have a concrete reason for not buying) as if we do not know the real reason, and then use a simple five-question, post-visit survey to uncover the buyer's genuine issues. Sometimes, they just didn't like you; so, if you're the only one completing the follow-up, you'll never get them to return.

This, plus the urgency of reconnecting with Be-Backs before they buy elsewhere is what drives my current Be-Back process:

Stauning's 6-Day Be-Back Process

This process assumes the floor sales team is collecting phone numbers, email addresses and mailing addresses of all Ups. Where this is not the case, obviously disregard those related activities.

- Day 0 – Survey Call – Customer Service Representative (CSR)
- Day 0 – Email and/or Card – Salesperson
- Day 1 – Phone Call – Salesperson
- Day 2 – Phone Call – Manager
- Day 3 – Email – Salesperson
- Day 4 – Phone Call – Salesperson
- Day 5 – Email and/or Card – Manager or Owner

After six days of no contact, my recommendation is to move on to the living. Placing these non-customers into an active broadcast status and sending them your monthly specials via email will guarantee they put you in their spam folders. Of course, if you're a master at old-fashioned networking, then sending these folks a couple of handwritten cards (perhaps on Days 90 and 180; and/or on their birthday, if you know it) complete with a request for referrals is not a wasted activity.

Use caution with your Be-Back process. If the prospect failed to buy because they feared sales pressure, and you bombard them with insincere calls, emails and cards, you're likely to never earn their business.

Now, let's break down this process and add some word tracks:

Day 0: Today is Day 0. You caught a fresh Up and put them in the CRM. They took the demo drive but claimed they didn't like the vehicle. You failed to get them to demo anything else despite your solid needs analysis, and they didn't come inside for the write-up. In fact, they left the dealership without speaking to a manager. The first contact attempt should come from a CSR who will conduct a quick, five-question survey meant to uncover the real reason they didn't buy today.

Time is of the essence and waiting even a few hours to make this call could lose you the deal; so, I prefer the survey call come within an hour of the dealership visit. The CSR should read the notes in the CRM and speak with the salesperson or manager before making the call to be sure they understand the issues from the dealership's point of view.

The goal of this call is to uncover the real reason the prospect did not buy – the goal is not to sell a car – though as you'll see in the survey, if the CSR feels he or she can generate a return visit, they should. As with all contact processes in this book, the next steps are created once you reach the prospect. For example, if the CSR discovers the customer bought elsewhere, there's no need to follow the rest of this Be-Back process, is there?

The survey call is a soft approach that disarms prospects and uncovers the path your team needs to follow to get the Be-Back to return. Assigning this call to someone with a pleasant voice and with no "skin in the game" – perhaps a BDC agent specifically assigned to make these calls or a bored receptionist – gives you the best chance of disarming a potentially defensive or even hostile prospect. Done right, the survey call takes just a few minutes to complete:

CSR: "Hi Mr. Jones, this is Mary, the Customer Experience Specialist for ABC Motors. Would it be okay if I asked you a few quick questions about your visit today to help us better serve our customers in the future?"

Prospect: "Sure."

CSR: "Thank you; I just have five quick questions. First question: on a scale of 1 – 10, Mr. Jones, can you please rate the vehicle you test drove today?"

Prospect: (answer)

CSR: "Thank you. Second question: Mr. Jones, on a scale of 1 – 10, can you please rate how you feel you were treated on this visit by your salesperson, Mike?"

Prospect: (answer)

CSR: "Thank you. Third question: If there was one primary reason you chose not to buy, what was that reason?"

Prospect: (answer)

CSR: "Thank you. Fourth question: On a scale of 1 – 10, please rate your overall experience in shopping with us?"

Prospect: (answer)

Based on the prospect's answers to this point, your CSR must choose one of the following two questions to ask as the fifth and final question:

CSR (When the responses have been mostly positive): "Great, so glad to hear you felt you were treated right. Final question: When were you planning to return to complete your purchase?"

CSR (When the responses have been mostly negative or neutral): "Thank you. Final question: What one thing could we have changed about the experience that would have had you rate us a 10 and make you a proud owner?"

It's critical to remember that the person on your team making this call only asks questions and takes notes on the prospect's answers. Short of asking those prospects with a positive experience when they planned to return, they should never try to do anything to sell the vehicle or even overcome customer objections.

After the call, the CSR gathers the customer's answers and sends them to the respective sales manager (via entering them in the CRM). Based on the responses, the sales manager can either call the prospect directly or can give the prospect back to the salesperson to call. Of course, if the salesperson was the issue, the manager should make the call.

If the CSR reaches voicemail or otherwise does not connect with the prospect, then the process continues, and the salesperson should be assigned the task of generating a follow-up email and/or card. I write "and/or" because it's perfectly okay to do both. The card is a simple thank you card with a quick handwritten note asking for a return call. Be sure to get this out in today's mail (if possible) and include another business card when you send this:

Mr. Jones,

It was a pleasure serving you today; and I wanted to thank you for giving me a chance to help you find the perfect vehicle. I'm hopeful you'll call me when you're ready to move forward, as I *truly look forward to doing everything possible to become your friend in the car business.*

Best wishes,

Mike
(555) 555-1212

Your Day 0 email should include similar sentiments; though it shouldn't copy the text above verbatim. Additionally, feel free to include more information in the email, as long as you can keep it brief and on-point. Your email will likely be read on a smartphone and no one wants to receive a book from you. Just thank the prospect and invite them to call you.

Day 1: This is the first day after the prospect's visit; and if they didn't connect with you or the CSR yesterday, the salesperson should make the call today. Holding to the strategy of trying to get the customer to take a five-question survey after the CSR failed to get the customer to call back yesterday is a waste of effort at this point.

While this call is made by the salesperson, it's prompted by a manager in most successful dealerships. That is, a sales or finance manager is assigned the task of making sure the salesperson makes this call. Why? So it will get made, of course. Additionally, the sales or finance manager usually has information they want the salesperson to share with the prospect. Information that they developed with their peers when reading the CRM notes during an old-fashioned Save-a-Deal Meeting this morning.

Trade value was too low? The used car manager may tell you that she's willing to pay more if you can get them back in today. New car priced too high? The new car manager may have another $500 available to make the deal (if it can happen today). Payments too high? The finance manager may be able to shop the loan with another lender who considers the buyer to be a Tier 1 borrower.

Of course, we're going on what the prospect told us yesterday and our instincts regarding the reason they didn't buy. So, using your notes in the CRM and your gut, develop a plan before the call. The goal of this Be-Back call is to get the customer to return... today... with a firm appointment (so we can be ready for them).

What do you say when you connect with the prospect? You thank them for giving you a chance to help them; you let them know you're ready to help them further; and you address the concerns they had yesterday:

Salesperson: "I wanted to thank you for giving me a chance to help you with your new vehicle. It was a pleasure to meet you and your husband yesterday; and I look forward to helping you move forward with your purchase. It looks like we have a buyer for your trade-in and we'd like to take another look to try and get you more money for it. Let's do this; let's schedule a quick appraisal this morning so we can get you in and out in no time. Tell me, does 10:15 or 10:45 work better for you?"

Of course, if you reach voicemail, your goal changes from getting the prospect to return to the dealership to getting the prospect to call you back. This means giving less information and simply asking for a return call:

Salesperson: "Hi Mrs. Jones. This is Mike over at ABC Motors and I wanted to thank you for giving me a chance to help you with your vehicle search. It was a pleasure to meet you and your husband yesterday; and I look forward to helping you move forward with your purchase. I've actually got some great news about your trade-in that I'd like to share; so, please call me back today at 555-555-1212. Once again, this is Mike with ABC Motors and my number is 555-555-1212. Thank you and talk to you soon."

Day 2: The CSR called two days ago and left a voicemail; the salesperson called yesterday and left a voicemail. We've also sent at least one email, and still the prospect has not called us back or stopped in. It's time for the manager to call. But... which manager? The manager with the great news, of course!

This call is simple and whether it's a live call or a voicemail, the tone is the same: excited because we have great news. If it's a live call and the prospect pushes back on returning, it's important for the manager to uncover the real objection and address it, if possible.

Day 3: This is a short email or text (if you have permission to text) asking the prospect to call you back so that you can share some great news with them.

Day 4: This will be your last call to the prospect, and given that they've not responded to any of your previous messages, be sure to use a generic shame attempt to drive a return call if you reach their voicemail:

> Salesperson: "Hi Mrs. Jones, this is Mike over at ABC Motors and I just wanted to apologize for whatever I did or said that's going to keep you from buying from us. I work hard for every customer, and I feel like I failed you somehow because you won't return any of my calls. Will you do me one favor and call me back to let me know the one thing I need to work harder on so that I can better help the next customer who walks through our doors? I would really appreciate it. My number is 555-555-1212; again, this is Mike over at ABC Motors and my number is 555-555-1212. I look forward to speaking with you."

The goal, after all, of any voicemail is to drive a call back. Played correctly and sparingly, shame messaging works quite well at driving return calls.

Day 5: A week ago tomorrow, a prospect shopped on your lot. They were entered in the CRM and didn't buy. Your team has made numerous attempts to reconnect with them to no avail. Chances are good that they've either already bought, or they lost their new car fever. Regardless, a letter or card from the face of your dealership (usually the general manager or owner) can help your current and future sales in a few ways:

- The prospect could respond to let you know about a salesperson or manager who needs additional training;
- If they bought your same brand from a competitor, this letter could encourage them to service with you;
- If they bought a different brand, this letter could encourage them to buy from you the next time (which, of course, could be just weeks away if they're a multi-vehicle household); and
- If they haven't bought, this letter could encourage them to give you another chance.

The letter needs to come from your heart and should encompass your dealership's tagline or motto about service, customers, etc.; so, it doesn't make sense for me to provide an example here. (You need this to sound sincere, and it certainly won't sound sincere if you and the dealer across town both send the exact letter you copied from a book.) Your letter should simply say:

- Thank you
- I wish we'd done a better job of helping you
- I take full responsibility for our inability to assist you
- We want to get better; will you help us
- I'm here if you want to vent about or praise anyone

Additionally, it should include your personal cell phone number. Few prospects will use it, but the ones who do use it likely need to be heard.

Bought Elsewhere

If at any time during the Be-Back process you discover that the prospect has bought elsewhere, do not simply thank them and hang up. Instead, it's time for a quick courtesy survey, "to help us better serve our customers in the future."

You'll want to learn what they bought, where they bought it, and why they didn't buy from you – and you'll want to include this information in the CRM. If you'll do this, you can create an activity for 24 or 36 months from today, and then make what sounds a lot like an owner-marketing call:

Salesperson: "Hi Mr. Jones; this is Steve Stauning with ABC Motors. You probably don't remember me, but we looked at a Honda Accord together a couple of years ago. As I recall, you ended up buying a Camry, is that right?"

Be-Back: "That's correct..."

Salesperson: "Great. Now, this is going to sound kind of strange, but my general manager wanted me to call you today because we have a buyer and immediate need for a Camry like yours and ..."

You can learn the rest of that talk track and how to answer any objections you're likely to receive in the "Assumptive Selling and Your Database" chapter.

Additionally, scatter a couple of thank you cards (where you know their address) in this process. Sending one today with a simple, "I'm glad you found a vehicle; I'm hopeful you'll consider me again the next time you, your family or your friends are looking for a vehicle" can go a long way toward selling them their next vehicle and driving referrals. (Yes, as I wrote earlier, you'll be asking for referrals from buyers who bought elsewhere – especially if you pay a bird dog fee.)

20

ASSUMING THE REFERRAL

Outstanding! You just closed a sale – your customer bought, and you gave them a great experience in the process. Guess what? You now have permission to ask for a referral... or ten!

You may recall the couple dozen times I referenced the desire people have for a friend in the car business; but, in case you do not, let me repeat myself: everyone wants a friend in the car business. Moreover, everyone wants to be able to recommend their friend who sells cars. They know car buying is stressful and sometimes risky, and they now get to confidently recommend someone who can help their friends and family buy their next vehicle.

You've just made a new friend who can now count you as their friend in the car business; make sure he or she knows that you cannot wait to do everything you can to help your new friend's friends and family.

To ensure you cover all available referral channels with your new buyer, use the time your customer is waiting on the F&I office to connect on social media (you're going to take a pick of them and their new vehicle and you want to tag them in it); and... ask for the referral, assumptively!

Salesperson: "By the way, nearly all of my sales come from repeat buyers and the referrals they send me. As you know, I'll certainly take great care of the friends and family members that you're going to send my way. I can't thank you enough for trusting me today and in the future."

Now, hand them a few cards; and, if you pay a bird dog fee, be sure to highlight that here.

Be Their Friend...

When I advise you to become everyone's friend in the car business, I'm not just regurgitating a slogan. I mean *be their friend*. Be is a verb: it means to happen; to occur. In other words, you must truly become their friend in the car business.

This means, when they're trying to book a service appointment and they reach you by mistake, you book the appointment for them. It means when they're still waiting on their title and your title clerk is giving them the runaround, you go stand on the general manager's desk and demand (in a friendly she-is-still-my-boss sort of way) that your customer get their title ASAP. This means when they still can't pair their phone to their SUV, you drive out to see them on your way home and pair it for them.

This means going out of your way to keep them happy with any vehicle they purchase – even if it's not from you. (Just as you would for a close friend who asked for help or advice.) You are, after all, their friend in the car business. Now act like it.

If you believe that this whole "friend thing" is too much work, remember that repeats and referrals often close at rates 4-5 times higher than Traditional Ups, they take less time, pay you higher grosses and give you perfect CSI. I'll bet you can make the time…

Post-Sale Follow-Up

Just a quick note about your post-sale follow-up to be certain you're clear on the goals. The post-sale satisfaction of your buyer is all that's important today, tomorrow and years from now. It's not about *getting* a perfect CSI score, but about *earning* a perfect CSI score.

Your first post-sale message to your buyer (I recommend a phone call) should thank them (again) for trusting you; wishing them happy roads ahead and reminding them they can call you at any time for anything… and mean it.

If they call you in two weeks about a strange noise coming from the air conditioner, handle it. If they have a We Owe that's still owed, handle it. If they forgot how to sync their phone to the vehicle, offer to drive to their home to do it for them… then do it.

Serving your buyer after the sale like they've never been served before will earn you their repeat business and their referrals. (Your letter or card asking for referrals will arrive a few days after this call.)

The Referral Call

For assumptive sellers, asking for the referral at the time of delivery is relatively easy. You can watch for visual cues and body language; and easily segue into your request at the most opportune time. Phoning your buyer out of the blue and asking for these is often more difficult.

The key for the referral call is to offer to do your customer a favor first; this way, they'll be more likely to want to do you one. Let's walk through a sample call:

Salesperson: "Hi Mr. Jones, this is Steve at ABC Motors and I'm calling to see if you need my assistance with anything on your new GX. Was there anything else I can help you with?"

Customer: "No, I believe I've figured it out."

Salesperson: "Outstanding, that's great. I assume it's running great and just wanted to be sure you'd received everything you needed from us. Is there anything we still owe you?"

Customer: "Nope, everything is great"

Salesperson: "Excellent, I am so glad to hear that. Most of my customers are either repeat business or referrals from satisfied customers like you. In fact, as long as I have you on the phone, who do you know that might be in the market for a vehicle?"

If the customer does give you the name of someone looking, ask for contact information and thank them. Of course, the response is usually something like "not off hand" or "not really;" in this case respond with:

Salesperson: "No worries, I understand; though if you wouldn't mind, I would consider it a personal favor if you could pass my name and contact information over to any of your friends or relatives who are in the market for a vehicle. I promise to treat them right and get them a great deal; and I'll even send you a $100 Starbucks gift card (or whatever legal bird dog reward you offer) if they buy from me."

If you don't offer a bird dog fee, simply end with "I promise to treat them right and get them a great deal."

Of course, as their friend in the car business, if the customer responds to your original questions that there are remaining issues or promises that have not been kept, you must be ready and willing to help.

Salesperson: "I'm sorry to hear that – that's definitely troubling. Can you provide me with all the details so that I can help you with this?"

Take your time and gather all the information... now, go solve it. Your referral request is going to have to wait a bit, as this customer is not likely to go out of his way to send business to you until his issues are resolved. Of course, once the customer is satisfied with the outcome, you may ask for the referral... because you earned it by proving you truly are his friend in the car business.

21

ALWAYS BE A GREEN PEA

As a final thought on Assumptive Selling, I'd like to leave you with this lesson: Always be a Green Pea.

For most automotive sellers stuck in the middle of the pack, their best months in the business are not only behind them, they are way behind them. Their best months in the business occurred when they were being called Green Pea, getting their necktie cut and finding themselves the target of most pranks and the butt of most jokes.

Today, they're selling eight to twelve vehicles a month and, as expected, they're not very happy with the car business. They can still remember that first or second month in the business when they sold sixteen or twenty… they remember it because it was their best month ever.

Their early success came from being new and not knowing any better. They listened to their managers, they followed the approved sales processes, they studied the product, they devoured any sales training they could find, and they assumed everyone on the lot was a buyer. They did everything right because they didn't know any better.

Then, like Skynet, they became self-aware. One day, they stopped listening to their managers, they started freelancing with every Up, they quit studying the product, they ceased looking for sales training, and they knew everyone on the lot was a deadbeat tire-kicker until they proved themselves worthy of buying. They ended their winning streak and settled into average.

They're seasoned; and now they know too much.

If you want to sell 30, 40 or even 50+ vehicles each month, it's time to go back to your roots… it's time to start acting like a Green Pea. This means you:

- Listen to your managers;
- Stick to your processes;
- Study the product daily (especially your pre-owned inventory);

- Seek out and devour any sales training you can find; and
- Assume everyone is a buyer who is buying today…

… because they are.

Good Selling!

GRATITUDE

When you take on anything big (like writing a book) there is an opportunity cost involved. That is, you give up the opportunity to do something else to do the big thing. For me, that something else usually involved my family. That's why I'm forever grateful to my beautiful wife, Michelle, and the three wonderful men we raised for their never-ending support of these efforts.

A lot went into writing this book, and there's certainly no way to thank everyone who had a hand in it. Just as with my first book, *Sh*t Sandwich*, inspiration and ideas came from both good and bad examples. (If you're a new salesperson, you should reread that sentence to understand that inspiration and ideas come from everywhere.)

While friends and clients have asked me for years to write a book of automotive retail best practices, it was Michael Glassman from Glassman Automotive in Southfield, Michigan who finally pushed me over the edge with his, "I wish you'd just write a damn book!" It was about the seventh time he mentioned it over the course of the previous six months, so I figured there must be something there. (For my digital marketing friends, you could say giving Michael credit is a lot like last click attribution.)

Of course, I'd be remiss if I didn't mention at least some of the people in and around the automotive industry who've provided advice, support and guidance over the years (and examples for this book). Initially, I planned to name as many as I could from my list of industry contacts, though this created a list of literally more than 1,000 names. Filling a book with 1,000+ names (more than 2,000 additional words) seemed silly; so, I tried to narrow it down to 100.

That was a complete waste of time, as nearly every name I cut kept making it back on the list! In fact, it proved impossible to remove even 9 names from the list, let alone 900! (Yes, this means I'm remiss, as I won't be mentioning any of you who've helped me so much over the years.)

So... know this: If we've ever met or if I've ever read your writings or watched you deliver a presentation (including a quick sales meeting at the tower), you've influenced me, and that influence spilled over into this book. For that, I thank you.

Steve

NOTES

Chapter 2
[1] Blum, Andrea "Dearborn car salesman sets world record for most vehicles sold in a year" *Dearborn Press & Guide* 9 Feb 2018: *PressAndGuide.com* Web. 25 Jun 2018

Chapter 3
[2] Wilson, Amy "Employee turnover costs dealers billions" *Automotive News* 23 Jan 2017: *AutoNews.com* Web. 25 Jun 2018

Chapter 4
[3] Totka, Megan "Under Promise, Over Deliver: The Must-Do's of Customer Retention" *Buisness.com* 22 Feb 2017: *Business.com* Web. 25 Jun 2018

[4] Shulzhenko, Mary "5 Major Reasons Why Unhappy Customers Don't Complain" *Provide Support Blog* 1 Nov 2017: *ProvideSupport.com* Web. 25 Jun 2018

[5] Roesler, Peter "American Express Study Shows Rising Consumer Expectations for Good Customer Service" *Inc.* 18 Dec 2017: *Inc.com* Web. 25 Jun 2018

[6] Freeman, Karen; Spenner, Patrick' Bird, Anna "Three Myths about What Customers Want" *Harvard Business Review* 23 May 2012: *hbr.org* Web. 25 Jun 2018

Chapter 6
[7] Cox Automotive Brands "2016 Car Buyer Journey provided by Autotrader and Kelley Blue Book" *Autotrader* Apr 2016: *b2b.Autotrader.com* Web. 25 Jun 2018

[8] DrivingSales Whitepaper "Competing on Consumer Experience" *DrivingSales* 13 Oct 2015: *go.DrivingSales.com* Web. 25 Jun 2018

Chapter 10
[9] Brenan, Megan "Nurses Keep Healthy Lead as Most Honest, Ethical Profession" *Gallup* 26 Dec 2017: *news.Gallup.com* Web. 25 Jun 2018

Chapter 12

[10] "The Ultimate Contact Strategy" *Velocify* Unknown: *pages.Velocify.com* Web. 25 Jun 2018

[11] Schwartz, Barry "More Isn't Always Better" *Harvard Business Review* Jun 2006: *hbr.org* Web. 25 Jun 2018

GLOSSARY

This glossary is meant as a reference for readers of Assumptive Selling and is not a complete guide to all the industry-specific terms you'll hear in automotive retail; merely a short list of those terms used in this book.

Addendum – An addendum is a sticker or card attached next to the manufacturer's (Monroney) label for new cars or next to the window sticker on used cars that details any dealer-installed accessories and/or market pricing adjustments.

Allocation – While a precise definition of allocation and the way vehicles are allocated to dealers can differ from OEM to OEM, the general definition of this is the new vehicle inventory the OEM allows a dealer to purchase. For some OEMs, the allocation may refer to what is forced upon a dealer more than what the dealer actually wants to order.

APR – Annual percentage rate; the interest rate.

Back-End; Back – This term refers to the F&I functions in a dealership, and most often is used to identify the gross profit made in the business office.

Bait and Switch – A very old-school (and illegal) practice of advertising a low price on a given vehicle that's often not in-stock (the bait) only to switch the customer to an inferior or higher-priced vehicle when they arrive.

BDC – Business Development Center; Call Center.

Beacon; Beacon Score – A credit score generated by Equifax to provide the dealer's lenders with insight on a buyer's credit worthiness. Sometimes just referred to as "Beacon" as in "What's his Beacon?"

Be-Back – Describes someone who's been in the dealership but did not buy. The term originates from the prospect's promise that they'll "be back."

Bird Dog – The term bird dog can refer both to the person who sends you referral business and the fee you pay for these: "did you pay him his bird dog?" Originates from the term for hunting dogs who can retrieve prey for the hunter.

Book of Business – There are multiple definitions of this term; though as it's used in Assumptive Selling, it's meant to describe everyone in your sales funnel (including prior customers).

Box, The – Finance office; business office.

Business Office – Any office or area that houses the F&I managers.

Buy-Here-Pay-Here – Describes a dealership that caters to subprime customers and most often carries the loans on the vehicles they sell.

Car Drunk – When a buyer is presented with too many choices, they will often get confused and need to go home to make their decision. This is sometimes called being car drunk.

CRM – An acronym for Customer Relationship Management; though it's most often used in automotive to describe the software the dealership uses for managing customer contacts.

CSI – Customer Satisfaction Index. Refers to the rating system most OEMs use to grade a dealership's performance (and the performance of the individual salespeople and managers) based on buyer responses to survey questions. Also called survey or SSI (Sales Satisfaction Index).

Dealer Principal – The owner of the dealership.

Demo Drive – Test drive.

Desk Log – Generally a record of everything that's happened and is happening today in the dealership on the sales side of the business. Used most often to record the Ups and track the progress of a deal.

DMS – Dealer management system. Basically, the accounting software (and sometimes hardware) that the dealership uses to track most everything related to conducting business.

F&I – Finance and Insurance.

FAB – Feature, Advantage, Benefit. A FAB Statement is a way to present a vehicle's feature (like run flat tires), the advantage that it provides (allows you to drive an extra 50 miles on a flat tire), and how that benefits the buyer (you'll be able to make it safely home or to the shop should you ever get a flat tire).

Five-Pounder – Pound stands for $1,000 in this example and it refers to how much profit you made on a car deal. A five-pounder has $5,000 in gross profit (usually only on the front, though most dealers will either combine front and back to describe the profit or break them out and describe them both). Can be any number followed by pounder; though we referenced a five-pounder in the book.

Floorplan – Refers to the money the dealership borrows to finance vehicle inventory. The dealer pays interest on this until a vehicle is sold and the floorplan is reduced.

Front-End; Front – The gross profit made on the sale of a vehicle, not including F&I (which is the back or back-end).

Get-Me-Done – Someone with poor credit who is desperate to buy a vehicle.

Green Pea – A salesperson new to the car business.

Gross(es) – The gross profit of a deal; the difference between what an asset cost and how much it was sold for. The gross profit is used to pay salaries and all other business expenses. Whatever remains after that is called net or net profit.

Hat Trick – Three vehicles sold in one day by a single salesperson.

Instant Retargeting – An effective way of presenting the online visitor an offer as soon as they leave your website (usually via website pop-under or in an adjacent tab in the browser) with the intention of generating an incremental sales lead.

Lay Down – A buyer who agrees to everything and accepts your first offer.

Mini – The smallest commission a salesperson can earn on a sale presented as a flat amount (sometimes called a flat). Minis are paid on car deals with little or no front-end gross.

MMR – The Manheim Market Report provides an accurate estimate of what a dealer can expect to get for a vehicle sent to auction.

Monroney Sticker; Monroney Label – The Monroney label or sticker (often just called the window sticker) is a label required to be displayed on all new vehicles sold in the US. It includes the listing of options and other required information about the vehicle. It's named after the late Mike Monroney, a former United States Senator from Oklahoma.

MSRP – Manufacturer's Suggested Retail Price

Needs Analysis – The step in the road-to-the-sale where the salesperson attempts to gather information from a buyer related to the buyer's situation and their actual vehicle needs and wants.

OEM – Original Equipment Manufacturer. Toyota, Chevrolet and other new car manufacturers are often referred to as the OEM by dealers.

Old Car Dog – Seasoned salesperson.

One-Price Store – A dealership that does not negotiate. Sale prices are generally marked on every vehicle and the price you see is the price you pay.

Orphan Owner – Describes a sales customer who bought from the dealership and their salesperson no longer works there, as well as a current service customer who bought their vehicle elsewhere. In other words, they are without an assigned salesperson in the CRM; they are orphaned.

Pack – Describes the amount of marketing and overhead costs allocated to a vehicle. The total pack reduces the commissionable gross on a deal like this: A vehicle is sold for $2,000 gross profit, though because it has a $500 pack, the commission is calculated on only $1,500.

Pencil; First Pencil – The offer or worksheet presented to a buyer in the write-up. The first pencil is the first worksheet or offer the dealership presents.

Phone Up Card – Often referred to as a call guide as it helps guide the salesperson or BDC agent on the best way to answer a call so that it ultimately results in a shown appointment and a sold vehicle.

PMA – Primary Market Area. The marketing and sales territory assigned to a dealer.

Road-to-the-Sale – The steps, in order, necessary to sell a car.

ROI – Return on investment.

Sales Desk; Sales Tower – The area where the desk/sales managers sit when penciling deals.

Sales Funnel – This is a visual representation of every buyer and sales prospect the salesperson is working with or has worked with in the past. The bottom of the funnel represents those closest to buying, while the top of the funnel represents those who've just bought (and were moved from the bottom of the funnel back to the top) as well as those who might just be starting their research.

Save-a-Deal Meeting – Usually a meeting of sales managers (new car, used car, finance) where every lost deal from the day before is reviewed and an action plan is developed for most of these.

Service Walk – The part of a traditional road-to-the-sale where the salesperson introduces the new buyer to the dealership's service department.

Showroom Log – Like a desk log, but in most CRMs, displays just those customers currently at the dealership.

Skating – When one salesperson attempts to sell or does sell a customer or Up that belonged to another salesperson.

Soft Pull – An inquiry into a customer's credit worthiness that does not impact their credit score (the way a hard pull would).

Sticker – Usually the MSRP of a vehicle. "Selling it for sticker."

T.O. – Stands for turn over and is most often used to describe an instance where the salesperson could not close a deal and needs a closer or manager to take over. In Assumptive Selling, most all connections between a manager and a buyer are sometimes referred to as a turn over or T.O. because when sales managers meet the buyers early in the process, it's proven to generate more sales and bigger grosses.

Tire-Kicker – A non-buyer; someone just browsing the lot looking at window stickers and kicking tires.

Trade Walk – There are two definitions of trade walk that are important for salespeople to know. As used in Assumptive Selling, the conversation a salesperson has with the buyer outside while walking around the buyer's trade and gathering information is called a trade walk. A more traditional definition of a trade walk is a daily gathering of salespeople outside to review the trades purchased the day before (so that they'll know how to sell them). Great salespeople use both types of trade walks to help them sell more cars and earn more gross.

TT&L – Tax, title and license.

Up – A prospect.

Up Bus – A fictional mode of transportation that "delivers" the Ups to your dealership.

We Owe – Something promised during the sale that cannot be delivered until later. For example, if you promised to add window tinting and special-order floor mats, you wouldn't delay the sale and delivery of the vehicle, you'd just provide the customer a "We Owe" form detailing what you still owe them and then schedule them back into the dealership when you can provide these.

Made in the USA
San Bernardino, CA
17 July 2018